PASSCODE TO THE THIRD FLOOR

PASSCODE TO THE THIRD FLOOR

AN INSIDER'S ACCOUNT

of

LIFE AMONG NORTH KOREA'S POLITICAL ELITE

THAE YONG-HO

TRANSLATED BY ROBERT LAULER

Columbia University Press
New York

Columbia University Press
Publishers Since 1893
New York   Chichester, West Sussex
cup.columbia.edu

Library of Congress Cataloging-in-Publication Data
Names: T'ae, Yŏng-ho, 1962– author. | Lauler, Robert, translator.
Title: Passcode to the third floor : an insider's account of life among North Korea's
political elite / Thae Yong-ho ; translated by Robert Lauler.
Other titles: 3-ch'ŭng sŏgisil ŭi amho. English |
Insider's account of life among North Korea's political elite
Description: New York : Columbia University Press, 2024. |
Includes bibliographical references.
Identifiers: LCCN 2023040380 | ISBN 9780231198868 (hardback) |
ISBN 9780231552844 (ebook)
Subjects: LCSH: Diplomats—Korea (North)—Biography. | Political refugees—
Korea (North)—Biography. | Political refugees—Korea (South)—Biography. |
Korea (North)—Politics and government. | Korea (North)—Social conditions.
Classification: LCC DS934.6.T3413 A3 2024 | DDC 951.9304—dc23 /eng/20231206
LC record available at https://lccn.loc.gov/2023040380

Printed in the United States of America

Cover image: Photo of Thae Young-ho

CONTENTS

ACRONYMS

Workers' Party of Korea	WPK
Organization and Guidance Department	OGD
Communist Party of China	CCP
Democratic People's Republic of Korea	DPRK
Pyongyang University of Foreign Studies	PUFS
Pyongyang Foreign Language Institute	PFLI
Ministry of State Security	MSS
Ministry of People's Security	MPS
Propaganda and Agitation Department	PAD
Social Security Department	SSD
Non-Proliferation Treaty	NPT
Defense Security Command	DSC

A NOTE ON ROMANIZATION

This book generally abides by the Revised Romanization system created by the South Korean government.

Names are notoriously tricky to transliterate because of the several Korean-to-English transliteration systems currently in use and existing Romanizations of names that have more or less become standardized. Most of the names of well-known figures (Kim Il-sung, Syngman Rhee, Park Chung-hee) have been standardized in the literature, so there is no need to transliterate them in another way in texts for general readers. Sometimes names have various spellings in wide use, depending on the source (e.g., Jang Song-taek, Jang Song-thaek, Chang Song-taek). In this book, well-known North Korean names follow the spellings commonly used in English-language news media. Lesser-known names follow Revised Romanization rules, with some caveats. The last name Lee or Yi in the South Korean dialect is commonly Romanized as Ri in the North Korean dialect, and thus North Korean people with the last name Lee are in general rendered as Ri in this book. Those with the last name Pak have all been changed to Park for consistency. The last name O has been rendered as Oh throughout the book, given the common usage of Oh in the English-language context.

Well-known place names (such as Pyongyang) follow standardized spellings. Geographical names are not fully transliterated but rather written out in a form common in news media (South Hwanghae Province as opposed to Hwanghaenam-do or Hwanghaenam Province).

CHRONOLOGY

1962: Born in North Korea's capital city of Pyongyang

1974: Entered the English Department at the Pyongyang Foreign
    Language Institute (middle school)

1976: Began studying abroad in China

1980: Graduated from the English Department at a middle/high school
    affiliated with the Beijing Foreign Languages University

1984: Graduated from the Pyongyang University of Foreign Studies
    (PUFS)

1988: Graduated from the English Literature Department at the Beijing
    Foreign Languages University

October 1988–1996: Worked in the European Department in the North
    Korean Ministry of Foreign Affairs

1996–1998: Served as a third secretary at the North Korean embassy in
    Denmark

1998–2000: Served as a second secretary at the North Korean embassy in
    Sweden

2000–2004: Worked as the head of the United Kingdom and Northern
    European Bureau in the European Department of the Ministry of
    Foreign Affairs

2004–2008: Served as a counselor at the North Korean embassy in the
    United Kingdom

2008–2013: Worked as the deputy director of the European Department in the Ministry of Foreign Affairs

April 2013–Summer 2016: Served as the deputy ambassador at the North Korean embassy in the United Kingdom

Summer 2016: Defected to South Korea

January 2017–Present: Adviser to South Korea's Institute for National Security Strategy

May 2018: Resigned from advisor position at the Institute for National Security Strategy

April 2020: Elected to South Korea's National Assembly

PREFACE TO THE ENGLISH EDITION

I t is May 2023. I am writing this preface in my office at the National Assembly of Korea. Five years have passed since I first published my memoirs in Korean under the title *3cheung Seogisirui Amho*.

I was in London as the North Korean embassy's deputy ambassador until the summer of 2016, when I defected from the UK to South Korea. This book was my first achievement after my defection. The publicity I gained from the book was a major driver in my being elected to South Korea's National Assembly in April 2020.

I was elected to the National Assembly just four years after I had settled in South Korea—truly a miracle for someone who had defected from the North. Even more miraculously, I was elected by the constituents of Gangnam's Gab District, the most affluent district in South Korea. This was the first time that a North Korean defector had ever been directly elected to the South Korean National Assembly. Many South Koreans wondered why a conservative political party had nominated a former high-ranking diplomat from North Korea, a "commie," in an electoral district where it would be sure to win. However, anyone who knew me and read my book could easily connect the dots and figure out that *3cheung Seogisirui Amho* played a vital role in my nomination and election. I was living proof of how powerful a book can be.

3cheung Seogisirui Amho was first published in May 2018. At the time, the April 27 Inter-Korean Summit at Panmunjom between South Korean president Moon Jae-in and North Korea's Kim Jong-un had created euphoria for peace. The Moon administration and the ruling Democratic Party widely promoted Kim Jong-un's promise that he would denuclearize his country and that the threat of nuclear war on the Korean Peninsula would simply evaporate. Many Koreans cheered joyfully. They had trembled anxiously over nonstop North Korean nuclear and missile tests less than a year before; perhaps it was only natural for them to be thrilled by North Korea's promise of denuclearization. The entire world seemed to welcome the Panmunjom Declaration.

As a former high-ranking diplomat in North Korea, however, I knew that Kim was running a big scam. I found it impossible to even contemplate that Kim would give up his nuclear program. I found it unfortunate that the South Korean government and many of its people fell for Kim's scam. At a seminar held at the National Assembly on May 14, 2018, I publicly stated that no one should believe Kim would give up his nuclear weapons and that North Korea would never denuclearize itself. And, for the first time, I recommended that people read my autobiography, *3cheung Seogisirui Amho.*

South Korea's conservative-leaning media outlets, which viewed the April 27 Panmunjom Summit negatively, headlined what I had said. Meanwhile, the Democratic Party criticized me for killing the euphoria celebrating inter-Korean peace and reconciliation. I was treated coldly by many at the Institute for National Security Strategy (INSS), where I worked at the time. INSS is a research institute affiliated with South Korea's intelligence agency, the National Intelligence Service. People working there must share the viewpoints of the presidential administration in power. Many viewed my publicly stated convictions that the Panmunjom Declaration was "a fake peace show" and "a fake denuclearization show" as politically charged. For an advisory researcher at a state-run research institute to say anything that could lead to political strife between the right and the left was not tolerated. Soon after, the INSS demanded that I submit in advance all plans of my activities, such as interviews with the media or lectures, so they could be approved beforehand. For the very first time, I felt my freedom was being restrained once again, despite freedom being my core reason for defecting to South Korea.

The post of an advisory researcher was a cushy gig. It came with a good salary that ensured a comfortable life in South Korea. The job was guaranteed until my retirement if I kept my mouth shut and went along with the government's policy. However, I could not silence myself and move on while witnessing a massive scam that concerned the denuclearization of North Korea, an issue that could decide the fate of the Korean nation itself. To continue watching without saying anything went against my personal and professional conscience as a former North Korean diplomat. Eventually, I decided to resign from the INSS and submitted a letter of resignation.

The news that I had resigned from the INSS broke almost immediately. When I arrived home that evening, my wife expressed disappointment at my making such a big decision without discussing it first. Yet she did not chide me. My wife had already witnessed the suffering I experienced over several days when I watched news programs showing Koreans fervently cheering in support of the Panmunjom Declaration. She is also from a high-ranking family in North Korea, and she had worked at the Ministry of Trade, so she knew that North Korea would never give up its nuclear weapons. Following my exit from the INSS, my wife and I were preoccupied with only one matter: how would we support our college-age children? In the end, I gave my family some relief by saying: "We risked our lives to come all this way to South Korea in search of freedom. There is nothing more difficult than that in this world. I am still healthy and can perform any job."

Despite the brave face I put on for my family, I was full of worries deep inside. I was unemployed for the first time in my life and had no clear way to earn a living. Gradually, however, a miracle started to occur. After my harsh criticism of the Moon administration's "show of denuclearization," many people throughout South Korea eagerly bought my published memoir. More than one hundred thousand copies were sold in just a few months. In general, books related to North Korea do not sell well in South Korea, but mine sold exceptionally well. I was swarmed by requests for lectures, as the readers of my book wished to listen my experiences and ideas in person. As royalties from my book and lecture fees flowed in, my life became comfortable once more.

My experience lends credence to a common Korean saying that posits that human beings do not die easily. Those who believed that North Korea would never give up its nuclear weapons program read my book, which confirmed their belief that Kim Jong-un would not denuclearize his country. Yet the "show to bring about denuclearization" went on. On June 12, 2018, a U.S.–North Korea summit was held in Singapore, and President Donald Trump and Kim Jong-un signed the Singapore Joint Statement. Kim once again promised to denuclearize the Korean Peninsula, a statement applauded by Trump. I was stunned to witness even the United States being deceived by Kim's denuclearization scam.

However, U.S. hopes for denuclearization did not last long. Secretary of State Mike Pompeo visited Pyongyang in July 2018, less than a month after the Singapore Joint Statement was announced. He proposed that North Korea make a basic road map for denuclearization based on the statement agreed upon in Singapore. But North Korea then asked to discuss normalization of the relations between North Korea and the United States first, based on the sequence of items placed in the agreement. In short, negotiations hit a roadblock from their very start because of opposing viewpoints on what issues to discuss first.

In fact, if negotiations had continued in line with the Singapore Joint Statement, the priority should have been on improving U.S.–North Korea relations and establishing a peace regime, followed by discussions on the denuclearization of North Korea. The United States, however, believed that North Korea needed to give up its nuclear ambitions first, before an improvement in U.S.–North Korean relations and the establishment of a peace regime could take place. In any case, North Korea's request to talk about denuclearization later was part of a strategy to work the negotiations in favor of the DPRK, including the partial lifting of sanctions on North Korea and the elimination of joint military exercises conducted by the United States and South Korea. Pompeo must have thought he had been deceived. Thus, he insisted on prioritizing discussions on the denuclearization issue.

In response, North Korea said that Pompeo was "gangster-like" because he refused to implement the agreement made in the Singapore Joint Statement. Pompeo's response to the slur made a splash in the media. He said that if those demands "were gangster-like," then "the world is a gangster." The Singapore Joint Statement was essentially dead within a month of its signing.

Despite this course of events, the United States and North Korea did not give up on the negotiations. In February 2019, Trump and Kim sat face to face once again in Hanoi, Vietnam, but eventually failed to come to a final agreement. North Korea's show of making efforts to denuclearize, which began in April 2018 in Panmunjom, ended ten months after the curtain rose. It did not last even one year.

What went wrong?

In June 2019, after the breakdown in talks in Hanoi, Trump and Kim met again at Panmunjom, but again failed to make a breakthrough. Why do North Korea and the United States keep failing to come to agreement during negotiations despite decades of nuclear talks and certain moments of progress?

The answer to that question is in my book.

The United States and South Korea have talked with North Korea for decades with the expectation that a solution could be achieved if they negotiated well and provided incentives for North Korea to denuclearize. North Korea has consistently deceived the United States into believing that sufficient incentives will lead to denuclearization. During the recent round of negotiations, North Korea did not conduct nuclear or missile tests, so the United States focused on managing the situation rather than achieving actual denuclearization through negotiations.

Readers of this book will be able to comprehend why North Korea is unable give up its nuclear weapons. Readers will also learn details about what kind of negotiating tactics North Korea uses in its talks with the United States.

As long as the Kim Jong-un regime exists, I am confident that North Korea will never denuclearize. The total collapse of the Kim regime is the only way to achieve denuclearization in the DPRK. My book is based on truths that I witnessed while working as a diplomat in North Korea and abroad; within its pages, readers will come to understand North Korea's foreign policy–making process as well as I do.

Thae Yong-ho
May 20, 2023
Seoul, Republic of Korea

PROLOGUE

WHAT WILL I DO NOW?

After my wife and I made the decision to leave North Korea and go to South Korea, my wife began to hoard books related to bread-making out of the idealistic notion that we could make a living by opening a bread shop in Seoul. Defecting from North Korea served as a reality check. While we would be gaining our freedom, we had no idea how we would make a living. Both of us sighed heavily when looking at our two sons, whom we would need to send to college.

In one corner of the North Korean embassy in the United Kingdom, I combed through the internet without my colleagues' knowing. I found out that the South Korean government's financial support for defectors was no more than a settlement payment of seven million won per person, along with a housing support payment of KRW thirteen million. While that was not a small amount of money, it meant that going forward we would have to be "self-sufficient," to borrow a phrase commonly used in North Korea.[1] I couldn't track down any particular stipulations regarding the lending of money, either.

I did not expect the South Korean government to give me a job. My wife and I would have to find a way to make money while raising our kids. If nothing else worked out, we decided we would open a laundromat or run a convenience store. All countries treat first-generation immigrants as second-class citizens. But, we figured, what could be worse than becoming second-class citizens? It would be no shame to us because we would be giving freedom and a chance to live well to our second-generation immigrant kids.

My mind went blank the moment I stepped onto South Korean territory. I felt like I was walking in a dream. My feet didn't seem like my feet. The National Intelligence Service (NIS) agents who came out to meet us didn't say anything to me. They looked tense. We went through the airport procedures and got into a car. The mountains and fields I could see out the car window looked like North Korea. I thought to myself I should have come to South Korea sooner; yet all I really wanted to do was quickly get to a bed and sleep.

I struggled to fall asleep, however. To this day, I still sometimes dream of being chased by a North Korean team of agents tasked with my arrest, but I had that nightmare continuously the first several days after I arrived in South Korea. I would spend all night being chased by the arrest team; when I opened my eyes, I came back to reality and the fact that I was in South Korea. A North Korean soldier who defected across the Joint Security Area said he felt a sense of relief while looking at the South Korean flag hung up in his hospital room. I know that feeling.

From the summer to late December 2016, I was interrogated by the NIS while suffering constantly from my nightmares. One NIS agent asked me why we had hoarded so many books about bread-making. When I responded that it was to make a living, he told me that there was an enormous number of bakeries already in Seoul and that such clumsy thinking would make it hard to make a living. While I was being interrogated, one thought never left my mind: What will I do now?

Fortunately, the South Korean government gave me a position that far surpassed what I deserved, as an adviser-researcher at the Institute for National Security Strategy. While I could not muster the courage to say it then, it was a job I had dreamed about since around the time I decided to defect. It was also a place where I could exert the last of my energy into the cause of bringing about unification. I no longer worried about what I would do.

When we arrived in South Korea, my older son was twenty-six years old. Around thirty years ago, when I was his age, I was full of certainty and enthusiasm about my "socialist motherland." That was when I began work as a "red warrior" in North Korea's foreign ministry. I hope readers of this book think of my life as just the fate of a person born in North Korea.

Things have changed now compared to that time. I have a new motherland, South Korea, along with the overwhelming task of helping to unify the Koreas. I have also regained the certainty and enthusiasm of that twenty-something young person who, thirty-odd years ago, was in the prime of his youth. My new goal for my motherland is a gift that has been returned to me despite the passage of time. The path ahead for me leads in only one direction: toward unification.

TRANSLATOR'S ACKNOWLEDGMENTS

The translator would like to thank Chris Green, Jacco Zwetsloot, Randi Lauler, two anonymous reviewers, and staff at Columbia University Press for their support in the translation and editing of this book.

I

AT THE HEART OF PYONGYANG'S LEADERSHIP

1

NORTH KOREA'S PATH
TO NUCLEAR WEAPONS

KIM IL-SUNG: "INVITE THE POPE TO PYONGYANG"

I started my career as a North Korean government official after my second time studying abroad in China. On October 25, 1988, I received orders to manage British and Irish affairs in the European Department of the Ministry of Foreign Affairs. At the time, South Korea was full of lingering excitement over the 1988 Olympics, but North Korea's focus was on preparing for the following year's World Festival of Youth and Students.

I was twenty-seven years old. As I watched the ongoing preparations for the festival in Pyongyang's Mangyongdae District, I promised myself that I would sacrifice my energetic youth for the "socialist motherland." I was unaware at the time, however, that the excessive preparations for the festival would lead to a disaster for the North Korean economy, and that— along with the collapse of the Eastern Bloc—the burdens of this economic collapse would bring about the "Arduous March."[1]

Kim Yong-nam was the minister of foreign affairs at the time, but real authority in the ministry was held by First Vice Foreign Minister Kang Sok-ju. Discipline in the ministry was very strict. All work in the organization was handled in militaristic fashion, but the ministry's employees were diplomats, which meant there were many people who were ideologically flexible. In fact, I received a great deal of advice from diplomats more senior than me.

What still leaves a deep impression from that time is the atmosphere of the "party criticism sessions" held within the ministry. During these sessions, which were held every Saturday, senior ministry officials actively engaged in self-criticism as well as criticisms of one another. When party cells conducted presentations on the written works of Kim Il-sung and Kim Jong-il, records of the Supreme Leader's virtues, or the recollections of anti-Japanese guerillas, session attendees earnestly took part in criticism of one another.[2] It was unimaginable for party members to come together after the presentations and simply repeat what they had heard, which is more common now.

At each session, everyone was required to prepare and present self-criticisms in front of the group. Then, one by one, the other attendees would criticize whoever had presented. Without any prodding, everyone enthusiastically rose to the occasion and criticized other members of the group. Party members seemed to view mutual criticism sessions as opportunities to show off their loyalty to the party. In or around 1992, Kim Jong-il used the Workers' Party of Korea (WPK)'s Organization and Guidance Department to conduct a full-scale "re-inspection" of Kang Sok-ju.[3] When Kang was subjected to a mutual criticism session, a woman among the attendees cried as she criticized and condemned him. Kang was punished with "revolutionization" at a farm, returning to his post about one month later.[4]

Criticism sessions are at the core of how North Korea's society of oppression is maintained. Self-censorship, along with mutual censorship, are used to create a type of human who bows down to the regime. This reality, however, was something that I realized only later; at the time, I felt that criticism sessions were a fundamental part of adhering to a desirable life as a party member.

The criticism sessions held each week at the foreign ministry have changed considerably with the passage of time. Nowadays, a lot of people doze off during the meetings. During my time, however, it would have been unimaginable for anyone to doze off during a criticism session—even for a moment. The atmosphere was too tense for something like that to happen. Everyone was full of enthusiasm, almost as if they could see the zenith of communism before them.

On November 9, 1989, around a year after I had joined the foreign ministry, the Berlin Wall—the symbol of division between East and

West Germany—fell. North Korean diplomacy, for its part, was in crisis around that time. Eastern Bloc countries had fallen in rapid succession, and the crackdown at Tiananmen Square took place in June 1989. North Korea's leadership had been hoping that the international environment would improve after the World Festival of Youth and Students, but it became more pressing and hazardous for the country with the start of the 1990s.

In September 1990, South Korea and the Soviet Union established diplomatic ties. In October, a united Germany emerged, and that same month South Korea and China agreed to establish trade liaison offices in their two countries. In South Korea, the Roh Tae-woo administration's "Nordpolitik" was gaining steam, and it was only a matter of time before China would establish full diplomatic relations with South Korea.[5] In North Korea, the foreign ministry seemed despondent for a while. Ministry officials conducted meetings all through the night. They did not know how to deal with the quickly changing state of affairs.

In December 1991, the Soviet Union, which had served as North Korea's protector, collapsed. Almost nobody in North Korea thought socialism had been defeated, however. They did not believe, moreover, that North Korea had lost the systemic and ideological competition with South Korea. Rather, North Koreans believed that the sudden collapse of the Soviet Union was a temporary stumbling block. That being said, the country's isolation only grew worse. The only nation North Korea could rely on was China, but in August 1992, South Korea and China finally established diplomatic ties. When the two countries established relations, foreign ministry officials shed tears of rage. This is not hyperbole at all on my part. North Korea, and the country's diplomacy, was being besieged from all sides.

One story demonstrates how hemmed in Kim Il-sung felt at the time. The North Korean leader actually examined the possibility of meeting with Pope John Paul II. He had seen news stories showing the enthusiastic response the pontiff received when he visited other countries and hoped that North Korea could extract itself from diplomatic isolation if the leader of Catholicism visited the country. Kim Il-sung ordered Minister of Foreign Affairs Kim Yong-nam to take measures to invite the pope, and in 1991, the foreign ministry created a task force aimed at inviting the Holy Father to Pyongyang. I was a member of this task force.

Fearing an Increase in "Real Christians,"
Kim Jong-il Expresses Opposition

The task force divided up roles and responsibilities. The foreign ministry would deal with protocol for the pontiff's visit, while the WPK's United Front Department (UFD) would handle preparations for religious events.[6] As it happened, I was assigned to work with UFD officials. I found the attitude of the UFD representatives to their work thoroughly disappointing, however. They simply spent their days reading books and chatting among themselves. They would have faced prompt disciplinary action if they had been part of the foreign ministry.

After watching them for a couple of days, I quietly asked them why they were not doing work to prepare for the events.

"Comrade Kim Jong-il has already decided that the visit by the pope to our country will not go forward. There's no need to proceed with it, but we have no choice but to remain here because the Supreme Leader has told us to. [You] at the foreign ministry should try your best [to prepare for the events]," they told me, referring to Kim Il-sung.

In short, all authority in the country was already in the hands of Kim Jong-il, which meant there was no way the pope's visit to North Korea would go ahead. That being said, it was clear even to me that a visit by the Catholic leader could greatly help ease North Korea's diplomatic isolation. The UFD officials, however, thought differently: "If the pope comes here, the UFD and Ministry of State Security have to deal with the consequences.[7] The foreign ministry has no idea whether there are religious people in our country or not, or how many there are if they exist. Who will take responsibility for what could be a dramatic increase in Catholics after the pope's visit?" Since childhood, I had received education telling me that religion was bad. North Korean movies such as *Chae Hak-shin's Family* and *Village Shrine* cultivated antireligious sentiment in me. I refused to believe the claims being made by these UFD officials that there could be religious people in North Korea.

To prove that religious people existed in the country, North Korean authorities even brought a North Korean who believed in Catholicism to the Vatican. The Vatican had demanded that the country allow them to meet with a real Catholic, and the WPK's Korean Catholic Association (KCA) responded by finding an elderly woman. The Social Security

Department had looked into the country's resident records and found someone who had been a true believer up until the outbreak of the Korean War.[8]

Cadres from the KCA went to the woman and asked her whether she "still believed in God." With a serious look on her face, she responded by saying, "How could I believe in God when there's the *Suryong* [Kim Il-sung] and the Workers' Party?" This relieved the officials, but they nonetheless pressed her further: "You can speak honestly. We are asking because we need to send someone who believes in God to the Vatican in Rome. Finding a true believer would actually help the Workers' Party and the nation." It was only then that the woman spoke frankly, saying, "Once God enters your heart, He never leaves." The cadres asked her how she maintained her faith all those years, and she took them to a wall behind her house. It was clear from the atmosphere emanating from the altar in front of the wall that it was a place of worship.

The officials, now certain that the old woman was a believer, told her that she "must head to the Vatican as a member of a delegation and in the interests of the revolution." As she gazed up at the sky, she responded by saying, "Lord, after praying hard to you my entire life, you have [finally] called [for your] little lamb." Flustered by this, the cadres reminded her again that "God did not call you. You are heading to the Vatican in the interests of the Revolution." However, the woman still seemed to believe that it was God who had called her to join the delegation. She further told them that "even my son doesn't know that I pray here every night, so please don't tell him."

The old woman ultimately joined the delegation to the Vatican and testified that North Koreans enjoy freedom of religion and that families set up altars for worship. In line with Catholic decorum, she also paid her respects in front of the pope. Vatican officials believed her, saying it was clear that she was a true believer just by looking at the expression in her eyes. This whole experience gave the WPK a keen lesson about the "perils" of religion. It was also the reason UFD officials were unenthusiastic about efforts to invite the pope to North Korea. North Korea's leadership was afraid that if the pontiff came to Pyongyang, it would create a wave of enthusiasm for Catholicism. The task force that had been given the job of inviting Catholicism's leader was quietly dismantled two months after its creation.

BEHIND THE TWO KOREAS SIMULTANEOUS ENTRY INTO THE UNITED NATIONS

Ultimately, Kim Il-sung's attempt to invite the Pope went nowhere, and North Korea's diplomatic isolation continued to deteriorate. By the 1990s, I think Kim Il-sung was experiencing his final failures in life. In early 1991, China gave North Korea some thoroughly unexpected news. In summary, this is what China said:

> The Soviets have established diplomatic relations with South Korea, which has led to major changes in the structure of power in Northeast Asia. China has decided to establish diplomatic relations with South Korea in order to prevent the United States from being the sole bene- ficiary of the future state of affairs in Northeast Asia. However, China cannot just rashly move ahead and establish diplomatic relations with South Korea. South Korea is not even a member of the United Nations, which poses a legal issue for China to recognize it first. China plans to establish diplomatic relations with South Korea only after the two Koreas have joined the United Nations. As such, China hopes that the Workers' Party of Korea rescind its policy of opposing the creation of two Koreas and take part in the process of having the two Koreas enter the United Nations simultaneously.

Sometime later, the Soviet ambassador to North Korea gave the country a similar message. It was clear that China and the Soviet Union had come to an agreement with South Korea and the United States about having the two Koreas enter the United Nations (UN) simultaneously. Kim Il-sung had long opposed the parallel entry of the two Koreas into the UN, calling it a scheme by the imperialist nations to create two separate Koreas. It was not surprising, then, that the North Korean leader was up in arms after hearing about the messages. Kim Jong-il, on the other hand, believed that North Korea's entry into the UN was inevitable; yet he had a difficult time persuading his father. When North Korea refused to accept the Chinese-Soviet proposal, the two countries made their demands even clearer:

> We hope that our Korean comrades view the situation rationally. At the UN General Assembly meeting planned for September 1991, South Korea

and the United States will attempt to push forward the South's entry into the UN. We cannot just stand by North Korea's side and rashly oppose South Korea's entry into the UN. If North Korea agrees to join the UN, however, we can negotiate with the United States about having the two Koreas enter the UN at the same time. If North Korea opposes entry into the UN to the very end, South Korea may be the only country that becomes a member. If that happens, South Korea will become the only government on the Korean Peninsula recognized under international law. We must prevent this from happening. There is no avoiding the simultaneous entry of the two Koreas into the UN.

Kim Il-sung flew into a rage when Soviet foreign minister Eduard Shevardnadze visited North Korea in September 1990 to inform him that the USSR had established diplomatic relations with South Korea. Even more enraging to Kim was the fact that Shevardnadze said the two Koreas' entry into the UN must not be postponed any longer. During the first high-level inter-Korean meeting held in October 1990, Kim Jong-il proposed, as part of an effort to come to an agreement, that the two Koreas simultaneously enter the UN as "one entity." This proposal went nowhere, however, because of opposition by the South Korean government. Even China was against it. North Korea's strategy of using inter-Korean talks to prevent the two Koreas from simultaneously entering the UN had ended in failure.

In May 1991, Malta—which held the presidency of the UN General Assembly at the time—sent a message to North Korea. In the message, the Maltese government asked the North Korean government to make a final decision on the UN issue because the Maltese foreign minister—as chair of the UN General Assembly—planned to visit North Korea and meet Kim Il-sung. A task force was created in North Korea's foreign ministry, and I was selected to be an interpreter and guide for the Maltese foreign minister. From that point on, everything proceeded in line with Kim Jong-il's agenda. Sometime later, Kim sent an order to the foreign ministry: "The Supreme Leader [Kim Il-sung] has decided to agree to the simultaneous entry of the two Koreas into the UN. We will now get what is owed from the Chinese and the Soviets. The Chinese and the Soviets must now ensure that North Korea and the United States establish diplomatic relations and the [foreign ministry] must make certain that this happens."

On May 27, 1991, North Korea's foreign ministry announced that the two Koreas would join the UN simultaneously. There was, however, a major problem standing in the way. If North Korea was the first to apply for entry, it would contradict everything it had said before. North Korea had long claimed that the simultaneous entry of the two Koreas into the UN would be the start of a perpetual division of the Korean Peninsula. That being said, North Korea found it difficult to wait until South Korea submitted its own application for entry into the international body. Indeed, it would be a major embarrassment for North Korea if, after South Korea's entry into the UN, the United States prevented North Korea from entering the organization.

North Korea conducted discussions with China and the Soviet Union about how best to join the UN. The Soviet Union told North Korea that while the United States said that it supported the simultaneous entry of the two Koreas, American officials had not given any real guarantees to that effect. North Korea received a promise from the USSR and China that they would accept South Korea's entry into the UN only if the United States first accepted North Korea's application, which the North Koreans planned to submit before South Korea.

Kim Jong-il reported to his father that North Korea would be the first to submit its application for entry into the UN. The elder Kim was very angry at first but eventually calmed down and agreed with his son's logic—that doing so would surely prevent South Korea from being the only Korea to join the organization. In July, in a move that the United States and South Korea did not see coming, North Korea submitted its entry application to the UN before South Korea. The issue of the two Koreas' entry into the UN passed through the UN Security Council in August and was adopted unanimously during a General Assembly meeting in September.

South Korea and the international community welcomed the simultaneous entry of the two Koreas into the UN. For North Korea, however, it was not a happy moment. The North Korean people were informed about it through a brief media report. Kim Il-sung's long-standing policy of opposing the concurrent entry of the two Koreas into the UN had, at that moment, completely fallen apart. As soon as North Korea submitted its application for UN membership before South Korea, Kim was weighed down with responsibility for the perpetual division of the Korean Peninsula.

There is something in all of this that I am still curious about. South Korea had moved aggressively to ensure that the two Koreas entered the UN simultaneously; however, why did the South Korean government submit its application after North Korea? Was it to prevent themselves from being blamed for causing the division of the Korean Peninsula? It is a mystery to me.

At the time, North Korea's foreign ministry was worried that South Korea would submit its application first and then mobilize the United States to block North Korea's application. The Roh Tae-woo administration's foreign policy of Nordpolitik suggested that South Korea was supportive of North Korea's entry into the UN. However, the United States, which had gradually been raising issues regarding North Korea's nuclear development program, may not have been so supportive.

As Kim Jong-il made his decision on the UN entry issue, he demanded that the Soviet Union and China support the establishment of diplomatic relations between North Korea and the United States. This completely broke his father's second principle of opposing the "cross-recognition" of the two Koreas. Cross-recognition meant that the Soviet Union and China would recognize South Korea at the same time that the United States and Japan would recognize North Korea.

Up until that time, all North Korean school textbooks stated that the country opposed the simultaneous entry of the two Koreas into the UN because it was a scheme to create two separate Koreas. The WPK now needed to explain away why the country had acquiesced to the concurrent entry of the two Koreas into the UN and why it had ignored the principle of cross-recognition. As a matter of fact, before becoming members of the UN, West and East Germany had first concluded a basic agreement before announcing to the world that their relationship was a "special one"—not just a regular relationship between two normal countries.

The two Koreas, however, became UN members without any treaty or agreement of any kind; moreover, the two countries were still in an armistice. North Korea was also faced with the problem of making its people understand that the two Koreas were not actually two separate countries. This issue was resolved with the signing of the Agreement on Reconciliation, Non-Aggression, and Exchanges and Cooperation between South and North Korea in December 1991. This treaty, also called the Inter-Korean Basic Agreement, stipulates that the two Koreas have formed "a special relationship constituted temporarily in the process of unification, not being a relationship between states." In reality, the agreement was akin to having your doctor prescribe medicine for you after your death; for North Korea, however, it was an opportunity to rationalize the simultaneous entry of the two Koreas into the UN.

The remaining issue facing North Korea involved receiving support from the Soviet Union and China to establish diplomatic relations with the United States and Japan. That was the only way for Kim Jong-il to achieve his initial goal of cross-recognition of the two Koreas. However, the USSR, which had already established diplomatic relations with South Korea, responded passively to North Korea's demand for cross-recognition. China, meanwhile, simply complained that while "we are doing the best we can to bring about cross-recognition, the United States and Japan have no intention to recognize North Korea."

When the Soviet Union collapsed the same month the Inter-Korean Basic Agreement was concluded, North Korea found it even harder to get help from its Cold War–era ally. China, for its part, moved to establish diplomatic relations with South Korea without even obtaining a promise from the United States that it would establish relations with North Korea. From Kim Il-sung and Kim Jong-il's perspective, the USSR and China were no longer trusted allies. In fact, China refrained from mediating the establishment of relations between the United States and North Korea, siding instead with the United States. The Chinese threw more salt into North Korea's wounds by saying that the DPRK would need to resolve questions surrounding its nuclear program before relations with the United States could be established.

An unexpected piece of good news arrived for North Korea's leadership as it was still getting over the "traitorousness" of the Chinese and Soviets. In November 1992, the Italian government proposed to send its ambassador in China, Oliviero Rossi, and Pini, the head of the Asia Section in Italy's Ministry of Foreign Affairs, to Pyongyang to discuss ways to improve the two countries' bilateral relationship. I do not remember Pini's full name.[9]

While South Korea had established diplomatic relations with North Korea's major allies China and the Soviet Union, North Korea had failed to establish official ties with any Western power such as the United States or Japan. At that point, North Korea's foreign ministry made a "contrarian" report to Kim Il-sung and Kim Jong-il:

> The establishment of official ties between South Korea and China will push new vitality into North Korea's diplomatic efforts. While we have long released a great deal of propaganda regarding our self-reliant foreign policy, the international community views us as a satellite of the USSR and China. Now, however, the Soviet Union has collapsed, and China and South Korea have established official ties. This presents us with the opportunity to clearly show how independent we are as a country. Moving forward, our country's international status will only strengthen further. From this point on, we will spur forward efforts to develop relations with Europe, Asia, and Latin American countries while opening the door to dialogue with the United States.

Kim Il-sung and Kim Jong-il ordered the foreign ministry to proceed as it wanted. Previously, in September 1992, the director of Italy's International Exchanges Finance Group, Carlo Baelli, had been invited to North Korea to negotiate a loan worth one hundred million dollars. Also in 1992, North Korean diplomats had moved to establish official ties with the eleven countries newly independent from the USSR. It appeared that North Korea was repairing the diplomatic hole that the collapse of the Soviet Union and the Eastern Bloc had created; in reality, however, the North's diplomatic efforts saw almost no tangible results.

It was under these circumstances that the Italian government proposed to send its ambassador to China on a trip to Pyongyang. Both of the Kims were naturally pleased to hear this.

As an aside, Ri Jong-hyeok, who was the North Korean representative for the Food and Agricultural Organization (FAO) in Italy, was considered to be very good at his job. Ri was the son of Ri Gi-yeong, a writer who had decided to leave South Korea for North Korea and a former vice chairman of the Korea Asia-Pacific Peace Committee. The younger Ri is sometimes seen in meetings held between the two Koreas.

The socialist and communist parties have traditionally been a powerful force in the Italian parliament. Following the end of the Cold War, Italy's parliament demanded that the government consider establishing diplomatic relations with North Korea. The Italian government, for its part, was faced with having to decide whether to loan North Korea one hundred million dollars. The moment seemed ripe for some kind of diplomatic breakthrough between the two countries. Kim Il-sung, full of excitement, said: "Italy is a strongly independent country of Western Europe. That Italy would send an ambassador to our country is not just an attempt to get a 'quick whiff' of our circumstances. The simultaneous entry of the two Koreas into the UN marked the start of an era of 'two Koreas.' Italy wants to establish relations with both Koreas and deal with them diplomatically on an equal basis. If things work out, we can establish official ties with Italy. I will meet the Italian ambassador personally." It was clear that Kim Jong-il was also excited. He handed down a detailed order to the foreign ministry that read:

> The Supreme Leader has great expectations for the visit by the Italian ambassador and his entourage. The WPK will provide everything needed to ensure we establish diplomatic ties with Italy. Make sure that the ambassador and his entourage are housed in the top floor of the luxurious Koryo Hotel and that their vehicles and meals are the finest we can provide. First Vice Foreign Minister Kang Sok-ju must handle their viewing of performances at the Central Committee's Mokrangwan state guest house, not the Mansudae Art Theater. I will ensure that the entourage will be able to see the Pochonbo Electronic Ensemble and the Wangjaesan Light Music Band in performance.
>
> The ambassador and his entourage will be most interested in what kind of economic relationship they can form with us. I will speak to Bureau 39 in advance, so take the ambassador's entourage to the Muncheon Smelting Facility in Gangwon Province and show them the gold bullion storage facility.[10] They will be amazed when you show them the storage facility and will become very interested in us. Use a helicopter when going to the Muncheon Smelting Facility. The roads are not great, and if we use vehicles, they will discover the dilapidated state of our country.

Kang Sok-ju, the first vice foreign minister, had been sentenced to "revolutionization" during a "censorship review" after being criticized by Kim Jong-il in the fall of 1992. Kang, who had been cleaning up excrement in a pig pen in a farm near Pyongyang, was reinstated about a month later by

Kim. He returned at a point when the Italian ambassador was set to arrive soon, and his relationship with Kim Jong-il was distant at best. Despite this, the North Korean leader gave him an important job during the visit, promising that the Pochonbo Electronic Ensemble and the Wangjaesan Light Music Band would be placed at his disposal. The two bands were, in actuality, Kim Jong-il's *Gippeumjo*.[11] Kang, for his part, was in the position of having to show off his loyalty to Kim.

Kang gave Kim Heung-rim, the head of the foreign ministry's European Department, the job of managing the day-to-day activities of the entourage. Choe Son-hui and I were chosen to be interpreters: Choe would handle interpretation for the ambassador's wife, while I would handle interpretation for the ambassador and Pini. Choe is now seen frequently on South Korean television. She has been promoted to first vice minister of foreign affairs after serving as the vice minister of foreign affairs handling North Korea's relations with North America.

The day before the ambassador and his entourage landed in Pyongyang, Kang held a meeting in his office. In a very excited voice, he gave the following order to Kim Heung-rim and me:

> You both know how much interest the Supreme Leader [Kim Il-sung] and Great Leader Comrade [Kim Jong-il] have in this visit. I'll get straight to the point. I must report to the Great Leader Comrade on a continuous basis, which means we must observe everything that the ambassador and his entourage do. The Supreme Leader and Great Leader Comrade both want specific information about each member of the delegation. From the moment they arrive, report to me in detail about their sentiments, hobbies, and family relationships. The Supreme Leader may demand a report on the delegation's movements through Jeon Hui-jeong, the director of the Foreign Affairs Bureau of the Presidential Department. It will be a major problem if reports go directly to the Supreme Leader before the Great Leader Comrade. Make sure to remember this. The party's internal reporting system dictates that the foreign ministry will report everything to the Great Leader Comrade first and then he will report to the Supreme Leader. You must make sure to adhere to this system.

I had been aware that all information had to first be reported to Kim Jong-il since the late 1980s, but I had not experienced such a thing myself.

The trip from the Pyongyang airport to Koryo Hotel was thirty minutes by car. I had to do my best to grasp the backgrounds of the people in the delegation during that time. The ambassador and his wife spoke in Italian inside the vehicle. I did not know what they were saying, but the wife did not appear to speak Italian fluently. I asked where in Italy she was from, and she answered saying she was Egyptian, not Italian. She also mentioned that she was a cousin of Boutros Boutros-Ghali, the UN secretary-general at the time.

Upon arriving at the Koryo Hotel, I spoke a bit with Pini, the director of the Asia Section of the Italian foreign ministry, while everyone checked in. I sensed that he knew Korean, so I asked him whether he spoke the language. He answered that he spoke a little bit. When I asked where he learned it, he answered that he spoke a bit because his wife was Korean. That led to a more extended conversation.

"When your plans to visit North Korea were announced, did the South's embassy in Rome stay silent? I would assume that you have deep relations with the South's embassy," I said.

"I'm married to a Korean woman, but I believe that, politically speaking, we need to treat the North and South equally," Pini answered. "I did meet with the South Korean ambassador in Rome before coming to Pyongyang. He asked the reason for my visit to the North and requested that we provide the results of the visit here to the South Korean embassy."

I asked what his Korean name was, and I think he told me it was Lee Gi-ju. During the conversation, the hotel staff was pestering me to take a phone call. It was Jeon Hui-jeong, the director of the Presidential Department's Foreign Affairs Bureau, calling for an update. Having received an order to make sure no updates should be given to Kim Il-sung first, I made the excuse that I needed to go up to the hotel rooms with the delegation. After that, I gave a report about the delegation to the foreign ministry's task force.

I took Jeon Hui-jeong's phone call only after I had confirmed that my report had made it to Kim Jong-il. Jeon was normally a calm person and would never raise his voice to another. But when I picked up the phone, he reprimanded me in an annoyed tone: "What's your name and position? Why haven't you been answering my calls? When did you join the foreign ministry? Are you asking for trouble? The Supreme Leader is waiting for his report!" Jeon, of course, knew that all reports must go to Kim

Jong-il first. However, it was natural for him to feel annoyed and anxious when Kim Il-sung demanded an update. "I apologize. I didn't know I had a phone call as I was busy helping the delegation get settled into their accommodations," I explained. I heard later that the two Kims were happy that the ambassador's wife was the cousin of Boutros-Ghali; however, they were unhappy to hear that Pini's wife was South Korean.

Two days later, Kim Il-sung met with the ambassador's delegation. "The Cold War has ended, and the North and South have all become members of the UN, so it is now time for Italy and North Korea to move away from the bloc mentality and establish diplomatic relations," Kim Il-sung emphasized during the meeting. However, the Italian ambassador remarked, incongruously, "North Korea must first resolve suspicions surrounding its nuclear program through the International Atomic Energy Agency or the United States before Italy can establish diplomatic relations with North Korea." As this showed, the Italian government had sent its ambassador to North Korea to better understand whether the DPRK would settle suspicions surrounding its nuclear program rather than to discuss establishing diplomatic relations with the country.

The day after the meeting with Kim Il-sung, the delegation visited the Muncheon Smelting Facility in Gangwon Province. The delegation flew there by helicopter as ordered by Kim Jong-il. Workers at the facility gathered to watch as the helicopter made its landing. Almost all of the workers at the facility seemed to have stopped work and gathered for the event. Officials at the smelting factory were curious to see how important the delegation was because, in their words, a helicopter had "never landed here before."

The facility's manager served as a guide for the delegation. He explained how gold and zinc were produced and even showed how gold bullion was made by pouring gold into crucibles. As a joke, the ambassador asked me to give him one piece of gold bullion, but Kim Heung-rim, the head of the foreign ministry's European Department, answered instead of me. "We'll give you ten pieces of gold bullion if we establish diplomatic relations with Italy," he said smiling, which gave the ambassador a big laugh.

The last remaining item on the delegation's schedule—per an order by Kim Jong-il—was to visit the storage facility for gold bullion. The facility's manager, however, seemed to think that the delegation's visit was over and prepared to say goodbye. Kim Heung-rim quietly asked the manager whether he had received an order to show the delegation the gold bullion storage area.

"There is no gold in the storage facility," the manager stated. "All the gold bullion produced here is immediately taken to Pyongyang. The gold bullion the delegation saw today was made especially for their visit out of ore collected after production was stopped a couple of days ago. If we could produce gold bullion every day like today, would our country be in such difficulties?"

Kim Jong-il was unaware of this situation. It was mortifying that a helicopter had been used to transport everyone to the facility. Even the Italian delegation was confused and appeared to question why they had been taken all that way to just see how gold bullion was produced. Italy was a modernized country that North Korea had no hope of catching up to. It was a mistake for North Korea's leadership to have even thought that they could show off their country's economic strength with gold bullion to people from such an advanced nation. In my view, even if we had shown the members of the Italian delegation hundreds of pieces of gold bullion, it would not have elicited much of a reaction from them.

That evening, a banquet was held for the delegation at the Mokrangwan state guesthouse. Kang Sok-ju was already there when I entered the banquet hall, along with some cadres from the WPK's International Department and the Cabinet. The delegation members sat in special guest seats, while Kang Sok-ju, Kim Heung-rim, Choe Son-hui, and I sat down between them. Pretty young girls were seated beside Kang, the ambassador, and Pini to wait on them.

Seeing them, I thought of the *Gippeumjo*, something I had only heard about through rumors. Curious, I began by first looking closely at each of their faces. They were very pretty. Soon, I found myself feeling shy and awkward even just meeting their eyes. I also thought about Kang's comment to me before the banquet had started: "The Great Leader Comrade [Kim Jong-il] will be watching the banquet through closed-circuit television. The banquet must be full of excitement. That's why interpretation will be important. You must ensure that there is a merry atmosphere." After the food was served, the *Gippeumjo* girls poured wine for the ambassador and his entourage. It was the first time I experienced sitting between such pretty girls for a meal. Some time into the meal, a performance began.

The music and dancing were performed by the Pochonbo Electronic Ensemble and the Wangjaesan Light Music Band. At first, the bands played North Korean songs, but later they moved to jazz and disco music, with the bright lights on the ceiling dimming to dark neon. Then dancers wearing racy clothes appeared on the stage. It felt as though I had been transported to Broadway, something I could only experience in American movies. Every time the performers switched turns, male staff waiting nearby gave us flower bouquets and told us to give them to those on stage.

These days, various North Korean–style dances are available to watch on YouTube. The dancing I saw that day was almost like those YouTube dances, yet also very different. The music I saw at the event was more unrelenting, and the clothes the performers wore were much racier—even more revealing than bikinis. The atmosphere was out of the ordinary, with the performers wearing black caps and black socks and even holding onto black dancing sticks.

The Mokrangwan state guest house, where the banquet was held, is inside the headquarters of the WPK's Central Committee. The WPK has long promoted communist morality and revolutionary culture and art while calling capitalist culture and art corrupt and decadent. I felt as though I was watching "corrupt and decadent culture and art" at the venue espoused by party officials to be the center of communist morality and revolutionary culture and art.

When I saw suggestive dances in American movies and other places, I was able to watch them lightheartedly. However, I felt like I was committing a crime by watching North Korean women reveal their belly buttons and raise and lower their legs while wearing bikinis that exposed the outlines of their bottoms. I think I was still just a simpleminded communist at the time.

At some point, however, the atmosphere among the delegation grew uncomfortable. The ambassador clapped along with the dancing, but Pini looked uncomfortable and made no effort to join in the excitement. After the performers disappeared from the stage, music began emanating from the stage. The music was good for social dancing and signaled that it was time to raise the excitement level.

The young women sitting next to the ambassador and Pini asked them to dance. The ambassador and his wife went to the dance floor and danced the waltz and tango. Pini, however, did not leave his seat and sat like a stone, even though the girl next to him repeatedly asked for a dance. Kang gave me a signal to encourage the Italian diplomat to dance. The Italian ambassador had already suggested that Pini should dance, but Pini responded with a comment that immediately washed away the banquet's merriment: "I'm uncomfortable here because I'm not accustomed to being at *gisaeng* parties."[12] Pini spoke in English, but his pronunciation of *gisaeng* was clear to any Korean speaker. I suddenly felt my heart sink and tried to read what the girl sitting next to Pini was thinking. If Kim Jong-il found out that Pini had mentioned "*gisaeng* party," it would become a serious problem. The ambassador, for his part, gave Pini a look that suggested something unnecessary had been said. Kang and Kim pretended not to hear Pini's comment and engaged in conversation with the ambassador. While the music and dancing continued, I had no heart left to watch or listen to it. I only realized that the performances had ended when it was time to hand flower bouquets to the performers.

After the banquet, I returned to the foreign ministry and wrote a report. Kang Sok-ju, Kim Heung-rim, and Chae Son-hui were also at the ministry building. The banquet had not been just any old banquet for us. Our "Report on Progress During the Mokrangwan Event" was filled with only the good things that had happened: "The banquet was full of excitement. Ambassador Rossi and Section Chief Pini said that it was the first time they had seen such a performance. They said that the state of our artistic culture is very high and that it was much better than Italy, which is the home of vocal music." Kim Heung-rim and I were unsure of ourselves even as we submitted the report. If someone in the delegation were to tell the press later that they had seen a performance of Kim Jong-il's *Gippeumjo* in North Korea, it would be a big problem. It was too terrible to imagine. If that were to happen, and Kim Jong-il were to hand down official criticism, we would face terrible punishment.

Luckily, the delegation kept their mouth shut about the performance to the press, but I am still unclear why Kim Jong-il decided to hold an evening banquet that resembled a "*gisaeng* party." Would it not have been better to show the delegation *Sea of Blood, The Flower Girl*, or another revolutionary opera that would have been better received by the Italians? For some time, I thought of the performers at the banquet dancing in very revealing clothes. I wonder if their parents knew that their precious daughters were stuck in the headquarters of the WPK's Central

Committee, dancing every night in such shows. What would they think if they did know?

In his own way, Kim Jong-il tried to provide the very best welcome for the delegation but ended up revealing the scandalous realities of the country's leadership. Even after the delegation returned to Italy, North Korea and Italy failed to establish official diplomatic relations. The main reason was the first North Korea nuclear crisis in March 1993, but I wonder if it was also related in some way to the sudden *Gippeumjo* performance. It was not until January 2000—eight years later—that Italy and North Korea finally established official diplomatic ties.

MAO ZE-DONG TELLS KIM IL-SUNG TO "STOP DREAMING ABOUT NUCLEAR WEAPONS"

In January 1993, South Korea and the United States officially announced the restart of the "Team Spirit" exercises, which had been suspended for a year. North Korea took that as a pretext to announce its exit from the Non-Proliferation Treaty (NPT) in March. This marked the moment when the North Korea nuclear issue—which had been simmering for decades—came to the fore, leading to the first North Korea nuclear crisis. That crisis continues to this day, three decades later.

The North Korean nuclear issue has deep historical roots and needs to be understood from a historical perspective. Here, I would like to explain the origins of the issue and the process in which North Korea ended its membership in the NPT.

Kim Il-sung experienced the psychological power of nuclear weapons during the Korean War. While UN troops advanced all the way to the Yalu River after the successful Incheon landing, the war began to turn against the UN when the Chinese communist army got involved in the war. The retreating main forces of the U.S. military became surrounded by Chinese troops at the Chosin Reservoir. In North Korea, rumors began suggesting that U.S. president Harry Truman was planning on dropping nuclear bombs in Manchuria or the northern part of the Korean Peninsula.

While Kim Il-sung, along with Mao Ze-dong and Stalin, did not believe such reports, ordinary North Koreans fled southward out of anxiety and fear bred by the possibility that nuclear weapons would be used. This, at least, was what I learned from the education I received in North Korea. My father and grandfather told me similar stories, with sayings like "We all die if the United States drops nuclear bombs on us" and "The entire family can't flee, so the sons must survive and carry the family forward." According to them, these sentiments were rife among North Koreans at the time of the Korean War. I am aware, of course, that many of those who fled southward did so out of a desire for freedom, not because they were afraid of nuclear bombs. Indeed, most South Koreans probably think this way. I was born after the Korean War, so I cannot say for sure which belief is closer to the truth. My point, however, is that the fear North Koreans felt toward nuclear bombs was even more intense than we can imagine.

Kim Il-sung seems to have viewed the fear North Korean people felt toward nuclear weapons from a different perspective. The North Korean communist party's control over the people at the time was weak compared to now. The WPK was unable to prevent people from fleeing no matter how much its propaganda told people to refrain from going south because the United States "could never drop nuclear weapons." Party officials could never have put everyone who wanted to flee up against a wall to be shot. Kim Il-sung, who had to watch helplessly as lines of people fleeing southward, saw with his own eyes the power of nuclear weapons: not the physical or military power of the weapons, but the psychological power they had over people. It was from that time that Kim decided to develop nuclear weapons and obsessively tried to obtain them.

In March 1953, in the midst of the Korean War, North Korea concluded an agreement for the "peaceful use" of nuclear power with the Soviet Union, and by the late 1950s, the country had built a nuclear research center focused on the development of a nuclear bomb. Kim's decision to build a research center for nuclear weapons—even as North Korea was still in a state of destruction from American bombings during the Korean War—shows clearly how much Kim was obsessed with nuclear weapons.

The Soviet Union, however, did not allow North Korea to develop nuclear weapons. The Soviets were firm in their position that they should be the only country in the communist bloc to possess the technology to develop nuclear weapons. The Soviets built nuclear power plants in other communist countries while restricting access to technology, raw materials, and even the plants' operators; moreover, any and all nuclear material was brought back home. That is why North Korea, China, and other communist bloc countries sent researchers to a nuclear research facility in Dubna to learn about nuclear power. North Korea reportedly sent around thirty physicists—mainly students in the physics and mathematics departments at Kim Il-sung University—to the center in 1956. While they went to the center under the pretext of learning about nuclear power, they had received an order from the party to "study with the development of nuclear weapons in mind." This marked the moment when North Korea really began its development of nuclear weapons.

The country moved one step further down the path of nuclear weapons development when it built a nuclear power research center in Yong-byon, North Pyongan Province, in 1962. With its existing technological and economic conditions, North Korea faced difficulties in building a nuclear reactor, however, because it lacked a heavy chemicals industry. In June 1963, the country received a mini-reactor for research purposes (IRT-2000) from the Soviets. North Korea was completely dependent on the Soviet Union for everything nuclear.

At the time, China was hurrying to develop its own nuclear weapons, but Mao Ze-dong refused to adhere to Soviet-mandated restrictions. The country publicly dismissed the Soviet's claim to a monopoly on nuclear technology and attempted to create its own nuclear weapons. Kim Il-sung stood with Mao on this issue, despite the fact that North Korea was the only communist country left in the world still receiving massive amounts of aid from the Soviet Union. Kim thought that communist countries other than the USSR needed to develop nuclear weapons to fight the Americans. He calculated that if China took the lead in developing the weapons, North Korea could follow in its footsteps.

In the October 28, 1963, edition of the *Rodong Sinmun*, North Korea published an article criticizing the leaders of the Soviet Union as "modern-day revisionists." The editorial stated: "The Soviet Union has unilaterally shredded the agreement made with its paternal countries and has more or less ended its economic and technological cooperation with them. It likes to boast about its support and is using it for political interference and economic pressure." At the time, the Soviet Union was making significant progress in concluding an agreement to end nuclear testing with the United States, the UK, and other countries with nuclear weapons, and it had been trying to bring the Chinese into this agreement. From the outside looking in, the Chinese and the Soviets appeared locked in an ideological conflict; in reality, however, the Chinese had expressed opposition to the Soviet's policy of monopolizing nuclear weapons development. Kim Il-sung's support for Mao was part of his strategy to have the Chinese aid North Korea's own development of nuclear weapons.

On October 16, 1964, China succeeded in testing a nuclear weapon, becoming a de facto nuclear-armed state. While Kim Il-sung may have been elated to hear this, he realized that his initial calculation was wrong. At a meeting with Mao in Beijing on April 18, 1975, Kim quietly asked him, "How much did it cost to develop a nuclear warhead?" Mao told an official at the meeting to tell Kim how much it cost. The official said he heard that it had cost a total of two billion dollars. The meeting was replete with Chinese alcoholic spirits and a congenial atmosphere, but Mao told Kim the following in a harsh tone: "North Korea should stop even dreaming about obtaining nuclear weapons. While China was developing nuclear weapons on its own, its relationship with the Soviets worsened and its economy got so bad that tens of millions of people died of hunger. If a country as small and economically weak as North Korea tries to develop nuclear weapons, it will eat away at the economy and people's lives will become more difficult. That will make it impossible to maintain its socialist system."

Mao made this statement not out of concern for North Korea's economy or the continuation of its regime. It was clear that Mao intended to prevent North Korea from developing nuclear weapons. While Kim evasively told Mao that it was not his country's intention to develop nuclear weapons, on the train ride back to North Korea Kim held a meeting of the party's political bureau and said the following: "Did you all hear what Mao told me? The biggest enemy preventing us from making nuclear weapons in the future is not the United States, it's China. In short, the biggest barrier we have to overcome is China. China will oppose us becoming a nuclear armed state until the very end, and if that is the case, we won't be able to develop nuclear weapons. As such, we need to proceed in cooperation with China."

The exact expression Kim used for "proceed in cooperation" was a North Korean expression meaning to "coax somebody into doing something." This story of the conversation between Kim and Mao is even in a North Korean novel. I remember this novel being about the secret history behind North Korea's nuclear weapons development. I, too, have long been aware of this story.

KIM CALLS FOR THE DENUCLEARIZATION OF THE KOREAN PENINSULA WHILE SECRETLY ATTEMPTING NUCLEAR WEAPONS DEVELOPMENT

After returning home, Kim, who was now certain that China would be of no further help to North Korea's nuclear development goals, created a detailed strategy. This strategy was implemented gradually over a long period, but its outlines are as follows.

The first part of his strategy was the removal of tactical nuclear weapons from South Korea. In the beginning, North Korea called for negotiations with the United States through China and the Soviet Union. The response from those two countries was cold, however, expressing doubt that the United States would listen to what they had to say. The Soviets expressed even more opposition to North Korea's request than the Chinese. The Soviets believed that if they demanded that the United States remove nuclear weapons from South Korea, the United States would demand that the Soviets remove nuclear weapons from the Eastern Bloc. At around this time, the Soviets were in the middle of negotiations with the United States about the removal of tactical nuclear weapons from Europe.

Kim decided not to rely on either the Soviets or the Chinese and instead to proceed to remove tactical nuclear weapons from South Korea by himself. He claimed that North Korea had received authority or sovereignty from the Soviet Union and China with regard to the nuclear issue. Right after his visit to China in the mid-1970s, Kim started calling for the denuclearization of the Korean Peninsula. His strategy was to develop nuclear weapons while using the slogan of denuclearization to prevent the United States or China from becoming suspicious. In 1980, North Korea, along with Japan's socialist party, announced a joint declaration calling for the denuclearization of the Korean Peninsula. In 1985, North Korea again called for denuclearization and lasting peace on the Korean Peninsula. In December of the same year, North Korea signed the NPT.

Kim's second strategy was to receive a U.S. promise to refrain from using nuclear weapons against North Korea. The logic he used was as follows:

The United States claimed that it had removed nuclear weapons from South Korea, but North Korea had no way of confirming this. And even if it was true, North Korea was still within targeting range of American nuclear weapons. If the United States refused to recognize North Korea and make this pledge, Kim would have no choice but to develop nuclear weapons.

With these two strategies in mind, North Korea put all efforts into secretly developing nuclear weapons. North Korea's development of nuclear weapons might have proceeded smoothly if not for the crisis caused by the fall of the Soviet Union and the eruption of the Gulf War. As the United States claimed victory in that war in February 1991, it declared nuclear nonproliferation as its highest priority for national security and foreign diplomacy. At around the same time, the Soviet Union was falling apart. The United States wanted the tactical nuclear weapons located throughout the fifteen federal republics of the collapsed Soviet Union to be gathered in Russia before being destroyed.

As the Russian nuclear issue proceeded in a way to America's liking, the United States gradually started to focus on how to resolve suspicions surrounding North Korea's nuclear weapons development. For Kim Jong-il, it was important to stall the United States as long as possible while soothing American concerns about the country's nuclear program. Kim used inter-Korean meetings to relieve pressure exerted by the United States. In fact, the card North Korea has always pulled out when it faces isolation and crisis has been inter-Korean talks.

Representatives from the two Koreas announced a plan for the denuclearization of the Korean Peninsula on July 30, 1991. On September 28, the United States announced that it would remove all tactical nuclear weapons throughout the world as part of its efforts to prevent the proliferation of nuclear weapons. While the United States and North Korea held different calculations in all of this, they appeared to agree on the idea of denuclearizing the Korean Peninsula. On December 13, the prime ministers of the two Koreas signed the Inter-Korean Basic Agreement, and on December 31, the two sides signed the Joint Declaration on the Denuclearization of the Korean Peninsula.

A situation similar to what happened during the negotiations surrounding the declaration of the denuclearization of the Korean Peninsula in December 1991 reappeared in 2018. The biggest barrier to progress in the 1991 negotiations surrounded the selection of places in North Korea to be inspected by the international community. The South Koreans wanted to inspect places it had selected, but the North Koreans strongly opposed this, calling the plan an infringement of its sovereignty. Ultimately, the final denuclearization declaration included a compromise stating that the sites to be inspected were to be selected by the South Koreans and then agreed upon by both sides.

Choe Woo-jin, a vice minister in the North Korean foreign ministry, who had succeeded in narrowing the final agreement to just those sites agreed upon by both sides, received high praise from Kim Jong-il. Within the foreign ministry, people compared the Korean Peninsula denuclearization declaration to students and teachers agreeing beforehand on what problems should be in a university test. In short, they viewed the declaration as a victory for North Korea.

At the time, North Korea had neither nuclear weapons nor any places to test nuclear weapons. Then, why did North Korea oppose the compulsory inspections proposed by the United States and South Korea to the extent it did?

During the inter-Korean talks, the South Koreans argued that they must have the authority to select sites for inspection. Officials in the North Korean foreign ministry's International Treaties Department thought there would be little issue in agreeing with the South Korean proposal, given that North Korea, as a signatory to the NPT, would have to open up the Yongbyon nuclear site to the IAEA (International Atomic Energy Agency) if requested to do so. However, members of the foreign ministry's Human Rights Department, Ministry of State Security, and other agencies strongly argued that the South Koreans should not be given the authority to select the sites for inspection. If that happened, they argued, the South Koreans could eventually ask to inspect the country's political prisoner camps as well.

Going forward, the final step in eliminating North Korea's nuclear weapons would be confirming the complete, verifiable, and irreversible destruction (CVID) of the weapons. However, given that North Korea has an uncountable number of so-called "special-use areas" for political prisoner camps and exclusive use of the Kim family, the country will never accept CVID.

Even during the inter-Korean summit on April 27, 2018, the two sides failed to discuss a specific road map for the dismantling of North Korea's nuclear program.

If, during a summit between the United States and North Korea, a compromise were brokered to limit the sites for inspection to just those agreed upon by both sides, this would be nothing more than a sham agreement. All that would happen is that we would find ourselves knee-deep in another nuclear crisis in a couple of years.

KIM JONG-IL SAYS NORTH KOREA WILL DESTROY THE WORLD IF IT LOSES IN A WAR

While the international community was mesmerized by the nice-sounding call for denuclearization, the United States was an exception. American leaders never stopped viewing North Korea with mistrust, given their suspicions about North Korea's nuclear development. Ultimately, America was right. The Kim family never had any intention of giving up nuclear weapons development.

In December 1991, the Soviet Union officially dissolved, and Kim Il-sung asked the following questions during a meeting with Korean People's Army cadres and former anti-Japanese revolutionary fighters: "Now, even the Soviet Union has been destroyed and China has attached itself to South Korea. How will we realize unification of the fatherland going forward? If the South Koreans and the Americans attack us, can we fight and win using only our strength alone? Tell me how you really feel." The military cadres and anti-Japanese revolutionary fighters told him: "Don't worry. We have been preparing for unification of the fatherland for decades and we will absolutely win."

After hearing this, Kim Il-sung asked another question: "Haven't we already gone through the war [Korean War] to liberate our fatherland? War did not work [in our favor] as we had thought. If we were to lose [in a war], tell me honestly what you think we should do." While everyone was hesitating to answer this question, Kim Jong-il stood up and said loudly, "We will destroy the world if we lose the war."

Then Kim Il-sung banged his hand onto his desk and said with satisfaction, "That's the answer I wanted to hear. If we lose, we must destroy the Earth. There is no need for a world without us."

From early 1992, the WPK began holding lectures that included this anecdote. The party aimed to ingrain in the minds of all party members that North Korea must develop nuclear weapons. At the time, even I thought that there was no need for a world without North Korea and that there was no other way to ensure North Korea continued to exist than for the country to possess nuclear weapons.

However, North Korea made it known that it would accept inspections of its nuclear program by the international community. In January 1992, South Korea and the United States declared they would suspend their joint Team Spirit military exercises. This provided North Korea with the pretext to conclude an agreement focused on nuclear safety with the IAEA. In short, North Korea permitted a nuclear inspection team to visit the country. The United States and South Korea claimed that North Korea had allowed the inspection as compensation for the American removal of nuclear weapons from South Korea and the suspension of Team Spirit exercises. However, the seeds of future conflict remained because the biggest issue surrounding the resolution of the nuclear problem was mutual inspections by the two Koreas, which the North Koreans did not accept.

In May 1992, North Korea submitted its first report regarding nuclear material to the IAEA. Up until that point, everything had been implemented based on the Korean Peninsula denuclearization declaration. It seemed as though even the United States would no longer apply any pressure on North Korea.

However, North Korea's first report submitted to the IAEA caused a problem. In the report, North Korea claimed that it possessed ninety grams of plutonium; however, the United States counterclaimed that North Korea had already extracted ten to fourteen kilograms of plutonium. The United States claimed that if North Korea was not transparent on this issue, it would be clear evidence that the country was developing nuclear weapons. The international community pressured North Korea to dispel these suspicions.

These suspicions were right on the mark. Nuclear specialists in North Korea's Ministry of Atomic Power Industry (MAPI) had believed they could fool the IAEA and the United States by reducing the amount of nuclear material declared, given that calculations surrounding nuclear material are very complicated. Kim Jong-il may have wanted to report even lower numbers. In fact, the North Korean foreign ministry engaged in a dispute with MAPI over how the nuclear material was calculated. However, the foreign ministry was unable to overturn an order by Kim

Jong-il that instructed officials to hide the real amount of nuclear material that had been extracted.

With a bitter taste in its mouth, the foreign ministry submitted the first report to the IAEA, and the issue exploded. Kim Jong-il, who had made the decision to submit the report after receiving reports on everything, tried to evade blame, placing responsibility for the issue at the feet of MAPI and the foreign ministry. Kim was extremely angry and claimed that the submission of the first report to the IAEA created more problems than it resolved.

Alarm bells rang in the foreign ministry. Criticism first centered on the ministry's treaty and regulations department, which had managed relations with the IAEA. Oh Chang-rim, the head of this department, saw his position fall in the ministry. Choe Woo-jin, the head of the Fatherland Unification Department, also saw a fall in influence. Choe's department had managed the adoption and implementation of the denuclearization declaration and issues surrounding the suspension of the Team Spirit military exercises. Choe had personally argued that if the denuclearization declaration was adopted, it could lessen the pressure exerted by the United States. Kim Jong-il also criticized the foreign ministry's American Department and Kang Sok-ju, who had managed the submission of the report.

Although Kim's attempt to submit false nuclear material figures to the international community on the basis of MAPI's reports was ultimately revealed, it would have been impossible for North Korea to submit accurate plutonium measurements. Doing so would have meant that North Korea would effectively be giving up on its plan to develop nuclear weapons. With North Korea refusing to explain suspicions surrounding the nuclear material, the United States and South Korea announced the resumption of Team Spirit exercises and demanded that North Korea acquiesce to nuclear inspections. In response, North Korea exited the NPT, which led to the start of the first North Korea nuclear crisis.

THE GENEVA NUCLEAR AGREEMENT WAS A DECEPTION TO STALL FOR TIME

A high-level meeting between the United States and North Korea was held in Geneva in July 1993. The United States threatened that war would be inevitable if North Korea did not accept special inspections. Robert Gallucci, the head of the American delegation, said that the two countries had tried everything to avoid armed conflict but ultimately failed. Kang Sok-ju and other North Korean delegates at the meeting believed that war would be unavoidable upon their return to North Korea, even though they did not express this outwardly. In short, war was inevitable unless North Korea yielded.

Kim Jong-il called for Kang and asked in detail about what Gallucci had said and about his behavior. After confirming that the United States was intent to push ahead with war, Kim was anxious. Real authority had shifted to Kim from his father more than ten years before the elder Kim's death in 1994, so that Kim Il-sung was nothing more than a figurehead at that point.

Following the meeting in Geneva, American media outlets reported that President Bill Clinton was moving forward with plans to strike the Yongbyon nuclear site. South Korean president Kim Yong-sam desperately opposed the Clinton administration's "surgical strike" plan. The situation was akin to a tinderbox. Then, former American president Jimmy Carter announced he would travel to North Korea to end the crisis, and in June 1994, the former president met with Kim Il-sung. Carter told Kim that America would end its sanctions on the country and provide light water for its nuclear reactor. Thanks to Carter's mediation, an inter-Korean summit was scheduled, but then Kim suddenly died.

The entire world predicted that, with the death of Kim Il-sung, North Korea would not last much longer. That prediction, however, was made without much knowledge about the country. Kim Jong-il was already wielding real power in the country in April 1980, when I matriculated into the Pyongyang University of Foreign Studies (PUFS). Kim Il-sung was no more than a symbolic figure in the country.

On July 8, 1994, when Kim Il-sung's death was announced, I received an urgent message to report to the foreign ministry's meeting hall. Kim's death was reported on TV. Everyone was crying as they left the meeting hall. My mother went with other women of similar age in her neighborhood to Kim's statue in Pyongyang's Mansudae and cried there for a while before returning home. Every day, officials from the foreign ministry headed up to the statue of Kim Il-sung in Mansudae with flowers to pay their respects and to shed tears. There was crying everywhere. The memorial period was set at one hundred days, and every day I went to Mansudae to cry or participate in memorial ceremonies.

I believed that the fervor surrounding the commemoration of the late North Korean leader would die down after a hundred days. Soon after the end of the hundred days, however, the authorities began holding criticism sessions aimed at assessing everyone's attitude during the mourning period for Kim Il-sung. In tandem with this, the authorities began another campaign of purges. Important members of each of the foreign ministry's departments were unable to go home as they worked to deal with various international issues. Several people were caught up in the purges.

Four employees of the foreign ministry's Domestic and Foreign Affairs Department were found to have played cards while working overnight and were expelled to a region outside Pyongyang. One employee of the Telegram Clearance Department was also expelled from the capital city after mumbling to himself after reading a telegram sent from the North Korean embassy in China. The telegram read: "Flowers are being sent to be placed at the statue of Kim Il-sung by way of Koryo Air." Without thinking, the employee mumbled to himself, "The Chinese must be earning a lot these days selling all these flowers." A member of the International Propaganda Department was expelled from the city for moving to a new home during the memorial period, while yet another was expelled for having gone to a sauna because they had a headache. Even today in North Korea, government and party officials face scrutiny about what kind of attitude they showed when Kim Il-sung or Kim Jong-il died.

In any case, Kim Il-sung's meeting with former U.S. president Carter achieved some results. In October 1994, the U.S.–North Korean Agreed Framework, otherwise known as the Geneva Nuclear Agreement, was signed. The agreement called for North Korea to abandon its nuclear development, promised that the United States and South Korea would provide economic and security guarantees, and called for efforts to achieve the complete normalization of U.S.-DPRK relations along with continued inter-Korean talks. The "first North Korean nuclear crisis" thus appeared to be at its close.

As is now well known, however, the Geneva nuclear accords were nothing more than North Korea's deceptive attempt to stall for time. As Kang Sok-ju was leaving negotiations in Geneva, Kim Jong-il gave him the following order: "What we need is time. Buy us more." From the beginning, Kim had no intention of adhering to the accords and was just trying to buy more time. There is an example I can give here that shows how deceptive North Korea's attitude toward the negotiations really was.

The core of the economic guarantees promised by the United States and South Korea was to build a light-water reactor in North Korea, and negotiations soon began on building this reactor. Experts from North Korea's Ministry of Electronic Industry took part in the negotiations, but they were in an uproar after reading the Geneva agreement, saying that the "foreign ministry had made mistakes in the negotiations." What they said, in summary, was: "How do you expect to get anywhere by making an agreement to just build a light water reactor? What funds will there be to build a substation, nuclear fuel rods, and power transmission systems? There's nothing in the agreement about these things. The agreement would be perfect if South Korea or the United States promised to provide support to build the substation and power transmission facilities and purchase nuclear fuel rods. You must renegotiate." The foreign ministry responded by telling the experts that they should "just stay quiet if they did not know that the country was in the midst of a deception to buy time." Not one person in the ministry believed that North Korea would abide by the Geneva accords. Up until that point, North Korea had claimed internationally that the country's goal was not nuclear development but denuclearization of the Korean Peninsula; internally, however, officialdom preached the opposite: "We must have nuclear weapons at all costs." While not an official order, it was considered a tacit set of instructions to follow.

FOREIGN DELEGATION EXPRESSES DISMAY AT THE REALITY OF NORTH KOREA'S RURAL AREAS

North Korea succeeded in buying time through the Agreed Framework. The United States made an agreement with North Korea because it believed that the country's economy would fall apart if its nuclear development was delayed just a little longer. American officials thought that once the DPRK's economy collapsed, its ability to develop nuclear weapons would evaporate. The United States, for its part, had made the agreement to buy time for itself as well. In fact, North Korea's economy was on the verge of collapse at the time. As an official in the foreign ministry, I saw the miserable conditions of the economy with my own eyes.

The year 1994—when the Agreed Framework was signed—was a truly unlucky year for North Korea. Kim Il-sung died in July, and in August, North and South Hwanghae provinces suffered massive flood damage. North Korea's food shortages had begun in the early 1990s, but these shortages grew worse as floods ravaged the country. North Korea did not have the ability to get through this difficult set of circumstances by itself. It badly needed food aid. However, nobody was able to propose to Kim Jong-il that the country needed to ask the international community for food. Making such a "wrongheaded" proposal would lead to a purge or worse; yet Ri Su-yong, who had been watching over the brothers Kim Jong-chul and Kim Jong-un in Switzerland, braved a minefield and made the proposal anyway. Ri is, at the time of this writing, the vice chairman of the Seventh Central Committee of the Workers' Party of Korea.

Ri admitted to Kim that North Korea may give the impression that its economy is in dire straits if it pleads for food aid from the international community; at the same time, however, the country could expand its exchanges and contact with the Western nations, thus serving to move North Korea out of its "diplomatic isolation." The focus of Ri's proposal was on ending North Korea's diplomatic isolation, not obtaining food aid, so it would not hurt Kim Jong-il's pride. Kim, who had been meeting frequently with Ri about his children, judged that his ambassador to Switzerland had a point and ordered him to "move forward with it."

In August 1994, Ri arrived in North Korea along with representatives from various international organizations. The foreign ministry immediately formed a task force, and I was selected as a member from among staff in the ministry's international organization and European departments.

Because this was the first time such an undertaking had occurred, there were no "speech scripts" or "activity plans" available, no documents used by ministry officials to prepare to explain about the country's circumstances to a foreign audience. The task force decided to create plans "on the go" as they met with representatives from international organizations. Up until that point, I had only talked to foreign dignitaries about North Korea's "brilliance"; I felt terrible as I showed the devastation and bleak realities of North Korea's flood-damaged areas to foreigners for the first time.

The delegation was appalled at what they saw. They had had no idea that North Korea's rural areas, which had been promoted as a "socialist paradise," were so backward. The foreign dignitaries shed tears as they saw children afflicted with malnutrition lying in hospitals, preschools, and day-care centers. I, along with North Korean foreign ministry representatives in the delegation, could not help but cry at what we all saw. What we witnessed tore away the veil that had covered what had been promoted as socialist cultural rural areas and a socialist paradise.

The international community was shocked by the realities of North Korea as described by those in the foreign delegation. International agencies and global nongovernmental organizations sent food to North Korea after their representatives saw emaciated children dying of starvation. The international community's distribution of food aid to North Korea right after the Agreed Framework led to a period of warming relations between the country and the West. It was just what Ri had told Kim Jong-il would happen.

KIM JONG-IL EXCITED BY THE UK'S PROPOSAL FOR "SECRET CONTACT"

I had the opportunity to see firsthand the warming atmosphere between North Korea and the international community following the arrival of food aid to the country. In January 1995, the foreign ministry received a telegram from the embassy in Beijing saying that the British government wanted "secret contact" with North Korea. The telegram expressed hope that department heads from the foreign ministries of the two countries could meet in March at the British embassy in Geneva. The British embassy in Beijing, which relayed the message, also requested that the proposal be kept secret.

The content of the telegram was immediately sent to Kim Jong-il. He appeared excited, and I heard that he told Kang Sok-ju: "It is interesting that of all the Western countries, the British—who are the closest allies of the United States—have reached out to us first. They have likely consulted with the Americans. Now that the door has been opened with the nuclear agreement the Americans have concluded with us, they are sending the

British to test the waters. There's nothing wrong with that. We may even be able to establish diplomatic ties with the UK. Once that happens, other European countries will follow. We may even be able to smooth the road to establish ties with France." Noteworthy here is that Kim expressed an interest in establishing relations with France, something that I will come back to later in this book.

A delegation was immediately formed after Kim ordered the foreign ministry to go ahead with the meeting with the British. Apart from myself, the head of the European Department, Kim Chun-guk, and the head of the UK and Northern Europe Department, Mun Bong-nyeo, were selected to join the task force. My overseas travel up until that point had been limited to Beijing and Moscow; it was the first time in my life that I was heading to a Western country, and I lost sleep thinking about it.

At 10 A.M. on Tuesday, March 21, 1995, the North Korean delegation was sitting in a meeting room at the British embassy in Geneva. Han Chang-hun, who was a counselor at the North Korean representative office at the UN in Geneva, had joined our delegation. On the British side, we sat across from the head of the foreign ministry's Asia and Pacific Section, the director of the Korea Section, and Jim Hoare, who was part of the research and analysis cadre of the British diplomatic service. Jim later became the first chargé d'affaires at the British Embassy in Pyongyang. I called him "James Ho."

The main point made by the British during the meeting was as follows: "Our two countries have had zero exchanges for too long. The UK welcomes the decision made recently by North Korea to conclude the Geneva accords with the United States as part of its efforts to become a member of the international community. We believe without a doubt that the two countries will establish diplomatic relations based on North Korea's sincere implementation of the nuclear agreement." In short, the British were saying that the two countries could establish relations if North Korea sincerely implemented the Agreed Framework. While they did put forth conditions, the British proposed to gradually improve the relationship over time—a traditional British way of conducting diplomacy.

The North Korean delegation responded to the British as follows: "During the Cold War era, our two countries had very distant relations. Now, however, the Cold War system has fallen, along with the blocs based on ideology and [political] systems. Now, even the UK has no need to align itself with the confrontational policies the United States has toward North Korea. We hope that the UK, befitting a permanent member of the UN Security Council, can act freely when it comes to policies toward North Korea."

The British delegation responded with this proposal: "We do not know much about each other and have many policy differences because our two countries have not had contact nor conducted dialogue in a long time. Let's conduct at least two official dialogues per year to expand our communication." There was no reason for us to refuse. The two delegations ended the meeting with a promise to conduct the next one in Beijing that coming autumn. After receiving a report on the results of the meeting, Kim Jong-il ordered talks to continue with the British while "pushing forward" to establish official ties between the two countries.

I participated in the second round of talks with the British delegation in the fall of that year. On December 12, 2000—five years later— North Korea and the UK finally established diplomatic relations. As it happened, I participated in the final meeting with the British right before the official establishment of relations. I am deeply entwined with the UK on several personal levels: I witnessed both the beginning and the finishing touches of the establishment of official ties and, later, succeeded in receiving asylum while working as deputy ambassador at the North Korean embassy in the UK.

THE SWISS TRY TO GAUGE
NORTH KOREA'S GENUINENESS

The Swiss were undoubtedly aware of our entry into their country, given that we had conducted a secret meeting with the British in Geneva. The Swiss authorities even proposed that we meet with them and tour a nuclear power plant. We decided to accept the proposal, even though we did not really know what their intentions were.

A day after the meeting with the British, Swiss officials allowed us to tour a nuclear power plant about a hundred kilometers from Geneva. It was a first for me and very different from what I had imagined. There were hundreds of tourists at the power plant, most of them students. Their guide was explaining how safe nuclear power plants were.

After touring the plant, we had a sit-down meeting with the Swiss, who seemed keen to emphasize the peaceful and safe use of nuclear energy. Reading between the lines, however, they were really telling us the following:

Getting a light water power plant from the Americans will not resolve North Korea's energy problem. You have to be able to transport the electricity produced in the plant, but there is nothing about this in the U.S.-DPRK agreement. Nuclear fuel rods are another issue. Even we Swiss import nuclear fuel rods from France. The cost [for purchasing the fuel rods] is covered by electricity bills. What funds does North Korea plan to use to pay for nuclear fuel rods? Your electricity bills don't even reflect the costs of producing electricity; they're just collected for symbolic reasons, right? Running a power plant means you have to stop its operation on a regular basis to repair it. In Switzerland, the American company Westinghouse, which built the power plant, manages the repairs. In North Korea's case, you'll have to regularly accept help from South Korean or American technicians to repair your plant. Did you know about all these issues before signing the agreement with the Americans?

On the face of it, the Swiss appeared to be pointing out that North Korea would be reliant on South Korea and the United States for its energy needs despite the import of a light-water power plant. From a different perspective, what they were saying could have been something else entirely. The Swiss may have been trying to ascertain whether North Korea—already cognizant of all these issues—was just running a scam to buy time, or whether it was the Americans who were conning the North Koreans.

The North Korean delegation responded to the Swiss as follows: "We will deal with whatever issues arise after the light water power plant is imported into the country. The electricity produced by the power plant will be a tremendous help to our country's economic development, so we can modernize transmission and transformation facilities even if we have to borrow funds. The nuclear fuel rod issue can be discussed with the United States on a separate basis later on." We gave the Swiss a very diplomatic answer with just the right amount of ambiguity. When we reported the results of the meeting to Kang Sok-ju upon our return to Pyongyang, he said we had done a good job, noting, "The Americans used the Swiss to try and figure out our intentions." The experience taught me yet again that diplomacy is war without gunfire.

WHY BIGWIG RI SU-YONG WAS SO POWERFUL

My relationship with Ri Su-yong, North Korea's ambassador to Switzerland, deepened even further through the secret meeting we held with the British in Geneva. Ri, who was a close confidant of Kim Jong-il, is someone to keep an eye on because he has continued to play a similar role under Kim Jong-un. Back in Switzerland he used an alias, Ri Chul.

Ri took our delegation to several famous locations in Switzerland, including the Interlaken ski resort. During the evening, he even made beer-cheese fondue at a pub. The conversation at the pub focused on North Korean diplomacy. What surprised me was that, despite his high rank, he listened intently to the ideas and opinions of young diplomats like me. And he did not just listen: he spoke in detail about his own thoughts as well. I concluded that he was quite personable.

When the delegation prepared to leave Switzerland to go back to North Korea, we received a lot of requests from the embassy staff to take things back to their homes. Ri, however, scolded them for "making trouble for someone who has visited Switzerland for the first time" and gave the delegation one of his leather bags. It was high-quality and must have been priced in the hundreds of dollars. He expected us to put the things the embassy staff wanted to send back in the bag; it was a gesture aimed at satisfying both the staff and the delegation, including me.

I met Ri later by chance when I was returning to North Korea from a trip abroad. He appeared suddenly when I was waiting for a flight at Frankfurt Airport in Germany. He took all of us to a pub in the airport, buying us beer and even handing out money for us to spend. After that, I saw him each time I traveled to Switzerland. There was a time when we rode in a car for hours on end together. I snoozed, unable to fight off my fatigue, but I never once saw him take a nap. I was impressed by his attention to his duties: receiving reports from embassy staff or handing down new orders, all while on the move.

I have no idea when Ri looked after Kim Jong-il's sons, Kim Jong-chul and Kim Jong-un. I knew that from the early 1990s, he met frequently with Kim Jong-il and that Ri had tremendous influence on the North Korean leader. Most of Kim's orders to the foreign ministry went through Ri. How Ri interpreted Kim's orders probably made a difference in the direction of the ministry's activities. While such influence could have come from Ri's relationship with Kim's children, I believe that Ri nonetheless possessed tremendous talent.

Ri received permission from the North Korean leader to do many things that the foreign ministry itself would have been unable to do out of fear. One prominent example was a measure that allowed diplomats and their families working abroad to take off their Kim Il-sung badges when required. In North Korean terms, this was a revolutionary change.

North Korean diplomats had long been strictly prohibited from removing their Kim Il-sung badges in any situation. Taking off the badge—whatever the cause—was a serious offense that warranted immediate punishment. My understanding is that Ri proposed to Kim Jong-il the following: "Based on my experience of working as ambassador in Switzerland, the wages of the diplomats are so low that we have to shop in inexpensive places. It's no shame to shop in such cheap stores, but it is regretful that the badges of the Supreme Leader are worn in such places. [Wearing the badges] also puts us in a disadvantage while flying planes because it makes us easy to spot by the southern puppets [South Koreans]." That Ri could bravely raise such an issue with Kim was because he travelled to Switzerland so often with Kim's children. The rule requiring Kim Il-sung badges to be worn at all times was likely very troublesome for him given that he needed to hide the identities of Kim's children while abroad. Ultimately, however, his successful proposal allowed all North Korean diplomats and their families to take off the badges when needed.

Ri also raised the issue of insufficient living expenses among diplomats with the North Korean leader. The monthly wages of North Korean diplomats were pitiful compared to those enjoyed by Western European or even South Korean diplomats. The issue had not been raised to the WPK because, compared to ordinary people, diplomats were already living "lives of luxury." While Ri's mention of the issue did not lead to an immediate rise in the pay of North Korean diplomats, their wages were adjusted every dozen or so years to match international commodity prices and the commodity prices where the diplomats resided.

KIM JONG-IL'S "ZHU BA-JIE" STYLE OF PRACTICAL DIPLOMACY

Right after Kim Il-sung's death in August 1994, the foreign ministry conducted a massive reorganization. The Nonaligned Countries Department was abolished, and the International Agency Department was reduced in size to become just one department. Kim Gye-gwan, who rose from being an adviser to nonaligned countries to the upper leadership of the foreign ministry, became the head of the ministry's American Department.

The Western European Department, where I had worked, was combined with the Eastern European Department to form a new European Department. Up until the reorganization, the Western European Department had a smaller number of staff and less work than the Eastern European Department. It was, in short, an easily forgotten part of the foreign ministry, but as part of the new European Department, those who had worked there grew in status. They took over important posts in the new combined department, including its directorship. The American Section, which was a part of the Americas Department, became a separate organization, the American Department. Meanwhile, the head of the Japan Section of the Asian Department became a vice minister, and an expert on Japan became the vice department director of the Asian Department.

This massive reorganization of the foreign ministry was done in accordance with Kim Jong-il's so-called Zhu Ba-jie diplomacy. Zhu Ba-jie diplomacy called for a shift from diplomacy based on ideology to diplomacy focused on achieving practical benefits. Like Zhu Ba-jie, a character in the Chinese novel *Journey to the West*, diplomats were to pretend to be honest, ignorant, depressed, and even foolish to obtain everything they could. Kim Jong-il's move to this kind of diplomacy was interconnected with the changes of the times. As he experienced the simultaneous entry of the two Koreas into the UN, the fall of the Soviet Union, the establishment of diplomatic ties between China and South Korea, and the first

North Korea nuclear crisis, Kim Jong-il came to understand the weaknesses and limitations of the Chinese and the Soviets.

Kim believed that North Korea had to join forces with enemies regardless of ideology if the country expected to obtain its own advantages. He knew it was important to maintain one's principles on the inside while never showing outwardly what North Korean diplomacy is pursuing or its strategies and objectives. Everything must be opaque; if North Korea was to obtain practical benefits, it must boldly make contact with countries it deemed enemy states, including even the United States and Japan.

The emergence of Zhu Ba-jie diplomacy meant that Kim Il-sung's policies regarding the nonaligned movement had ended with his death. Kim Il-sung's style of diplomacy had been part of a global revolutionary strategy to join forces with nonaligned countries to remove any American influence throughout the world. His son revised North Korea's diplomatic direction through the use of a strategy to place a check on the United States vis-à-vis the Europeans. In short, the elder Kim's revolutionary diplomacy strategy had been replaced by one that aimed to keep the United States in check.

Kim Jong-il also presented a "global multipolar strategy," which argued that the global order should be multipolar instead of a unipolar one centered on the United States. France, England, Germany, and other western European countries key to the European Union served as an important pillar of this multipolar strategy. The focus of expertise in North Korea's foreign ministry moved from Soviet and nonaligned movement experts to those with expertise on the United States, China, Japan, and Europe. Those with expertise in Asia, Africa, the Middle East, and Central America were gradually pushed to the background.

"COMRADES, DON'T LIVE LIKE ME"

In 1995, North Korea's situation began to grow dramatically worse. The foreign ministry was no exception. Paper was no longer being supplied for us to write up documents. The WPK called for "self-sufficiency." The foreign ministry built its own paper-making factory. I found out only then that scrap paper could be placed in a tank and treated with a chemical reagent to create paper to write on. This method created very low-quality paper, but it gave us material to create documents. The foreign ministry even created a place for people to take baths because most of its staff could not do so at home.

From early 1995, there were many times when even Pyongyang-based food distribution centers did not have any rice to hand out. The foreign ministry did not hand out rice directly but gave staff distribution cards that they then took to receive rice at local distribution centers. This was before the rise of black markets, so if you could not obtain rice from your distribution center, there was nowhere else to get it.

The foreign ministry adopted emergency measures that provided free lunch to staff suffering from difficult living conditions. This lunch, how-ever, was nothing more than corn soup. Diplomats who had accumulated foreign currency through their stays abroad lived reasonably well. Those without such experiences had to survive on one bowl of soup handed out every day at the ministry's cafeteria. There were around forty people in the ministry's European Department, and around five of them frequented the ministry's "cafeteria to help the poor." While I had never worked abroad, I never fell to such depths of eating the ministry's soup because we received support from my wife's family.

Everyone else brought lunch boxes to work. A common word for lunch box in Korean is a word borrowed from Japanese, *bento*, a linguistic remnant of the Japanese occupation of Korea. Despite its origins, North Koreans use the word without shame. Recently returned diplomats from abroad would put together two lunch boxes with rice and side dishes for their less fortunate colleagues. The country's economic difficulties were felt by everyone, but people cared about each other a lot.

Probably the happiest part of the day for me was lunchtime. Around ten people would sit down together in the large office room to eat the side dishes they had brought; it could not get any better than that! I remem-ber one of my colleagues who particularly liked lunchtime. He was over seventy years old and about to retire. Even before the strike of 12 P.M., he would pester everyone to gather around with their lunch boxes. He may have done that because he was only able to bring rice most of the time due to his own financial difficulties.

This elderly man would be the first to arrive at work to clean up the office and was a hard worker. I respected and liked him. One day after lunch, however, he let out a sigh while telling us: "Comrades, don't live like me." Then he began to complain in detail about his own circumstances.

It turned out that he had gone to Europe to study during the Korean War and, after his return to North Korea, took up work at the foreign ministry. He had lived his whole life without concern over money while making trips between Pyongyang and other countries every three or four years. He thought of Kim Il-sung as God and repeated the Ten Principles for the Establishment of a Monolithic Ideological System every evening.[13] He fell asleep only after reflecting on whether he had spent his day in accordance with the teachings of Kim Il-sung and Kim Jong-il.

In the late 1980s, he was a counselor at an embassy abroad. The ambassador, party secretary, and security officials at the embassy focused on making their own money, ignoring their official work. They bought cigarettes in cheap countries and resold them for a profit. It was a time when Eastern Bloc countries did not interfere in the business practices of North Korean diplomats.

The man was unable to look past such behavior, which contradicted the teachings of the Supreme Leader, or Kim Il-sung. When it came time to conduct a self-criticism session one Saturday, he criticized the ambassador, saying, "The Supreme Leader told us not to conduct business at the embassies, but some Comrades are breaking this rule." It made things awkward for the ambassador and other staff who had earned money through private business.

One day, the ambassador called for the man. He gave him a passport and told him to buy some cigarettes in a nearby country and then sell them. The ambassador was essentially telling the man to make some money. The man refused the ambassador's offer, telling him he did not know what the ambassador was talking about. Everyone else did business selling cigarettes on the sly, but the man stuck to his guns and lived in accordance with the teachings of the Supreme Leader until he returned home.

Several years after the man returned, however, North Korea's Arduous March began. All those who had earned money abroad—in violation of the Supreme Leader's teachings—were able to bring lunches to work, but this man had no money to bring anything more than rice. He had little time left before retirement, and he was unhappy thinking about what life would bring him after he retired.

While listening to the elderly man's story, I felt that his comment, "Don't live like me," exemplified an old man expressing regret too late in life.

THE REASON NORTH KOREAN DIPLOMACY APPEARS SO STRONG

After I arrived in South Korea, I found that North Korean diplomacy was highly regarded. I, too, felt proud about being a member of the foreign ministry when I was in North Korea, even finding myself expressing awe at North Korea's diplomatic skills. However, I never imagined that North Korean diplomacy would be so highly regarded in South Korea.

There are a number of reasons why North Korean diplomacy is strong. As the expression "brinkmanship diplomacy" suggests, North Korean diplomacy is conducted in desperation because it is aimed at survival of the country. That cannot help but make it strong. Diplomatic policies stay in force for long periods of time, and the foreign ministry places a premium on diplomats' building expertise in their fields. Diplomatic policies are not pulled from their roots even if administrations change, and diplomats are not sent here or there to build broader experience.

North Korea is a dynastic country, which means that the leaders of the country's diplomacy and security can stay in their posts for twenty or even thirty years. Kim Il-sung and Kim Jong-il, for example, were accomplished veterans who experienced all sorts of hardships from a diplomatic and national security perspective. I would like to go into detail about one example here.

Kim Jong-il had a negative view of Soviet general secretary Mikhail Gorbachev's Glasnost and Perestroika policies and criticized them as an attempt to destroy the communist system. At the height of confusion and disorder in the Soviet Union, on August 19, 1991, a hardline faction of the Soviet communist party calling itself the State Committee on the State of Emergency initiated a coup. They claimed that Gorbachev's health issues made him unable to continue as president and deployed airborne troopers and tanks into Moscow. The coup forces went on the radio to claim that Gorbachev's policies of reforms and opening would lead to the disintegration of the Soviet Union and that the Soviet military now needed to rise up to take control of the situation.

That evening, North Korean radio reported in detail about the State Committee on the State of Emergency declaration. Just listening to the announcer's voice made it clear how much North Korea's leadership wanted a coup in the USSR. It was an expression of the North Korean leadership's rage at Gorbachev for being captivated by the Roh Tae-woo government's Nordpolitik and forming diplomatic ties with South Korea. Events within the North Korean foreign ministry that day were tinged with urgency. The Soviet ambassador in Pyongyang visited the foreign ministry to alert North Korea's leadership about the policies of the coup forces. The ambassador expressed support for the coup and said that the "red flag of the revolution" could not be taken down. Foreign ministry leaders and members of the ministry's Soviet Department (Department No. 3) stayed at the office until late into the night to provide reports on the situation to Kim Jong-il.

On the morning of August 20, Kang Sok-ju received a call from Kim. The North Korean leader, who I had thought would welcome the coup given his unflattering opinion of Gorbachev, issued the following order in a calm and composed manner:

> The document the foreign ministry sent to me says that the coup forces will succeed, leading to a stabilization of the situation in the USSR. I don't think success will be easy. The coup can only succeed if citizens and laborers are deployed to organize rallies in support [of the coup]. Deploying airborne troops and tanks is the way soldiers in capitalist countries run a coup. A communist party must never do such a thing. It should instead hold a communist party rally to criticize Gorbachev and conduct mass rallies with civilians and laborers. That the "State Committee on the State of Emergency" has failed to move the party in this regard means that the Soviet communist party has already been turned. The coup will likely fail given that the "State Committee on the State of Emergency" did not deploy party members and because of its reliance on the military. Make sure we don't make it seem we openly support the coup.

From that very afternoon, North Korean media outlets began reporting on events in the USSR without any analysis or editorial commentary. People not in the know were confused as to why the North Korean communist party had failed to announce a declaration supporting the coup. On August 21, three days after the start of the coup, Muscovites were shown on top of tanks and armored cars. The special forces tasked with silencing demonstrations had refused to attack fellow Russians, and the coup had fizzled out in three days. Kim's prediction had been right on the mark.

KANG SOK-JU NUDGES OUT KIM YONG-SUN

Of course, Kim Jong-il's diplomatic perspective and judgment were not something he had been born with. He had cultivated his skills during his lengthy experience on the front lines of diplomacy. Foreign ministers in North Korea can stay in their positions for ten or twenty years if they do not fall astray of the leader. This is not something easily accomplished by diplomats in liberal democracies and can be seen as a strength of North Korean diplomacy.

North Korea's diplomacy also became stronger as it helped overcome crises that threatened to pull the country apart. North Korean diplomats could not make heads or tails of the series of crises they faced, from the fall of the Eastern Bloc and disintegration of the Soviet Union to the simultaneous entry of the two Koreas into the UN, the establishment of relations between China and South Korea, and the first North Korea nuclear crisis. The diplomatic establishment's expertise was so concentrated on China, the USSR, and the Eastern Bloc countries that it had few people who could negotiate with Western countries.

For North Korean diplomats, resolving the nuclear crisis was unavoidable; however, even among those in the foreign ministry there were splintered views on what to do. Choe Woo-jin and others placed importance on inter-Korean talks and the role of South Korea. They believed that inter-Korean talks could be used to achieve a joint declaration with South Korea about denuclearization and, once that happened, North Korea could obtain South Korean support to have the United States declare the nonuse of nuclear weapons against North Korea. In their view, all of this would ultimately lead to the possibility of the United States and North Korea establishing official ties.

Kang Sok-ju, meanwhile, believed that there were limits to what inter-Korean talks and the use of South Korea could achieve. He thought that North Korea must raise tensions to force the United States to come to the negotiating table. The WPK Central Committee's secretary for international relations, Kim Yong-sun, agreed with Kang on this and said that his department would take the lead in managing U.S.-DPRK relations.

There was a time when Kim Jong-il was unable to make up his mind on the direction of the country's diplomacy regarding the nuclear issue. By the 1990s, the issue was being discussed through the IAEA, with the United States lurking behind the scenes. Kim was unsure whether to give the baton to Kang Sok-ju or Kim Yong-sun to resolve it. In short, he was unsure whether North Korea should resolve the nuclear issue through cooperation with the international community, led by the IAEA, or through bilateral negotiations with the United States.

Most people thought that Kang was smarter than Kim Yong-sun. At the working level, Kang's foreign ministry was a much better operation than the party's international relations department run by Kim. Kang, however, was not one to just follow orders. He would at times find creative ways to deal with things. With this in mind, Kim Jong-il decided to implement a two-track strategy: give control over negotiations with the international community, including the IAEA, to Kang, while allowing Kim Yong-sun to manage relations with the United States.

In January 1992, Kim Yong-sun visited the United States to meet with Undersecretary of State Arnold Cantor. Kim proposed something striking: "We want to establish U.S.-DPRK ties in return for not demanding the withdrawal of American troops stationed in the South." However, the meeting did not lead to a written agreement or a declaration. Kim Jong-il viewed Kim Yong-sun's team as incompetent. The North Korean leader finally determined that while the nuclear issue should be resolved through bilateral talks with the United States rather than negotiations with the IAEA, Kang should lead the charge, not Kim Yong-sun.

Aart from Kang, there was no other person in North Korea who could have resolved the first North Korea nuclear crisis. Kim Jong-il did not just give Kang new marching orders, however. At the time, the North Korean leader was planning changes to the foreign ministry because he thought that the ministry had responded poorly to the succession of crises in recent years. Kim was very unhappy with the ministry for, in his view, sparking the first nuclear crisis following the first report the ministry submitted to the IAEA. The North Korean leader planned to revive discipline in the ministry by knocking down one of its bigwigs. That bigwig was none other than Kang Sok-ju.

POWERFUL KANG SOK-JU NUDGED ASIDE AS KIM JONG-IL REASSERTS DISCIPLINE IN THE FOREIGN MINISTRY

In September 1992, Kim Jong-il found his chance to reassert discipline in the foreign ministry. A regular board of governors meeting of the IAEA was held in Vienna, Austria. One of the major items on the agenda was examining the implementation of North Korea's nuclear safety agreement. Three-party talks among South Korea, North Korea, and the United Stataes were also held, and the head of the North Korean delegation was a foreign ministry counselor named Oh Chang-rim.

The head of the South Korean delegation proposed to Oh that they hold an unofficial meeting over a meal. The South Korean intention was likely to open up lines of communication with North Korea to prevent the United States and North Korea from shutting South Korea out of negotiations. Oh sent a telegram to the foreign ministry saying it would "be good" to meet with the head of the South Korean delegation to "find out what kind of information is being shared" between the United States and South Korea. Kang, who thought it was not a bad idea, sent a report to Kim Jong-il by email saying that he would order Oh to meet with the South Korean delegation. This was at a time when there were still no clear plans among North Korean leaders as to how to resolve the nuclear crisis, and opinions were split between those who called for working with South Korea and those who believed it better to conduct bilateral negotiations with the United States. Choe U-jin, who believed that North Korea should use South Korea to achieve its aims, also held considerable influence at this time.

For some reason, Kim Jong-il's confirmation about Oh's meeting with the South Korean delegation was slow in coming. There was no way to know, but the North Korean leader may have been out on an on-the-spot inspection somewhere, or perhaps he was deep in thought about what to do. A day passed, until finally Kim sent down a signed document stating, "There is no need to meet with the South's delegation." Kang immediately ordered that a telegram with Kim's order be sent to the North Korean representative office in Austria.

At the time, North Korea's foreign ministry used a shortwave wireless communications system due to security concerns, despite the existence of wired communications and international phones. Shortwave wireless telegrams had to go through the North Korean representative office in Moscow before reaching Austria. There were only two times a day when the telegrams could be sent. As a result, Oh Chang-rim was unable to receive Kang's telegram before his scheduled meeting with the South Korean delegation.

Oh, believing Pyongyang had no instructions to give him, went ahead and met with the South Korean delegation. The results of the meeting were sent back to Pyongyang. His actions, however, went against foreign ministry policy. Oh was supposed to have waited until he had received a specific order; if there was no order, he should not have met with the South Koreans.

Oh's actions put Kang in a difficult position. He had been given an order by Kim Jong-il to avoid meeting the South Korean delegation, but he now had a telegram that said his delegation had met with the South's officials. Kang was forced to report the truth to Kim because there was no way of hiding it. The North Korean leader was extremely angry, asking why the foreign ministry had gone ahead with meeting the South Korean officials when he had told them not to. Kang responded that he had made a serious mistake and blamed the slowness of the wireless communications system. The North Korean leader gave Kang a ferocious scolding, further fueled by his previous intention to reestablish discipline at the foreign ministry: "How can you use the wireless communications system as an excuse? If you had any intention to implement my order, you should have immediately called Oh Chang-rim to stop him [from meeting the South's delegates]. You're telling me that you acted in accordance with the rules, but if you intend to do your work this way, I have no interest in seeing any documents from the foreign ministry. You'll just have to do everything yourself!" Kang continued to make his report by phone. Kim was heard slamming his phone receiver down. From the next day, the foreign ministry was no longer able to submit reports to Kim through email. The North Korean leader had shut off his computer.

Several days later, a WPK Central Committee inspection team showed up unannounced at the foreign ministry. The inspection team was made up of forty people, including staff from the Central Committee's Organization and Guidance Department and the International Department. The head of the inspection team was the deputy head of the party's International Department, Kwon Min-jun. Kang was stripped of his position and kicked out of the ministry. Kwon took over Kang's role.

Each member of the inspection team took up positions in each of the foreign ministry's departments. The inspection team started by going through a document with a record of all Kim Jong-il's orders. In North Korea, government departments are required to organize and record all of the leader's orders and the results of their implementation. This document, called the "orders implementation ledger," is the first thing inspection teams look at when they conduct investigations. This ledger records where the orders were sent, what discussions were conducted about their implementation, and how the orders were implemented over time. Updates to the record are made once every hour without fail because any delay, however brief, would lead to trouble.

NORTH KOREAN DIPLOMACY IS BUILT THROUGH PURGES

Across all the departments of the foreign ministry, the orders implementation ledger filled the space of several books over the course of a year. The European Department, where I was, was investigated intensively by the head of the WPK International Department's Foreign Policy Section. At the end of a month of investigation, a criticism session was held at the lecture hall in the foreign ministry. The session was led by the secretary of the Central Committee's Economic Affairs Department, who was supported by Kim Yong-sun, the head of the Central Committee's International Department. Party members in the foreign ministry shed tears while criticizing Kang Sok-ju and Oh Chang-rim for so poorly carrying out orders by Kim Jong-il. Some ministry department heads who had ill feelings toward Kang even called for his expulsion from the party.

It appeared that, at the very least, Kang would be expelled from Pyong-yang as punishment.

Kim Yong-sun could not hide his personal animosity toward Kang during the criticism session. When Kim was the vice director of the Cen-tral Committee's International Department, Kang was just the manager of European affairs in the foreign ministry. As Kang rose to become a first vice minister of the foreign ministry, his status grew more powerful than Kim's. Kim seemed unsettled by this. He criticized Kang during the session by saying: "Comrade Kang Sok-ju has become arrogant. He sits in the very front during party politburo meetings even though he is not a member of the politburo. The place he sits at is for politburo mem-bers. Does he not know where he should sit?" A considerable number of people, however, believed that Kang would not have sat in such a seat of his own accord. Kim Jong-il frequently asked Kang's opinion during the meetings, so—according to them—Kang had no choice but to sit close to the North Korean leader.

Ultimately, Kang was punished by being sent to a rural area for "revo-lutionization," while Oh Chang-rim was expelled with his family to Pyeo-ngseong, South Pyongan Province. Kang was forced to work on a farm, clearing up pig droppings. Yet Kim Jong-il did not plan to completely shove him off the platform; the North Korean leader simply wanted to reassert discipline over him. Kang handwrote a letter to Kim begging for forgiveness and, around a month later, Kang was returned to his former position. Kang's punishment further cemented the foreign ministry's focus on direct dialogue with the United States. Choe Woo-jin, who sup-ported inter-Korean talks, slowly lost influence.

Meanwhile, the instigator of the furor, Oh Chang-rim, settled down in Pyeongseong. He was an able diplomat and possessed the internal strength to soldier on regardless of what befell him. When the Arduous March began in the late 1990s, Oh and his wife began making bread and selling it on the black market. His bread was a hit and became so famous that it came to be called "Oh Chang-rim Bread." Both he and his wife have since died.

Later, the resurrected Kang headed up North Korea's "brinkmanship diplomacy." Purges are an embarrassing part of North Korean life, but they are also a reason that North Korean diplomacy is strong. Of course, purges are little more than shock treatment: they may create strength tem-porarily, but there is no guarantee that strength will continue forever.

RI YONG-HO SACRIFICES SLEEP TO READ AMERICAN BOOKS ABOUT NUCLEAR NEGOTIATIONS

While Kang managed negotiations with the Americans, Ri Yong-ho—who was North Korea's foreign minister at the time of this writing—handled the behind-the-scenes work. His rise and development as a diplomat happened within the foreign ministry. Up until the 1990s, North Korea, which had conducted diplomacy mainly with the USSR, China, and the Eastern Bloc during the Cold War, had nobody versed in military arms reduction–related issues who could talk with Western nations. In 1990, however, an official message arrived at the foreign ministry from the UN saying that the United States was conducting a six-month-long arms reduction expert training program and requested that each UN member nation send one person to participate.

Ri, who was the head of the foreign ministry's Military Arms Reduction Bureau, took this message to Kang to ask whether he could participate in the program. The bureau, nestled inside the ministry's International Agency Department, had nothing to do and was a place to idle one's time away. Nobody in the ministry wanted to work there. Everyone was unclear why Ri Yong-ho, the son of Ri Myeong-je, a powerful member of the elite who headed up the "Third-Floor Secretariat," was even working in that department.

Foreign ministry rules required that no fewer than two people could be sent abroad for training. Kang fell into deep thought because it was exceedingly rare for anyone to be sent alone to a training program outside the country. Kang knew he needed to adhere to the rules, but he could not outright refuse a request from the son of Ri Myeong-je. Kang reported to Kim Jong-il that he "intended to send Ri Yong-ho to an American training program focused on arms reduction," along with a comment that Ri was Ri Myeong-je's son. Kim, who held Ri Myeong-je in very high regard, immediately authorized the plan.

Ri Yong-ho participated in the U.S. arms reduction expert training program in 1990, visiting a wide range of think tanks over the program's six-month period. He brought back a bag full of books when he returned to Pyongyang. At the time, few people thought that a nuclear crisis would explode between the United States and North Korea. Ri predicted such an event before many others and read all of the nuclear negotiations–related books written by American scholars that he had brought back, even staying up nights to get through them.

Sometime later, the IAEA raised suspicions about North Korea developing nuclear weapons, leading to the start of the first nuclear crisis. American media outlets reported that the United States soon planned to conduct a surgical strike against the Yongbyon nuclear facility. Most people in North Korea believed that "at last, war is coming." Even the foreign ministry was taken aback by the unfolding events, but while everyone else was unsure what to do, Ri Yong-ho took charge.

He argued that "North Korea must bring events to the brink of war by exiting the NPT and declaring a quasi-state of war." That someone as normally calm and moderate as Ri could argue for such a hardline approach was based on a certainty about what to do bred through skill and experience. As the first nuclear crisis unfolded as Ri had foreseen, it also ended in a way that North Korea desired. North Korea's strong diplomacy had once again displayed its staying power.

THE PURGE OF MY SUCCESSFUL FATHER-IN-LAW THROWS DARKNESS ON MY FUTURE PATH

Even while working at the foreign ministry, I had no hope that I would be called to serve in Europe. Up until the 1990s, diplomats could be expected to be sent abroad after three or four years in the job if they were proficient in a foreign language. In the European Department where I worked, most of the diplomats had studied the language of a specific European country such as Danish or Swedish. They found it easy to get called out for foreign service. For people who had studied English like me, however, it was harder to be sent to Europe unless you were the child of a party cadre. It was much easier to be sent to Africa or Asia. There was another reason that made it difficult for me to serve in Europe: my father-in-law, who had been caught up in the storm of purges that came after the "Frunze Military Academy Incident," was exiled to an area outside of Pyongyang.

North Korea has long used purges to deal with threats to its system. As unrest increased in North Korea following the collapse of the Eastern Bloc and the disintegration of the USSR, Kim Jong-il needed something new to create fear among the people. One step he took was using the Frunze Military Academy Incident. Frunze is an old Soviet military academy named after one of the founders of the Soviet Red Army. From 1986 to 1990, around 250 North Korean military leaders studied at the school. Right after the fall of the Eastern Bloc in the late 1980s, North Korea rushed to extract its students from the USSR and Eastern Europe. North Korea's leadership was concerned that the movement toward reforms and opening in those places could find its way into North Korea through the students. To the leadership, it appeared that those who had studied at the Frunze Military Academy were critical of North Korea's dictatorship.

In early 1992, I visited Russia as a member of a foreign ministry delegation. Moscow looked extremely depressing, unlike what I had seen in the movies. There were demonstrations almost daily in the city's main square. The display cases at stores were completely empty, and in the subways and underground walkways, women and the elderly were standing around trying to sell shoes, butter, bread, and coats.

The delegation visited the resting place of Lenin in the Kremlin, but there were few other people there. The socialist Soviet Union—built by people who risked their lives like Pavel Korchagin, the protagonist of the socialist realist novel *How the Steel Was Tempered*—was lifelessly collapsing before our eyes. When the delegation returned to Pyongyang, several people asked me about the situation in Russia. I could not get myself to tell them anything. Doubts formed in my mind: If the Soviet Union and Eastern Bloc have already fallen, how will North Korea survive? This sense of doubt shifted to concern about my own family.

THE FRUNZE INCIDENT KNEECAPS SOLDIERS WHO STUDIED IN THE USSR

The Frunze Military Academy Incident was launched in February 1993 with the purge of members of the Ministry of the People's Armed Forces who had studied at the academy. A former KGB operative who had defected to North Korea reportedly turned over a list of pro-Soviet, anti–North Korean regime soldiers to the North Korean authorities. North Korea's leadership spread the message that it had discovered a secret KGB spy ring within the military. By 1998, many people had been thrown out of the military, arrested, or even executed.

The sparks from this incident flew into the eyes of all those who had studied abroad. From the viewpoint of the North Korean authorities, these people had committed the crime of experiencing life outside of the country. Even Oh Geuk-ryeol, a member of the revered "anti-Japanese partisan bloodline," became someone Kim Jong-il guarded against because he had graduated from a Soviet air force university. In 1988, the head of the Soviet military's politburo visited North Korea and met with Oh, who was then the chairman of the general staff. The North Korean leader even installed listening devices in Oh's office and car to monitor his every word.

My own father-in-law, Oh Gi-su, suffered punishment when a delegation from the Soviet Military Academy visited North Korea in 1989. It was only a couple months after I had married his daughter. He was proficient in Russian and met with the Soviet delegation as president of the Kim Il-sung University of Politics. He toured various places in North Korea with them and told them about his time studying abroad in the USSR as a way to express his fondness for the country. He also did this to stay loyal to Kim Jong-il's order to ensure that the delegation's trip to North Korea went well.

The North Korean military's security command, which caught my father-in-law's comments on tape, reported to the North Korean leader that Oh had an extraordinary affinity for the USSR. Without any stated reason, my father-in-law was relieved of his presidentship in 1990 and demoted to deputy director of the Victorious Fatherland Liberation War Museum. Oh's fall from grace was even reported in South Korea through a Yonhap News article published on July 5, 1999. The article stated, quoting defector Choe Ju-hwal, that it was unclear why Oh had been suddenly relieved of his presidentship at the university to become deputy director of the museum. Choe, who was once a military officer assigned to the North Korean embassy in the USSR, is now the chairman of the Association of North Korean Defectors in South Korea.

Oh Gi-su was promoted again in 1994 to be chairman of the Korean People's Army Sports Guidance Committee, but in 1995 he was suddenly discharged from active service and assigned as vice chairman of the people's committee in Deokseong County, South Hamgyong Province. My understanding of why he was exiled is as follows.

Oh was staying at the Seosan Hotel on the outskirts of Pyongyang while preparing for the Military World Games, which were scheduled to be held in Belgium. He had dinners with military officers on a frequent basis and, one day, made comments that showed "pessimism" about North Korea's situation, which were caught on tape. To be clear: he had not criticized or condemned North Korea's situation, just voiced pessimism. He had not even made any comments attacking Kim Jong-il. It was fortunate that he was not thrown out of the party; he was simply demoted to become the vice chairman of the people's committee in Deokseong County. His children and their significant others were not affected.

Apart from my father-in-law, I knew another person who was exiled because of the Frunze incident. Choe Gwang-su had been working in the Arab Department of the foreign ministry. He had studied in Syria during his youth and graduated along with me at PUFS. One day, he told me that his older brother had been arrested because of the Frunze incident and that he was being forced to move back to his hometown of Hamheung. He was to divorce his wife, whom he had married in Pyongyang, and leave for his hometown by himself. Eom Chul-ho, who worked in the foreign ministry's Diplomatic Delegation Bureau, was also exiled from Pyongyang after divorcing his wife. Eom, like Choe, had studied in Syria and graduated along with me at PUFS.

It was typical during the course of the Frunze Military Academy Incident that if a direct family member or sibling was arrested, you would be exiled out of Pyongyang, and if a wife's relatives were arrested, the husband would have to divorce the wife. Most of the men exiled who were already married left for exile by themselves. They would have no heart to bring their wives to such hard-to-live places given that their wives had been born and raised relatively stress-free in Pyongyang. In many cases, the men would then marry women in their new homes, thus becoming the head of two different families.

A number of people in the foreign ministry were thrown out of their jobs or suffered in some way as a result of the Frunze incident. I was also fearful of what could befall me. Those who had studied abroad and their families suffered from extreme levels of anxiety because they never knew if they would be accused of being part of a spy ring or "anti-regime forces." The "Russia Kazan International Student Incident" was one example of this. Kazan is the capital of the Republic of Tatarstan in the Russian

Federation. From the late 1980s, dozens of North Korean students studied at schools in this city. They were accused of gathering to discuss the fabrications surrounding the North Korean regime and, on their return to North Korea, holding frequent meetings to plan a conspiracy against the state. In my view, it was a ridiculous accusation. All of the students who studied in Kazan were arrested, however, and their families were exiled to the provinces. My friend, Kim Jeong-ho, studied in Kazan while attending PUFS. After returning home, he worked in the Ministry of Trade, and his wife was one of my colleagues at the foreign ministry. Kim was arrested as part of the Kazan incident and was eventually killed by firing squad. His brother-in-law is Yoon Yeong-il, the former chief representative at the French embassy who was called back to North Korea when Jang Song-taek was arrested and then killed in December 2013.

KANG MYUNG-DO'S DEFECTION OPENS THE DOOR TO MY FIRST POSTING ABROAD

Given this atmosphere of purges, I thought it unimaginable that I would be sent to an embassy abroad. Call it fate, but I was nonetheless offered the opportunity to do so.

In 1994, Kang Myung-do, who was a relative of Kim Il-sung on his wife's side and the son-in-law of Premier Kang Song-san, defected. He had graduated some years before I did from the Pyongyang Foreign Language Institute.[14] Kang's defection was never made public to ordinary people, but the foreign ministry and other ministries involved in foreign affairs were ordered to delay any travel, work-related or otherwise, of the children of party cadres. I was simply an English major—not the child of a party cadre—thus making it unlikely for me to be sent to Europe; however, with that order, all the barriers in my way to such an assignment disappeared.

When the foreign ministry replaces diplomats already abroad, they select their successors six months in advance and begin the onboarding process, which includes background checks. In my case, all my colleagues in the European Department conducted a review of my "working attitude." Five or more of them signed their names and placed their thumbmarks on certificates of guarantor. Moreover, people from all areas of my life—stretching back to secondary school, university, and later life with whom I had studied or worked—signed certificates saying that I would not switch allegiances.

In order to be selected as a diplomat in North Korea, you have to have your second cousin on your father's side, first cousin on your mother's side, and first cousin on your wife's side in the country's "core class."[15] No one among your relatives should be a criminal or have strayed politically by being expelled from the party at any point. In short, it is not enough that you are loyal to the regime; the dozens of people in your entire family need to have no traces of ideological flaws.

Following the background check, a document is created that needs to be signed by the director of the cadre (human resources) department in the foreign ministry, the party secretary, a first vice minister, and the head of the foreign ministry before being submitted to the cadre department of the Central Committee. This department then sends an official to the foreign ministry to review, in its totality, the documentation created thus far on the candidate. If no problems are found, the section head of the cadre department conducts an interview with the candidate before a final review by the party committee's vice director and director. Only after receiving confirmation from Kim Jong-il can the candidate be confirmed as a diplomat. This whole process is so complicated and thorough to be unimaginable in South Korea.

I AM TOLD TO LEAVE MY SICK SIX-YEAR-OLD BEHIND

My hiring process began around June 1995, at a time when the children of party cadres were not allowed to leave the country because of Kang Myung-do's defection. I was the only English major in the European Department. My selection to go abroad was like a gift from heaven. In January 1996, I was told by the Central Committee Cadre Department that I had been assigned to the North Korean embassy in Denmark as a third (recruitment-level) secretary.

One problem remained. North Korean diplomats are not allowed to take their children abroad with them. Children about to enter elementary school or currently attending elementary school do not have permission to live in other countries. The authorities do this to ensure that children get their elementary education in North Korea, but the rule is torture for their parents. Students above the age of fourteen who are in fourth, fifth, or sixth grade of higher middle school are not allowed to leave the country, either.[16] They are not allowed to leave because they must prepare for the college entry exam three years before they take it. University students, meanwhile, are not allowed to leave because they are considered adults who no longer need their parents.

Children allowed to go abroad with their parents are those not yet preparing to enter elementary school and those in the first, second, or third years of higher middle school. In addition, if a family has two children, only one is allowed to leave the country. This applies even to families with twins. The reason children in the first, second, and third years of higher middle school are allowed to leave the country with their parents is because they can reenter North Korea before the start of college.

At the time, we had yet to have our second child and our first was just six years old. He was about to enter elementary school so was not allowed to leave the country. The Central Committee Cadre Department and the foreign ministry told me that the "Supreme Leader [Kim Il-sung] has ordered that the children of diplomats must receive their primary education in the fatherland because elementary level education—when children learn their native language—is an important part of a child's developmental process. You must leave your child here in Pyongyang."

My son was suffering very badly from a disease we had not been able to cure since he was three years old. I tried to uncover every opportunity I could to ensure he would join us abroad. I obtained a document showing my son's diagnosis from a university hospital and pleaded with the Central Committee Cadre Department: "If my six-year-old can't receive care from his parents, his disease could get worse enough to threaten his life. I want to take my child with me to cure him of the disease once and for all." I finally received permission to do so only after an official with the cadre department assigned to my case had met with the university hospital doctor to confirm my story. That is why my wife and I were able to take our son to Denmark.

2

NORTH KOREAN DIPLOMACY DURING
THE ARDUOUS MARCH

PHOTO OF A NORTH KOREAN DIPLOMAT
SMUGGLING CIGARETTES RELEASED
TO THE WORLD

Once I finished my preliminary education and preparations to go abroad, my family and I arrived in Copenhagen, Denmark, in June 1996. Later, after my defection to South Korea, some media outlets reported that I studied in Denmark as preparation to serve as an interpreter for Kim Jong-il, but this is not true. These reports seemed to have confused me with Ha Sin-guk, who served as a counselor in Denmark before me and later became Kim Il-sung's Danish interpreter. He is proficient in English and even worked with me in the UK later on.

Soon after I arrived in Denmark, the North Korean embassy in Sweden got into trouble. The staff at the embassy included Ambassador Kim Heung-rim, counselors Han Chang-yeop and Jeon Deok-chan, a secretary, an encryptionist, and a wireless communications operator. The secretary and the encryptionist were arrested in Tallin, the capital of Estonia.

They had taken a car on a passenger ship and headed to Tallin Port. There, they purchased a large number of cigarettes, loaded them in the vehicle, and then tried to sail back to Sweden by way of the passenger ship when they were caught and arrested. North Korean diplomats had long been engaged in such smuggling activities. Now two of them had been caught in the act.

At the time, North Korea was at the height of the Arduous March. Months would pass before diplomats received their wages. Ambassador Kim Heung-rim told his staff: "The motherland is having great difficulties, so we can't ask it for handouts. Let's earn our own foreign currency to run the embassy and fix up the building." Kim was an expert on Sweden and had been my direct superior while in Pyongyang. It was not his style to just sit on his hands when he served as a department director at the foreign ministry. He knew no bounds.

Kim observed that cigarettes were expensive in Sweden and decided to bring in cheaper cigarettes being sold in nearby countries on the Baltic Sea and sell them to a group of Swedish smugglers. From late 1995 until early 1996, the embassy sent its staff almost every month to Estonia, Latvia, and Lithuania to purchase and bring back cigarettes, earning tens of thousands of dollars in the process. The money was used to repair the old embassy building and was divided equally among the diplomats for their living expenses. In any case, it was akin to a miracle that the embassy staff was able to repair the embassy building by themselves.

For Kim, the risks to his career that he took in this endeavor were emblematic of North Korean–style patriotism. The foreign ministry, for its part, told all of its embassies to "learn from the spirit of self-sufficiency shown by the representative office in Sweden." North Korean authorities outwardly promoted "self-sufficiency" and "encouraged loyalty"; however, what they were really saying was to keep the embassies running even through illegal activity. The logic was this: if embassy officials were caught in the act, it would be their problem; if they were not caught, the fruits could be enjoyed by both the embassy staff and the motherland.

The embassy in Sweden, however, had overreached. Swedish authorities knew about the embassy's activities from early on. They shut their eyes to what was going on a few times but then decided to shut down the smuggling ring, perhaps because they believed the illegal activities were getting out of hand. Yet Swedish authorities knew they could not just arrest embassy diplomats, who enjoyed special diplomatic privileges. The country's intelligence agency evidently decided to stage a crackdown in Estonia, a country with which North Korea had no official diplomatic relations. Lithuania and Latvia, countries also frequented by embassy staff, had official ties with North Korea.

Swedish intelligence officials gave Estonian authorities a heads-up about what the North Korean embassy was doing. As soon as the secretary and the encryptionist drove their vehicle onto a ship at Tallin Port, they were arrested by local customs agents and police. The two were unable to claim diplomatic immunity in the country, leaving them open to arrest. After forcing the North Korean diplomats off the boat, local authorities opened the trunk of their vehicle and the box of cigarettes. This scene was caught by photojournalists, who had been tipped off about the sting, and released to the world.

SWEDEN'S NORTH KOREAN EMBASSY DECIMATED THROUGH ARRESTS, EXPULSIONS, AND IMPRISONMENT

The arrested North Korean diplomats were stripped of their cigarettes and held in custody until they were expelled from Estonia back to Sweden the next day. Even before this incident, Sweden had experienced several other incidents involving North Korean diplomats. In 1976, Gil Jae-kyeong, who was the ambassador to Sweden at the time, was expelled for involvement in an illicit drug-smuggling ring. In 1996, Kim Hyeong-gu, a counselor at the North Korean embassy in the Czech Republic, was arrested and served jail time for entering Sweden with drugs and a fake passport.

In July 1996, the Swedish government expelled most of the diplomats at the North Korean embassy, including Ambassador Kim and Counselor Han. Only Counselor Jeon Deok-chan and the embassy's wireless communications expert were left because they had had no involvement in the cigarette-smuggling ring. Jeon had arrived in Sweden only about a month before, and the wireless communications officer was not involved in the smuggling because he lacked a diplomatic passport.

Ambassador Kim later served as ambassador to Italy and then became the head of the economic section of the foreign ministry before dying of stomach cancer. Han Chang-yeop served as Kim Il-sung's and Kim Jong-il's interpreter; he was the son-in-law of a cousin of Jang Song-taek. Han had a promising career as a diplomat, but the smuggling incident forced him out of the foreign ministry and into the Overseas Activities Bureau of the Ministry of People's Armed Forces as a guidance officer. He seems to have staged a comeback later with a posting as a trade officer at the North

Korean embassy in Cuba; however, he was later taken to a political prisoner camp along with the elder sister of Jang Song-taek's wife. It is unclear
whether he is still alive.

The only remaining diplomat at the embassy in Sweden was Jeon Deok-
chan. He had majored in the Norwegian language and had poor English
skills. Soon, I was transferred to the embassy in Sweden with instructions
to provide support until new staff could be posted there. My transfer happened in July 1997 and forced me to leave my family in Denmark. It was the
same month the diplomats at the embassy in Sweden had been expelled.

A couple of days after I arrived in Sweden, the chairman of the Sweden-
Korean Association, Thomas Rönström, visited the embassy and told
me: "I came here because I couldn't stand how Swedish media reports
on the North Korean diplomat cigarette-smuggling incident every day.
The Swedish government is perpetrating a campaign against the Republic
[North Korea] by fabricating smuggling incidents. I plan to submit a letter of protest in the name of the Sweden-Korean Association demanding
an immediate end to this. We will also release a statement to the media.
My daughter cries every day while watching TV. She feels it's unfair that
the Swedish government is criticizing and attacking the honorable North
Korea." He then made a request for the "North Korean embassy to officially deny the cigarette-smuggling incident." I had mixed feelings. The
North Korean embassy in Sweden was prohibited from contacting the
media after the smuggling incident, either to confirm or deny what had
happened. If I went ahead and denied the Swedish government's claims as
Rönström demanded, more information about the incident could come to
light. I responded to him:

> The cigarette smuggling really happened. America's measures to pres-
> sure the North through sanctions are at their zenith, which has led to the
> Arduous March in our motherland. In fact, there is no money available
> to maintain the embassy's facilities. The embassy staff could not just sit
> around waiting to die. They had to find ways to survive. I hope you can
> understand the situation. This is not the time to fight with the Swedish
> government, but rather to ignore it and stay quiet. There are ebbs and
> flows in any revolution. We are now facing an ebb in the revolution. We
> will soon overcome the current difficulties and reemerge as the Eastern
> bastion of socialism.

Upon hearing what I said, Rönström was forced to accept that the cigarette smuggling had been real. He also expressed agreement about ebbs and flows occurring during a revolution. Rönström told me his organization would not release a statement of protest against the Swedish government. After meeting with him, I found myself thinking that anything North Korea did could be easily rationalized by using America's "confrontational policies" toward North Korea.

JANG SONG-TAEK ARRESTED FOR USING A FAKE PASSPORT IN NORWAY

Something else happened just a couple days after my arrival in Sweden. Jeon Deok-chan asked me to do something with him, telling me simply to change into "work clothes." We took a car ride of around fifteen minutes to a medium-sized, two-story house. Jeon then proposed that we clean the inside and outside of the house. I asked whose house it was. He told me:

> We can't talk about anything we see here to anyone else. That would mean the end of both of us. This is Jang Geum-song's house, the daughter of comrades Jang Song-taek and Kim Kyong-hui. She goes to middle school here. She's in Pyongyang now because of school vacation, but she'll return in late August right before school begins. Until that time, we need to come here once a week to clean up the house and mow the lawn. Once Jang returns, she'll visit the embassy frequently. You must give her a deep bow when you see her, and always call her "General Comrade" when you refer to her.

It was only then that I remembered Jang Song-taek had once been arrested in Norway. It had happened five years earlier, in December 1991. I had just gotten to work at the foreign ministry office when I was told to prepare for an important meeting by European Department director Kim Heung-rim. At around 9 A.M., we headed down to the meeting room of the foreign ministry together and met with the chargé d'affaires of the Swedish embassy in Pyongyang. What he told us was shocking: "Yesterday, the Norwegian police arrested a North Korean living in Oslo for carrying a fake passport. The man in question claims he is Jang Song-taek, the brother-in-law of Kim Jong-il, and is demanding that we tell the North Korean foreign ministry that he is being detained." According to the chargé d'affaires, the message had come from the Norwegian authorities. Sweden was the only country in northern Europe that had an embassy in Pyongyang. The Swedish diplomat continued: "Norway seems to think that the man is Jang Song-taek. However, it is puzzling why a high-ranking North Korean official would use a fake passport to enter Norway. The Norwegians are requesting that the North Korean ambassador to Sweden be sent to Norway to confirm whether it is Jang Song-taek or not. They also would like us to tell you that possessing a fake passport is considered a criminal act." While interpreting for the chargé d'affaires, I remember thinking how truly ridiculous it all sounded. Who would dare to pretend to be Jang after being caught using a fake passport? Why, for that matter, would Jang go all the way to Norway? I could not believe what the chargé d'affaires was telling us.

In North Korea, it is typical for a foreign ambassador's request to confirm something ridiculous like this to be met with a North Korean official's immediate refusal to discuss it. What surprised me, however, was how Kim Heung-rim answered: "We shall confirm this. However, we request that you inform the Norwegian government to refrain from publicizing this to the media until it can be confirmed." The Swedish chargé d'affaires then got up, telling us that the issue needed quick action as it was an "urgent problem."

After the meeting, Kim told me to keep the issue tightly under wraps and then headed to the office of First Vice Minister Kang Sok-ju. Sometime later, Kim returned and told me to "quickly prepare a document we will submit to the General [Kim Jong-il]." The foreign ministry had not yet started using computers. All documentation was written up by hand before being sent for final confirmation by the North Korean leader. A document would go through revisions as it traveled up the line from the department heads and vice ministers to Kang Sok-ju and foreign minister Kim Yong-nam. Only after a document was signed off by the foreign minister could the final typed version be sent by fax to Kim Jong-il.

The final document regarding Jang Song-taek's arrest was prepared in this way before being sent to Kim. Only a few hours later, however, the North Korean leader had given an order to Kang Sok-ju, and Kim

Heung-rim again called in the Swedish chargé d'affaires. Kim told the Swedish diplomat: "The Norwegians have Jang Song-taek in their custody. We hope that the Norwegian government will refrain from publicizing this to the media and that they will immediately let Jang go. If the Norwegian authorities alert the media or charge him with a crime, South Korea, the United States, and other enemy forces could use it in anti-Republic propaganda. That would quickly and uncontrollably aggravate the state of affairs on the Korean Peninsula. We hope that the Norwegian government resolves this issue with an eye on ensuring peace is maintained on the peninsula."

The Swedish chargé d'affaires, who wrote down exactly what Kim had said, promised to inform the Norwegian government immediately. A "confidential telegram" from Jeon Yong-jin, who was the North Korean ambassador to Sweden, arrived in Pyongyang that afternoon. Jeon was Jang Song-taek's brother-in-law. The confidential telegram he sent was used only when there was something to report that only the ambassador knew about. Jeon's telegram was essentially a belated report on the situation. He wrote in the telegram that he had departed for Norway after receiving word that "Jang XX" was being detained in an Oslo police station.

At the time, it took almost a day for the North Korean embassy in Sweden to send a telegram to Pyongyang. The telegrams had to be sent through a shortwave wireless communications device that delivered messages via the North Korean embassy in Moscow. Both sender and receiver had to line up the time a telegram would be sent. Meanwhile, the Swedish chargé d'affaires in Pyongyang had informed the Norwegians of what to do through a few phone calls. North Korea's outdated communications system was exemplified by the reliance on telegrams to communicate between the country's embassies and the foreign ministry in Pyongyang.

The next day, the Swedish chargé d'affaires told the foreign ministry, "The Norwegian government has prudently accepted the North Korean government's demands despite the fact that the incident is criminal in nature. As requested, the incident will not be publicized, and Jang Song-taek has been handed off to the North Korean ambassador to Sweden, who has arrived in the country." At the time, I did not understand why Jang had gone all the way to Norway and why Kim Heung-rim had not been surprised about hearing that Jang had been arrested.

I thought I could piece together the puzzle as I cleaned Jang Geum-song's house in Sweden: Jang Song-taek had come to Sweden to meet his daughter. He had wanted to go to Norway to see the sights, but there was no Norwegian embassy in North Korea. As a result, he had been unable to acquire a visa and used a fake passport instead. Of course, this was just my own speculation on what happened, but it seemed to make sense.

Jeon Deok-chan and I cleaned Jang Geum-song's house without fail once a week. When late August rolled around—signaling the start of the school semester—Jang's daughter was nowhere to be seen. Only her body-guard had returned to Sweden. We went to her school and told them, "Something has come up so Jang Geum-song cannot attend school." The two of us also closed her bank account. Jeon's English was so poor that I helped with interpretation when required.

I found myself with mixed feelings as, for around two months, we cleaned up Jang Geum-song's house and dealt with other chores here and there. I had heard vaguely that Kim Jong-il's children were studying in Switzerland but now found that Jang Song-taek's daughter was studying abroad as well. I had gone through many hoops just to get my own child out of the country. I briefly grew very angry as I thought about how the Kim family and their relatives were able to do something that I had fought like hell to achieve. I found myself suddenly disgusted with both Kim Il-sung, who required the children of diplomats to attend elementary school in North Korea, and Kim Jong-il, who sent all his kids abroad for study. This feeling of dissent did not last long, however.

In early September 1996, Choe Chun-yeong, a Swedish language expert, arrived in Sweden as the new counselor, and I returned to Denmark. Later, I heard stories about Jang Geum-song on a frequent basis. Jang Song-taek's daughter never returned to Sweden. I heard that she transferred to a school in France as perceptions of North Koreans had grown worse in Sweden because of the cigarette-smuggling incident.

Jang Geum-song was registered as a child of one of the embassy staff while in Sweden and attended an international school in Stockholm. She had one bodyguard, along with a female cook caring for her. I heard that she would occasionally stop by the embassy, which was on the way to her school. Jang would sometimes bring buckwheat cold noodles her cook had made to the embassy. Her parents would take turns to see their daughter in Sweden. All of this happened before I arrived in Sweden, but it seemed to me that the embassy staff in the country had to suffer quite a bit. It was all very clear to me the difficulties involved in taking care of Kim Jong-il's cousin, younger sister, and brother-in-law, who dropped by the embassy at unpredictable times. Ten years later, in 2006, Jang Song-taek's daughter committed suicide in Paris.[1]

In 2009, when Kim Jong-un first appeared on the scene, his name was not made public. He was just called the Comrade General. Upon hearing his title, I immediately thought back to Jeon Deok-chan's comment that we call Jang Geum-song Comrade General. It seemed to me that all of the children in Kim Jong-il's family had that title.

I recently read Ri Han-yong's book, *Royal Family*. Ri, who is now deceased, was a cousin of Sung Hye-rim, the mother of Kim Jong-nam. The book describes Kim Jong-nam's early years. Whenever his son's birthday rolled around, Kim Jong-il made Kim Jong-nam wear a military uniform. At first, the younger Kim wore a military uniform with general insignia, the next birthday he wore the uniform of the *Wonsu* (Marshal), followed by the *Daewonsu* (Grand Marshal or Generalissimo). Everyone had to call Kim's son *Wonsu* and *Daewonsu*.

I found it ridiculous at first to hear that everyone had to call Jang Geum-song Comrade General, even though she was just in secondary school. I soon found myself more comfortable saying it, however, when I saw all my colleagues say it, and even more after hearing the embassy children calling her Comrade Older Sister. Using the title soon became natural for me.

AFTER TRYING TO SCROUNGE UP FOOD AID HERE AND THERE, I SHED TEARS AT DENMARK'S PROMISE TO PROVIDE AID

At the time, many North Koreans were suffering from hunger. There were even rumors that hundreds of thousands of people had died of starvation outside of Pyongyang. Denmark, however, was a very peaceful and wealthy country. The state handled everything related to education and public health, with citizens enjoying more or less free education and free medical care. I could find no trace of the gap between the rich and poor in capitalist societies that I had learned about in North Korea. Bicycles, which North Koreans considered an important piece of property, were lent out for free in Danish cities.

The contrasts between the two countries were even more stark to me than before because I had shown foreign delegations around parts of North Korea on almost a daily basis in the past. I felt guilty for seeming to live in luxury in plentiful Denmark while North Koreans suffered through the Arduous March.

At the time, North Korea was actively engaged in diplomacy with the United States. This was due to the Clinton administration's policies, which were aimed at giving North Korea a "soft landing" following the signing of the Geneva nuclear agreement in September 1994. America, not China, was helping North Korea to overcome its economic troubles.

From early 1996, the United States began sending food aid to North Korea. The North's diplomatic objectives shifted to resolving the economic crisis it faced by acquiring as many "practical benefits" as it could. The leadership signaled the start of a "war to save socialism." North Korean leaders handed down almost daily orders to North Korea's foreign consulates to send back food.

As a third secretary, I worked hard to acquire food along with Ambassador Ri Tae-gyun from the first day I arrived in Denmark. We visited the Asia Bureau and International Cooperation Bureau of Denmark's foreign ministry along with the local Red Cross and other private-sector charity organizations to request that food aid be sent to the DPRK. North Korea's foreign ministry sent us orders every day telling us to focus on sending as much rice and medical supplies as possible back home, given that the "motherland was enduring the Arduous March."

The North Korean embassy in Denmark moved aggressively to respond to this call to arms. I remember that everyone worked really hard. The head of the Asia Bureau at the Danish foreign ministry even told Ambassador Ri that the "North Korean embassy is the hardest working foreign delegation in Copenhagen."

Perhaps thanks to our efforts, the head of the Ministry for Development Cooperation, Poul Nielson, contacted Ambassador Ri in September to propose a meeting. During the meeting, Nielson told us: "We have a high regard for the activities of the North Korean embassy. The Danish government has decided to send one million dollars' worth of food to

North Korea through the World Food Programme. We will also contribute food aid to North Korea through international agencies each year going forward." I shed tears uncontrollably upon hearing what he said. I saw the ambassador tear up as well. Seeing us tear up, Nielson broke off his comments for a time before saying that he believed that North Korea would overcome its current difficulties. We cried out *Manse!* (Hurray!) upon our return to the embassy. While North Korea received small amounts of food aid from some countries through international aid organizations, none had provided so much at once like Denmark. I pictured joyous people in my country receiving food aid.

DEJECTION AT KIM JONG-IL'S PURCHASING OF LOCAL SPECIALTIES WHILE ORDINARY NORTH KOREANS STARVE TO DEATH

We reported the news immediately to Pyongyang. A day later, a telegram arrived saying that the authorities held the embassy's activities in high regard. A telegram was sent out to all North Korean embassies saying: "Make sure to show results at a time when the motherland is suffering difficulties by displaying a high level of loyalty, just like the staff at the embassy in Denmark."

In September 1996, as we were enthusiastically engaged in efforts to secure food aid in Denmark, an incident involving a North Korean submarine occurred in Gangneung, South Korea. Danish media reported heavily on the South Korean military's efforts to hunt down the crew up until early November. Media outlets cited reports coming from Seoul that several armed North Korean agents had been killed, several had run away, while others had committed suicide by blowing themselves up. The Danish foreign minister called in Ambassador Ri to strongly protest the incident. The embassy, however, had little choice but to neither confirm nor deny that the provocation had occurred and instead highlighted the "uniqueness" of the state of division on the Korean Peninsula. Quietly, we feared that the Danish government might end up suspending its food aid to North Korea. Danish diplomats, however, responded to the incident in a way we had not imagined: "As we witnessed the country trying to hold on to dear life with its requests for food aid, we thought that North Korea wouldn't last much longer. It's true that we murmured among ourselves that way. However, it appears that given its agents readily blow themselves up instead of returning home, North Korea's collapse is not imminent."

Leftist figures in Denmark encouraged us by saying, "The only real army on Earth is North Korea's army. The South Korean military is nothing compared to North Korea's." Each time I heard words of support, I felt for the submariners who had died, but also felt proud. The submarine incident in Gangneung showed the world that North Korea continued to maintain a strategy to communize the South; however, I think it also showed the strong mentality held by North Korean soldiers. The incident appeared to play a significant role in quieting the idea that North Korea would collapse soon.

Despite the embassy's initial worries, our relationship with Denmark remained smooth, and food aid continued to pour into North Korea. We continued our momentum by reaching out to nongovernmental organizations, ultimately bringing in hundreds of thousands of dollars of food aid a year from the Danish Red Cross and Caritas Internationalis.

I felt our efforts were worthwhile because we enabled food to be sent to starving members of our society. That being said, a sense of shame toward the North Korean regime was already building in my heart. While North Korean diplomats sought every opportunity to send even limited amounts of food back home, "purchasing teams" sent out from Pyongyang showed interest in only the items they needed to buy for the Kim family. Of course, it was not all their fault. They were just following Kim Jong-il's orders.

One time, a purchasing team arrived to buy cows and bull sperm for Eungok Farm, which is where the beef and dairy products for the Kim family were produced. Another delegation came to purchase the wooden tiles to be placed on the floor of the Gumsusan Palace of the Sun.[2] Yet another time, a delegation arrived to buy Danish beer for cadres to drink after an event to honor the third year since Kim Il-sung's death. All of the delegations purchased goods that had no relation whatsoever to improving the food situation of ordinary people.

I was the only person who could provide English interpretation among the embassy staff in Denmark, which meant that I supported the activities of each delegation. I, along with other embassy staff, was tortured by having to do this. While drunk, some of my colleagues asked candidly whether they had to do such work while people were dying of starvation at home. Outwardly, Kim Jong-il worried about the lives of his people and soldiers, but he was actually focused only on ensuring his own family lived well. Party cadres were no different.

HWANG JANG-YOP'S DEFECTION

In February 1998, while my own sense of shame toward Kim Jong-il and the North Korean system was deepening, Hwang Jang-yop applied for asylum at the South Korean consulate in Beijing.[3] When the global media began publishing reports about Hwang, I still could not believe what had happened. Hwang was the founder of North Korea's Juche ideology. His defection essentially meant the exile of the Juche ideology from the country.

The North Korean embassy was peppered with calls inquiring whether Hwang's defection was true or not. In line with an order from Pyongyang, the embassy responded that Hwang had been abducted by South Korea's intelligence agency and warned that if the South Koreans did not release Hwang immediately, serious consequences could not be avoided. The atmosphere at the embassy was a mix of sadness and anxiety. The ambassador immediately called a meeting and issued the following order: "The actions of the southern puppets [South Korea] have gone too far. We must mobilize the Danish government and leftist organizations to conduct an operation to rescue Comrade Hwang Jang-yop." The ambassador quickly moved to meet with the Danish vice minister of foreign affairs and requested that the Danish government release a statement condemning the abduction by the "southern puppets." Meanwhile, I went around to the leftist political parties to request that they issue condemnations or write letters of protest.

A few days later, the embassy received a call from the North Korean embassy in France telling us to stop all efforts to release Hwang because an "important document" would be sent by fax. The document was said to be an order from Pyongyang. Everybody gathered in front of the fax machine. "Hwang Jang-yop has turned his back on the revolution and gone to the side of the enemy. Stop the campaign to release him and focus your external activities on emphasizing that 'all cowards should leave [North Korea] if they want.'" Upon reading the document, the ambassador sank down to the ground with a thud. It was something I still vividly remember and will never forget.

A few days after that, we received a message from the Central Committee in Pyongyang. We were ordered to immediately hold a party meeting where we were supposed to send the "resolution" of all party members back to Pyongyang. The meeting's topic was "All cowards should leave if they want. We will protect the red flag." When the party meeting was held, all party members expressed great anger and criticized Hwang. The conclusion of the meeting was: "Hwang Jang-yop has left, but we will protect the red flag until the very end."

I also made my voice heard during the party meeting, but when I arrived home, I fell into thought for some time. Every North Korean knew that Hwang had created Juche Thought.[4] That the person who created the ideological foundations for the North Korean regime had defected would inevitably have a major impact on the country's elites. I had met Hwang several times while working at the foreign ministry. I knew his character. When a delegation of politicians from Western Europe visited Pyongyang, I handled his interpretation during their meetings with him.

Hwang was a sensible and logical person. He knew how to treat other people. If a meeting involved a meal, he would tell me—the interpreter—to start eating first and would ask foreign dignitaries to wait until I had finished. He gave me a clear impression of being a good person. Hwang was very different from other cadres, who couldn't care less whether I ate or not because they wanted to tell foreign dignitaries as much as they could about their activities.

It was only after I arrived in South Korea in 2016 that I found out that Hwang had been buried in the national cemetery in Daejeon, not the one in Seoul. I feel that he should be moved at some point to the national cemetery in Seoul. I also hope that a cemetery can be created in Pyongyang once unification is achieved to honor those who fought for the democratization of North Korea.

Hwang's defection set off yet another storm of purges in North Korea. The Juche Thought Research Institute in Mangyungdae was shut down and its building handed over to the military. Most of the institute's personnel were sent to political prisoner camps. The only people who avoided punishment were the children of high-level cadres, such as the son of Vice Premier Kim Chang-ju, who was part of Kim Il-sung's bloodline. Kim Jong-il, for his part, criticized the research institute for conducting both academic research and overseas activities. "Overseas activities are the site of fierce struggles against the United States and the southern puppets, but the Juche Thought Research Institute, as an academic institution, was involved in the distribution of propaganda about the Juche ideology internationally, which allowed Hwang Jang-yop to do whatever he pleased," Kim claimed. "Going forward, the distribution of propaganda concerning Juche Thought internationally will be handled by the foreign ministry given its experience and awareness regarding the struggle against our enemies, while academic research will be handled by the Academy of Social Sciences." In line with Kim's order, activities concerning the distribution of Juche Thought–related propaganda is, to this day, being handled by the Seventh Bureau (the International Propaganda Department) of the foreign ministry, while academic research on the ideology is being managed by the Academy of Social Sciences.

SELLING 120 TONS OF NORTH KOREAN STAMPS TO SWITZERLAND AND THEN SELLING THEM AGAIN TO DENMARK

It was the summer of 1997. The Central Committee's Propaganda and Agitation Department had told us that the head of the Korea Stamp Corporation (KSC) was to head to Denmark and ordered us to support his activities as best we could. Sometime later the KSC director arrived at the embassy in Denmark. He looked like a gentleman in his late sixties. He had worked for decades as the head of the publishing division in the Propaganda and Agitation Department and had not been the head of the company for long.

The day after he arrived at the embassy, he woke up at 6 A.M. and cleaned the yard in front of the embassy by himself. He even washed my official car. The director continued to do such things despite our telling him not to. He was the model of the "Central Committee worker" that was common to see in North Korea.

KSC's main task was earning foreign currency by selling North Korean stamps abroad. The company was, in fact, the cash-earning branch of the Foreign Languages Publishing House (FLPH). The FLPH is, in turn, part of the WPK's Propaganda and Agitation Department and publishes introductory material about the Juche ideology in foreign languages. In short, the publishing house would make the stamps, and KSC would sell them. This system was set up by none other than Kim Jong-il.

I became livid when I heard the reason for the KSC director's visit to Denmark. Four tons of North Korean stamps had been sent to a Danish stamp company, but the North Koreans had yet to receive payment. I did not understand what had happened. The payment was equal to only $600,000. It would have made more sense for four tons of stamps to equal $60,000,000. In any case, receiving payment for the stamps should have been a piece of cake.

I was the only person at the North Korean embassy with proficient English. I visited the Danish stamp company with the postmaster. I had planned to protest a great deal, but when the Danish company representatives saw the postmaster, they were very angry, calling him a crook and a fraudster. When I heard the explanation from the Danes, I was taken aback. According to them, what had happened was as follows:

> KSC had agreed to give exclusive rights to the sale of the stamps in Europe to the Danish company, which had received four tons of stamps. The Danish company had even taken care of the transportation costs and, in expectation of selling the stamps, they had sent samples to the national postal services of each country in Europe. Not one national postal service expressed interest in purchasing the stamps, however. It turned out that a stamp company in Lausanne, Switzerland, already had an exclusive contract with North Korea for the sale of the stamps. In fact, the Swiss company had more than 120 tons of North Korean stamps in its possession.

"Stamps are like currency. How can 120 tons of stamps be printed with a view to be sold in the global market? It is also illegal to be giving out exclusive sales contracts helter-skelter. Take back the North Korean stamps because we do not need them anymore," the Danish company representatives demanded.

They were right. Stamps are similar to currency, and selling more than a hundred tons of stamps is pretty much the same as having made a transaction with an equal amount of currency. The postmaster responded poorly to the complaints raised by the Danish company, however. He told me to try haggling with the Danish company representatives, saying, "If we can't receive $600,000, let's try to get $100,000 or even $60,000." I was forced to interpret what he said, but the Danish company representatives said they would not give him any money.

The postmaster was in a corner. I asked him if taking the stamps back and selling them in North Korea would be alright. He responded that North Korea already had storage facilities full of stamps and that if we could not get any money here, it would put him into a very tight spot if he had to bring them back. I was feeling the pressure, so I told the postmaster the following: "How could you print so many stamps to earn just a little bit of foreign currency? If we sell our stamps at such low prices, people in other countries will not take us seriously. Our country is at risk of collapsing, so why print so many stamps? What do you have to say to that?"

He responded with a sigh: "I have no choice because I am just following orders from my superiors." I realized that I was working for a leader who would sell anything just to earn foreign currency and who would shake the very foundations of the country for such aims. I suddenly grew sad about the position I was in. To this day, companies in Denmark and Switzerland probably still have stamps that they have been unable to send back to North Korea.

SEEING *THE TAE BAEK MOUNTAINS* ON DANISH TELEVISION

My sense of shame toward the North Korean regime continued to deepen. One day in 1997, I saw a South Korean movie for the first time in my life. This was at a time when hundreds of thousands of people were dying of hunger after the start of the Arduous March. I still remember each scene and word from the movie.

I had been looking through a local Danish newspaper when I saw that Danish TV would be showing a South Korean movie on TV at 9:00 that night. Usually, embassy staff would have dinner before heading back to the office to work into the night; that day, however, nobody was working late. I suspect they were sitting quietly at home watching the South Korean movie.

The movie was titled *The Tae Baek Mountains*. I was surprised at what it portrayed: the struggle waged by partisans with the Workers' Party of South Korea before and during the Korean War. As I watched the partisans risk their lives to fight for their own land, I was reminded of my grandfather's and father's generations. My grandfather was a poor tenant farmer and was illiterate but joined the Communist Party after hearing they were giving away land for free. He sided with the North Korean communists during the Korean War. My grandfather's and father's generation believed until their deaths that socialism and communism were "science."

At first, I could not tell whether the movie was praising or criticizing communism. The communist characters were portrayed as morally superior, while the anti-communists were shown as immoral people. The movie's broader message was truly profound, however. The film portrayed communists as expressing a just idealism, yet these same people would mercilessly eliminate all those who thought differently from them—it was very much like North Korea. At the time, North Korea had created the *Simhwajo*, leading to a massive purge in which people were arrested or sent to political prisoner camps. Those of us working abroad were afraid for our families at home.

The final scene of the film was especially impressive. Kim Beom-woo, played by actor Ahn Seong-gi, tells the leader of the local Communist Party committee, "You all will fail because you don't think human life is precious," while Yeom Sang-jin, played by Kim Myeong-gon, wonders "where everything went wrong" as he observes the endless purges. I saw myself reflected in these two characters.

As soon as I arrived in South Korea in 2016, I lodged a request with the National Intelligence Service to meet with Im Gwon-taek, the director of the film. I wanted to ask him how he had been able to express the message through a single movie that the system and ideological confrontation between the two Koreas had ended. I was amazed that he had made such a judgment way back in 1994 when the movie was made.

I finally met with Im on March 17, 2017. I got an unexpected response from him to my question: he told me that he had received a great deal of criticism from right-wingers along with interference from the government during the making of the movie. He said, however, that he had wanted to settle his own thinking toward communism, which his family had supported at one time. Im had even traveled to North Korea in the 2000s to see for himself the society his relatives had sacrificed their lives for. What he saw, however, was the delusions of communist society and, for him, the unbelievably dreary and disappointing realities of North Korea.

THE *SIMHWAJO* INCIDENT

At about the time I viewed *The Tae Baek Mountains* on Danish television, all people in North Korea could talk about was who would be arrested or sent to a political prisoner camp during the night. From 1997, a massive purge called the *Simhwajo* Incident began.[5] The purges lasted almost three years, finally ending around the year 2000. North Korea's food situation had worsened even more by 1996, and by around 1997, groups of people died of hunger in areas outside of Pyongyang. Government food rations were suspended even in the capital city.

As people's anxiety gradually rose, Kim Jong-il got a brilliant idea: instigate an incident that would shift people's attention somewhere other than the country's economic woes. Choe Mun-duk, who was the head of the General Political Department at the Social Security Department (SSD), and others took the lead in the purges.

Choe organized the *Simhwajo* in the SSD, which looked into the personal information of everyone in the country. The *Simhwajo* looked particularly into the histories of people who were in high-level positions in the WPK Central Committee, including what they did during the Korean War and whether they had any blanks in their records. Seo Gwan-hee, who was the secretary of agriculture in the Central Committee Secretariat, was the first to be arrested and executed. Then, the corpse of the former minister of agriculture, Kim Man-geum, was dug up and shot with bullets. During partywide criticism sessions, the two men were targeted for having failed to properly implement the "*Juche* Farming Method," which the authorities claimed had led to the famine.[6]

The *Simhwajo* also discovered a massive spy ring within the party's leadership. Several high-level officials—including Mun Seong-sul, the chief secretary of the WPK Central Committee's headquarters party (committee); Seo Yoon-seok, the chief secretary of Pyongyang's municipal party committee; Pi Chang-rin, the chief secretary of South Hwanghae Province's party committee; Kim Gi-seon, the chief secretary of Gaesong's municipal party committee; and Rim Hyeong-gu, the chief secretary of Gangwon Province's party committee—were ensnared in the purges. Diplomats were also caught up in the purges. Foreign ministry staff—including the sons-in-law of Mun Seong-sul and Pi Chang-rin, the daughter of Kim Man-geum's cousin, and the son of Rim Hyeong-gu—were taken to political prisoner camps. Rim Jin-su, the son of Rim Hyeong-gu, once served as a counselor at the North Korean embassy in Jamaica.

Nationwide efforts to seek out former members of the Northwest Youth League led to punishments for many people. North Korea claims in its propaganda that the South Korean army and U.S. military formed the Northwest Youth League during the Korean War. When workers at the Hwanghae Iron and Steel Complex took steel sheets and equipment out of their factory to sell to China, North Korean authorities deployed a tank into the city to spread fear while soldiers threatened the workers with violence if they did not put back the things they had stolen. Cadres at central government agencies in Pyongyang were frozen in fright, while ordinary people were too afraid to complain about the lack of rice.

While anxiety was suppressed only by fear, the *Simhwajo* Incident did appear to have stabilized the regime. Kim Jong-un awarded Choe Mun-deok and other cadres in the Social Security Department the honorary title of Hero of the Republic. That being said, the social impact and repercussions of the incident were massive. Inevitably, there were complaints. Of course, nobody could make their complaints openly, which meant that only those with unquestionable social status could lead the way. Hwang Sun-hui, a former anti-Japanese guerilla fighter who had looked after Kim Jong-il when he was a baby, is said to have sent the North Korean leader a letter saying that she thought the *Simhwajo* Incident "went overboard." Other former anti-Japanese guerillas also began expressing doubts about the extent of the purges.

Kim, who was certain that stability had been restored in the country, then turned his sights on Choe Mun-deok and the SSD. He ordered the Ministry of State Security along with the military's Military Security Command to investigate the *Simhwajo* Incident and the SSD. Choe and other leaders of the purge were executed, while others were let off with lesser punishments. They were all accused of killing innocent people by fabricating evidence during the purge.

While it was too late to make any real difference to the victims, North Korean authorities held a general party meeting to announce publicly the "injustice" of the *Simhwajo* Incident, and surviving victims of the purge were returned to society. On Kim Jong-il's orders, the SSD was renamed the Ministry of People's Security.[7] Through a supreme commander directive, Kim released those who had been held in political prisoner camps under the pretext of freeing them from the unfair and false charges that had put them there in the first place. The measure, however, was meaningless to those who had already suffered greatly. Many victims saw their families torn to pieces, suffered from mental illnesses, or found themselves at the mercy of serious diseases. Most of the victims married before the purge had been forced to divorce their partners, which meant they had no families to go back to. Victims found the destruction of their families the most difficult thing to bear. Those who lost their homes because of imprisonment were put into group housing after their release and given small amounts of rice and cooking oil.

Diplomats who had been imprisoned also returned to society and to their jobs at the foreign ministry. The son-in-law of Pi Chang-rin later even served as ambassador to Malaysia, but Mun Song-sul's son-in-law reentered society with a disease, forcing him to leave the diplomatic service.

THE DEATH OF MY FRIEND KIM CHUN-GUK

My second son was born in June 1997 while I was working in Denmark. The age gap between my first and second child was seven years.

There was a reason the age gap between the kids was so wide. My parents had told me that I must have at least two children, and three years after we had our first, they began to make it known that it was time for a second to be born. While things have changed now, North Korean diplomats could only bring one child abroad with them at the time. One friend of mine who had twins was forced to leave one child in Pyongyang before departing for a consulate in South America. The entire family was in tears as they left.

My wife and I decided to have our second child abroad so we would not have to go through such pain. That is why we waited seven years.

After I was appointed to my position in Denmark in June 1996, I told the ambassador, Ri Tae-gyun, that we would be having one more child. While it was against the rules to have another child while abroad, that is how determined I was to have another child. After I defected to South Korea, Ri criticized me and my defection through *Urriminjokkiri* (literally, "among our people"), a North Korean media outlet aimed at South Korean readers. Regardless, I feel both grateful and sorry toward him to this day.

My wife soon became pregnant. Her pregnancy was against the rules and, what is more, there was no money for her to get prenatal exams, which meant she never went to a hospital. She visited the hospital only once—when she delivered the baby.

The North Korean government does not handle the medical costs for its diplomats abroad. All costs associated with hospital stays and surgical procedures must be paid by the diplomats themselves. As such, diplomats undergo very rigorous health screenings before they are sent abroad. These screenings essentially tell those who suffer from illnesses or poor health they will not go abroad. That being said, going abroad brings opportunities to earn money, which means diplomats fabricate medical screening documents to show perfect health even though that may not be the case.

In January 2016, the ambassador to Italy, Kim Chun-guk, died at his post. He was my best friend. Kim had died a painful death after suffering for months with liver cancer. South Korean media coverage questioned how an ambassador failed to receive any health screenings, going to the hospital only during the terminal stage of the disease. While he likely did not take as good care of his health as he should have, I think he probably was unable to go to the hospital because there was no money available to do so.

GERMANY HANDS OVER A LIST OF STUDENTS WHO STUDIED IN EAST GERMANY

Amid the massive purges of the *Simhwajo* Incident was another purge called the German Foreign Exchange Student Incident. While, again,

North Korean authorities later called it an "unjustified affair" and released all those involved, the purge was, in its totality, particularly ridiculous.

Following Germany's reunification in 1990, the German government stated that while it respected the agreements and relations the old East Germany had with other countries, it refused to honor the old diplomatic relationship with North Korea. Until formal diplomatic relations could be reestablished, Germany and North Korea agreed that the existing North Korean embassy would maintain its status as an Office for the Protection of the Interests of the DPRK, but the special status and rights of new diplomats and of the embassy building would stay in effect only temporarily. Germany's government wanted to use the old East German embassy in Pyongyang, while North Korea's government had no intention of discontinuing use of its embassy building in Berlin. Because both embassies were large, the agreement met both of their interests. The old East German embassy in Pyongyang became the Office for the Protection of the Interests of the Federal Republic of Germany, while the North Korean embassy in Berlin became the Office for the Protection of the Interests of the DPRK, with China acting as a protecting power. Instead of the title "ambassador," the heads of these offices are called "directors."

One day in the late 1990s, the head of the Office for the Protection of the Interests of the Federal Republic of Germany visited the North Korean foreign ministry. He brought with him a list of hundreds of North Korean students who had studied in East Germany and requested that the ministry give him the addresses and contact information for the students as Germany planned to "develop bilateral relations by forming relationships with former exchange students." This was a common way to invigorate diplomatic exchanges. The North Korean security officer watching over the German diplomatic office, who heard about the request from the German diplomatic office's interpreter, told the interpreter to steal the list. The interpreter had no need to steal the list, of course—he simply made a copy and gave it to the security official.

At that time, the Military Security Command was more or less fully in charge of managing cases regarding "internal spy networks." One prominent example was purges related to the Frunze Military Academy. At the same time, the Ministry of State Security was facing criticism from Kim Jong-il for failing to produce results. The security ministry, now armed with its unexpected new gift, told Kim that it had acquired a list of people who were part of a spy ring from Germany. The ministry then went ahead and arrested most of the students on the list who had studied in Germany during the 1980s.

Kim Kwang-sik, a colleague of mine who headed up the German Section in the European Department of the foreign ministry, was arrested. His family was not expelled from Pyongyang; luckily, they continued to live in the capital city without any trouble. This spy ring case was different from the Kazan or Frunze Military Academy purges. I heard that Kim's family was allowed to stay in Pyongyang because his case was still in the "preliminary examination" stage; however, his relatives continued to reside in the capital city years after his arrest.[8] The incident came to a quick end, relatively speaking, because it was, from the beginning, a rather hastily thrown together, thinly fabricated spy case. By the early 2000s, most of those caught up in the incident, including Kim Gwang-sik, were released back to society. Some of those former students, however, never returned because they did not survive the forced labor and stress they faced in the political prisoner camps.

"PLEASE GIVE US A BOAT TO TRANSPORT CHEESE"

Good fortune sometimes appears from the most unlikely of places. One day, I received a call from the Danish Red Cross. A Danish company wanted to give North Korea feta cheese it had planned to send to Iran; the cheese had become stuck in a port storage facility because of the European Union's trade sanctions against that Middle Eastern country. The sad part was that North Korea had no boat to pick up the cheese. I reported the news to Pyongyang but got a predictable response: "There's no way to send over a boat, so get support from the Danish government to provide transport."

Feta cheese is considered one of humankind's oldest cheeses. It was apparently first developed in Greece and the Balkans. That area is very rocky and mountainous, meaning it is hard to raise cows. Feta cheese is made out of the milk from lambs and goats, which gives it a salty taste; however, it is full of nutrients. I thought that it would greatly improve things in North Korea if malnourished children could eat even just a little bit of the cheese. I felt my heart racing with excitement just thinking about it.

I requested a meeting with the head of the cheese company. At the time, I was the only person available to conduct such activities because other staff had been pulled out of the country owing to financial issues. I remember telling the head of the cheese company: "I want to thank you for providing [the cheese to us] for free. However, we currently do not have any boats or money to bring the cheese back to the country. You may have seen on TV, but hundreds of thousands of our children are suffering from malnutrition. If we can get the feta cheese to our country to save our dying children, our people will never forget your help. Imagine that it was your own children dying of hunger. Please help us."

After hearing this, the CEO stayed silent for a while. He finally told me that he would let me know what they would do after discussing the issue with his board of directors. Two weeks later, I got a call from the CEO asking to meet at a restaurant. I sensed it was a good sign. After all, when someone asks to have a meal, not hold a meeting, it is typically to give you good news. I felt ecstatic.

When I got to the restaurant, the CEO, along with his entire board of directors, was there. He politely rose to his feet and promised me that his company would send 3,200 tons of feta cheese to North Korea for the children. The price for one kilogram of feta cheese—without shipment costs to the consignee—was more than ten dollars. That meant the cheese alone cost more than thirty-two million dollars; including transportation costs, the total expenses equaled around thirty-three million. I felt myself about to tear up, but I resisted the urge and simply found myself thanking them profusely several times.

KIM JONG-IL SAYS, "GIVE THAE YONG-HO ANYTHING HE WANTS"

Sometime later, the promised supply of cheese arrived at Nampo Port in North Korea. The cheese could be stored for a long period of time because it was packaged well. I learned this later, after I returned to the DPRK, but the entire saga was reported to Kim Jong-il, and he was so happy that he called in Kang Sok-ju and told him: "I have been hit with anxiety each time I've gone out to personally observe military units. The food situation is terrible. I would have liked to give them some good news each time I go out but was frustrated because there was nothing. The foreign ministry has done a really great job. Call back Thae Yong-ho to Pyongyang, commend him, and give him anything he wants."

Kim's order led to my return to Pyongyang in early February 1998. At the time, I had already left Denmark and was working as a second-grade counselor at the North Korean embassy in Sweden. By late 1997, North Korea had significantly reduced the number of its embassies to save money. Embassies in Poland, Yugoslavia, and Denmark were shut down. In January 1998, Ambassador Ri Tae-gyun became the North Korean representative for UNESCO in France, while I was sent to Sweden.

When I received the order to return to Pyongyang, I was filled with anxiety. I did not know why exactly I was being called back. A telegram arrived saying that the authorities wanted to "confirm something in regard to the supply of Danish cheese"; however, if that was all it was, I would have been the only person to be called back to Pyongyang. I could not understand why Baek Seung-cheol, a colleague at the Swedish embassy, was being called back as well.

At the time, purges related to the *Simhwajo* Incident were in full stride. Baek and I were the only two people at the Swedish embassy who had studied abroad. I had studied abroad in China, but Baek, who had studied in Russia, was even more anxious about what lay in wait. Baek had graduated from a university of foreign languages in Sinuiju with a degree in the Russian language, and then was selected to participate as an exchange student to study Swedish at a foreign language university in Moscow while studying at PUFS. He failed to get posted abroad after the Kazan exchange student incident; then, in 1997, restrictions on his foreign service were lifted. We had not heard of any former foreign exchange students being caught up in the *Simhwajo* Incident but nonetheless found it difficult to erase our fears.

That both of us were being sent back to North Korea meant that one of us was going to be purged. It was also a signal for us to watch the actions and words of the other. If one person was to defect on the return home, the other person would get punished. We did not know who the target of the purge was, so neither of us could make a run for it based on speculation alone.

Baek tried to be dignified, saying he had never participated in any political meetings during his time abroad. I also felt the same way. We agreed to accept whatever investigation we would be thrown into together and boarded a plane for Beijing. There were a total of five people working at the North Korean embassy in Sweden at the time: Ambassador Son Mu-sin, counselors Jeon Deok-chan and Choe Chun-yeong, Third Secretary Paek Seung-chul, and me. Given that two members of the embassy staff—and those earliest in their careers—were being sent back only served to increase our anxiety.

NONE OF US KNEW WHETHER WE WERE JUST BEING TRANSPORTED OR BEING TAKEN TO AN INTERROGATION

We stayed in Beijing one day after our arrival. The next day, Baek Seong-cheol suddenly said he wanted to call the husband of one of his wife's siblings as we waited to board our flight to Pyongyang. North Korean diplomats are not allowed to make calls to Pyongyang for personal reasons while abroad; the authorities forbid this as part of efforts to prevent the leaking of classified information. The husband of one of his wife's siblings was Kim Yong-nam, who was the head of a trading company under the auspices of the Sports Guidance Commission's Mass Games Creative Group. Kim had graduated a year before me at Pyongyang University of Foreign Studies, so I also knew him well.

North Korean custom requires that when two people are traveling abroad, one person is appointed the "head of the team." If Baek wanted to make a call to Pyongyang, he needed permission from me because I, albeit a colleague of his, was the "team leader." His request put me in a difficult position. If Baek sensed something awry during a call with his relative, he might decide to defect without returning to North Korea. If I told him not to make the call, I would feel sorry and Baek would be unhappy.

After some thought, I allowed him to make the call but only on the condition that I would be right beside him. Baek's relative asked him when he would arrive in Pyongyang and said he would meet Baek at the airport with his wife. The luster returned to Baek's face as he relaxed for the first time in a while. That made me anxious about what would happen. Even if I had wanted to make a call to Pyongyang, I could not. If someone in North Korea wants to make or receive an international call, they cannot do it from an ordinary telephone; they must have access to an international telephone. Kim Yong-nam had one of these in his office because of his position as head of a trading company, but none of my relatives did.

The next day, we boarded an Air Koryo flight, which took us to Pyongyang's airport. Kim Yong-nam and his wife, along with some colleagues of ours from the foreign ministry, were there to meet us. The first thing we asked when we arrived was: "Who will be purged"? It turned out Baek was the one. I asked a colleague at the foreign ministry what mistake Baek had made and whether it was because there was a purge of former exchange students to the Soviet Union. I was told that Baek's father had been arrested and executed by the Social Security Department. Baek, who heard about this turn of events from Kim Yong-nam, shed tears wordlessly as he looked up at the sky.

It was not clear what had happened. Baek's father had longed to work as a secretary to the chairman of South Pyongan Province's people's committee, a position akin to a provincial governor in South Korea. The head of the committee had seen the younger Baek and, liking his handsome and tall appearance, made him his son-in-law. In North Korean parlance, Baek and his wife were the "children of a cadre household." Around the time Baek was posted to Sweden, his father was working in a military armaments factory in North Pyongan Province as a party secretary. The factory was massive. The family was on cloud nine.

Given his position, I could not believe that Baek's father had been executed. His arrest and execution had its origins in his sensible and good-natured attempt to improve the poor food situation among the factory workers. When government rations were suspended, the workers had to fend for themselves to get food. Military munitions factories had to continue operating despite it being the Arduous March period, and Baek's father came up with a creative plan to solve the food shortage. He earned money to buy food by cutting up artillery shells and selling the iron powder to China. It was, for a party secretary, a very clever thing to do.

When the trade official in charge of selling the iron powder to China continued to siphon off money, however, Baek's father was forced to fire him. The trade official wanted to take revenge and told the authorities that the factory's party secretary was selling iron powder to China as part of an effort to send important military secrets to South Korea's intelligence agency. Baek's father was then arrested and interrogated by the *Simhwajo*. The interrogators tortured him, demanding that he hand over a list of spies. When the elderly man died during his torture, the *Simhwajo* ended up blaming everything on him. *Simhwajo* officials closed the case after fabricating a document saying, "The party secretary was executed after confessing to all the crimes." On the back of the trumped-up charges, North Korean authorities had no choice but to call back Baek's son as well.

Baek and I first headed to the foreign ministry to report our arrival in the country. The cadres looked at us, seemingly unable to find words to say. Later, a colleague in the cadre department told me: "You did a good job bringing back Baek without any incident. Baek was the first former exchange student to Russia who had been sent abroad in almost ten years, and if he had defected, dozens of former exchange students to Russia in the foreign ministry would have been unable to go abroad for a long time. I got very little sleep, worried that Baek would defect after the telegram telling him to come home was sent."

A couple of days later, Baek told me that he needed to go quickly back to his hometown because his mother was living alone. He also told me that he would write a letter to his wife telling her not to worry and to return quickly to North Korea and asked me to take it to her on my return to Sweden. It made me sad. Concerned that an entire family could defect, North Korean authorities typically make up a pretext to bring the head of the household back first. Then, the remaining family members are ordered to return home to "save" the head of the family. Baek's family was no exception to this common ruse.

THE DANISH CHEESE BECOMES A "GIFT FROM THE GENERAL" AND GOES TO THE MILITARY INSTEAD OF CHILDREN

There were two reasons why I had been called back to North Korea by the party. The first was, unknown to me at the time, facilitating the safe return of Baek Seong-cheol. The second was regarding my part in sending Danish cheese to North Korea.

The cadres at the foreign ministry, who had seemingly nothing to say when Baek and I reported our arrival in North Korea, could not repress their happiness at every opportunity they had when we met alone. The foreign ministry had failed to prepare an appropriate "birthday gift" for Kim Jong-il, who celebrated his special day on February 16. The Ministry of the People's Armed Forces called in military cooks to try the cheese and even conducted a training for how to cook it. People thought it tasted like salted tofu. Every time Kim Jong-il visited a military base, the feta cheese was distributed to the soldiers as a "gift from the General." In short, the cheese Denmark had sent to feed malnourished children was being used to strengthen the North Korean military.

Kang Sok-ju told me: "The General has given you high marks for making a special contribution to the strengthening of the Korean People's Army during the Arduous March period. He has also ordered that you shall be provided with anything you wish. What are your requests to the party?" I was confused about what to say. All I had done was work hard to get food for starving North Korean children. Those efforts had brought me good fortune, but I was somewhat put off by Kim Jong-il's praise that I had given a "great contribution to the strengthening of the Korean People's Army." North Koreans frequently tell each other that they must answer very carefully when faced with this kind of situation.

There are set criteria for receiving commendations in North Korea. You can receive a Labor Hero Commendation if you bring in more than one million dollars in aid. While I could have asked for such a commendation, I would have been a bit embarrassed to do so. I was not comfortable asking for such a commendation given that I had just been doing what the foreign ministry had long been involved in: bringing in food aid for North Koreans. Instead, I told Kang that I would like my wife to become a party member. He said he would give this request to Kim Jong-il.

The next day, Kang called me into his office and said: "I reported to the General about your request. He said that your ideological foundation is very strong given that, despite your great accomplishment, you have simply asked for your wife to become a party member. He ordered for your wife to receive a 'frontline membership' to the party while you will be given a Kim Il-sung watch. Measures to this effect will be implemented shortly." I responded politely, saying, "I will repay the trust and consideration the Dear General [has in me] with loyalty." Kang again praised me, telling me to work even harder going forward.

A couple of days later, on February 16, a commendation ceremony was held at the lecture hall at the foreign ministry. I was given a watch with Kim Il-sung's name inscribed on it. My wife was given "frontline membership" in the party in Sweden in accordance with a special order from Kim Jong-il. "Frontline membership" is given to soldiers on the front lines who greatly distinguish themselves in battle as a way to boost morale.

WIVES OF DIPLOMATS TAKE RISKS ALONG WITH THEIR HUSBANDS

In North Korea, there is a saying that, translated into English, roughly means: "Only by becoming a party member can you fulfill your expected role in society." South Korea has a similar saying that is used about people who begin to meet expectations set by their relatives or peers after failing to do so.[9] Men can become party members relatively easily if they join the military, but many diplomats avoid the military and graduate from foreign language schools before heading to foreign language universities, or the foreign literature or international relations departments at Kim Il-sung University. Those with these kinds of backgrounds are called *jiktongsaeng*, or students who enter university directly from secondary school. They have to work in the same job for four to five years, or even more, before they can become party members.

In the case of the wives of diplomats, however, they experience an end of their working lives once they go abroad with their husbands. They do not really have the opportunity to become party members because they are unable to work for very long in one job. For the wives of counselors who are on their first stint abroad there is less stigma despite their lack of party membership. Wives of higher-level diplomats, including ambassadors, however, are typically in their forties or fifties, and if they are not party members, they experience a loss of face. For example, if the wife of a counselor is a party member, but the wife of a higher-level diplomat is not, only the counselor's wife can attend party meetings with her husband. Party meetings are a frequent part of life at a foreign embassy, and there is nothing more embarrassing than not being able to attend them if you want.

My wife joined North Korea's trade ministry in 1989 and went with me to Denmark in 1996. Given that there are many men in the trade ministry waiting for party membership, it is not easy for a woman with even seven to eight years of work experience to apply for party membership. It seemed as though my wife would never become a party member because she was traveling with me every three to four years to this destination and that. That is why I asked Kim Jong-il to make my wife a party member.

After I received a Kim Il-sung watch, there was a drinking party with my colleagues. They teased me for not asking for a house. In fact, my parents were living in a small house in Pyongyang's Gaeson District, and it would have been nice to give them a bigger place. It did not seem right, however, to ask for a new house while I was living in comfort abroad and the rest of the country was suffering from the Arduous March.

While in Pyongyang, I saw friends and did some errands. Then it was time to return to Sweden. My heart was heavy thinking about having to give Baek Seong-cheol's letter to his wife. The foreign ministry said it would not send the order for Baek's family to return by telegram; rather, Son Mu-sin, the ambassador to Sweden, would have to deliver it verbally. Kim Yong-guk was tasked with escorting Baek's family back to Pyongyang. Kim had completed an interpreter training course in Sweden and is now a counselor at the embassy in Sweden. Some diplomats are given the opportunity to enter interpretation training courses after entering the foreign ministry following their graduations. This allows them to learn foreign languages while at consulates abroad.

I gave Son a call after I arrived in Beijing. I told him I was the only one returning, and he responded with a sigh, asking how he would break the news to Baek's wife. I was met by Son's wife and Counselor Choe Chun-yeong at the Stockholm airport. Even my wife did not know I was returning.

When I arrived at the embassy, Yong-bok, Baek's son, bounded out thinking that, because I was there, his father had returned, too. He yelled out, "Dad's back!" Then, Baek's wife appeared. Seeing only me get out of the car, she immediately asked why her husband had not returned with me. I could not think of what to say, so I suggested we head inside to talk, but she suddenly began to cry loudly as if she already knew what had happened.

Things did not improve even after we had calmed everyone down and entered the embassy. Half of the staff was in tears, while the other half was busy caring for Baek's wife. I gave her Baek's letter. She stopped crying then, knowing that her husband was still alive. Baek's wife said she had thought her husband had been arrested by the Ministry of State Security and was dead. She resolutely decided, after hearing that her husband was alive and that he had gone back to his hometown, that she would return home and take things as they came with her husband.

I frequently witnessed purges while working at the foreign ministry. If a couple was caught up in one, the person who could remain in Pyongyang generally chose divorce. Baek's wife was the first person I had ever seen who said she would follow her husband to his hometown. She stood by her word despite pleas by her family for her to stay in Pyongyang. She went to her husband's birthplace of Dongrim County, in North Pyongan Province. I heard that both Baek and his wife went through a lot of troubles before they were able to return to Pyongyang.

It was only after Kim Jong-il criticized the "injustice" of the *Simhwajo* Incident, and then announced a decree forgiving all the victims, that Baek and his family returned to Pyongyang. I heard that Baek and his family chanted "Long Live General Kim Jong-il" when they found out that his father's criminal charges had been dropped. However, I suspect that there was still sadness and even resentment in Baek's heart about what had happened to his father. As of this writing, Baek is still loyal to the North Korean regime, working as a counselor at the embassy in Sweden. He is protecting the faded "red flag" until the very end.

THE ELECTION OF KIM DAE-JUNG: A WELCOME YET CONFUSING DEVELOPMENT FOR NORTH KOREA

Aid from the international community, including Denmark, saved North Koreans who were on the brink of dying from starvation. The aid was undoubtedly a good thing from a humanitarian perspective. That being said, the aid gave the North Korean economy room to breathe, and after taking a breath, it again focused all its resources on the secret development of nuclear weapons. While ground was broken on the construction of the light-water reactor in August 1997, full-fledged construction work did not begin until September 2001. This was most likely because of American-style stalling tactics. America's calculation was that it could delay North Korea's nuclear weapons development on the pretext of constructing the light-water reactor, in the hope that North Korea's economy would collapse first.

Then, an event occurred that was shocking and strange for North Korea. In the December 1997 South Korean election, Kim Dae-jung was elected president. At the time, I was working at the North Korean embassy in Denmark, and his election came as a shock even to me. For decades, North Korea had spread propaganda that Kim was a friend of North Korea, given his leadership in South Korea's struggle for democracy. North Korean leaders had intentionally lionized him as part of efforts to realize their strategy of uniting the two Koreas under the red flag. Kim was commonly referred to as "Kim Dae-jung *Seonsaeng*," a polite form of address used in both Koreas. The authorities also produced a number of movies portraying his struggle to bring democracy to South Korea.

North Korea's leadership had, until that time, considered members of South Korea's democracy movement to be on their side and had maintained a strategy of bringing about unification under communism with the support of those in the movement. For North Korean leaders, the election of Kim was a major accomplishment from the perspective of their strategy to unify the two Koreas under the banner of communism. However, nobody in North Korea knew whether his election would be beneficial to North Korea. That uncertainty forced North Korean leaders to revise their strategy of "unification under communism."

Immediately following his inauguration, Kim espoused the so-called Sunshine Policy, essentially a policy of engagement toward North Korea. In its first order following Kim's election, North Korea's leadership told consulates throughout the world, including the one in Sweden, to actively criticize Kim's Sunshine Policy. From that point on, North Korean diplomats attacked the Sunshine Policy, asking who was supposed to engage with whom under the new policy, and questioning whether the Kim administration's engagement policy was in fact just aimed at achieving "unification through absorption."

North Korea also mounted a show of force aimed at undermining the Sunshine Policy. On August 31, 1998, North Korean authorities launched the *Gwangmyeongseong 1*. While the country claimed that it had succeeded in launching a satellite, South Korea considered it to be a delivery vehicle for missiles. That is why South Korea called the *Gwangmyeongseong 1* the *Baekdusan 1* (or *Daepodong 1*).[10]

NORTH KOREA RESPONDS TO THE SUNSHINE POLICY WITH MISSILE LAUNCHES

Global media outlets chatted excitedly that North Korea had conducted a test launch of a missile. The North Korean embassy in Sweden received a short order from Pyongyang to "just respond that it was a launch of a satellite." The day of the launch, Ambassador Son Mu-sin and I were in Copenhagen to present our credentials to the Danish king.

Two days later, on September 1, Son and I visited the Danish foreign ministry and were told: "North Korea has broken rules regarding missile restrictions. The Danish government strongly protests this." Son responded by saying it was the peaceful launch of a satellite, not a missile; however, Danish foreign ministry officials went on: "Even if it was a satellite, North Korea must go through procedures to alert the international community before the launch. If a country just launches missiles willy-nilly, a major incident could happen if it hits a passing passenger airplane. North Korea is truly an unpredictable country."

Son, however, refused to take this criticism sitting down, responding: "What is so unpredictable? Russia, China, Japan and other neighboring countries all launch satellites, but none of them have ever told us in advance. That's why we never feel the need to let other neighboring countries know beforehand."

It was only on September 4, after we had returned to Sweden, that North Korea officially announced that it had succeeded on August 31 in launching a "multi-level launch vehicle" into orbit. South Korea, the United States, Japan, and other countries then proceeded to consider sanctions against North Korea. The Korean Peninsula Energy Development Organization, or KEDO, canceled the signing of a resolution agreeing to share expenses to support the building of the light-water reactor, while Japan announced that it was suspending food aid to the country. The U.S. Senate adopted a resolution saying that North Korea must first promise to suspend its missile exports before the legislative body would provide a budget to supply North Korea with heavy fuel oil.

The international community was split on whether North Korea's satellite launch had been a success. Two weeks after the launch, the United States announced that the satellite failed to reach orbit, yet stated that North Korea had, through its launch, shown that it had the capacity to "deliver a warhead toward a ground target slightly farther away." North Korea, for its part, argued that the satellite was currently "in orbit," while Russia claimed that it had confirmed that North Korea's first domestically made satellite launch was successful.

In fact, North Korean diplomats had been anticipating among themselves that the door to reconciliation might open even while they were criticizing the Sunshine Policy on orders from the leadership. The international community was providing North Korea with food aid, while Kim Dae-jung, who had called for reconciliation and cooperation with North Korea before his election, was pushing forward earnestly with his Sunshine Policy. What, then, was Kim Jong-il's motivation for launching a missile in such a situation? While it was clear he intended to show that North Korea would never abandon its nuclear program, that was not all. Kim Jong-il already had another calculation in mind.

SECRET MISSILE NEGOTIATIONS
WITH ISRAEL IN SWEDEN

In January 1999, the Swedish embassy received a telegram from Pyongyang telling us to confirm whether there was an Israeli ambassador to Sweden. We checked and confirmed that there was. The next telegram from Pyongyang was, even for me, extraordinarily shocking. Ambassador Son and I were told to meet with the Israeli ambassador and conduct "secret missile transaction negotiations." It was only then that I was able to understand Kim Jong-il's intentions in shooting off the missile during such an atmosphere of peace and reconciliation.

Son was not an English speaker, so I came along as an interpreter and negotiated with the Israelis about a place to meet. For security reasons, I contacted the Israeli ambassador directly without going through a secretary. After calling the ambassador and telling him that I was the "secretary to the ambassador from the DPRK," I said: "I was hoping you could meet with Ambassador Son in a quiet place." The Israeli ambassador responded by saying, "Let's meet after I contact my home country and get permission."

A couple of days later, the Israeli ambassador gave me the address of a café in Stockholm for us to meet. He was waiting for us at the designated time at the coffee shop. I noted that all four of his guards were women. Son went straight to the point: "The satellite our Republic launched a couple of months ago went into orbit. This could have a major impact not just on Northeast Asia but also on the state of affairs in the Middle East." The Israeli ambassador's face grew serious. "Why is that? Get to the specifics." Son again went straight to the point:

> Many countries have an interest in our missile technology, including nations like Iran. They continually ask us to give them our missile technology. As you know, our economic situation is extremely difficult. We are at the point where we have to sell our missile technology to protect our country.
>
> If we export our missile technology to the Middle East, this will ignite a new missile competition, and this will threaten Israel's security as well. We don't desire this. You could say that our two countries have many things in common. We face a military threat from the United States, while Israel is surrounded by hostile Arab countries. Countries like us must do whatever is necessary to keep the peace. If Israel can help us, we can rethink the issue of exporting missile technology to the Middle East. We hope that we can come to a mutually agreeable settlement on this.

The Israeli ambassador then asked, "How are you saying we could help you? Tell me in detail what you have in mind." Son spoke candidly: "We are negotiating with Middle Eastern countries for one billion dollars. If Israel gives us one billion dollars, we will not export the missile technology." The Israeli ambassador then said, "I can't say anything because this is an unexpected proposal. I will contact you after reporting home."

"THE DEAL IS OFF IF YOU CAN'T GIVE US ONE BILLION DOLLARS CASH"

The meeting that day ended with just an exchange of opinions. We immediately sent the results of the meeting to Pyongyang. Ten days later, I was contacted by the Israeli ambassador, and we met in another coffee shop. "The Israeli government has examined North Korea's proposal seriously and has decided to accept it in principle. However, we cannot give you one billion dollars in cash. We can provide supplies such as food, fertilizer, medical goods, or other items North Korea requests of an equal value. We can also provide the latest technology for North Korea's farming or industrial sectors if that is what is desired."

Son, however, told the Israeli ambassador, "What we want is not goods, but cash." The back-and-forth between the two men continued:

"Cash won't work. America will oppose it even if we try. The United States is Israel's ally. If America opposes it, there's nothing to be done. We hope North Korea can understand this."

"The DPRK needs foreign currency. We require it to rebuild our economy. Only then can we efficiently and systematically purchase goods. If Israel can't give us cash, then we will have to negotiate with countries who say they can."

"I hope North Korea prudently considers this issue. Taking cash off the table means that we can provide goods equal in value to higher than one billion dollars. If North Korea exports missile technology to the Middle East, this will cause a serious problem. It could cause the suspension of the ongoing efforts to implement the Geneva nuclear agreement and could cause a serious security threat to North Korea."

"The Geneva nuclear accords came about through demands by the United States. We have suspended nuclear development in line with the accords. We've lost a lot [more than we've gained]. If the United States breaks the agreement first, that's not a problem for us."

The Israeli ambassador said that he would report the meeting to his government and would meet us again upon further orders. Meanwhile, Pyongyang told us to "stick to demanding cash going forward, and clearly show them that we're not interested in anything but cash."

Another ten days later, we received word from the Israeli ambassador that Israel's position had not changed. It had grown more hard-line:

We regret that North Korea refuses our proposal for the provision of goods. If this negotiation goes well, Israel could become the catalyst for normalizing relations between the United States and North Korea. Look at China. Israel played a significant role in the final period of normalization of relations between the United States and China. As a result, there were changes in even China's one-sided policy of support for Arab countries. If North Korea changes its one-sided policy of support toward the Arab countries, you can obtain many things. However, if the DPRK chooses to move away from Israel, the relationship between North Korea and the United States will become uncomfortable.

Son expressed a hardline position as well: "We regret that Israel refuses to accommodate the DPRK's proposal. If we were able to come to a mutual agreement this time, Israel's security situation would have grown much more peaceful. It's unfortunate that the DPRK's refusal was deemed unacceptable."

There was no further contact between North Korea and Israel in Stockholm after that. North Korea's attempt to acquire one billion dollars from Israel had failed. I have no idea whether North Korea went ahead and obtained one billion dollars from Iran, Egypt, or another country in return for missile technology.

There is something I realized late in the game. Did Kim Jong-il really expect to obtain one billion dollars from Israel when he ordered our negotiations? On reflection, I do not think that was the case. Kim seems to have been certain that Israel would exchange information with the United States once North Korea began negotiations with Israel.

At around that time, North Korea was already preparing for summit-level talks with South Korea. Kim may have thought that if he hinted at the possibility that North Korea would sell its missile technology to the Middle East, the Americans would have no choice but to support inter-Korean talks. The United States, for its part, probably needed to use South Korea to ensure that North Korea was tangled up in inter-Korean talks, with a view to prevent North Korea from selling its missile technology. In fact, what Kim Jong-il needed most to overcome North Korea's economic troubles was not the sale of missiles but rather summit talks between the two Koreas. The North Korean leader needed to manufacture a situation in which the United States would have no choice but to agree to an inter-Korean summit, and he may have done just that by engaging in missile talks with Israel. If Kim did in fact operate along those lines, it would have been a very meticulously thought-out strategy indeed.

ENCOUNTERING A SOUTH KOREAN
DIPLOMAT AT THE SAUNA AFTER
THE YEONPYEONG NAVAL INCIDENT

There were only five staff members, including the ambassador, at the North Korean embassy in Sweden. We had to deal with issues relating not only to Sweden but also Norway, Denmark, Iceland, Finland, Latvia, Lithuania, Estonia, and Ireland. When I was in Sweden, Ireland and Estonia did not have diplomatic relations with North Korea. I was in charge of affairs concerning Denmark, Ireland, Finland, Lithuania, Latvia, and Estonia. Given that the embassy in Sweden was in charge of the affairs relating to nine countries, Ambassador Son and I would visit the other eight countries at least once per year to give them an update on North Korea's positions and to find ways to improve bilateral relations.

The North Korean embassy's main task was to analyze the state of affairs in countries it managed. The embassy building did not have internet, which forced staff to travel to a nearby library every day to research the state of affairs in each country online and then report the results back home. It would have been nice to have had a subscription to a newspaper, but financial constraints made it possible for us to subscribe only to one Swedish newspaper. The financial situation at the embassy became so bad that, at one point, the five families living at the embassy's dormitory did not have access to hot water. After thinking long and hard, Ambassador Son came up with an idea: take baths at a nearby "health center." Sweden was typical of countries that have good welfare for its people. Paying five hundred dollars every six months got us access to the center, which had a gym, swimming pool, and sauna. During the winter, we would all pile into a car every other day to go to the health center.

The health center is where I met the first South Korean diplomat I had ever seen. It was also the first time that I had ever met a South Korean. The North Korean embassy staff typically traveled around in threes or fours; the South Korean diplomat, however, seemed to be single, which may have explained why he always came to the health center by himself. We all stayed clear of each other because inter-Korean relations had soured as a result of the First Yeonpyeong Naval Incident in June 1999. We did meet him, purely by accident, in the sauna one time. The reader may have a hard time imagining diplomats from the two Koreas sitting in a sauna together in bathing suits, staring blankly at each other. I wanted to ask the South Korean diplomat a lot about his country, but I never had the courage to do so.

Ambassadors from the two Koreas also encountered each other during an event hosted by the Swedes. Ambassador Son's only foreign language was French, so I frequently accompanied him as an interpreter. At the time, South Korea's ambassador was Son Myeong-hyeon. Ambassadors from other countries introduced North Korea's Ambassador Son to the other Ambassador Son, telling him to "talk often" to his South Korean counterpart and saying that the South Korean ambassador's daughter, Son Ji-ae, was the head of the CNN office in Seoul. The two ambassadors simply greeted each other, nothing more.

PHONE CALLS FOR THE SOUTH KOREAN AMBASSADOR AT THE NORTH KOREAN EMBASSY

Thanks to his daughter, the South Korean ambassador was a popular figure among diplomats in Sweden; in short, a lot of people wanted to talk to him. Both Korean ambassadors had the family name Son, which led to some awkward calls to the North Korean embassy from people looking for him. When the secretaries of other nations' ambassadors were told to "set up a golf game with Ambassador Son," they would first call the North Korean embassy. That was because the number for the North Korean embassy was higher up on the phone number list for diplomats than the South Korean embassy's number.

When a caller would ask to set up a time to play golf with "Ambassador Son," North Korean embassy staff, who even then did not know anything about golf, would respond curtly that it was the North Korean embassy the caller had dialed. Whenever we received a call like that, we would think: "Diplomats from South Korea must have nothing to do. All they do every weekend is go around and play golf." While we knew that the foundation of diplomacy was social gatherings, we could not help but complain, nonetheless.

In March 2000, South Korean President Kim Dae-jung announced the outlines of the Sunshine Policy in Berlin. North Korea's criticism toward the policy intensified. The country's concerns also deepened. In May 1999,

NATO forces led by the United States had destroyed the Chinese embassy during a bombing of Belgrade, the former Yugoslavia's capital. China, however, was not able to make much protest against the United States. Russia, Serbia's ally, simply observed the U.S. attack. China and Russia, in short, were unable to speak out against U.S. actions.

The atmosphere surrounding the U.S. presidential election was also disadvantageous toward North Korea. There was a very high possibility that the Republican candidate would win. The Republican Party had announced that it did not "recognize the Geneva accords." It was clear that U.S.-DPRK relations would worsen further if the Republican Party candidate won the race. North Korea, which still needed considerable time to prepare for a nuclear test, required time to breathe. Kim Jong-il judged that he could probably get through the difficulties he faced for a couple years at least if he successfully utilized Kim Dae-jung's Sunshine Policy and proposal for talks.

WE TELL SWEDEN THAT THE INTER-KOREAN SUMMIT WAS THANKS TO KIM JONG-IL

On June 13, 2000, Kim Dae-jung and his entourage landed at Pyongyang's Sunan Airport. On that day, Ambassador Son and I were in Lithuania to present our credentials. Watching CNN through a TV at a hotel in Lithuania, I saw Kim Dae-jung get off the airplane and shake hands with Kim Jong-il while hundreds of people welcomed him waving flowers. It gave me a considerable shock: "How can inter-Korean relations flip 180 degrees like this so quickly?"

As I watched Kim Dae-jung—the South's military supreme commander, who was considered our enemy up until that point—inspecting the North Korean military honor guard, I thought: "How can [Kim Jong-il] give him such a grand welcome?" Even Ambassador Son questioned the move: "We've been criticizing the South's Sunshine Policy as a policy of unification by absorption. Now we'll have to say that this inter-Korean summit was thanks to Chairman Kim Jong-il's courageous decision." And that is how Son explained the significance of the inter-Korean summit to the president of Lithuania.

Two days later, on June 15, the two Kims announced a joint declaration. The declaration stated that the two Koreas agreed to "resolve the question of reunification independently" and that there was a "common element in the South's concept of a confederation and the North's formula for a loose form of federation." The impact of the June 15 Joint Declaration was stunning: everyone we met asked us whether unification was just around the corner. North Korean diplomats knew, however, that the inter-Korean summit was no more than a move by Kim Jong-il to overcome North Korea's current crisis.

Right after the June 15 Joint Declaration, Kim Jong-il made a gesture for cooperation toward Russia as well. On July 19, 2000, Russian president Vladmir Putin visited Pyongyang for two days. It was the first visit by a Russian or Soviet leader to North Korea. Kim made a trip to Russia from July 26 to August 18 the next year.

Kim and Putin announced joint declarations during both trips, but the Moscow declaration was more significant. The most important part of the declaration was the construction of a railway that would connect the Korean Peninsula to Russia and Europe. It was certain that North Korea would reap massive economic benefits following both the start of inter-Korean economic cooperation and the construction of a trans-Korean railway (that would then be connected to the Trans-Siberian Railway) Kim appears to have held considerable hopes regarding the plan. A year after his trip to Russia, in August 2002, Kim visited Russia's far eastern region to negotiate issues concerning the implementation of the Russo–North Korean agreement.

The construction of the trans-Korean railway was impossible, however, because of the North Korean regime's inability to accept even things delivered to it on a silver platter. Russia had a clear intention to build the railway, while South Korea was always ready to lend support. The Russians had plans to open a logistics route connecting the Trans-Siberian Railway and the South Korean railway system to ship large-scale freight, such as containers or coal. The country further planned to straighten out the railway built during the Japanese occupation period and construct many new tunnels and bridges.

The problem, however, was that most of North Korea's defense forces are located on railways along the country's eastern seaboard. In the belief that the reason the Korean War had turned against North Korea was because of the Incheon Landing, North Korea's military leadership had spent decades building many defenses on the eastern coast along the railway. The construction of a trans-Korean railway system along with the modernization of North Korea's railways would require a massive relocation of these defenses.

North Korea's military leadership had long known that it had to maintain its own survival. It would be close to impossible for the military alone to relocate the bases. Even during the construction of the Gaesong Industrial Complex, the military leadership had gone through fire to relocate and build new bases. It was thus not surprising that military leaders opposed the construction of a trans-Korean railway and the relocation of military bases.

While solving the issue of relocating the military bases would have led to progress, North Korea did not have the economic power to do so. That is why Kim Jong-il was unable to push back against the military leadership's opposition. The plans to modernize the railway on the eastern seaboard naturally lost steam. Later, North Korea agreed to modernize only the railway linking Russia's Khasan to Najin Port in North Hamgyong Province. South Korea and Russia, both in the dark about the factors influencing North Korea's decision making, still held out great hope for the creation of a logistics route that would traverse the two Koreas.

A simple search on Google Earth shows what I am talking about here. There are numerous airports big and small near North Korea's railway on the eastern coast. Even now, North Korea makes gestures toward South Korea and Russia, making it seem like the construction of a trans-Korean railway is possible. Of course, such a thing is not completely impossible. South Korea and Russia would just have to pay for the relocation costs for the countless military bases on North Korea's eastern seaboard.

SEVERE ELECTRICITY SHORTAGES MAKE CANDLES A POPULAR GIFT FROM ABROAD

Unlike in Denmark, North Korean diplomats in Sweden were unable to make much progress in efforts to send food back home. In June 2000, I received an order to return home. It was the same month as the inter-Korean summit between Kim Dae-jung and Kim Jong-il. Generally speaking, North Korean ambassadors spend around four to five years abroad, while all other diplomats spend about three to four years. Diplomats who work longer periods abroad are generally those affiliated with special agencies such as the Reconnaissance General Bureau, or they are working on special projects given out by the WPK's "Third-Floor Secretariat."[11] The Third-Floor Secretariat is a powerful agency akin to the Blue House's Secretariat in South Korea.[12]

North Korean diplomats typically begin preparations to return home after their third year abroad. Some diplomats try to delay their return to Pyongyang at least a few months by doing behind-the-scenes projects with the foreign ministry's cadre department or powerful cadres.

Normally, I would have had to return to North Korea at the end of 1999. I had been posted to Denmark in June 1996 and had spent much longer than three years abroad. However, two factors lengthened my time in Europe: I had moved to the North Korean embassy in Sweden when the embassy closed in Denmark in late 1997, and I had received a special commendation from Kim Jong-il for pushing through the donation of cheese from Denmark. I had thus reaped the benefit of an extra year and three months living abroad.

North Korea has shortages of everything. It is human nature for diplomats to purchase as much as they can when they return from a posting abroad. While it depends on where diplomats are stationed, they generally try to acquire gifts, foodstuffs, and electronics to take home.

Diplomats, along with their wives, each prepare gifts for their parents, siblings, relatives, and friends. Anyone who does not get a gift will be very hurt. People prefer gifts that are hard to find in foreign-currency stores in Pyongyang or that are more expensive than those sold domestically, such as cooking oil, sugar, condiments, televisions, video players, and cameras.

Costs to transport these goods back home are considerable. North Korean authorities allow diplomats to transport 150 kilograms of air freight from their posts to Pyongyang free of charge. This amount, however, is not even enough to transport clothes and household goods. That is why many diplomats use savings to pay to transport their goods back by a container or a container pallet. My wife and I did not have much to take back, so we just sent it in three or four container pallets to Nampo Port. Many diplomats, however, send back their stuff in an entire container.

I remember purchasing about ten boxes of candles to bring back home. Pyongyang experienced frequent blackouts at the time. Now, many Pyongyang homes have solar panels and even twelve-volt rechargeable lights imported from China, which means candles are not much of a necessity anymore. Even in the early 2000s, however, families that had candles were considered wealthy. Ordinary families typically created lamplights with tissue wicks dipped in cooking oil. While it may appear that a major shift has occurred in how people deal with electricity outages, North Korea's electricity situation has not improved that much over the past two decades. People have simply shifted from candles and makeshift lamplights to solar panels and rechargeable lights. This shows, nonetheless, how hard North Koreans have worked to overcome their country's electricity shortages.

The diplomat who took over my post in Sweden was Choe Gwang-il, who served as a secretary at the embassy in Libya and at the foreign ministry's Situation Analysis Department. He had graduated two years before me at the Pyongyang University of Foreign Languages, and during his time in college he had caused a major uproar due to the "Kim Song-ae watch affair." I will go into more detail about this incident later in the book.

I spent a month handing over my duties to Choe. I transferred my duties related to Denmark and Norway during our visits there, but I simply handed over documents to Choe related to my activities in Ireland, Lithuania, Latvia, and Estonia. Choe later died of liver cancer while abroad, and his body was returned to Pyongyang.

3

SAVED BY SOUTH KOREA

MY FATHER-IN-LAW IS HELPED BACK TO HIS POSITION BY JANG SONG-TAEK

After packing up and sending our things back from Sweden, my family took a plane to Beijing and then a train to Pyongyang. We arrived at Pyongyang station in July 2000. I had returned to Pyongyang twice during my time abroad, but it had been four years since my wife and older child had been back. It was the first time my younger child, who had been born in Denmark, set foot in the country.

Our relatives, including my mother, older and younger siblings, cousins, father- and mother-in-law, and my wife's siblings, were waiting in front of the station for us. It had been five years since I had seen my father-in-law since his fall from grace in 1995 landed him in Deokseong County, South Hamgyong Province. At the end of 1999, he returned to Pyongyang in accordance with Kim Jong-il's orders and was living in his son's house. He told me that Kim Jong-il's brother-in-law and close adviser, Jang Song-taek, was the one who suggested to the North Korean leader to let him return. My father-in-law had been close with Jang since his time as president of the Kim Il-sung University of Politics.

About three months earlier, South Korea's Yonhap News Agency reported that my father-in-law had been demoted after being caught on tape by the Military Security Command. While I cannot be certain whether Jang saw the report and then suggested to Kim Jong-il to let my father-in-law return to Pyongyang, I heard that Jang saw Kim, who did not seem to be in a good mood, and told him earnestly:

Oh Gi-su [my father-in-law], who served as the president of the Kim Il-sung University of Politics, is currently being revolutionized in Deokseong County, South Hamgyong Province, due to a conspiracy by Lee Bong-won, the head of the Organization Department in the Ministry of People's Armed Force's General Political Bureau. The basis of the evidence received by the Military Security Command from Lee Bong-won is nothing more than the fact that Oh had studied in Russia. [His punishment may be due to] biased judgment. It's unclear what Oh's mistake was, and he is already sixty-seven years old. I was hoping to have him return to Pyongyang now because he's already done a lot of self-reflection.

Hyeon Cheol-hae, the director of the Standing Bureau of the National Defense Commission, who was there with Jang, joined in to support the proposal. Hyeon's father and Oh's father had both fought with Kim Il-sung against the Japanese. Based on those ties, Hyeon and my father-in-law attended the Mangyungdae Revolutionary School after liberation, and during the Korean War they both served in Kim Il-sung's personal guard.

Much to the surprise of those listening, Kim Jong-un said, "Is Oh Gi-su all the way down there? Send him back to the military with another star or let him decide what he wants." The Ministry of People's Armed Forces moved quickly. My father-in-law was taken in a respectful manner back to Pyongyang and given the following proposal:

You were a lieutenant general [major general in South Korea] when you left the service, so if you want to rejoin the military as the General [Kim Jong-il] ordered, you must add another star to become a colonel general [three-star general]. There is only one position befitting a colonel general and that is the manager of the National Archival Facility in Jagang Province. If you want to serve your country as a soldier to the very end, you can become a colonel general and head to Jagang Province; otherwise, you can live comfortably for the rest of your days with your son. It's up to you.

My father-in-law, who had spent all his life as a soldier, wanted to serve again. However, his children implored him to come home: they were worried that, having returned to Pyongyang by a thread, if he went back to the military and committed an infraction, he would no longer have any chance for redemption. He listened to them, abandoning the new posting to the military. I think that he made the right decision. In North Korea, even successful people can suffer a backslide at any moment. Jang Song-taek, who helped my father-in-law regain his status, is evidence of this phenomenon. Jang looked as if he would enjoy wealth and prosperity to the end of his days; who would have thought that he would be executed at the hands of Kim Jong-un?

Upon meeting my younger child for the first time, my relatives said that we had "earned" another baby while in Denmark. My father was just barely able to come out and meet us as he had suffered from a stroke and was half-paralyzed. Everybody was facing difficulties but was happy to see us return home.

THE VIGOR RETURNS TO PYONGYANG AFTER THE JUNE 15 JOINT DECLARATION

Upon our return home, an energetic spirit came alive among our relatives, who had been living in difficult conditions. I realized anew the great power all the money we had saved abroad could have. We had all we could ask for. My father liked beer, and I bought him a can every day. At the time, you had to have foreign currency in hand to buy beer. It was a tremendous luxury to be able to drink a can of beer before dinner every day. My wife purchased fruit and sugared cookies from the local market for my father and mother. We had an unlimited supply of things to eat every day. My wife told me that she wanted to be the daughter-in-law to my parents that she had not been able to be for the past several years.

One day, my mother quietly made a request to my wife: "Circumstances here are really tough these days. There are many people who can't get enough to eat. If you go and buy all this food from the market every day, the neighbors could start to resent us. That's why you need to wrap up the food you buy in several black vinyl bags. That way no one will know." In fact, my mother said that people would look carefully at what my wife had bought every time she returned home. It was the first time in North Korean society that the divide between the haves and have-nots was increasing. People viewed those who lived well with great disdain.

I proposed to my mother that we should hand out one package of Chinese-made udon noodles to each of the thirty-six neighboring families in our apartment. She agreed to the plan with delight. My wife also suggested that we buy Chinese-made materials to make skirts for the elderly women in our neighborhood. It was only after we had handed out the noodles and the materials for the skirts that everyone's thinking about us changed for the better. Even the expressions of people looking at us changed. They would even offer help to my wife when she needed to lug something heavy up the stairs of the apartment.

While working as a diplomat abroad, I had returned to Pyongyang twice, in 1997 and 1998. The atmosphere in Pyongyang was now different compared to those two times. The country's circumstances had improved a great deal. While there were still shortages of food and electricity, the depressed expressions I had seen before on the faces of many people were gradually getting better. It seemed as though everyone had new hope for the future.

Right after the announcement of the June 15 Inter-Korean Joint Declaration, there were rumors every day of another meeting between the two Koreas. Many people who had been sent to political prisoner camps during the *Simhwajo* Incident were allowed to return to Pyongyang and their jobs. With the June 15 Joint Declaration, North Korea was able to recover its vigor, a little less than ten years from the start of the country's crisis years in the early 1990s. Ri Seon-gwon, who represented North Korea in high-level talks in January 2018, said that the "June 15 Joint Declaration era" was "priceless" and that he "missed it." His comment clearly shows the significance of the June 15 Joint Declaration era in North Korean society.

THE AUTHORITIES CAREFULLY INVESTIGATE MY LIFE ABROAD BEFORE MY APPOINTMENT TO HEAD THE FOREIGN MINISTRY'S NORTHERN EUROPEAN SECTION

North Korean diplomats undergo two stages of screenings upon their return from abroad. First, the ambassador and party secretary of the embassy where they were posted write up reports about the diplomat and transmit them to the Central Committee's Organization and Guidance Department as "confidential documents." If there are negative things in the reports, the diplomat can face difficulties during his or her self-criticism sessions on their return to North Korea. That is why diplomats try to maintain friendly relations with both the ambassador and the party secretary at their international posts. Self-criticism is a key concept in understanding North Korean society. Broadly speaking, it means for someone to "analyze results and come to conclusions about one's activities and life, and identify experiences and lessons that can help improve one's activities and life in the future."

In the past, ambassadors and party secretaries would not show the content of the documents they wrote to the people they were writing about. More recently, however, they show the documents to the diplomats in question and even ask whether they agree with what has been written. It is not typical for someone to write badly about another person they have worked with for years, and most of the time ambassadors and party secretaries just say the diplomat has been "very loyal to the Supreme Leader and the party." Doing this, of course, is against the rules.

The next step for a diplomat just returning from abroad is to conduct self-criticism sessions in Pyongyang. When diplomats arrive back to Pyongyang, they first go to the Central Committee's Cadre Department to report that they have returned. This department then writes up a document that states the diplomat has been relieved from their position on this or that date. The period between being relieved and acquiring a new position is called "the period of non-assignment." During this period, diplomats must conduct self-criticism sessions according to established procedure. After conducting self-criticisms at a special department in the Central Committee's Organization and Guidance Department—called the Overseas Party Life Guidance Section—diplomats typically then go to the Overseas Department in the Ministry of State Security to conduct another self-criticism regarding their time abroad. If no issues are found during this process, diplomats are assigned to their new posts. If issues are found, however, they are either "revolutionized" or put into a Ministry of State Security prison.

I did not have any major issues crop up during my self-criticism sessions. I had already received a Kim Il-sung watch from Kim Jong-il, which likely ensured I would receive high scores when it came to my "political and ideological life" and how well I had "carried out the tasks of the revolution." I did find it slightly unpleasant, however, to be persistently asked by the official in charge of my Ministry of State Security self-criticism session whether I had had any "contact" with South Korean diplomats or civilians. I had not, and told him so, which ended the self-criticism sessions I needed to do for the WPK and the Ministry of State Security.

LONG-TERM PRISONERS SENT BACK TO NORTH KOREA DONATE MONEY THEY EARNED IN SOUTH KOREA, AND REGRET THEIR DECISION TOO LATE

Right before I rejoined the foreign ministry's European Department, a total of sixty-three South Korean "unconverted long-term prisoners," included Kim Seon-myeong, crossed over the Thirty-Eighth Parallel and arrived in Pyongyang in September 2000.[1] Most of Pyongyang's population came out into the streets to welcome them. North Korean media claimed that their return was the "first victory" following the June 15 Joint Declaration and called on North Koreans to learn from the "unyielding beliefs" of the long-term prisoners. North Korea gave all of them Motherland Unification Awards along with membership in the WPK.

North Korea failed to predict how quickly South Korea would send the ex-prisoners over and had not yet prepared apartments for them. Kim Jong-il ordered party vice ministers to hand over their apartments, and a massive revamping of the apartments began. The ex-prisoners were overtaken by emotion seeing that party cadres were giving up their own homes for them; however, until the renovations were complete, they all had to stay in Pyongyang's Koryo Hotel.

Some of the ex-prisoners still had relatives in North Korea. They were not allowed to go meet them outside of the hotel; instead, their family members came to meet them. Soon, various rumors began to circulate. A colleague of mine at the United Front Department (UFD) told me: "The economic circumstances of each of the ex-prisoners are different. It seems some of them made money in the South. Perhaps they worked here and there after getting an early release from prison. Others seem to have lived in extreme poverty before coming here." Some of the ex-prisoners who appreciated the nice welcome by the North Korean authorities brought all the money they had with them and donated it to the WPK. They believed the fantasy that North Korea provided its people with all the necessities of life. In their minds, they did not need any money because North Koreans no longer worried about "what to wear, what to eat, or where to live."

Gradually, the children and relatives of the ex-prisoners began to reveal what they really wanted during their meetings. They quietly asked whether the ex-prisoners had brought back anything from South Korea. When they said everything had been donated to the party, all hell broke loose. The ex-prisoners did not understand that money was important even in North Korea. While the party was taking care of their necessities, they had to have money to take their relatives out for meals on the weekend or to buy things they needed at foreign-currency shops or local markets. The ex-prisoners did not know that the party was not in the habit of just giving out money. That being said, they could not go back to WPK officials and ask for their money back.

Faced with this new understanding, the faces of some of the ex-prisoners darkened. The faces of others, however, lightened up because they had hidden their money without giving it to the party. The ex-prisoners gradually came to know the realities of North Korea, which were wholly different from what was on North Korean TV or in the newspapers. They came to understand that money, not "belief," was the currency required to be treated as a person, but this realization came too late for some.

In 2002, I joined British diplomats to visit Kim Seon-myeong, who was famous for having been held in South Korea as the world's longest jailed prisoner. Jim Hoare, who was the chargé d'affaires of the British embassy in Pyongyang, said he wanted to meet with Kim. What the British wanted was clear. Kim had lived in North Korea for more than a year, and the embassy wanted to hear his thoughts about life in the country. The ex-prisoners were handled by the UFD. The department told me it would be alright for the British diplomats to meet with Kim. Kim was living in a nice house and was doing a lot of "external activities," which meant there was nothing to worry about.

After setting up an appointment with the UFD, I, along with Hoare and a female third secretary named Kennedy, visited Kim's house in Ansandong, an area of Pyeongchon District in Pyongyang. As we had heard,

Kim's house was furnished with good-quality furniture. Kim had been called the "unmarried grandfather" in South Korea but had gotten married after arriving in North Korea. His wife was beautiful.

Hoare asked Kim specific and direct questions about his life: "I've heard a lot about you. Now that you've lived in both Koreas, which one is better? Everyone in North Korea is watched by the authorities; is that also true in your case? Are there any difficulties you've experienced in your life here? Do you believe that North Korea has human rights?" Kim made the pleasant-sounding comment: "After coming to the Republic, I've gotten married and am living happily." He also spoke frankly about his childhood in South Korea, the forty-four years he spent in prison because of his beliefs, and his meeting with his mother after being released from prison. It seemed to me that the British diplomats were very moved by what he said.

KIM SEON-MYEONG EXPRESSES A DESIRE FOR MONETARY COMPENSATION FROM SOUTH KOREA

After several hours of conversation, Hoare started to get up when Kim asked him a question: "Do you know if Amnesty International in London has sent me any money?"

Even I was taken aback by the sudden mention of money. Hoare was even more disconcerted and sat back down. Kim proceeded to take out two large albums from a bookshelf. One was filled with pictures taken when he was in South Korea, the other with South Korean newspaper clippings about himself. As he showed us the pictures and newspaper clippings, Kim gave us the following explanation.

He had become a prisoner of war in October 1951 after joining the North Korean "volunteer army" following the outbreak of the Korean War. Kim had received fifteen years in prison after a trial at the Seoul High Military Court, but in 1953, he was charged with being a spy and sentenced to be executed. Later, his sentence was changed to life in prison, after which he spent forty-four years in jail, until 1995. After his release, Kim was visited by "human rights lawyers." They told him that because there was no law that applied to "spying" when he was sentenced, he should petition for compensation from the government. Then, Amnesty International got involved. Kim was told that the organization had combed through South

Korean and American archives to find evidence of the existence of a law related to spying but had come up empty.

Kim said he had had some concerns before his move to North Korea. He was in the middle of a lawsuit against the South Korean government for compensation. Kim was not sure whether to wait for the resolution of the lawsuit to get his compensation before heading to North Korea or to wait in North Korea for the judgment. His lawyers promised to send him the compensation if he won in court. Kim believed them and headed to North Korea.

When he heard that representatives from the British embassy in Pyongyang wanted to see him, Kim thought it was Amnesty International trying to give him the compensation from the South Korean government. When he found out that the meeting had nothing to do with that, he looked extremely disappointed. Hoare also expressed his great regret and promised to look into the issue.

There are documentaries and movies about Kim's life in both Koreas. The North Korean novel *Son of the Fatherland* is about his life as well. To this day, I am still curious what differences there were between the North Korea he believed in all his life and the North Korea he experienced. Why, moreover, did he wait with such anxiousness near the end of his life for the South Korean government's money? He died in 2011, leaving no indication as to whether he just wanted to receive an apology from the South Korean government or whether he had gained a new realization about the value of money in North Korea.

THE KIM DAE-JUNG GOVERNMENT REQUESTS THAT EUROPEAN COUNTRIES ESTABLISH DIPLOMATIC RELATIONS WITH NORTH KOREA

In October 2000, the Third ASEM Summit Meeting (a summit between leaders from Asia and Europe) took place in Seoul. Inter-Korean relations had been improving gradually following the June 15 Joint Declaration; however, neither North Korea's foreign ministry nor its foreign embassies had been doing much regarding the meeting. The prime ministers of the UK, Germany, and Spain, who were participants in the ASEM Summit

Meeting, all expressed plans to establish diplomatic relations with North Korea around the time they arrived in Seoul. That is when North Korea's diplomatic corps suddenly started getting busy.

It was an unexpected development even to Kim Jong-il. He pressured Kang Sok-ju to get a handle on what was going on and report to him. An order was immediately handed down to North Korea's embassies in each European country, and information began to pour in from several places. The gist of the reports was this: "Before the ASEM Summit Meeting, the South's government requested that EU countries without official ties with the DPRK form diplomatic relations with us. The South's goal is to guide the DPRK to reforms and opening, and it requested that the EU countries finalize their plans to establish ties with the North at around the time of the ASEM Summit Meeting in October if possible."

Based on this information, the foreign ministry submitted a document to Kim Jong-il that read: "It seems crystal clear that following the adoption of the June 15 North-South Joint Declaration thanks to the General [Kim Jong-il]'s determination and unyielding efforts, the Republic's status has soared in height and now even European countries that have blindly followed America's policy of isolating the DPRK for decades have started forming their own policies toward us and are deciding to establish diplomatic relations with our country."

In November, the UK, Germany, Spain, Belgium, and other European countries sent letters requesting the start of negotiations for establishing diplomatic relations with North Korea. Kim Jong-il ordered the foreign ministry to conclude the negotiations as soon as possible. North Korea sent letters back to the European countries saying that the country accepted the negotiation proposals and wished the negotiations to begin as quickly as possible. The European countries responded with a proposal to start the negotiations in December. The foreign ministry proposed to Kim Jong-il that a delegation—made up of Kim Chun-guk, the head of the European Department; me, the head of the UK Section; and Park Gang-son, another staff member in the UK Section—be sent to the UK, France, Spain, Germany, Belgium, and the Netherlands. Kim granted permission soon after. Later, Park Gang-seon conducted activities related to the Third-Floor Secretariat in Austria before being called back in 2014 and executed.

IN A RUSH TO FORM TIES, THE UK TELLS THE NORTH KOREAN DELEGATION TO USE THE "AMBASSADOR'S CORRIDOR"

The North Korean delegation visited the UK first. The UK pressed North Korea to start negotiations quickly since the two countries were already holding two regular meetings a year. The delegation arrived in London on December 6, 2000. At the time, there was a North Korean representative office in the London office of the International Maritime Organization, a UN agency that is responsible for regulating shipping. This representative office had a director and a vice director from North Korea's Maritime Monitoring Bureau. The vice director, Jeong Sun-weon, was a colleague of mine who had worked at the foreign ministry's International Organization Bureau.

In March 1995, I had participated in the first secret meeting with the British at the British Embassy in Geneva as part of a North Korean delegation. During that meeting, it was proposed that official talks be held at least twice a year, and I took part in the second meeting, held in Beijing in the fall of 1995. Official talks with the UK were held six more times before the North Korean delegation arrived in London in December 2000. The third meeting was held in Pyongyang, the fourth in London, and the meeting venue alternated between Pyongyang and London thereafter.

The North Korean delegation was fatigued in the run-up to the ninth meeting with the British, which was expected to be a "marathon" given what had happened during meetings in the past. We were resting at the hotel after a simple meal when suddenly a British official approached us. He handed over a document, saying that he had been asked to give it to us immediately. The document proposed breakfast together the next day, further noting that Jim Hoare, the head of the Foreign Office's North Asia and Pacific Research Group—along with the head of the British foreign ministry's Asia Section—would be attending. Everyone in the delegation tensed up. Originally, the plan had been for official talks to take place at 10 A.M. on December 7, 2000. Normal diplomatic conventions did not accommodate holding a "working breakfast." The proposal meant that something pressing was happening.

Everyone tried to go to bed and get some sleep, but nobody could. Everyone got up and discussed what the British proposal for breakfast could mean. We concluded that "if we do a good job, we might be able to bring about a basic agreement on establishing diplomatic ties during the negotiations." Remembering the first secret meeting I had attended with the British, I had a good feeling about what would happen, though I did not know exactly why. I found myself thinking that I might experience both the start and the finish of the process of forming official relations between the UK and the DPRK. I waited eagerly for morning, but the night seemed to go on forever.

At 8 A.M. the next day, our working breakfast with the British began. We focused on every word the British said to try and grasp their meaning. The British started out by saying, "When the North Korean delegation enters the British foreign ministry building, it will use the 'ambassador's corridor.' " North Korean delegations had up until that point just used the ordinary entrance to the building; they had never used this special corridor.

Inviting a delegation from a country without official ties to Britain to use the ambassador's corridor was essentially a diplomatic message saying that the British acknowledged the DPRK as an independent nation. While we understood the significance of this, the British used diplomatic rhetoric to beat around the bush. In short, they never said outright, "We acknowledge North Korea to be an independent nation."

Then, the British moved to discuss working-level issues related to establishing official ties. They asked us, "We'd like to quickly finalize the negotiations on establishing official relations; what is North Korea's stance on this?" and "Have you [the delegation] been given total authority to make decisions during the negotiations?" These were hard questions to answer even for the head of the delegation, Kim Chun-guk. North Korea's leaders had not given Kim, a department director in the foreign ministry, the authority to sign any document on behalf of the country. That authority would need to be issued by the DPRK's minister of foreign affairs, but the delegation had failed to prepare such a document, thinking that the British would not speed through the process so fast. On the spot, our delegation conducted an internal discussion. We decided to tell the British that we had the authority to proceed and report the situation at the meeting later. That moved the meeting forward.

A DISPUTE OVER HAVING BRITISH
JOURNALISTS RESIDE IN PYONGYANG

The British were delighted. They proposed that the two sides start full-fledged discussions on establishing official relations at the official meeting scheduled to be held right after the working breakfast. The official talks, which began at 10 A.M. that day, focused on the dissemination of nuclear weapons and weapons of mass destruction; issues related to human rights; the issue of loans between the two countries; and issues related to ensuring peace in Northeast Asia. The British placed on the table agenda items that had absolutely no relation to the establishment of official ties, and officials from various foreign ministry departments came into the meeting to inform us of their country's stances on the issues. We could not just sit there and listen, so we gave them our official stance on each issue. Once we had finished giving our view, the British official in charge of that issue would leave and another would come to take his or her place. In short, the British seemed to be trying to build evidence that they had "informed North Korea about every concern that [the British government] has." North Korea's delegates, including Kim Chun-guk, were not the least bit impressed by this behavior.

On December 8, the second day of the negotiations, the two sides got to the point. The British raised three separate issues. The first involved the establishment of an embassy in Pyongyang and how long it would take for permission to build it; the second was an inquiry about whether British diplomats would be guaranteed freedom in their activities; and the third was whether British journalists could be posted in Pyongyang.

The British seemed to be hurrying through the negotiations process. The first two issues could be answered through communication with Pyongyang, but it did not seem likely that North Korea would agree to the third proposal, that British journalists be posted to Pyongyang. From North Korea's perspective, allowing foreign journalists to reside in the country would be no different than agreeing to allow spies in the country. The North Korean delegation responded that discussing the issue of journalists during a meeting focused on establishing official relations went against diplomatic conventions. Our logic as stated to the British was as follows: "The establishment of diplomatic relations refers to mutual acknowledgment as nations and a commitment to develop bilateral relations. Relations between countries cover all spheres, including politics, economics, culture, and media exchanges. We do not understand why you are making the nonessential issue of posting journalists [to Pyongyang] as a precondition to establishing relations."

The British responded with an attempt to get us to understand their position: "We understand what you are saying. However, if British journalists are not allowed to be posted to Pyongyang after the establishment of official bilateral ties, our media will criticize the government. This issue is a very important one."

The North Korean delegation then made this rebuttal: "The North Korean foreign ministry deals with relations between countries and does not deal with issues concerning the posting of journalists. The Korea Central News Agency [KCNA] deals with media-related issues in North Korea. Going forward, you and KCNA can move forward naturally with discussions on journalist exchanges once diplomatic relations are established. We believe that Britain is the only country on Earth that would make the issue regarding the posting of journalists a precondition for establishing relations."

The British did not respond for a while. Then they suggested that a statement be included in the negotiation document saying that the two sides would continue to discuss the issue after they had established official ties. We accepted this, thinking that it would be acceptable to the North Korean leadership. With that, all the basic issues had been agreed upon. Now, all that was left was for each government to sign off on the agreement. The North Korean representative office at the International Maritime Organization would send the results of our meetings to Pyongyang, but as time was of the essence, we also sometimes used the hotel fax machine to inform North Korea's leadership of what happened.

A BRITISH REPRESENTATIVE TELLS US THAT THE ESTABLISHMENT OF BILATERAL RELATIONS IS THANKS TO SOUTH KOREA'S SUNSHINE POLICY

As the meeting wound to a close, the British suddenly told us that foreign intelligence agencies were putting out feelers at the hotel where we were staying to figure out what was going on and that we should not use the hotel fax, but rather the special international phone line in the British foreign ministry. The British seemed very sensitive to the risk that the secret meeting could be found out. After that, we established contact with Pyongyang in a room provided by the British. Pyongyang had ordered us to report at any time of the day because the leadership was closely watching the situation. We could sense that Kim Jong-il was waiting every day for our reports.

We sent the final agreement to Pyongyang on the evening of December 10, along with a request for authority to sign the document. On the afternoon of December 11, we received an order from Pyongyang to sign the agreement. When we told the British, they said that an undersecretary in the foreign ministry named John Kerr would sign the document on the morning of December 12 and that a joint press conference would be held afterward.

At 11 A.M. on December 12, Kim Chun-guk and I entered the signing ceremony room through its left entrance while John Kerr entered through the right entrance. Though it was customary for only the representatives who sign the document to enter the room, Kim's only foreign language was Italian, so I joined him to sit at the table where the signing would occur. The two sides signed the document and then exchanged their copies. Camera flashes erupted in unison. It marked the moment when the UK and the DPRK officially established diplomatic relations.

John Kerr stated, "At this moment, the remnants of the Cold War between our two countries has collapsed," and praised South Korea, saying, "South Korean President Kim Dae-jung's Sunshine Policy is the reason our two countries have been able to establish diplomatic relations." Meanwhile, Kim remarked, "Today is a very significant day, for we have removed the legacy of the Cold War between our two countries" and "the DPRK will place all its efforts into developing the relationship between our two countries going forward."

KCNA and other television stations reported on the establishment of relations between the two countries. The North Korean announcer's high-pitched voice rang throughout the country. The announcement showed symbolically that North Korea, less than ten years after the country faced diplomatic isolation following the establishment of relations between China and South Korea, and despite the fall of the Eastern Bloc and the collapse of the USSR, had escaped from this isolation.

"QUICKLY ESTABLISH RELATIONS REGARDLESS OF THE INSULTS AND BEFORE THE BUSH ADMINISTRATION COMES TO POWER"

Following the establishment of UK-DPRK relations, the North Korean delegation was about to head to Spain on the morning of December 13, 2000, when we received a message from the International Maritime Organization's North Korean representative office. We were told, "An urgent message from above came down on the wireless saying that the delegation's work is being highly regarded. As such, it should finalize negotiations with other countries and then return home." The phrase "from above" referred to Kim Jong-il.

Energized by this message, the delegation then proceeded to visit Spain, Belgium, and the Netherlands. An unpredicted issue arose, however. These countries said that they would establish relations with North Korea on the condition that their ambassadors in South Korea would also serve as ambassadors to North Korea. This demand, however, was unacceptable to North Korea at the time.

Similar proposals had been made when Kim Il-sung was alive. Some countries proposed that their ambassadors in South Korea would also serve as ambassadors to North Korea. However, Kim responded to these proposals by saying, "Sending an ambassador based in Seoul to Pyongyang would mean acknowledging that Seoul is the center, and I could never accept this, even if it means ending relations with those countries." That is why North Korea was unable to accept such a proposal.

The Belgians now demanded that their ambassador in Seoul be accepted as the new ambassador to North Korea and that diplomatic relations could be established only on the condition that neither side would set up an embassy in their respective countries. At a meeting concerning the establishment of diplomatic relations, telling the other side that they must accept the posting of this or that ambassador, or raising the condition that there will be no need to establish an embassy, is an insult toward the other country. The demand was so insulting, in fact, that the North Korean delegation simply stormed out of the meeting room. On reporting what had happened to Pyongyang—namely, that we had taken a stand on principle—we expected to be praised by the leadership.

When the report of what we did was made known to Kim Jong-il, however, he responded in a way we had not anticipated. He called Kang Sok-ju and said:

> Why is the delegation doing things this way? Do they not know the state
> of international affairs? People expect the Republican Party's Bush to win
> and implement hardline policies, so we need to quickly establish rela-
> tions with European countries before the Republicans put together their
> foreign policy. Do you think that Europe will want to establish ties with
> us once the Republican administration pressures [them not to]? Who
> cares if European countries want to send their ambassadors in Seoul or in
> China to present their credentials [to us]? Send a telegram immediately
> telling the delegation to finish the negotiations on establishing [these]
> diplomatic relationships.

Kang, of course, could not tell Kim that instructions not to accept ambassadors from Seoul had been made by Kim Il-sung. If he had, there is little
doubt that Kang would have been verbally abused by the North Korean
leader. The North Korean delegation received a telegram from Pyongyang
right before it was to leave Berlin, telling us to return immediately to Spain,
Belgium, and the Netherlands and unconditionally establish relations
with those countries. Without much choice, we contacted those countries
again, only to find that they were all on Christmas holiday. Depressingly,
we were told that the negotiations could restart in early 2001.

Everyone treated us coldly upon our return to Pyongyang. Under
normal circumstances, we could have received at least the Order of the
National Flag First Class if not a Kim Il-sung watch. Kim Jong-il's criticism of us, however, washed away our achievements. Broadly speaking,
we were regarded as having done a poor job. Kang Sok-ju later conducted
a self-criticism during a criticism session held by the foreign ministry's
First Department party cell: "I failed to properly ensure that the delegation understood the ambitious international strategy of the General [Kim
Jong-il]. Before the delegation left for Europe, I should have explained to
them the situation regarding America's presidential election, but I failed to
do so. I made a big error by failing to completely explain to the delegation
about the General's strategy of quickly establishing relations with Europe
before the American hardline conservatives take power." The delegation,

however, had simply been loyal to Kim Il-sung's "dying instructions" that North Korea would not accept ambassadors based in Seoul. That loyalty cost North Korea the chance to establish relations with many countries in Europe by the end of the year 2000. Ultimately, North Korea established relations with those countries in the spring of 2001.

THE FRENCH REFUSE TO ESTABLISH
RELATIONS WITH NORTH KOREA

The George W. Bush administration came to power in 2001 and proceeded to invalidate the U.S.-DPRK Geneva Nuclear Accords that had been signed in 1994. In September of the same year, the 9/11 attacks occurred, and in October, the United States went to war with an attack on Afghanistan. In January 2002, during his State of the Union Address, Bush called North Korea, Iran, and Iraq the "axis of evil." Then, in March 2003, the United States invaded Iraq. If North Korea had not quickly established relations with Europe by early 2001, the country would have failed to do so with most EU countries—just as Kim Jong-il had said.

Several EU countries refused to establish relations with North Korea, including France, Ireland, and Estonia. Each country had different reasons for refusing to form ties with the DPRK.

France immediately criticized the UK, Spain, Germany, and other Western European countries when they announced they would establish diplomatic relations with North Korea. Per EU rules, European nations all had to come to an agreement on the issue of establishing relations with North Korea. At the time, France held the presidency of the EU. France argued that recognizing North Korea without clear evidence of the country's abandoning plans for nuclear development would make "nuclear suppression more difficult." In short, France claimed that other European countries were falling victim to North Korea's deceptions.

Ireland, which had long espoused policies of neutrality, said that it would delay negotiations on establishing relations because it needed to examine whether establishing relations with North Korea was in line with its own policies. When Ireland held the rotating presidency of the EU in 2003, it formed official ties with North Korea.

Estonia was a unique case. North Korea and Estonia had already signed an agreement regarding the establishing of diplomatic relations in Moscow in 1992. The person who signed the agreement for Estonia was the chargé d'affaires in Russia. Estonia later invalidated the agreement, saying it contradicted domestic law. In short, Estonian law stated that a chargé d'affaires could not sign such an agreement for the country. North Korea proposed multiple times that the two countries' ambassadors in Moscow or diplomats granted full authority to sign such agreements conclude a new agreement. Estonia, however, refused to go along, and the two countries have still not established relations.

The establishment of relations between France and North Korea is still "ongoing." More accurately, negotiations between the two sides have been suspended for a long time. When the second North Korea nuclear crisis erupted in October 2002, the French attitude was "I told you so!" The French said that they had been right all along about North Korea's pledge to abandon nuclear weapons and that other countries had been fooled by the DPRK. The French continue to adhere to this position, given that the nuclear crisis justified their decision to refuse forming official ties with North Korea.

France has long had a special relationship with the DPRK. During the Cold War, France was the only major Western European country to allow North Korea to open a mission in their capital. Former French president François Mitterrand, during his days as head of the Socialist Party, visited North Korea and met with Kim Il-sung. Given their long and deep relationship, it would have been natural for France to be the first European country to establish relations with North Korea; however, the French just do not trust North Korea.

In his thinking about relations with European countries, Kim Jong-il placed particular importance on Switzerland and France. He was interested in Switzerland because Kim Jong-chul and Kim Jong-un had studied there. North Korea tried but failed to establish a "non-visa" relationship with Switzerland.

NORTH KOREA'S SPECIAL "LOVE FOR FRANCE" HAS NO EFFECT

From the late 1970s, after establishing a representative office in Paris, North Korea purchased Western luxury items. France was the place where high-level North Korean officials had their medical operations. Kim Jong-un's birth mother, Ko Yong-hui, along with other members of the Kim family and high-level cadres such as the former head of the Ministry of People's Armed Forces, O Jin-u, received medical treatment there. For those leaders, if you were diagnosed with an incurable disease in North Korea, you would logically head to France.

Why did France allow high-level North Korean officials to do this? After my defection to South Korea, I met with a French diplomat who asked me how far North Korea had advanced in its nuclear and missile development. I responded, "The French intelligence service knows more than me about that," adding, "The country that has the most high-level information about North Korea is France." He seemed doubtful, so I proceeded to explain: "For decades, high-level North Korean officials have gone to France for medical treatment. While residing in French hospitals for months on end, they certainly talked a lot while in hotels or at hospitals. Your intelligence service would have bugged their conversations, no doubt. There would be a tremendous amount of information available in just those bugged conversations alone." He was unable to respond to this.

Even as late as 2008, the building where the North Korean representative office was located in France was really small. High-level officials from North Korea would have to stay in hotels. Representative office officials would cater to every need of the high-level officials as they traveled between the hospitals and hotels. The cadres also drank alcohol through the night frequently. I think that many secrets must have been revealed. The French must have received something in return for allowing these high-level officials to enter and leave the country as they pleased. I am certain that there is a massive amount of high-level information about North Korea in France. I believe that the French caught wind of North Korea's ambitions to develop nuclear weapons, which is why they have not established diplomatic relations.

Kim Jong-il spent considerable energy to establish ties with the French. If a North Korean wants to go to France, they must get a visa at the French embassy in Beijing. That is very inconvenient. Kim wanted to form diplomatic ties with the French even if he had to kowtow to them. Chae Su-hon, a vice minister of foreign affairs, did not know this and received harsh criticism from Kim as a result.

Chae went to France to negotiate the establishment of diplomatic relations. The French did not send someone of a similar rank to meet with
him; instead, a department director came out to meet him. Thinking that
he was practicing "independent diplomacy," Chae simply returned home
expecting praise.

When Kim heard that Chae had returned without holding any consultations at all with the French, the North Korean leader got very angry
with Kang Sok-ju. Kim demanded why the foreign ministry had not
ordered Chae to kowtow to the French to establish the relationship, and
why he had simply met with a mere department director. Chae wrote a
self-criticism and then returned to France. He applied for a meeting with
a department director, but the French told him that they had no interest
in meeting with him.

Once, Kim Jong-il also tried to buy a French Airbus aircraft. He needed
a private plane and was both distrustful of and repulsed by Russian air-
planes. Initially, he tried to buy a used American Boeing aircraft before
attempting to buy an Airbus but failed in the end.

NORTH KOREAN ART EXHIBITION OPENS IN THE KOREA SECTION OF LONDON'S BRITISH MUSEUM

Despite the hard-line Bush administration coming to power in the United
States, the British quickly moved forward with its engagement policy
toward North Korea. In March 2001, Foreign and Commonwealth Office
permanent undersecretary John Kerr visited the country, and in November of the same year, a joint British–North Korean art exhibition was held
in the Korea section of London's British Museum. I participated in the
exhibition as the head of a North Korean delegation. The other members of the delegation included Park Hyeon-jae, who later became North
Korea's ambassador to Uganda before retiring in 2012, and Li Dong-il,
who served as North Korea's vice representative to the UN.

When we arrived at the exhibition hall, there were a lot of British people, but more than half of those attending were overseas Koreans. Even
the South Korean ambassador to the UK was there. The British had simply told us that the event was being jointly held by North Korea and the

UK, and I had been under that impression before walking into the exhibition. I was taken aback. Later, I found out that the Korean section of the British Museum was being funded by South Korean companies. The British had, in short, held a North Korean art exhibition in the (South) Korean section of the museum and had even invited the South Korean ambassador and overseas Koreans living in the UK. Likely, it would have been natural for them to do this given that the event was funded by South Korean companies.

North Korea has long refused to participate in any events run jointly with another country if South Korea was involved, calling it a scheme to create "two Koreas." Permission was required from Kim Jong-il beforehand if a North Korean official had to attend such an event. I was troubled by my attendance yet could not leave because of the presence of the British foreign secretary. Despite my palpable discomfort, I stayed at the event.

After celebratory remarks were made, people began to view the artwork. After the event, however, the South Korean ambassador came over to the North Korean delegation, extending his hand in greeting. He suggested that we head to a quiet place to sit down and talk. Before the Kim Dae-jung administration came to power, North Korean diplomats would strongly rebuke any attempt for conversation if South Korean diplomats approached them. That was the rule. After the June 15 North-South Joint Declaration, however, this policy changed. We were told to respond naturally and with friendliness to South Korean diplomats in places we were observed by foreigners. This was part of North Korea's efforts to show that it was working hard to promote inter-Korean exchanges and cooperation. Even so, North Korean diplomats still needed prior permission to meet with South Korean diplomats; if suddenly faced with meeting someone from the South, we had to make a report after the meeting.

We were unable to push back against the South Korean ambassador's friendly request and went out to sit on chairs in the corridor. The ambassador grasped me by the hand and said: "Our policy toward the North has now changed. We do not want confrontation with the North. This is the truth. We want cooperation so we can all live well. Since coming to England as an ambassador, I've found there's really a lot to learn from this country. At the very least, as ambassador, I can get together funds to support scholarships for three or four students from the North. Send your students here. The DPRK needs to modernize quickly. I hope you'll explain to your leaders that all we want is peaceful coexistence."

The ambassador was a short, gentle-looking man, and his quiet way of speaking made me feel that he was speaking from the heart. He was none other than Ra Jong-yil. He was the first South Korean ambassador with whom I had a conversation at a public event abroad. Later, after I was appointed deputy ambassador to the UK, I attended a talk held between North Korean ambassador Hyeon Hak-bong and South Korean ambassador Im Song-nam. At another event, I had the opportunity to engage in a short friendly conversation with South Korean ambassador Hwang Jun-guk. Yet I never shared such a serious and long interaction with any of them as I did with Ra.

When writing up our reports upon our return home, we removed any mention of our meeting with Ra in the UK. Reporting the meeting would not have been a big deal because it had taken place in the presence of several people; however, doing so would have made things more complicated. We would have had to write in detail about what had been discussed, and the Ministry of State Security would have called us all in to confirm all the details of the meeting. In fact, many North Korean diplomats refrained from reporting coincidental conversations with South Korean diplomats. That was how much they were afraid and annoyed at the Ministry of State Security's prejudiced officials, who tended to badger diplomats about their meetings with South Koreans.

When Ra first started speaking, I thought he was a former member of South Korea's National Intelligence Service (NIS). When North Korean diplomats are about to head abroad, they are taught: "The South's foreign consulates have diplomats who are affiliated with the NIS. These diplomats are called 'white agents.' The diplomats the NIS dispatches abroad have distinguishing features. They will proactively approach our diplomats to introduce themselves, hand over their name cards, and suggest having a meal together. Diplomats with [South Korea's] foreign ministry, however, will not approach you that way. That's why you need to be careful of any South Korean diplomat who proactively approaches you. Most of them are agents with the NIS."

Ra approached me in a friendly manner. His way of speaking was so soft and quiet that I was not sure whether he was really an NIS agent. My curiosity on this matter was put to rest after I read his book *Inside North*

Korea's Theocracy: The Rise and Sudden Fall of Jang Song-taek while working as deputy ambassador at North Korea's embassy in the UK during the spring of 2016. His author profile revealed that he had once worked at the NIS. I slapped my knee in the realization that I had been right! After coming to South Korea, I had the chance to meet with Ra again, and we laughed as I told this story.

THE SWEDISH PRIME MINISTER CRITICIZES NORTH KOREA'S HUMAN RIGHTS RECORD DURING A MEETING WITH KIM JONG-IL

In the first half of 2001, Sweden held the presidency of the EU. Sweden is the only country in the world that has three representative offices on the Korean Peninsula: one in Seoul, another in Pyongyang, and yet another in Panmunjeom.[2] The Swedish ambassador to North Korea also represents the interests of the United States, which does not have any diplomatic relations with North Korea. While having embassies in Pyongyang and Seoul makes sense, some readers may be unclear why the Swedes have a representative office in Panmunjeom. That office houses a Swedish representative to the Neutral Nations Supervisory Commission.

Sweden takes pride in boasting that it has a special relationship with the Korean Peninsula and, as a mediator, the country has long had an interest in issues concerning the peninsula. In early 2001, the Swedish prime minister Göran Persson, then president of the EU Council, proposed leading an EU delegation to visit both Koreas.

North Korea was concerned about the international state of affairs at the time. George W. Bush's election as president had led to the start of neocons gaining power in the halls of American leadership. Kim Jong-il, for his part, was emphasizing that North Korea needed to firmly establish ties with Western nations before America's policies toward North Korea turned hard-line again. It was thus natural that Kim immediately accepted the Swedish prime minister's suggestion for the trip.

Kim told the foreign ministry, "The [changes in] American government's policies are worrisome. This will be the first time in our history that a Western prime minister will visit the country, so we need to use this opportunity to its fullest to ingratiate ourselves into the international community before the United States starts efforts to build support for sanctions on the DPRK." He ordered: "Reference material needed to prepare for the meeting should be submitted as quickly as possible." Immediately after this, a task force was formed in the foreign ministry with me as its leader.

The task force examined materials in the possession of the foreign ministry, and the North Korean embassy in Sweden sent us material to review every day. The materials covered a wide range of topics, including the politics, economy, culture, and military of Sweden, along with a who's who in Swedish acting and singing, the country's alcohol culture, its famous places, and anything else of importance. The task force summarized all this material and submitted a report to Kim Jong-il, who devoured it.

Then, the North Korean embassy in Sweden requested permission to install internet service in its compound. Having access to the internet would allow the embassy to collect much more material than could be found through daily trips to the library. Access to the internet would also massively increase productivity by providing embassy staff with an easier and faster way to search for information. North Korean embassies were prohibited from using the internet at the time. Having already experienced life in Sweden, I explained the positive aspects of the internet to Kang Sok-ju. Kang suggested that I create a proposal to explain how the internet could be used that could then be submitted to the North Korean leader.

After Kim read the report, he accepted the proposal. Starting in the first half of 2001, North Korean embassies were given permission to use the internet. Of course, given that the spread of the use of the internet was unstoppable, North Korea's foreign missions would have been allowed to get online within a couple of years. That being said, the closed nature of North Korean society meant that, barring special actions by the leadership, access to the internet among embassy staff would have been delayed even longer. To this day, ordinary North Koreans are not allowed to use the internet.

Swedish prime minister Göran Persson arrived in North Korea on May 2, 2001, for a two-day, one-night stay in the country. He was accompanied by European commissioner Chris Patten and EU Council Secretary-General Javier Solana. Their visit to North Korea led to a new shift in North Korea's human rights policies.

Persson remains the first and only foreigner to have officially and directly raised North Korea's human rights issues to the DPRK's supreme leader. Up until that point, the foreign ministry would not even consider inviting a foreigner who might bring up the issue of human rights to Kim Il-sung or Kim Jong-il. Even if such a figure were allowed to visit the country, they would never have been able to meet directly with the North Korean leader.

Persson, however, abruptly brought up the human rights issue during his farewell luncheon with Kim Jong-il, despite its not being on the official meeting agenda. The Swedish leader took considerable time to try and get Kim to understand the importance of resolving the country's human rights issues. He told Kim, "Even if the nuclear issue is resolved, the human rights issue will remain, which will make it hard for North Korea to join the international community." He also suggested, "North Korea's cooperation with the international community in the sphere of human rights will be a plus over the long term." In short, the Swedish leader was telling Kim that North Korea's failure to resolve the human rights issue would make it impossible for the country to receive support from Western countries. The comments were painful to hear as they were akin to a political attack on the DPRK.

KIM JONG-IL'S SCHEME TO SIT PERSSON ON "KIM DAE-JUNG'S SEAT"

I participated in the farewell luncheon at the Baekhwawon Welcome House as an interpreter. Kim Chul managed the interpretation between Kim Jong-il and Persson, while conversations between Prime Minister Yon Hyeong-muk and Secretary-General Solana were handled by Choi Son-hui. I interpreted for Foreign Minister Baek Nam-sun and Commissioner Patten. Kim Cheol was Kim Jong-il's personal interpreter and was working at the Central Committee's International Department at the time.

In fact, I was not just a participant; I was seated at the same table as Kim Jong-il. As I listened to what Kim was saying to Persson for around two hours, I could not help but be amazed by his cunning tricks. Initially, I had thought that the North Korean leader would adhere to what we had written for him to say. Kim, however, did not stick to the script at all. As he led Persson to a seat at the leader's table, Kim told the Swedish prime minister: "This is an historic seat that you will be sitting on. This is where President Kim Dae-jung sat when the June 15 North-South Joint Declaration was signed. History tends to be created when seated here. That is why I've deliberately put you here." Persson's face tensed up somewhat at hearing this, yet he happily said, "Ah, so this place and this seat is where you welcomed President Kim Dae-jung." From the get-go, Kim had found a perfect way to get the Swedish leader excited. It was the work of a veteran at these things.

Kim did not express displeasure at Persson's suggestion regarding North Korea's human rights record. In fact, he told the Swedish leader: "Given that our system is very similar to that of the old Soviet Union, there are many areas of our country that are hard to accept in the West. However, the floor is open to talk about human rights. Let's do it. That being said, because our two sides have different sociopolitical concepts regarding human rights, I don't expect agreement to come easily. If we narrow the differences we have through dialogue and communication, the human rights issue can eventually be solved. I wholeheartedly agree to dialogue."

Persson evidently felt that leaving a record in the meeting notes about his having "raised the human rights issue during an official dialogue with Kim Jong-il" was sufficient. Surprisingly, the Swedish leader showed immense happiness when Kim responded positively to his suggestion for dialogue on human rights. After the luncheon, the Swedish delegation told the foreign ministry that "Chairman Kim Jong-il responded that he accepted dialogue on human rights, which is akin to dialogue having started already" and that "we will take on all costs related to dialogue on human rights." The Swedes were encouraged and excited by what Kim had said.

"DEVISE FAKE MEASURES WHILE DRAWING OUT DIALOGUE ON HUMAN RIGHTS"

The Swedes, however, were mistaken. The North Korean leader had a different plan in mind. After the luncheon, he told Kang Sok-ju:

> I promised Prime Minister Persson that we would have human rights dialogue with the EU. Study how we can draw out human rights diplomacy. That Europe wants to engage in human rights dialogue is ultimately

aimed at digging into our internal situation, and that is not acceptable. Human rights are connected to national sovereignty. Europe could, however, get angry if we don't engage in dialogue. We need to maintain good relations with Europe to push back against the hard-liners in the United States. That's why you need to research how we can fool the Europeans. If we hadn't created the nuclear basic accords through talks with the Americans, how would we have gotten past that crisis and endured to this day? Find ways to fool the international community when it comes to the human rights issue.

Kim presented a direction for North Korea's human rights diplomacy, and the foreign ministry developed the logic and specific methods for this diplomatic strategy. The details of the proposal prepared during a foreign ministry meeting were as follows:

The General [Kim Jong-il] promised to conduct human rights dialogue with the EU when he met with Prime Minister Persson, so we can't go back to them and refuse to engage in dialogue. We suggest that first we tell the EU that our concepts of human rights are different from theirs, and that we should move forward one step at a time to discuss our different concepts of human rights. We will also delay progress in human rights dialogue by calling for advance contact and exchanges to cultivate experts in human rights. This will buy us several years.

From a long-term perspective, however, we can't simply rely on delaying tactics, so starting now we will prepare courts, prisons, and prisoners we can show foreigners. Going forward, once the conditions are ripe, it would be good to put in place many things for people to see, including some of the DPRK's judiciary facilities. If the United States and Europe join forces to mount a human rights offensive, we must take ultraconservative measures such as nuclear weapons tests. That would center their focus on the nuclear issue. If we raise tensions through nuclear crises, the United States will have no choice but to fall back on a "nuclear first, human rights later" policy. In short, nuclear weapons will completely muffle human rights.

Kim approved of the foreign ministry's proposal and sent down a separate order to the Ministry of State Security, the Ministry of People's

Security, the Central Public Prosecutor's Office, and the Central Court, instructing them to build courts, prisons, and other facilities that could be shown to foreigners. From the second half of 2001, North Korea began holding preparatory meetings for the start of a dialogue on human rights with the EU in Brussels. The country also sent human rights experts to the UK and Sweden to participate in human rights trainings and constructed a court and prison in Pyongyang's Mangyongdae District to show foreigners.

Persson also pointed out to Kim the weaknesses in North Korea's economy: "The socialist economic system has a number of drawbacks. North Korea must conduct reforms and open up to changing its economic system like China and Vietnam so its people can live well. North Korea has an educated workforce, and the party and state wield strong control over its people. The country will quickly have a working economy if it moves forward with reforms and opening up. Look at South Korea. It has become a global economic powerhouse in a short amount of time."

Kim calmly responded to Persson's comments. I was once again amazed at Kim's duplicity. "What you are saying is correct. Up until now, we have copied the Soviet system to the letter. It is all we know. That system has now completely collapsed, has it not? Like you said, I believe that the DPRK's economic system is weak. However, we don't have anyone who knows about the capitalist system even if we wanted to change the system and conduct reforms and open up. We must have this knowledge to change things, but even though we want to change, we can't. I would like Sweden to help us."

Upon hearing this, Persson showed great surprise, saying in earnest, "Ah, is that the case? Then, send your economic experts to Sweden. We will pay for North Korea's economic cabinet members to come to Europe to see and listen to explanations about Europe's market economy system." Kim then responded, "You have raised the issues of economic reform and human rights. Prime Minister Yon Hyeon-muk sitting here with us has been to Sweden and has said that it is a very developed country. I must also go to Sweden to see this development so I can work out a plan for economic reforms. I would like to visit Sweden. You should invite me as an official guest. During my trip there, I could also meet with other world leaders."

In fact, as Kim said these words, he had in mind a conference between the United States and the European Union set to be held in Sweden at the end of that year. President Bush was scheduled to be at the meeting. Kim was planning to receive an official invitation from Sweden to participate in the meeting, naturally gaining an opportunity to meet the American president.

Persson was very flustered after hearing this proposal. If he said yes, negotiations would have to start immediately about Kim's visit to Sweden. "I can't make the decision alone about having you visit the country," Persson said carefully. "I will give you my response after discussing it with our national assembly." Kim pressed on, pointing out that "because Sweden is a constitutional monarchy, the prime minister's word goes." Persson, however, did not feel he could extend an invitation to the leader of a country that suppresses human rights. During the inter-Korean summit in 2007, Kim requested that South Korean President Roh Moo-Hyeon stay another day in North Korea before pointing out that "as president you are the decision maker, are you not?" At that time, too, Kim had used the same tactic that he used to put Persson in a tight spot.

"DOES KIM DAE-JUNG THINK I'LL GO TO SEOUL? THAT'S REALLY FOOLISH."

Several hours into the luncheon, Persson asked Kim whether the North Korean leader had any message to give South Korean president Kim Dae-jung. The Swedish prime minister was scheduled to visit South Korea that afternoon following his time in Pyongyang. Kim did not skip a beat:

> Last year, President Kim and I brought about the June 15 North-South Joint Declaration. Now, however, the South seems to have changed. President Kim proposed to me that we solve the issue of unification together based on the spirit of "between just us Koreans,"[3] but recently the South has continued to press for reciprocity in their dialogue with us. Reciprocity is [a term that was] used by the West Germans when they absorbed East Germany. That the South is mentioning reciprocity means that they plan to absorb us into them.
>
> While giving us rice and fertilizer, they ask where the supplies are going and whether they've been distributed correctly. Why would we need to tell them about that? Reciprocity does not fit well with the spirit

of "between just us Koreans." The relationship between North and South is a special one that is heading down the path toward unification. We can't unify if the South treats inter-Korean exchanges and cooperation just like those between two separate nations. I would like you to tell President Kim Dae-jung to stay loyal to the spirit of the June 15 North-South Joint Declaration.

Kim spoke as if he genuinely wanted the unification of the Korean Peninsula, yet South Korea was engaged in a policy of unification by absorption. Persson showed surprise at Kim's words. "I also believe that unification by absorption is not possible on the Korean Peninsula. I will be sure to tell President Kim Dae-jung that you wish for him to abandon reciprocity and stay loyal to the spirit of June 15."

I have no idea whether Persson gave this message to the South Korean president. However, South Korea began to largely refrain from mentioning the principle of reciprocity during inter-Korean talks. Persson also asked Kim Jong-il when he planned to visit Seoul. Kim told the Swedish prime minister that he planned "to visit when North-South relations improve some more." However, after the meeting, the North Korean leader told Kang Sok-ju: "Persson raised the issue today of me visiting Seoul probably because he was asked to do so by President Kim Dae-jung. That means President Kim still believes that I could make the trip to Seoul. That's very foolish."

Kim Jong-il's duplicity was always like this. After I arrived in South Korea, I was very surprised to find that many people blindly believed a statement made by Kim Jong-il during inter-Korean talks that "American forces do not need to withdraw" from South Korea.

NORTH KOREA'S FIRST-EVER HUMAN RIGHTS–RELATED "CONTACT"; NO "DIALOGUE" OR "MEETING" ALLOWED

The preparatory meeting for human rights–related talks between North Korea and the EU was held in Brussels on June 13, 2001. Kim Jong-il's order regarding human rights diplomacy had led to the first meeting related to human rights in North Korean diplomatic history. The meeting came only around forty days after Prime Minister Persson's visit to North Korea. The dialogue was part of a tactic by North Korea to show that it was actively interested in participating in human rights talks.

I participated in the meeting as the head of the delegation and spent all day playing tug-of-war with the EU representatives. Near the end of the meeting, the EU side proposed that we add a sentence in the meeting document saying that "North Korea and the EU held its first human rights dialogue," but I argued until the very end that we had been engaged in "contact," not dialogue. In fact, the EU had backed off using a more formal term than dialogue to describe the meeting. The Europeans argued that, in reality, the two sides had spent all day in consultations that almost amounted to official talks, but—in consideration of North Korea's position—had proposed to use the term "dialogue" rather than "official talks." The EU representatives requested the North Korean side to yield a little bit on this issue. Despite the request, I held fast to the use of "contact" to describe the meeting. Because of this single word, the talks lasted until around 11 P.M. The EU finally retreated and agreed to my demand.

After the preparatory meeting in Brussels, North Korean authorities selected prisoners who could be interviewed by foreigners and even gave them the opportunity to practice the interviews beforehand. Over two years, from 2001 to 2002, French and German national assembly delegations visited North Korea to visit judicial courts and interview prisoners. In November 2001, exchanges in the human rights sphere between North Korea and Europe gradually picked up when a Swedish human rights lawyer visited the country and held talks with North Korean human rights experts.

However, North Korea's plans—which were aimed at delaying the international community's human rights offensive for several years— came up against an unexpected event that ultimately led to their failure. America's invasion of Afghanistan (in October 2001) and Iraq (in March 2003) after the 9/11 terror attacks of 2001 completely changed the EU's previously soft-line attitude toward North Korea. At a meeting of the UN Human Rights Council in March 2003, a joint resolution tabled by the EU and Japan demanding that North Korea improve its human rights situation was adopted for the first time in the council's history.

Kim Jong-il scolded the foreign ministry over this: "America's attack on Iraq with simple suspicions over weapons of mass destruction shows that the DPRK could be attacked solely on the pretext of human rights. That the UN Human Rights Council adopted the DPRK human rights resolution around the start of the Iraq invasion gives the United States the pretext to attack the DPRK militarily. What on earth is the foreign ministry doing?"

Ultimately, the foreign ministry's plan to get over the hump for several years ended in failure. The ministry was unable to defend itself against Kim's scolding. In the end, North Korea sent this official message to the EU : "During dialogue on human rights with the DPRK, the EU unexpectedly introduced the human rights issue on the international stage without any advance notice to us. This action has betrayed the trust between the two sides, and there is no longer any trust left. The DPRK suspends all human rights–related exchanges with the EU."

THE UN'S ADOPTION OF A NORTH KOREAN HUMAN RIGHTS RESOLUTION SHOWS THE FAILURE OF THE DPRK'S FABRICATED HUMAN RIGHTS DIPLOMACY

From that point on, North Korea closed the door on talking about the human rights issue and thoroughly adhered to a "strategy of disregard." The foreign ministry wrote a proposal that said, "Even if the EU, Japan, and others continue to pass human rights resolutions at the Geneva Human Rights Council, anti-DPRK human rights organizations and the pressure offensive toward the DPRK by Western countries will fall apart if we adhere to a 'strategy of disregard' and keep the doors closed [on dialogue about the issue] for around ten years." The proposal was sent to Kim Jong-il and met with his approval. However, North Korea's human rights strategy missed the mark, and in March 2014, the UN Human Rights Council released the "Report of the Commission of Inquiry on Human Rights in the Democratic People's Republic of Korea," which was a comprehensive investigation into North Korea's human rights abuses. Even from the perspective of an official in the DPRK's foreign ministry, Kim Jong-il's duplicity and time-delaying tactics were in a way incredible, as shown by the DPRK's efforts to conduct "human rights contact" with the Europeans.

From October 3 to October 4, 2002, a delegation led by U.S. Assistant Secretary of State James Kelly visited Pyongyang. North Korea reportedly admitted to Kelly during the visit that it was developing highly enriched uranium (HEU), but the truth of this is still a matter of debate. Of course, North Korea was in fact moving forward with developing HEU. This was confirmed when North Korea showed the American scientist Siegfried Hecker and others a centrifuge facility in November 2010. However, there is a difference between having developed HEU and having admitted to developing it. The situation at the time, as I know it, was as follows.

Kelly told Vice Minister Kim Gye-gwan and First Vice Minister Kang Sok-ju, "The United States has concrete intelligence regarding North Korea's HEU plans," and demanded that North Korea acknowledge those plans. Kelly even presented the foreign ministry officials with documentation to show that North Korea had imported special steel pipes from a foreign country. The pipes were required to develop HEU. The U.S official placed a great deal of pressure on the North Koreans. However, Kang retorted: "The American delegation has come here to negotiate, has it not? Yet, it seems like you have come to pressure us, rather than conduct negotiations. If the United States pressures the DPRK in this way, we could have something stronger than nuclear weapons [in our arsenal]." In the end, Kelly figured that Kang did not deny that the country was developing HEU.

When Kelly and his delegation returned to the United States, they announced, on October 16, that North Korea had admitted to developing HEU. That was the start of the second North Korea nuclear crisis. In February 2003, the IAEA passed the North Korea issue on to the UN Security Council, and when the DPRK restarted its reactor in Yongbyon, the North Korea nuclear issue returned to the same spot it had been around ten years prior. The next month, in March 2003, the Iraq War began.

KIM JONG-IL, FEARING THE IRAQ WAR, ORDERS THE OPENING OF NORTH KOREA'S EMBASSY IN LONDON

In April 2003, the United States, North Korea, and China held a three-party conference to find ways to resolve the second North Korea nuclear crisis. Throughout the conference, North Korea consistently held to a hard-line stance toward the United States. That was because Kim Jong-il felt he had something up his sleeve: the attitude of the British.

When the second North Korean nuclear crisis erupted, the United States was preparing for the war in Iraq. The British took the lead in showing support for America's position. If the UK had not participated in the war, the United States would have found it difficult to barrel through with attacking Iraq in the first place. North Korea conducted a close analysis of the actions taken by the United States and the United Kingdom. If, after the end of the Iraq War, all the war-related supplies were to head to the Korean Peninsula, that would be the end of North Korea. Indeed, the United States had already declared that Iran, Iraq, and North Korea constituted an "axis of evil." America's next target would naturally have been the DPRK.

Of prime importance, however, was the British attitude toward America's plans to engage in war on the Korean Peninsula. If the British refused to play along, North Korea would be able to adhere to hard-line pressure tactics in its confrontation with the United States. If the British supported America's plans, however, North Korea would have to retreat to a more flexible, dialogue-centered position. In early 2003, Kim Jong-il threw out some bait: he told London that the DPRK wanted to build an embassy there. If the British agreed to support the construction of an embassy, this would mean that the British opposed America's plans to wage war on the Korean Peninsula. It would also mean that North Korea could act boldly toward the United States.

The British actively supported North Korea's plans to build an embassy in London. Kim Jong-il decided that while the United States was taking a hard-line stance toward the DPRK, it would not attack North Korea as it had Iraq. Therefore, North Korea was able to play hardball during the three-party talks in April 2003.

When the three-party talks led to meager results, China came to the fore. In August 2003, China led a six-party conference that included the two Koreas, the United States, China, Russia, and Japan. Until the first session of the fifth round of talks in November 2005, the dialogue seemed to be making steady progress. North Korea acted with reckless bravado at each meeting, but at the second session of the fourth round of talks, in September 2005, the parties succeeded in adopting the September 19 Joint Statement of the Six-Party Talks. The main points of the statement were that the international community would provide security guarantees to the DPRK and that North Korea would abandon its nuclear weapons development in return for economic aid. Following the announcement of the joint statement, tensions surrounding the second North Korea nuclear crisis seemed to abate. The joint statement, however, was no more than a result of Kim Jong-il's duplicity and time-delaying tactics.

To this day, some in South Korea still argue that the responsibility for the breakdown of the September 19 Joint Statement falls at the feet of the United States. They claim that the Americans did not adhere to the agreement and pressured North Korea into having no choice but to develop nuclear weapons. Throughout this entire period, however, North Korea never stopped its efforts to develop nuclear weapons. In short, no statement or agreement would have been able to halt North Korea's nuclear ambitions.

MY FATEFUL RELATIONSHIP WITH JIM HOARE, THE FIRST BRITISH CHARGÉ D'AFFAIRES TO PYONGYANG

After establishing diplomatic relations with North Korea, the UK opened an embassy in Pyongyang in December 2001 and sent Jim Hoare to serve as its first chargé d'affaires. In October of the next year, David Slinn became the embassy's first official ambassador.

When I met Hoare again, I was struck by the mysteriousness of relationships and fate. I had participated in the first, second, and ninth conferences held between the British and North Koreans in the run-up to establishing official relations. As I mentioned previously, I had essentially participated in both the start and the finish of efforts to establish diplomatic relations between the two countries. Hoare, meanwhile, had been a part of all nine meetings between the two countries. He was then appointed the first diplomatic official to represent the UK in North Korea. For my part, I managed the construction of the North Korean embassy in the UK in 2003, and later worked there as both a counselor and deputy ambassador.

In short, Hoare built the British embassy in Pyongyang while I did the same for North Korea's embassy in London. I don't think that in all the world's diplomatic history there have been two diplomats like Hoare and myself who have first engaged in talks to establish diplomatic relations before turning to finalize the relationship through the building of embassies. I have no idea how the two of us came to lead the efforts to improve relations between our two countries over a period of close to ten years. That is why I was struck by the power of relationships and fate. Hoare and I are the only surviving participants of those marathon-like meetings between the British and the North Koreans.

Hoare is now working as a North Korea expert at Chatham House, the UK's largest think tank. We still ask about each other, and our families know one another. We both share a dream: to jointly write a history about the UK and DPRK forming official ties. I do not know when this dream will be realized.

The British did not use a new piece of land for their embassy in Pyongyang; rather, they borrowed several buildings owned by the German embassy. These buildings were formerly owned by East Germany. After German unification, the German government had no need to send a great number of diplomats to North Korea, so it rented out the empty buildings to the British and the Swedes. After German unification, North Korea also needed to reduce the size of its compound in Berlin, which it had owned ever since East Germany had been in existence. North Korea brought in a local hotel and health club company to take over the office building in Berlin.

The British had an easy time finding a building for their embassy in Pyongyang, but the DPRK had a much more difficult experience in the UK. North Korea decided to open its embassy in London in early 2003 and sent a team to the country to see the project through. Kim Changsik, an accountant in the foreign ministry's Foreign Currency Department, and I were selected for the team. Before heading to London, I met with First Vice Minister Kang Sok-ju to report our departure. During the meeting, he told me:

> We don't have a long time to do this. The United States looks like it will attack Iraq. The invasion cannot take place without Prime Minister [Tony] Blair's support. When you get to London, you must quickly set up the embassy and put up the DPRK flag. If the British actively help to set up the embassy, this means that the United States will not start a war on the Korean Peninsula. Send us frequent reports about what's going on in the UK. We will be able to judge whether we can take the initiative in our future relationship with the United States by what happens during the setup of the embassy.

I could fully understand what he was saying. However, it was my own opinion that the British had no reason to oppose the setup of a North Korean embassy in their country. I also met with David Slinn, the British ambassador to North Korea, before leaving Pyongyang. When I sounded out how things were looking in the UK, he seemed to indicate an active willingness to help.

THE BRITISH GOVERNMENT HELPS TO SET UP THE EMBASSY IN A RESIDENTIAL AREA ON THE OUTSKIRTS OF LONDON

To set up the embassy in London, Kim Jong-il set aside three million dollars. When I investigated the prices of real estate in London, I found that this would not be enough to afford a building in the city center. There was also nobody willing to hand over full ownership rights; the only option available was a long-term lease for a maximum of ninety-nine years. North Korea, however, wanted complete ownership of a building.

There were almost no buildings in London that could be used both as an embassy and as living quarters for staff. Unlike other countries, North Korea only sets up embassies when it can place both the embassy and living quarters in the same building. There are no exceptions to this rule, which, of course, is aimed at ensuring that staff keep watch over one another. As I tried to find a building that would meet our needs, I found myself looking at Ealing, a borough of West London. In fact, the building I found in Ealing was in a residential area that, by law, was unable to accommodate an embassy. Despite this violation of British law, the British government made some kind of arrangement and received permission for us to set up the embassy there.

This entire process of setting up the embassy required time to navigate procedural hoops, but I faced fiery demands from Pyongyang to set up the embassy as quickly as possible. The Iraq War erupted after I had just barely found a building for the embassy and was managing construction work to ensure that three families could both live and work there. North Korea's leadership worried that British participation in the war might put a halt to efforts to set up the embassy, but those worries turned out to be unfounded. The British spared nothing to help us set up the embassy, which opened in April 2003. Ri Si-yong, who would later become the ambassador to Germany, was appointed the chargé d'affaires ad interim, and Ha Sin-guk was appointed as the embassy's secretary. In August, Ri Yong-ho was appointed the first North Korean ambassador to the UK.

The money set aside for the embassy, which I had initially thought would be insufficient, turned out to be too much, since we had purchased a small single residence with a garden. The one million dollars that was left from the original three million was sent back to Pyongyang. After the embassy was up and running, I returned to North Korea. Later, I heard a story about British foreign ministry officials coming to the embassy and asking: "How did you set up an embassy in the UK given that you've been under American economic sanctions for a long time and your economic conditions are difficult? A lot of work must have gone into it. You must not have enough money to run the embassy, so how will you manage? We will research ways we can lend support." These officials were, in a sly way, trying to understand how North Korea came up with funds to conduct its activities abroad.

In the late 1990s, North Korea shut down its embassies in Denmark, Norway, Finland, Hungary, and the former Yugoslavia because of a lack of funds. Just a few years later, in the early 2000s, the DPRK set up embassies in the UK, Brazil, Mexico, Peru, the Democratic Republic of Congo, and Angola, among others.

DONATIONS FROM AID GROUPS USED TO COVER OPERATING COSTS FOR EMBASSIES

Some media outlets have reported that North Korea's foreign ministry earns money to run its embassies through illegal activities such as the sale of illicit drugs. From a foreigner's perspective, this may be an area of curiosity. The British foreign ministry officials who visited the embassy may have been curious about this as well.

Of course, some North Korean diplomats still earn foreign currency by trading in illicit drugs, ivory, rhino horns, cigarettes, and alcohol. Unlike in the 1970s and 1980s, however, these diplomats are not engaged in such illicit transactions as a matter of policy. After the start of the Arduous March in the mid- to late 1990s, Kim Jong-il ordered embassies with little diplomatic importance to shut down and other embassies to find their own ways to survive, because the party could no longer provide a budget for the foreign ministry. The foreign ministry, for its part, conducted organization-wide discussions on ways to earn foreign currency, but this did not produce any particularly good ideas.

When the international community began providing food aid to North Korea in the late 1990s, however, the foreign ministry found a way to earn a great deal of money. Generally speaking, the international community provides food aid directly to people suffering from hunger in the places they live. This is particularly true when dealing with areas where government control does not exist because of natural disasters or civil war. North Korea's government has strong control over its country, which means there is no need for the international community to do this. It thus makes sense for the North Korean government to receive food aid at the Nampo or Wonsan ports and then manage its own distribution of the aid throughout the country.

North Korea's government, however, forced the issue of having the international community pay for costs associated with distributing the aid inside the country, something that the international community accepted. International aid organizations gave the North Korean foreign ministry U.S. dollars to transport food to affected areas. The foreign ministry, in turn, crafted a "clever plan" to push the costs of transporting the aid to local authorities. In short, the ministry did not tell local authorities that the country had already received payment to cover the costs of transporting the aid. The local authorities happily paid for transportation because it enabled them to receive free food. Sometimes, aid distribution events were held in front of visiting foreign donors. This was how the dollars earmarked for distributing the food aid flowed into the foreign ministry's coffers.

The foreign ministry also looked for other ways to earn money. It leased out its embassy buildings and living quarters in Poland, Germany, Bulgaria, Romania, and Russia to local companies. It also began the practice of having travelers pay for passports, a service it had provided for free in the past. Tourist visa fees—with a visa going for ten euros each—became another major source of income. Around five thousand travelers from the West visit North Korea each year, and almost 300,000 Chinese travel to the country annually. That means that North Korea earns millions of euros in visa fees each year, and it's a big deal that just one ministry earns a steady income of millions of euros on an annual basis.

A "MIRACLE" HAPPENS TO THE PREGNANT WIFE OF A BRITISH DIPLOMAT IN PYONGYANG

After the British opened their embassy in Pyongyang, their very first request was to install a satellite communications antenna inside the embassy compound to communicate with their home country. Up until that point, other embassies in North Korea were allotted frequencies from the country's Ministry of Posts and Telecommunications (MPT) to talk with their home governments through shortwave wireless communication. North Korea's Ministry of State Security (MSS) was, of course, bugging those communications. North Korea had not allowed the embassies to use satellite communications because the MSS Radio Wave Monitoring Department (which focused on wiretapping) had no equipment to monitor satellite communications.

The MSS and MPT expressed opposition to the British request, saying that satellite communications were not permitted. The British, however, did not retreat. They brought out British foreign ministry regulations and said that there was no way that the British government would make an exception for North Korea and simply allow the embassy to use shortwave wireless communication. In short, the embassy demanded that communications between it and the home government must be conducted through satellite.

The North Korean foreign ministry was not allowed to make its own decision on whether to allow the British embassy to install a satellite communications antenna. When the British embassy's demand was seen by Kim Jong-il, however, the North Korean leader handed down an unexpected order: allow the British to set up the antenna, and later find a way to wiretap it. I am unaware of whether the MSS eventually found a way to wiretap satellite communications, but Kim's acquiescence to the British demand opened the floodgates: Russia, Poland, Germany, and other countries that had never raised the issue all demanded that they be allowed to use satellite communications. North Korea had no choice but to agree to the demands.

The next thing the British embassy requested was to allow its diplomats to travel back and forth to China through the bridge crossing in Sinuiju, a city located across from Dandong in China. This issue had long been raised by other embassies, but it was a "special privilege" given only to the staff of the Chinese embassy in Pyongyang. North Korea prohibited the use of the bridge crossing because diplomats could catch glimpses of North Korea's poverty-stricken realities if they traveled from Pyongyang to Sinuiju.

The British again took a hard-line position on the issue. They warned that North Korean diplomats in Europe could face restrictions on their activities if they did not resolve the issue. Staff working in the North Korean representative office at the UN in New York were, in fact, not allowed to go farther than twenty-five miles from the city center. The British threatened to start negotiations with the EU to impose a similar restriction on North Korean diplomats in European countries.

The foreign ministry sent a message to Kim Jong-il stating: "If we don't accept the UK's demand, our diplomats in Europe will face restrictions in movement. As such, it would be a good idea to allow [travel across the bridge] on the condition that the embassy must inform the foreign ministry of any travel plans to Dandong one week in advance." The North Korean leader, who was highly interested in maintaining diplomatic relations with the UK, may have faced a small dilemma. "Going forward, we need to move away from outdated Russian-style diplomacy and learn the diplomatic skills of English gentlemen if we are to [be accepted] by the West. Using the British embassy, we must accurately transmit the DPRK's stance to the Americans." Yet he also emphasized that the foreign ministry must ensure that British diplomats did not find out about the realities of North Korea.

Preventing anyone from finding out about North Korea's realities meant preventing everyone from entering or leaving from the Sinuiju route. North Korea's leadership found it unacceptable to have its own diplomats in Europe face restrictions, however. If that happened, Kim Jong-il's children residing in Europe would not be able to move around freely. The issue surrounding the British use of the Sinuiju route ultimately led to a collision between national interests and Kim's personal interests. The latter quickly won out. Kim soon announced his acceptance of the British demand. A rumor floated around the diplomatic quarter in Pyongyang:

"Since the establishment of the British embassy, tough issues that had remained unresolved for decades have gradually sorted themselves out."

Regarding North Korea's acquiescence to the British demand to allow travel through the Sinuiju route, I remember something that happened that I can only call a miracle. In 2002, there was a first secretary at the British embassy called John Dan. His wife was pregnant and had plans to give birth in China. She did not want to have her baby in a dilapidated North Korean hospital.

However, a month before her planned date for delivery, she suddenly started to get pains. And these pains, coincidentally enough, started on a Sunday. I was resting at home when I got a call from the interpreter at the British embassy. Dan had proposed to head to a North Korean hospital, but his wife had flatly refused, saying she would head to the UK after catching a flight in Dandong. Dan told the interpreter to "ask a favor of UK Department head Thae Yong-ho because he will resolve this"; he then put his wife in a car and, recklessly, zoomed off for Sinuiju.

Crossing over the Yalu River required advance notice of one week. Moreover, the border patrol never opened the bridge on Sundays. I was concerned about what would happen if the border guard refused to let Dan and his wife out of the country, leading to a problem with his wife's delivery. I felt a sense of urgency as my mind raced with all kinds of negative thoughts. I immediately went to the foreign ministry and made a call to the Border Control Department in the General Staff Department of the Ministry of People's Armed Forces, which had authority over the bridge on the Yalu River. I told them in detail what had happened and requested that they immediately open the bridge when Dan and his wife arrived in Sinuiju.

About an hour later, I received a call from the General Staff Department saying, "The decision has been made to allow them to leave the country, and [this decision] has been handed down to the sentry post on the Yalu River bridge in Sinuiju." Dan, without knowledge of any of this, was full of anxiety as he pulled up to the sentry post on the Yalu River bridge. When the car approached the sentry post, something happened that was almost impossible to imagine happening in the DPRK: The North Korean military officer and soldiers came over and told him to "quickly cross over the bridge" while expressing hope for an "uneventful delivery." The British diplomat shed tears thinking that something seemingly impossible had just happened as he crossed over the bridge.

A British aircraft was already in Dandong to take his wife to Beijing, where she received emergency treatment. Then the two returned to the UK. A couple of months later, Dan's wife headed back to Pyongyang with her new child. The British embassy held a large banquet to which I was invited. Jim Hoare and other members of the British embassy staff, including Dan's wife, took turns coming over to me and kissing me on the cheek. They thanked me multiple times. Dan, for his part, told me gratefully, "Mr. Thae, if it wasn't for your help, my wife and child would probably not be here today."

The incident was reported in the British media, and the BBC proposed making a special documentary about it. The North Korean foreign ministry, however, refused: although telling the world about a moving story of humanitarianism in North Korea would be a good thing, the documentary could focus attention on the closed nature of North Korean society. Later, Dan and his family left Pyongyang for a new posting in New York.

THE STORY BEHIND THE MAKING OF THE MOVIE *THE GAME OF THEIR LIVES*

This next story I want to share happened, I think, in early 2001, because it occurred right after North Korea formed official diplomatic relations with the UK. A representative from the Korea Film Export and Import Company, which was under North Korea's Ministry of Culture, came to the foreign ministry to meet with the person managing British affairs. As the head of Northern Europe and UK affairs, I met with him and heard why he had made the visit. I found his explanation fascinating:

Nicholas Bonner, the head of Koryo Tours in Beijing, along with British documentary director Daniel Gordon, said they want to make a movie in the DPRK. The story they want to dramatize is the DPRK's football team that performed miracles during the Eighth World Cup in England in 1966. The Korea Film Export and Import Company believed it was a good opportunity to improve UK-DPRK relations and suggested the movie project to the Ministry of Culture but was unable to receive permission. We would like the foreign ministry to receive permission from the General [Kim Jong-il] to move forward with this project.

Upon reflection, the issue at hand was not a particularly difficult one to resolve. Daniel Gordon and Nicholas (Nick) Bonner had for years been contacting the Korea Film Export and Import Company to try to produce a movie, and during that same time the foreign ministry had led efforts to form official ties between the DPRK and the UK. North Korea was a society where nothing works, yet nothing was impossible. Everything depended on how Kim Jong-il felt. Given that the North Korean leader was actively interested in improving the DPRK's relations with the British, the issue could be resolved simply by approaching it as a political rather than a cultural issue.

I wrote up a proposal focused on the positive impact the movie production would have on UK-DPRK relations. The proposal was sent to Kim Jong-il after receiving final approval in the foreign ministry, and sometime later the proposal was approved. Gordon and Bonner entered North Korea in April 2001 and were the first Western film producers to make a movie in the country. The resulting film was *The Game of Their Lives*, which was released in October 2002. The film was shown at the Busan International Film Festival and was even shown in South Korean theaters.

The story surrounding the North Korean football team that took part in the Eighth World Cup happened when I was just four years old. I have only very vague memories of it, but I did incessantly hear the story of their heroism while growing up. In the film, the North Korean footballers averaged a height of 162 centimeters. The team battled against the rough and ungentlemanly fouls made by the Soviet Union's soccer team, whose members dwarfed them in both stature and strength, and lost 0 to 3, but then tied with the Chilean team, which was ranked third in the World Cup. The North Korean team was scored on during a penalty kick, but toward the end of the match with the Chileans it turned the tables by scoring a goal that led to a draw.

During the final match of the preliminaries, the North Korean team claimed victory over the Italians with a score of 1 to 0. The Eighth World Cup, played in England, remains the only World Cup that England has won. That North Korea, a closed-off country located in the remote Far

East, won against as strong a competitor as Italy led to an outpouring of enthusiasm toward the North Korean team among the British.

The team received a passionate welcome home but could not escape the North Korean regime's requirement that they undergo self-criticisms. The team's failure to turn around a game against Portugal—initially leading 3–0 before losing 5–3—was particularly problematic. Some of the team members were suspected of drinking alcohol before the game with Portugal and were even accused of bringing local women into their living quarters.

Many of the team players were also the so-called sons of landowners. Families with money, after all, were the only ones able to raise their children as athletes. As such, the players had low *songbun*, or social status, and were the children of families that had a lot to hide. It is not clear whether some of the players did indeed hold a "promiscuous party" replete with alcohol and women; however, a couple of the players were sent to places outside of Pyongyang after the authorities judged during the self-criticism sessions that their "ideological armor was insufficient."

International football games are held every year apart from the World Cup, and when some of the footballers who were part of the "Miracle of the Eighth World Cup" suddenly disappeared, various rumors started to circulate internationally. One prominent rumor was that the team manager and players were "taken to the Aoji Mine." The movie *The Game of Their Lives* featured the recollections of eight North Korean players—including Park Du-ik, Park Sung-jin, Ri Chang-myeong, and Rim Chung-son—to shed light on the miracle of the 1966 English World Cup. The film showed the world that the players were not purged, as rumor had suggested, but were "still alive and well." That naturally pleased the North Korean government.

Daniel Gordon, the film's director, received an enthusiastic welcome when he visited North Korea after the movie's production. During the visit, a Korea Film Export and Import Company representative introduced me to both Gordon and Bonner. I am still in contact with them from time to time. Gordon later completed a trifecta of documentaries related to North Korea, including *State of Mind*, which followed the lives of two schoolgirls who participated in North Korea's mass games, and *Crossing the Line*, which featured the lives of American soldiers who had defected to North Korea.

BRITISH AMBASSADOR SAYS THAT THE BIGGEST ACHIEVEMENT DURING HIS TIME IN PYONGYANG WAS THE SOCCER GAME WITH THE NORTH KOREAN FOREIGN MINISTRY

The British embassy in Pyongyang used soccer to propose something unique and groundbreaking to North Korea. British ambassador David Slinn remarked that the North Korean foreign ministry restricted the activities of the Pyongyang diplomats too much and proposed that sports, including soccer, would help strengthen ties between the foreign ministry and diplomatic missions in the city. The North Korean foreign ministry judged that the British had a hidden agenda; namely, to increase contact with North Korean government officials with a view to gaining a better understanding what was going on in the country.

However, at around that time, Kim Jong-il wanted to kowtow as much as possible to British requests. After seeing Saddam Hussein's regime fall lifelessly to the ground during the war in Iraq, Kim was full of anxiety because he believed that the United States could do the same to North Korea. In his mind, one way of preventing the United States from attacking the DPRK was to improve relations with Europe. The foreign ministry, which was fully aware of Kim's concerns, decided to accept the British embassy's request regarding a soccer match.

In August 2003, staff from the North Korean foreign ministry and various European embassies in Pyongyang held a soccer match in Pyongyang's Neungrado District. The Russian embassy was the only diplomatic mission that did not participate, for reasons unclear to me. The match was aimed at strengthening ties between the two sides; yet it was also a competition tied to everyone's ego. The North Korean foreign ministry chose staff members who had some ability to play soccer and trained them for several days. Once they got on the field, however, those few days of training were clearly not enough. The European team included diplomats who were conducting humanitarian aid programs in Pyongyang, and they played so well the North Korean team did not have chance.

The North Korean team scored two goals in the first half. The North's team felt it had to win at all costs because the results of the match were to be reported to Kim Jong-il. The North Koreans were able to score two goals to tie with the foreign diplomats only after three members of the

North Korean national soccer team were put into the game disguised as foreign ministry players. The European diplomats complained to the referee after the game that the foreign ministry team had dishonestly used professional players. The North Korean referee insisted until the end that all the foreign ministry team's players were from the ministry. The referee himself was none other than Park Du-ik, a world-class soccer hero who had scored a goal against Italy during the 1966 English World Cup.

Later, Slinn recalled in an interview with a journalist that his biggest diplomatic achievement while in Pyongyang was the football game with the North Korean foreign ministry.

PROMOTING THE OPENING OF THE FIRST WESTERN MEDIA OFFICE IN PYONGYANG

British chargé d'affaires Jim Hoare met with me around June 2002 accompanied by a foreign journalist I had never seen. Hoare requested my help to open an office in Pyongyang for Associated Press Television News (APTN), which was broadcasting the Arirang performance to the world from Pyongyang at the time.[4] He introduced me to Rafael Wober, a British journalist who was APTN's Hong Kong bureau chief. My proficiency in English was probably the reason, but a lot of "projects" concerning the UK came knocking at my door. Wober explained what he needed: "I have consulted with the Korean Central Broadcasting Committee, which sponsors the stays of APTN journalists in Pyongyang, for the past several months about setting up an office in Pyongyang, but there has been absolutely no progress. When I appealed to Jim Hoare about this, he suggested we meet with the head of the British affairs department at the foreign ministry. That's why I'm here."

I then asked Hoare: "Isn't APTN a subsidiary of the U.S.-owned Associated Press? The DPRK and the United States do not have official ties. Do you think that setting up an office in Pyongyang for an American media company is possible? Moreover, this is an issue that the United States should be dealing with, so why is the British embassy trying to help?" His response was:

APTN is the U.S.-owned AP's video service company but, more accurately, it's a company created after AP merged with the British WTN. APTN is managed separately from AP and is a British company with its legal address registered in the UK. In fact, the APTN delegation should have made clear that it is not an American company when it entered the DPRK but failed to do so. The APTN team came to the DPRK because it was ordered to by the AP headquarters to cover the Arirang event in Pyongyang. While [APTN] does take orders from the AP as it is that company's subsidiary, its business side has no relationship with the United States whatsoever.

This all seemed very complicated to me. I thought that the way it was being approached from the start was wrong. Nonetheless, I felt they needed help, so I told the two men, "Let's meet again after I've looked into this a bit further."

Up until that point, the only foreign news agencies with offices in Pyongyang were China's Xinhua and CCTV, along with Russia's Interfax. These news agencies were allowed a permanent presence in North Korea on the basis of reciprocity when relations between the DPRK and Russia and China were good.

Western journalists, however, are considered scouting parties, shock troops, and spies who spread imperialistic ideology and culture into North Korea. North Koreans receive education to this effect from childhood. Yet Western journalists have been considered a necessity because even North Korea cannot live in complete isolation from the international community. While their entry into the country has typically been strictly restricted, foreign media outlets have been allowed to enter the country all at once for major events such as Kim Il-sung's birthday or a WPK conference. Even then, however, guides who act as interpreters follow them around everywhere, watching everything they do.

In April 2002, North Korea began the mass games and arts performance called Arirang in commemoration of Kim Il-sung's ninetieth birthday. Arirang is comparable to the revolutionary performance *Sea of Blood*, which caused a sensation in North Korea's cultural arts world in the 1970s. The following is a brief summary of what Arirang is all about: "Our nation is the Arirang nation. We have suffered from losing our country but met the 'Star of Korea' [Kim Il-sung] and reclaimed our motherland. With the start of the Kim Jong-il era, 'Songun Arirang' is now being performed. Our nation heads toward strength and prosperity as it thrives with the path open to unification."[5]

NORTH KOREA GIVES AP EXCLUSIVE RIGHTS TO LIVE COVERAGE OF THE ARIRANG SHOW TO BETTER PROMOTE IT

North Korea gave AP exclusive rights for live coverage of the Arirang performance to promote the show to potential tourists all over the world. AP then ordered its TV news subsidiary, APTN, to visit North Korea to both film and cover the performance. The APTN team resided in North Korea for more than a month to provide international audiences with news about the performance. It appears that was when APTN came up with plans to set up an office in Pyongyang.

North Korean media reported that the AP—an international news agency, and one owned by the United States, an enemy of North Korea— was covering the Arirang performance, an event that promotes the reign and achievements of the Kim family. In fact, APTN was a British company, but North Korean media's promotion of APTN as an American company was not completely wrong. The impact of this on North Koreans was more than the DPRK leadership had fathomed. When I came across the news story, I also asked myself, "Is this real?"

The Korea Central News Agency (KCNA) and the Korean Central Broadcasting Committee (KCBC) had authority over the setup of offices for international news outlets and issues concerning journalists residing in the country. The two agencies would first receive permission from the WPK Central Committee's Propaganda and Agitation Department before sending an application to the foreign ministry permitting a journalist to reside in the country.

The foreign ministry's media department would then decide whether to send the application up to Kim Jong-il. Once the report was submitted and Kim gave his approval, permission was then given to the journalists or news agencies to conduct their activities. Neither the Propaganda and Agitation Department nor the foreign ministry's media department held any discussions regarding APTN because it was an "American news agency."

I decided to help Jim Hoare and Rafael Wober with their request. Since the start of bilateral negotiations on establishing relations with North Korea, the British had persistently raised the issue of stationing journalists in North Korea. The foreign ministry proposed to discuss the issue after the establishment of diplomatic relations, so ministry officials felt there was a debt owed to the British. I felt the same, given that I had taken part in the negotiations at a working level.

APTN was, legally speaking, a British company with its legal address in the UK. In fact, it looked as though it would be alright to persist in saying that it was a British media agency. I discussed this with my department head and vice minister, and they told me to write up a proposal. I met with Hoare and asked him to have the British embassy create an official document certifying that APTN was a British, not an American, media company.

I decided to meet with Rafael Wober to better understand what kind of practical benefits would come from setting up an APTN office in Pyongyang. Wober invited staff from the foreign ministry's British affairs department along with a representative from the KCBC to a restaurant in the basement of Pyongyang's ice rink. He even prepared a bottle of high-priced British whiskey called Caol Ila. The name of the whiskey sounds similar to a phrase in North Korea, *goinda*, which refers to giving presents or bribes to curry favor with someone.

When I heard what Wober had to say, I felt that setting up an APTN office in Pyongyang would be beneficial to North Korea: "If you give exclusive rights to APTN for content produced by KCNA and other outlets, there will be benefits for both APTN and North Korea. When foreign media companies cite KCTV content, it is impossible for North Korea to watch over how it is used and to receive royalties. North Korea could earn foreign currency if APTN collects those royalties instead. APTN would provide the KCBC with free access to the TV news it transmits to the world."

KIM JONG-IL AGREES TO THE SETUP OF A PYONGYANG APTN OFFICE WITHOUT JOURNALISTS RESIDING IN THE DPRK ON A PERMANENT BASIS

Kim Jong-il viewed CNN, BBC, KBS, and other news agencies in his personal office, but North Korean TV could not use content from those agencies without breaking copyright law. If North Korea were to sign a contract with APTN, however, the country would likely be able to use all the content broadcast by APTN. There were also practical benefits to the KCBC as APTN would pay in foreign currency for its office, as well as the monthly wages of two North Korean employees, and provide a vehicle for work.

The obstacle facing us was stationing journalists in the country. North Korea would never allow such a thing. I made a counterproposal to Wober: "Setting up an office will be difficult if you insist on stationing journalists here. Let's start with having a DPRK employee take video, which he will then send to you. Let's do that for a couple of years, and then after building trust on both sides, we can decide on the issue of stationing journalists here." I continued: "Once an office is set up, APTN journalists and managers can easily obtain permission to visit the DPRK because they can submit an entry application stating they are visiting not to do a story but to visit the office. Once they have open entry into the country, they will be stationed more or less permanently here."

Wober was happy to hear the words "open entry into the country." He said he would discuss with his headquarters and then get back to me. A few days later, he contacted me saying that APTN had agreed to everything.

After consulting in person with my department director and vice minister, I wrote a proposal based on the discussions for Kim Jong-il. Here's a summary of the main points:

> The General [Kim Jong-il] has concluded that permanently stationing Western journalists is unacceptable, thus permission has not been given. Instead, it appears possible to station two KCBC journalists at the APTN office in Pyongyang to send [to APTN] only video required for our propaganda [efforts]. There will be no major concerns because the WPK's Propaganda and Agitation Department will inspect [all the materials] in advance. The British are very unhappy over the lack of progress on permanently stationing British journalists in Pyongyang, particularly given that the issue has been raised since the establishment of relations [between the two countries]. Setting up the APTN office may help to soften the unhappiness felt by the British.

When sending a proposal to Kim Jong-il, it was important not to say, "This person or country has long made this or that request and there are

various pros and cons, but there are more pros, so please give us permission." Writing up a proposal that way would be a recipe for getting
rejected. Rather, there needed to be evidence that the writer of the proposal had thought deeply about what has been allowed and what has
not been allowed from the perspective of maintaining the North Korean
regime. High-level foreign ministry officials did not oppose my proposal,
and Kim granted it his permission. That is how APTN's Pyongyang office
was set up. I still feel a sense of pride for helping to set up the first bureau
of a Western media outlet in Pyongyang.

NO ONE STEPS UP TO APTN'S FIRST INTERVIEW
OPPORTUNITY, SO I "UNDO THE KNOT THAT I TIED"

While South Korean media reported that APTN's Pyongyang bureau was
"established" in June 2006, they appear to have considered the establishment of the bureau to be the day when its official office was opened. The
bureau actually began its activities in the latter part of 2002. The office was
a busy place as the world's focus turned to North Korea following the start
of the second North Korea nuclear crisis in October 2002. The bureau
requested an interview with a spokesperson from the North Korean foreign ministry about the crisis. They appeared to have been ordered to do
so by their headquarters.

The department in the foreign ministry that handled media relations
was called the Press Department. However, nobody in the department's
staff would agree to an interview with a foreign journalist. Interview
requests kept coming in, but not one person in the entire ministry was
interested in doing it.

Anyone who conducted an interview with a foreign journalist would
be bugged by the MSS. The security agency, depending on its judgment
as to how important something was, would sometimes send the full
transcript of an interview to Kim Jong-il. That would mean the inter-
viewee could face either praise or criticism from the North Korean leader,
depending on how an interview went. The vice chair of the Committee
for Cultural Relations with Foreign Countries, Hong Son-ok—who also
served as vice chair of the Presidium of the Supreme People's Assembly—
provides an example of what praise from Kim could achieve: when she

was a departmental director at the foreign ministry, she told off the Russian ambassador, which gained her favor in Kim's eyes, leading to her rapid promotion through the ranks.

Russia had established diplomatic ties with South Korea in 1990, but despite having an embassy in Seoul, the Russians would at times ask North Korean officials about the state of affairs between the two Koreas. Once, the Russian ambassador in Pyongyang met with Hong, who was the head of the Motherland Unification Department in the foreign ministry, and asked her, "What is your evaluation of the Kim Yong-sam administration's policies toward North Korea?" Hong answered matter-of-factly, "Why are you asking me when the Russian ambassador in Seoul will know quite well about the South's policies toward the North?" Essentially, she had expressed to the ambassador North Korea's discontent about Russia's forming of diplomatic ties with South Korea.

The Russian ambassador left the meeting red-faced and without saying another word. Kim Jong-il, after receiving a report about the meeting, repeatedly praised Hong as smart. So, while anybody could have dreamed about landing a successful career on the back of Kim's praise of an excellent interview with a foreign journalist, nobody came forward to do an interview with APTN. They must have felt that the risks were just too great.

In the spirit of doing myself what others could not, I volunteered. That is how the APTN Pyongyang bureau's first interview in Pyongyang, and its first interview with a DPRK foreign ministry official, was broadcast across the globe.

After I defected to South Korea, the country's TV stations broadcast my interview with APTN several times. At the time, I was surprised that South Korean media had gotten hold of the file. That interview deepened my relationship with Rafael Wober and APTN's management.

KIM JONG-IL APOLOGIZES AFTER KOIZUMI'S AGGRESSIVE REMARKS ON THE JAPANESE ABDUCTION ISSUE

Kim Jong-il and Japanese Prime Minister Junichiro Koizumi announced the Japan-DPRK Pyongyang Declaration on September 17, 2002. The summary of the declaration published in the *Rodong Sinmun* noted, "The two sides [agreed] to focus all efforts on normalizing establishing diplomatic relations, for Japan to reflect and apologize for the damage and pain it has inflicted on the Korean people, and for the two sides to work to resolve the nuclear issue."

As a diplomat, I focused most of my attention on the statement in the agreement that read: "With respect to the outstanding issues of concern related to the lives and security of Japanese nationals, the DPRK side confirmed that it would take appropriate measures so that these regrettable incidents, that took place under the abnormal bilateral relationship, will never happen in the future." That sentence of the agreement essentially meant that Kim Jong-il officially acknowledged North Korea's kidnapping of Japanese nationals. It was shocking to me that Kim had signed such a declaration, given that he had long criticized South Korea for talks with the Japanese and had claimed he would never sit down with the Japanese without an apology or compensation.

The international media reported that Kim had apologized about the abduction of Japanese citizens and promised that it would never happen again. Even North Korea's foreign ministry had conflicting opinions about how to interpret the declaration and how to deal with its fallout. First Vice Minister Kang Sok-ju then held a lecture for the entire staff at the foreign ministry's lecture hall. His interpretation of the declaration was as follows:

Before Koizumi's visit to Pyongyang, there were several negotiations held about what issues would be prioritized for discussion during the summit, but [the two sides] failed to come to agreement. We plan to obtain economic aid from Japan through improvement in relations with the country. That will help resolve our economic troubles and weaken the American's pressure offensive against the DPRK. However, Japan held fast to its position that it would not budge unless the abduction issue was resolved. During the summit, Koizumi's persistence [on this issue] was stronger than expected. Japan made it clear, however, that if the DPRK accepts Japan's demands regarding the abduction issue, then they may yield on other issues.

According to Kang, Kim Jong-il knew that Koizumi would come out strong yet had nonetheless come to the summit with the intention to avoid mentioning the abduction issue himself. Instead, he had planned to place a single line about the abduction issue in the declaration to assuage the Japanese. The Japanese prime minister, however, kept to his hard-line stance. Kim was forced to mention the issue during the meeting, with the assurance the Japanese would yield on other issues and would provide economic aid: "I only found out about [the abduction issue] recently. Going forward, nothing like that will happen [again]."

By promising that no abductions would occur again, Kim's essentially made a de facto apology. For North Korea's supreme leader to apologize in front a *choppari* was something unacceptable and unimaginable to the North Korean people.[6] After the morning meeting with Koizumi ended, Kang went over to Kim and, with his hands clasped together while bowing, apologized to the North Korean leader: "General [Kim Jong-il], I greatly apologize to you as a diplomat-warrior. We should have ensured that the issue of the Japanese abductions did not arise, but we failed. I feel enormously guilty about this."

KIM SAYS THE *"CHOPPARI* CAN'T BE TRUSTED" AFTER PROMISED AID OF TEN BILLION DOLLARS DISAPPEARS FOLLOWING THE TRANSFER OF MEGUMI'S FAKE REMAINS

Unexpectedly, the North Korean leader gave Kang words of encouragement: "At the Revolutionary Martyrs' Cemetery, there are the remains of anti-Japanese warriors who died fighting against Japanese imperialism and who never received an apology from the Japanese imperialists. The *Suryong* [Kim Il-sung] failed to receive an apology from the Japanese during his lifetime. If, by receiving an official apology from the Japanese prime minister today, I can relieve the resentment held by our anti-Japanese warrior comrades, I can handle giving that level of apology to the Japanese prime minister. It's OK."

At that, Kang told us that he cried out "General!" while shedding tears. Kang then went on to explain the significance of the Pyongyang Declaration:

> The General's great accomplishment was to receive remorse and an apology from the leader of the Japanese government, the prime minister.

Even Park Chung-hee failed to receive an apology from a Japanese prime minister. Only the General, among all the national leaders of Asia who suffered at the hands of the Japanese, received an apology and remorse in writing from the Japanese prime minister. Japan has promised economic cooperation to compensate for the damage caused during its colonial rule. The DPRK will receive ten billion dollars at the very least. With ten billion dollars, we can modernize all of our country's basic infrastructure, including its roads and railways.

Even my heart leaped at the mention of ten billion dollars. My foreign ministry colleagues all showed a great deal of excitement on their faces. It was a massive amount of money. Later, however, the situation took a turn that we had not expected.

The international media intensified its anti-DPRK offensive, repeating that North Korea had officially acknowledged its abduction of Japanese citizens. Japan decided not to send five living former abductees returned to Japan by the DPRK back to North Korea. Following the Japanese government's judgment that the remains of Yokota Megumi, which North Korea had returned to Japan, were fake, the international media again rose in fury. North Korea claimed that Japan had fabricated and then distributed the story about the "fake remains of Megumi," but within the DPRK's foreign ministry there was criticism about North Korea's actions: "How could the remains be returned without knowing whether they are real or not, which led to this embarrassment? The remains shouldn't have been returned if there was no certainty about whether they were real."

At this, the staff of the Japanese affairs department in the foreign ministry gave this explanation:

Yokota Megumi died of a mental illness at the No. 49 Hospital. When the abduction issue became part of Japanese-DPRK talks, the party ordered her remains to be found. There were no accurate records kept about Megumi at the No. 49 Hospital, however. She died at a time when those who died at the hospital were buried in a mountain behind the hospital without even a funeral. The hospital authorities were put in a difficult spot. The authorities relied simply on the memory of a staff member to find the spot where they thought Megumi's remains were buried, and after looking around there they found some remains. Certain that the remains were Megumi's, the body was sent to Japan, but a DNA test revealed that it was not the case.

The gist of this was that North Korea had not deliberately sent fake remains to fool the Japanese.

Following the DNA results, Japan's offer of ten billion dollars disappeared, leaving only the abduction issue remaining between the two countries. Kim Jong-il abandoned efforts to normalize Japanese-DPRK relations, saying, "As expected, the Japs can't be trusted. The American bastards are better."

NORTH KOREA EMBARRASSED AFTER SENDING THE BONES OF ANIMALS TO THE BEREAVED FAMILY OF A BRITISH PILOT

There is another story related to human remains that concerns the British and is not well known. On May 4, 2011, North Korea returned the remains of Desmond Fredrick William Hinton through Panmunjeom. Hinton was a British combat pilot who had died during the Korean War. The North Korean media devoted significant coverage to the event. When North Korea and the UK had established diplomatic relations, the two sides had promised to find ways to resolve the issue of repatriating the remains of British soldiers; however, there had been little progress on the issue up until that point.

The British sent documents to the North Korean foreign ministry stating that a British combat pilot had been downed near Pyongyang during the war. The foreign ministry then sent these documents to the Panmunjeom Representative Office under the Ministry of the People's Armed Forces, which managed these kinds of things. One day, the Panmunjeom Representative Office sent a document to the foreign ministry suggesting that they had hit the jackpot: the office claimed that it had discovered the remains of the British pilot in Pyongyang's Ryongseong District. This claim was then immediately sent to the British embassy in Pyongyang through the foreign ministry.

Accordingly, the younger brother of the pilot, David Hinton, visited North Korea in early 2004 and visited the site where the remains of his older brother were found. The younger Hinton requested that the British government bring the remains back home for burial. The Panmunjeom Representative Office soon handed over the remains and other belongings to the family after holding consultations with the British embassy in Pyongyang.

Then, in August, the British embassy suddenly requested a meeting with the foreign ministry. A DNA test had found that the remains were that of an animal, not the missing pilot. I was stunned: this had come after the DPRK had been thoroughly embarrassed by the scandal involving "Megumi's fake remains." I did not think that North Korea would have deliberately tried to fool the British, but I nonetheless held my anger at bay as I forwarded the British protest over the remains to the Panmunjeom Representative Office. The response I received was ridiculously calm and confident: "We don't have any DNA testing equipment, so there's nothing to say. We did our best given that we found remains in the area where the plane went down. If it's not [the pilot's remains], then it can't be helped. Animal remains are occasionally found when searching for the remains of humans."

It was clear that North Korea would again face embarrassment if this incident was made public. High-level foreign ministry officials ordered that every measure be taken to ensure the British did not do so. I met with the British ambassador and told him: "The agency in charge has no DNA testing equipment, which seems to have led to what happened. I hope that bilateral relations will not be harmed by this incident." The British ambassador, for his part, responded in an unexpectedly calm manner: "We don't believe that North Korea deliberately sent us animal bones. We don't intend to make this a big issue, so don't worry too much." That concluded the animal bone incident, but I couldn't help sighing deeply in frustration at what had happened.

THE MINISTER OF FINANCIAL ADMINISTRATION IS EXECUTED AFTER NORTH KOREAN FUNDS EARNED THROUGH BUSINESS ARE FROZEN IN EUROPE

After Park Bong-ju became prime minister of the North Korean Cabinet in late 2003, the organization began implementing a major set of economic reforms. One of the Cabinet's plans for reform involved earning foreign currency by selling North Korean public bonds and domestic currency into the international financial market. Mun Il-bong, the minister of financial administration, actively moved forward with the plan, which involved printing large amounts of North Korean currency for him to take to Czechoslovakia and Austria to exchange for U.S. dollars and euros.

As part of the process of moving forward with the plan, Mun sent a "draft proposal for the General" to Foreign Minister Baek Nam-sun. The reason he had to send the proposal to Baek before reporting the plan to Kim Jong-il was that ministers had to conduct consultations in advance with the foreign ministry if they planned to go abroad. In late 2003, the head of the foreign ministry's European Affairs Department, Kim Chun-guk, held a meeting to review Mun's proposal.

At the time, the USD-KPW (Korean People's Won) exchange rate on North Korea's black market was KPW 1,500–1,700 to one USD. There was, in fact, no need to go to Europe to buy U.S. dollars at favorable rates. Essentially, Mun's plan was to buy massive amounts of dollars and euros at rates more unfavorable than the black-market exchange rate with a view to solving North Korea's foreign currency shortage. Such a proposal would make the European financial market happy, but it was clear that buying foreign currency in that way would lead to a fall in the value of North Korea's own currency. Indeed, North Korean currency was in the process of becoming as worthless as toilet paper. The proposal was not something the minister of financial administration should have been planning; indeed, he was essentially proposing to intensify the country's inflation rate.

Mun was not someone who had worked in financial administration from the get-go. He had rocketed up to his position as minister following his success in earning foreign currency while serving as a trade official at the North Korean embassy in Moscow. Starting in 2003, Mun issued public bonds and pressed people to buy them using the party's various organizations. The WPK promoted the purchase of public bonds by calling them "an expression of patriotism and loyalty" during every party meeting, and people who donated the public bonds they had purchased to the party were deemed as highly loyal to the regime. At the time, the leadership considered Mun to have raised the value of North Korean currency.

Mun, however, went a bridge too far in trying to show off his loyalty to Kim Jong-il. After Kim conducted an on-the-spot inspection of a military base, he would typically meet with the soldiers and try and solve their problems. Mun would later send a report to Kim saying, "The issue you were concerned about has been resolved." The problem was how Mun resolved the issues that had been brought up with the North Korean leader during his inspections. His ministry would print currency and sell it on the black market to obtain foreign currency. This foreign currency would then be used to buy food or textiles in China to give to the military so that Mun could say that the problem had been resolved.

At the time Mun proposed to sell North Korean currency in Europe, the entire WPK was engaged in a "Learn from the Ministry of Financial Administration" campaign. The minister had brought forward a ridiculous plan, but the foreign ministry could not express straightforward opposition to it. In a nutshell, Mun's plan was to earn foreign currency and donate it to the party. Moreover, Kim Jong-il had a great amount of trust in him. Foreign Minister Baek and First Vice Minister Kang Sok-ju were veteran diplomats and knew not to come forward and express outright opposition in these situations. Yet so many people expressed complaints during a meeting about the proposal that, ultimately, Kim Chun-guk was forced to take the lead and sent a message to the Ministry of Financial Administration that the foreign ministry was unable to acquiesce to Mun's proposal.

In response, Mun told Baek and Kang, "The foreign ministry does not consider the difficult situation the nation is in and rigidly goes by the book." Then, he went ahead and received permission for the proposal from Kim Jong-il on his own. While I am not sure how much money he took, Mun took several sacks of North Korean currency with him to Czechoslovakia and Austria and sold them before returning home. The results were painfully obvious: The value of North Korean currency tanked. People who said they wanted to buy North Korean currency in the European financial market disappeared. The whole operation was suspended after the end of 2007.

North Korea's international image took yet another hit as a result of this affair. The North Korean currency sold in Europe made its way back to the China–North Korea border, where it was resold and even distributed within North Korea itself. The country's inflation grew even worse.

The currency that Mun and his staff had failed to sell in Europe was at the center of yet another piece of ridiculousness. This currency was being stored at the North Korean embassy in Austria, but a great many people were eyeing it. How much money was being stored there was a secret, but everyone knew it was a lot. Some of the North Korean diplomats asked to change their monthly wages—which they received in foreign currency— to the North Korean currency stored by the embassy. Of course, what they wanted was to get a better exchange rate for their money than they could get on North Korea's black market.

North Korea also suffered an insult from a European reinsurance company. At the time, a North Korean state-run insurance company had brought a lawsuit against the reinsurance company in London. In July 2005, a North Korean Koryo Air helicopter had crashed. The North Korean insurance company requested that the European reinsurance company pay the insurance money with a small amount of euros. As I recall, the North Korean company requested forty million euros. After fabricating this incident involving a helicopter crashing over a storage facility holding humanitarian supplies, the North Korean company tried to obtain compensation for the humanitarian supplies as well. The company even fabricated an itemized list of the supplies in the storage facility. The European reinsurance company refused to provide the insurance money, saying it did not believe the incident had happened; with that, the two sides moved to court.

When the court's proceedings moved in a positive direction for the North Koreans, the reinsurance company said it would provide the insurance money not in euros but in North Korean currency. It was a major insult to North Korea, because essentially the European companies were saying that they would purchase North Korean currency at rock-bottom prices in the market. What was even more frustrating was that the North Korean insurance company had no way to accept the proposal. What would be the point of receiving currency with the same value as toilet paper? The court proceedings dragged on, but North Korea won and received the insurance money. Nonetheless, North Korean diplomats along with staff at the Korea National Insurance Corporation found themselves asking, "Is this what [our] country should be doing?"

At the time, I was a counselor at the North Korean embassy in London and received ridiculous proposals from several British people. They told me: "We have a lot of North Korean currency. We want to change it into dollars or euros on the North Korean black market. Can you help us? Let's do business together." I still remember feeling extremely puzzled about what to do with these proposals.

In 2007, the USD-KPW exchange rate on the North Korean black market skyrocketed to the point where one USD equaled KPW 3,000. The discontent North Koreans felt toward the country's inflation situation flew sky high as well. In 2007, Park Bong-ju was removed from his position as Cabinet prime minister, while Mun Il-bong was blamed for everything and executed. In short, he was suddenly put to death while just trying to fill Kim Jong-il's coffers with foreign currency.

The North Korean currency stored in the North Korean embassy in Austria, meanwhile, truly became worth less than toilet paper in November 2009. That was when North Korea conducted a major currency reform. The money in the embassy had been of intense interest to all the embassy's staff because they thought no one would know whether any of it had been taken. I think it probably took several days to destroy all that money.

AFTER THE RYONGCHEON COUNTY STATION EXPLOSION, CELL PHONES WERE PROHIBITED BUT THEN ALLOWED AGAIN AFTER A SUGGESTION BY RI SU-YONG

At around 1:00 P.M. on April 22, 2004, two months before I was sent to the North Korean embassy in England as a counselor, a huge explosion ripped through a side track at the Ryongcheon County Station in North Pyongan Province. This event became known as the "Ryongcheon County Station Explosion Incident." The incident was caused by workers conducting electrical work on the tracks in an unsafe manner. Sparks flew and they ignited a hundred tons of ammonium fertilizer imported from China. As a result of the blast, almost all the government buildings and private houses in Ryongcheon's county seat were flattened or had cracks in their walls. Dozens of people were killed instantly, while casualties numbered in the thousands.

Typically speaking, North Korea does not request help from abroad even during natural disasters or other crisis situations. This time, however, North Korean authorities took the rare step of quickly announcing the situation at the explosion site. They also acknowledged that the cleanup and rebuilding of the area was beyond the country's capabilities. North Korean leaders asked for help from the international community, including China and South Korea, and encouraged the humanitarian aid organization representatives at foreign embassies in Pyongyang to come and observe the site. Labor brigades were formed all over the country. Supplies sent in from all around the world found their way to Ryongcheon County. The labor brigades demolished all the buildings still standing after the blast and began to construct a new town.

At the time, international media reported that a train carrying Kim Jong-il from a visit to China had passed through the station just a couple of hours before the blast, raising the possibility of a "conspiracy to assassinate the North Korean leader." North Korea had, in fact, opened the site of the explosion to foreigners as a way to silence such rumors of an assassination attempt. International media outlets, however, continued to issue follow-up reports on the incident. There was even a report that claimed a train with Kim Jong-il on board was scheduled to pass through Ryongcheon County Station at around 1:00 P.M., which was when the blast occurred. British media claimed that a cell phone with tape on it was discovered at the site of the explosion, suggesting that a mobile phone was used to trigger the blast.

Decades later, a British investigative journalist named Gordon Thomas published a book called *Gideon's Spies: Mossad's Secret Warriors* that raised the possibility of another conspiracy: at the time of the blast, a train carrying Syrian scientists was passing through Ryongcheon County Station and Mossad agents with knowledge of this had triggered the blast.

I have not given credence to these kinds of conspiracy theories. The atmosphere in North Korean society at the time suggests that most North Koreans did not, either. It was strange, however, that right after the Ryongcheon County Station incident, North Korean authorities suddenly put an end to cell phone service in the country. Rumors circulated among the population that the measure had something to do with the blast.

It is true that Kim Jong-il ordered the suspension of cell phone use in the country to prevent future terrorist attacks, regardless of whether the blast at Ryongcheon County Station was really an assassination attempt. North Koreans naturally faced inconveniences as a result, and it had significant economic repercussions. North Koreans had been allowed to use cell phones in 2003, one year before the blast at Ryongcheon County Station. The cell phones were supplied by Loxley, a company based in Thailand. Each cell phone cost $1,270, a massive sum of money in North Korea. Based on current exchange rates with the South Korean won (KRW), the cell phones cost upwards of KRW 1,400,000. After cell phone service was suspended, North Koreans who had taken the big step of purchasing cell phones complained the state had just taken their money for nothing.

Cell phone service in the country was restated several years later following a suggestion by Ri Su-yong.[7] He had heard a suggestion from the secretary-general of the International Telegraph Union in Geneva that a well-crafted mobile telecommunications network could prevent terrorist attacks in advance and be an effective way to exert control over society. Apart from this, Ri also took notice of another way to use mobile phones: mobile telecommunications could provide new hope to a society that had lost its vitality and was stuck in its ways. After being introduced to Naguib Sawiris, the chairman of Egypt's Orascom, through the secretary-general of the International Telegraph Union, Ri grew even more certain that this was the way forward.

Ri then proposed to Kim Jong-il to build a mobile telecommunications network and received permission to do so. He was probably the only person who could raise such a sensitive issue to the North Korean leader, given that people have been executed in the country for just saying the wrong thing. I recall that mobile phone service was restarted at the end of 2008. Egypt's Orascom supplied the cell phones to the country. I think that North Korea's move to allow the return of cell phones was completely thanks to Ri.

4

NORTH KOREA USES THE BRITISH
TO CHECK THE AMERICANS

THE BATTLE TO BRING MY KIDS ALONG WITH ME
EVERY TIME I WAS POSTED ABROAD

In June 2004, I was sent to the North Korean embassy in the UK to serve as a diplomatic counselor. My posting came one year and two months after I had returned from setting up the embassy in London. My older child was fourteen years old, while my younger was seven. In principle, my second child was not allowed to travel with me because he was elementary school age, but my first faced no such restrictions.

North Korean diplomats must go through a complicated and scrupulous process if they intend to take their children abroad. First, they must write up a document telling the foreign ministry why they want to take their child abroad; this document is submitted to the Overseas Representative Office Guidance Bureau in the foreign ministry's Department No. 1. Other documents must be submitted as well, including a document that certifies the child's school grades; a recommendation letter that certifies the child's ideological status from a political organization such as the Socialist Patriotic Youth League; and a chart showing the child's physical health. Diplomats even resort to pretending that a healthy child is sick to ensure they can accompany their parents abroad. All that one needs to do is obtain a fabricated document stating the child's illness from a prestigious hospital, such as one affiliated with a university.

The documents examined by the Overseas Representative Office Guidance Bureau are then sent to the Cadre Department in the WPK's Central Committee. Once the documentation is approved, a "passport issuance notice" is sent to the foreign ministry. Once a passport is created, the child can accompany their parents abroad. However, the issues do not stop after this difficult process, or even after a child goes abroad with their parents. The child must return home if they are of elementary or higher middle school age, regardless of whether the parent still has time left at their post abroad.[1]

In early December each year, a message is sent to all ambassadors and party secretaries at each embassy abroad. The message instructs them to create and send a list of all children of embassy staff who are elementary or higher middle school age, and to have these children sent home by a certain date. The foreign ministry and WPK Central Committee have their own lists, which makes deliberate false reporting impossible. Parents with school-age children engage in various campaigns to prevent their kids from being sent back. The most common method is to turn a normal, healthy child into a sick child. Pleading that a child cannot be sent back because he or she is undergoing medical treatment sometimes works, but that's not always the case.

Diplomats first began expressing their discontent over the difficulty of taking their children abroad in the early 1990s. During the Kim Il-sung era of the 1980s, diplomats were allowed to bring only one child abroad; however, most diplomats did not raise much of an issue at the time. That was because the Nampo Revolutionary School was alive and well: the school took care of and educated the children of diplomats working abroad. While the school was up and running, many diplomats had no problem leaving their children in North Korea while they went abroad for work.

When the luster began fading from the Nampo Revolutionary School, however, diplomats who entrusted their children to the institution gradually disappeared. Meanwhile, grandparents increasingly took care of children their parents had to leave behind. These factors led to an increase in the number of diplomats who wanted to take their children abroad. Parents were even more eager to take their children abroad when a system was established that allowed students who had studied foreign languages abroad to transfer easily into the Pyongyang Foreign Language Institute (PFLI).

North Korean students begin focused study of foreign languages at foreign language academies during middle school. It is very difficult for students to gain entry or transfer into the PFLI regardless of how well they do during their elementary school years. However, it is relatively easier for students who have already studied abroad to transfer to the school upon their return. In short, parents could get their children into the school if they greased the wheels a bit. That is why diplomats went to such lengths to bring even just one more of their children abroad with them.

I also found myself unable to leave my youngest child in Pyongyang. While I can't go into the details, I was fortunate to be able to bring both of my sons with me to the UK.

FROM PYONGYANG TO LONDON BY TRAIN

When I found out that I could take both of my children to London, I got greedy. I believed it would be my last chance to travel with them, given that the criteria for diplomats to take their children abroad were constantly changing. My wife also wanted to show our children what the world was like. I decided to take a train from Pyongyang to London with my family.

Foreign ministry rules state that diplomats traveling from Pyongyang to Beijing must take a train, while those traveling from Beijing to London must fly. Diplomats are also given just enough money to cover their travel expenses. The foreign ministry has another rule: when diplomats are posted abroad, they must arrive at their overseas posting within a week. Diplomats recalled home from an overseas posting are given two weeks to travel; this extra time is given so that diplomats and their families can purchase goods to bring home. If the return trip requires a stopover in another country, diplomats must report this to Pyongyang immediately upon arriving at the North Korean embassy in the stopover country. All these rules are aimed at preventing diplomats from defecting.

When I reported my plans to travel by train to my superiors at the foreign ministry, I told them, "I will report each time I arrive in another country, so please don't worry if it takes longer than one week for my family to arrive in London." All of them expressed agreement to my plan, given that they had a great deal of trust in me.

I planned things so that the trains we took would only go through countries with North Korean embassies. It took close to a month to get to London, passing through Beijing, Moscow, Warsaw, Berlin, and Paris. From Beijing to Moscow, we had to ride inside a train car for five days straight. We rode the Russian Trans-Siberian Railway and stayed in each major European city we stopped at for two nights and three days until arriving in London a month later. I told Ri Yong-ho, the North Korean ambassador to the UK, that I was sorry it had taken so long. He just laughed, saying, "Your love for your kids is tremendous."

Even today, my kids still miss that trip. I've talked about it frequently with people I know in South Korea, and their reactions have always been almost the same: "The two Koreas must be unified quickly so we can all travel by train from Seoul to London."

Later, following our trip, North Korea intensified its surveillance over what routes the families of diplomats took when they traveled abroad. Colleagues who heard about my family's trip could not even dream of doing the same thing. I suppose that my family's trip by train from Pyongyang to London was the first and last time that something like that was permitted.

After arriving in London, we placed our children in elementary and middle schools near the North Korean embassy. I wanted them to learn English and about British society, including its politics, economy, and culture; however, they were still too young for that to happen.

THE POWERFUL RI YONG-HO APPOINTED AMBASSADOR TO THE UK

On December 1, 2004, South Korean President Roh Moo-Hyeon made an official visit to the UK. In mid-November, two weeks before the visit, the British foreign ministry made a dramatic proposal to Ambassador Ri: "We would like Ambassador Ri to attend the welcoming banquet for President Roh. We think it would be good to televise Ambassador Ri and the South Korean ambassador entering the banquet hall together and clapping to welcome President Roh to the UK. Even just showing the world Ambassador Ri sitting next to the South Korean ambassador would stabilize the situation on the Korean Peninsula and promote the image that the two Koreas are in sole control of the inter-Korean relationship."

At the time, the United States was increasing military pressure on North Korea by pushing forward a proposal that called for "destroying nuclear weapons first before implementing corresponding measures"—a tactic the United States used to solve the Libyan nuclear issue—along with the introduction of a bill for the North Korean Human Rights Act and the implementation of the Proliferation Security Initiative. North Korea was facing down these threats by arguing for "simultaneous measures" on the freezing of its nuclear weapons program, the signing of a nonaggression treaty, and the provision of economic aid. Regarding the British proposal, Ri sent the following report to Pyongyang: "If we participate in an event welcoming the South's president, we could give the impression that the South is the mainstay [of affairs] on the Korean Peninsula. However, I think we could deliver a blow to the American neocons if we show the world the two Koreas clasping hands together in the 'spirit of us Koreans' enshrined in the June 15 Declaration. I am wondering whether it would be good to accept the British proposal."

A week went by before a response came. It seemed that North Korea's leadership had deliberated quite a bit on the issue: "No matter how much the event can show off the 'spirit of us Koreans,' having a North Korean ambassador participate in a welcome ceremony for the South's president could give the impression to the world that [the DPRK] is being led around by the southern puppets. Make clear that we do not accept the British proposal." We let the British know how North Korea stood on the issue. They expressed deep disappointment, and even questioned why North Korea still failed to understand the hard-line position of the Americans.

As this incident shows, Ri was a sensible diplomat. He was thrown into the world's spotlight in September 2017 when he was in New York to attend the UN General Assembly as North Korea's foreign minister. When asked about what North Korea meant by its "highest level of countermeasure," Ri caused an uproar when he said, "In my view, I think it [the DPRK] will probably carry out an H-bomb test in the Pacific." The South Korean media along with major international news organizations, including Reuters, headlined Ri's remarks.

In fact, Ri is not particularly gung-ho for war. The Ri I knew spent all day in his office reading books. His skill and personality made him the envy of all North Korea's diplomats. While I worked under him, I never saw him express anger toward his underlings. Even if he had to press someone working under him about work, he did not speak in a direct manner; rather, he would beat around the bush to make the listener figure out what his point was.

As a matter of fact, Ri's appointment as ambassador to the UK was a major deal. In August 2003, when he was appointed to the position, North Korea was just about to take part in the first round of Six-Party Talks. Ri was the only qualified expert on the nuclear issue who could serve as the chief representative to the talks. Despite this, Kang Sok-ju sent Ri to serve as ambassador in the UK, while putting Vice Minister Kim Yong-il—an expert on France—in the role of chief representative at the talks. The move was a sudden and surprising one even to the staff at the foreign ministry.

The move signified that North Korea had completed its efforts to grasp what was happening on the international stage. In the UK, there were doubts being raised about the Iraq War, along with criticism toward Prime Minister Tony Blair's support of the American invasion. North Korea was certain that, without support from the UK, the United States would not be able to stage a military operation against the DPRK. Ri's selection as the ambassador to the UK was aimed at using the British to get a better read on America's calculations and to prevent the United States from provoking a war on the Korean Peninsula. These two reasons formed the core of what Ri and his staff at the embassy were to accomplish.

I heard that Kang Sok-ju told Ri the following, right before the new ambassador headed to the UK: "Make good use of the British to buy us a couple of years. Just two or three years will be enough. If you can do that, something big will happen, and I will call you back [to the DPRK]." Kang's mention of "something big" was North Korea's first nuclear test. As he had promised, Kang brought Ri back after the nuclear test.

KIM JONG-IL IS ENRAGED AFTER LEARNING WE WERE LEARNING GOLF FROM A "SOUTHERN PUPPET"

After my appointment as counselor at the North Korean embassy in London, I received a message from the Associated Press Television News (APTN) headquarters asking if they could do anything to help me. Given my status as a North Korean diplomat with very little money to run an embassy, I could not refuse their nice offer. I told APTN that the embassy needed a couple of notebook computers, and they happily agreed. My relationship with APTN continued right up until I defected to South Korea.

I visited Rafael Wober's house in London quite often. Wober mostly worked between Hong Kong and Pyongyang, meaning he was rarely in the capital city; however, his father welcomed my visits. I have a story I can tell about this. In March 2003, when I was in London to set up the North Korean embassy, at the height of construction work on the embassy's interior, an elderly man came to the embassy with a bottle of expensive British whiskey.

Given all the construction work, the place was full of dust, so there was no good place to sit down. I asked the elderly man who he was, and he answered that he was Wober's father. Wober, who was in Pyongyang at the time, gave updates to his father in London and appeared to have suggested to him to bring a bottle of whiskey to the embassy. I was really pleased to see Wober's dad. I may be the first North Korean person to have ever received two bottles of whiskey as gifts from both a British father and his son.

A year after I had been appointed as counselor, I played golf in the UK from the summer of 2005 to October of 2006. That year or so was the only time I played golf. After I defected, some South Korean media outlets claimed that I had "brought my golf clubs to South Korea" and that I was "crazy about golf" to the extent that I "always went to golf courses" during my time in the UK. That's not true. I did not bring any golf clubs with me, and I did not always go to golf courses. It is thus a far cry to call me "crazy about golf."

These media outlets probably sourced a Yonhap News article published on July 21, 2005. Here, I will reprint a portion of the article, which was titled "Ambassador Ri Yong-ho and his entourage learn the basics of golf as a group. . . . All are complete beginners and are taking pains to learn the sport."

> Staff at the North Korean embassy in the UK, including Ambassador Ri Yong-ho, have gained attention for learning how to play golf as a group. According to overseas Koreans in London on [July] 21, Ambassador Ri

joined a golf school run by an overseas Korean resident two months ago along with four other diplomats, and the group is working hard to learn the sport. Only seven North Korean diplomats work at the embassy building in Ealing, a residential area on the outskirts of London, meaning that almost all the embassy's staff has begun learning golf.

Ri and his staff have begun learning golf because they realized that not knowing anything about the sport in the UK would present restrictions on their diplomatic activities. Ri and his staff are all learning the sport for the first time and receiving education and lessons in the field from overseas Korean pro golfers.

As the Yonhap article reported, this was the first time I learned to play golf. Ri was the one who suggested that we all learn the sport. One day, he told me, "Golf is fun and is something we must learn as diplomats, so find a way for us to learn it." The first barrier we faced was money: golf clubs alone cost two thousand dollars, and lesson fees along with memberships to a golf club would cost, at the very least, more than five thousand dollars. That was too much money for North Korean diplomats.

After considering the issue for a while, I visited the London-listed gas and oil exploration company Aminex. At the time, the company was conducting gas-drilling negotiations with North Korea. I spoke with Brian Hall, the CEO of Aminex at the time, about our problem: "Our ambassador wants to learn golf. We need golf clubs and money for lessons. We were also hoping you could help with golf [club] memberships." The request was ridiculous, but Hall said he was willing to help. He told me to order everything we needed and then send the receipts to him. I went ahead and purchased one set of clubs for five staff members at the embassy. Hall helped set us up in the London Airlinks Golf Club, the closest one to the North Korean embassy.

The money-related issue was resolved, but now we had to find a place to receive golf lessons. After searching here and there, I asked an adviser to the National Unification Advisory Council (NUAC) in the UK, whom Ri knew. He connected me with a South Korean pro golfer named Kwon Jung-Hyeon, who provided golf lessons in the New Malden suburb of London. Ri, along with me and the other staff members, took lessons from Kwon for around a month. It was during these lessons that I met South Korean golfer Park Sae-ri. Amid the fun we were having learning golf, the embassy received an urgent order from the foreign ministry saying: "We have heard that you are playing golf. Is this true? We have also heard that you are learning from a southern puppet. Is that true as well? If true, immediately report back to us."

The foreign ministry never should have found out that we were learning golf. We knew that it was a major problem yet were clueless about how the foreign ministry had found out. We had learned golf under the strictest confidentiality. When we went online to see if any article had been written about it, we found that the Yonhap News article had been published several days earlier. We had no choice but to admit to what had happened. We wrote a self-criticism that can be summed up as follows: "While working as diplomats in the UK, we found we had no way to develop personal relationships without knowing golf. Faced with this difficulty, we wanted to start learning golf but found it difficult to find places to take lessons, which is why we began learning from a Korean with British nationality. He is not a southern puppet, but a British citizen. We have committed a grave error. We will not do so again. Please forgive us."

KIM JONG-IL AT ONE TIME LEARNED GOLF BUT SOON ASKED "WHAT'S THE FUN IN THIS?"

While we were fortunately able to smooth over the incident, it was still a wake-up call for us. We stopped the golf lessons immediately. Later, we found out that there was a particular part of the Yonhap News article that had angered Kim Jong-il: "With fluent English skills, Ambassador Ri is conducting active diplomatic activities following his appointment and is providing opportunities for North Korean public servants, teachers, and doctors to study in the UK. Ambassador Ri is a recognized expert on the United States and his father, Ri Myung-jae, a close confidant of chairman of the National Defense Commission Kim Jong-il, is the former vice director of the Workers' Party of Korea's Organization and Guidance Department."

Ri Myung-jae was the head of the Third-Floor Secretariat, which provided close support to Kim Jong-il. In short, he was one of North Korea's most powerful people. Kim was naturally furious that Ri's name and personal information had been reported in South Korean media. After receiving a report on the Yonhap News article, he immediately scolded Kang Sok-ju by phone: "There's been a report that Ri Yong-ho has not been working and instead is going around every day playing golf. What is this? Kang Sok-ju, did you know about this? They say he's been learning golf not from an English person but from a southern puppet. Have they gone mad? Moreover, how does the South's media know that Ri Yong-ho is Ri Myung-jae's son? Look into this immediately." Kim's outburst was why we at the embassy had received an urgent message from Pyongyang about our golfing activities.

Later, after I had defected to South Korea, I started to play golf and again realized how much fun it can be. My return to the golf course happened eleven years after I took my first golf lessons in the UK.

Some South Korean media organizations reported falsely that I had brought my golf clubs with me during my defection to the South. Some time ago, I had the chance to speak by phone with our former golf teacher, Kwon Jung-Hyeon. Even after eleven years, he remembered all the names of the embassy staff and even their children's names. He noted proudly that after our golf lessons had finished, he told others during a drinking session that he had taught golf to Ri Yong-ho, the foreign minister of North Korea, me, and even the children of embassy staff.[2] Nobody, he said, believed that it was true. During our phone call, he mentioned that teaching golf to North Korean diplomats was the happiest time in his life.

In South Korea, there have been rumors that Kim Jong-il had a golf handicap of fifty-six. Kim did in fact play golf for a time; however, that his handicap was fifty-six is a groundless rumor. Kim started playing golf because those near him suggested that he should. They told him: "General, you need to exercise. You don't like to work out, but golf is a fun sport for people who don't like exercise." Kim evidently thought it would not be a bad idea and ordered the construction of a golf course. He purchased golf clubs and distributed them to Kim Yong-sun and others so they could play golf every weekend.[3] Golf, however, is only fun after getting some lessons first. The North Korean leader just stressed himself out by heading out to the course without any lessons. His confidants were in the same position. Sometime later, Kim threw his golf club to the ground, saying, "What's the fun in this?"

THE THIRD-FLOOR SECRETARIAT: WHERE THE "OMNISCIENT LEADER" IS CREATED

Many South Koreans are familiar with the Workers' Party of Korea's Room 39. The organization serves as the party's financial directorate and was created to acquire foreign currency.

Ordinary North Koreans, however, do not know anything about Room 39, an organization that Ri Myung-jae once ran. Room 39 was so named not because it is on the third floor of some building; rather, it occupies a building with three floors. More specifically, the building that housed Kim Jong-il's personal office had three floors, and this building was frequently mentioned in North Korean media as the "headquarters of the Party Center, where General Kim Jong-il resides." The department in these headquarters that provides close support to the North Korean leader is called the Third-Floor Secretariat. A rough comparison with South Korea would have the Party Center's Headquarters as the Blue House, while the Third-Floor Secretariat would be the Blue House's Secretariat.[4]

Even Central Committee officials are unable to access the Party Center Headquarters without permission. On March 5, 2018, however, Kim Jong-un met with a special South Korean presidential delegation in these headquarters. That was the first time that North Korean media referred to the headquarters as the "main building of the Workers' Party of Korea."

In 2015, Third-Floor Secretariat officials accompanied Kim Jong-chul on a trip to London to see an Eric Clapton concert. Jang Ryong-sik, one of the people who accompanied Kim, had graduated from the Moscow Tchaikovsky Conservatory and had worked as the conductor for the Mansudae Art Troupe. Why would this person have been affiliated with the Third-Floor Secretariat?

Let's presume the following situation occurred: Kim Jong-il went to a music troupe and told them, "This song's chords should be like this, and its instrumental composition should be like that." Members of the troupe, unaware that Kim had been given preparation by Third-Floor Secretariat officials, would be completely surprised, asking, "How does he know all of this?"

In North Korea, a subservient relationship exists between the Kim family—or the "gods"—and various lower-ranking organizations. Barely any horizontal relationships exist in the society. North Korean government departments do not consult with one another. While procedures do exist to ensure a message goes up the line, the system was set up so that everything was reported directly to Kim Jong-il. For example, even if there was something that the foreign ministry and WPK International Department's Research Bureau needed to discuss, they did not hold a meeting. The foreign ministry and the bureau simply submitted reports separately to Kim. Issues regarding the United States, China, and Russia needed to be handled carefully from a security standpoint, and such issues must not be leaked outside the foreign ministry. In short, only Kim and the foreign ministry must know what is going on. Even though the WPK's Organization and Guidance Department (OGD) may have a tremendous amount of power, it cannot meddle with this system. There are real examples that show how tremendously powerful the OGD is. A mere official who heads the Overseas Party Life Guidance Section in the OGD can decide whether to purge a diplomat. The department has this level of power, yet it cannot meddle in foreign policy. The same goes for the WPK's International Department.

This system turned Kim Jong-il into a god. The North Korean leader would talk in specifics about an issue that even those directly involved had no idea about, and when he gave an order, they would ask themselves, "How did the General even know about that?" In fact, none of them knew that Kim had already received reports about the issue from different departments. Kim Jong-un has continued to use this system.

The reason the Third-Floor Secretariat is the most powerful organization in North Korea is that it makes sure this system works. For example, let's say that Kim Jong-un ordered the government to "create a plan to achieve unification by 2015." The Third-Floor Secretariat would send down an order to each department individually saying it was an order from Kim. The Ministry of People's Armed Forces would write up a plan to attack South Korea, the foreign ministry would concoct a proposal to overcome UN sanctions on the country, and so on.

During Kim Jong-il's reign, no one department had complete access to all aspects of a particular issue. All information—and authority—would be held by either the Third-Floor Secretariat or Kim Jong-il. That is why the Third-Floor Secretariat had so much authority behind the scenes, despite not having any ability to put together specific policies or proposals. It is thus understandable that Kim Jong-il was upset after hearing that personal details about the Third-Floor Secretariat's director, Ri Myung-jae, had been leaked to the wider world because of the "golf incident."

The current head of the Third-Floor Secretariat is Kim Chang-seon, who visited South Korea with Kim Yo-jong during the PyeongChang Winter Olympics in 2018. Kim Chang-seon's ex-wife, Ryu Chun-ok, is the daughter of Ryu Gyeong-su and Hwang Seon-hui, a husband-and-wife pair of anti-Japanese revolutionaries famous in North Korea. Ryu Chun-ok is also good friends with Kim Jong-il's sister, Kim Kyong-hui. Kim Chang-seon had a weighty role to play when a special delegation from South Korea (including Chung Eui-yong, the Blue House's national security adviser, and Suh Hoon, the head of the South's National Intelligence Agency) visited North Korea in 2018. He played the role of usher when Kim Jong-un and the special delegation met, and he participated in talks along with Kim Yong-chul, the vice chairman of the Central Committee of the Workers' Party, to then report the results of the discussion to Kim Jong-un.

KIM JONG-IL'S NUCLEAR STRATEGY TO "FAKE BOLDNESS WHILE TAKING EVERYTHING POSSIBLE"

It took one year and seven months for the first North Korea nuclear crisis to dissipate: from North Korea's exit from the NPT in March 1993 to the signing of the Geneva accords in October the next year. The second North Korea nuclear crisis, which was sparked by the Kelly delegation's visit to North Korea in October 2002, seemed to die down after around three years with the announcement of the September 19 Joint Declaration during the second meeting of the fourth Six-Party Talks in September 2005. Of course, there were some wrinkles along the way: North Korea's declaration on February 10, 2005, that it possessed nuclear weapons and, the same year, the U.S. designation of Banco Delta Asia (BDA, a bank based in Macao) as a "financial institution of primary money-laundering concern." In fact, the BDA issue became North Korea's excuse for launching a missile and conducting its first nuclear test sometime later.

After arriving in the UK in June 2004, I was able to observe the circumstances surrounding the second North Korea nuclear crisis, including the Six-Party Talks, with a greater international perspective than when I had been in Pyongyang. I genuinely felt that Kim Jong-il was a miracle worker. I found myself in awe of how he was able to deal with South Korea and the United States so well. Until the September 19 Joint Declaration was announced to provide a road map for denuclearization on the Korean Peninsula, the DPRK put on a show of confidence while taking all it could. Doing this was not easy. When George W. Bush was reelected in November 2004, there were expectations that America's policy toward North Korea would become even more hard-line.

North Korea's ability to navigate all this was possible because the DPRK's embassy in the UK, from Ambassador Ri on down, was able to understand American positions through the British. From late 2004, British politics had gotten messy as public sentiment grew that Prime Minister Tony Blair had exaggerated the threat posed by nonexistent weapons of mass destruction in Iraq. He was accused of misleading the legislature and the people in the run-up to the decision to participate in the war. The British were in a position where they could not blindly support U.S. hard-line policy toward North Korea. The UK government needed to show more support for the Roh Moo-Hyeon administration's North Korea policy, which had taken up where the Kim Dae-jung administration's "Sunshine Policy" had left off.

American pressure on North Korea continued even after the September 19 Joint Declaration; however, North Korea put on a show of confidence, to the extent it could, given that it had predicted America's next moves through the British. By 2006, North Korea had expanded its efforts to push back on the BDA issue. A total of $25 million of North Korean funds in the bank had been frozen. North Korea responded that it would not participate in the Six-Party Talks. On July 5, 2006, it tested the Daepodong 2 missile, followed by the DPRK's first nuclear test on October 9 of the same year. In short, Kim Jong-il's scheme to buy time succeeded in advancing North Korea's nuclear weapon development ambitions a major step forward.

Everyone at the North Korean embassy in London knew about North Korea's plans to denotate a nuclear weapon and had even held a meeting in advance to talk about how to deal with it.

CONCLUDING THAT "NUCLEAR TESTS WILL NOT INVITE AN AMERICAN ATTACK"

The topic of that meeting, "Will the United States attack us if the DPRK conducts a nuclear test?" may, at a glance, seem to be a difficult issue to unravel; however, we easily reached a conclusion. Considering the state of affairs in the UK, public sentiment growing more negative after the Iraq War, the failure to find weapons of mass destruction in Iraq, and the relationship between the UK and the United States, we concluded that the United States would never mount an attack on North Korea. The results of this meeting were immediately sent to Pyongyang.

We quickly came to this conclusion because the North Korean embassy had continued interactions not only with British government officials but also with staff at Chatham House and the International Institute for Strategic Studies (IISS). Gary Semore, the director of studies and a senior fellow for nonproliferation at IISS, had led an American delegation during negotiations between the United States and North Korea over a light-water reactor. Semore later replaced Mark Fitzpatrick as deputy assistant secretary for nonproliferation at the U.S. State Department and, in 2009, served as a special assistant to the U.S. president.

Ri Yong-ho met with high-level British and American officials to get a reading of America's policy toward North Korea. However, he was in too public and formal a position to hold deep conversations. Those he met were only interested in finding out more about North Korea's stance, not about sharing their own positions. As ambassador, all his meetings more or less fell into the trap of becoming "official talks." In fact, his meetings with a vice minister or department head at the British foreign ministry ended up becoming official conversations. Few of his meetings lasted more than forty-five minutes, which only left time for the two sides to share their views before it was time to part.

Ri felt there was a need to open new routes of dialogue. He told me to find new unofficial ways to communicate while he continued more official talks. As it happened, Jim Hoare, who had served as the chargé d'affaires at the British embassy in Pyongyang, had returned to the UK. He had a good reputation within British academia. I told Ri that I would turn Hoare into a route of unofficial dialogue and got permission to do so.

Hoare was retired following his return to the UK in 2002. He answered my questions in a serious and sincere manner, but he did not have a clear sense of the atmosphere within the British foreign ministry at the time. That forced me to find new routes for dialogue. Major opinions regarding North Korean policy at the British foreign ministry originated not from the ministry's Asia-Pacific Department but rather from the North Korea experts at the foreign ministry's North Asia and Pacific Research Group. Hoare had at one time led this group, and in 2004 Euan Graham and Michael Cohen were managing the UK's North Korea policy.

Initially, I went to Graham's office and suggested we engage in an unofficial conversation. He happily obliged, and from that time on, our place for conversations became St. James Park near the foreign ministry building. He made a good conversation partner. We walked around the park for hours at a time exchanging opinions on the status of the Six-Party Talks and differences of opinion between the United States and the UK. We both tried to make it seem like we were putting all our cards on the table while attempting to get a sense of what the other person was really thinking. That was just part of the job.

Later, Graham married North Korea expert Song Ji-yeong, a South Korean. He is currently at the Lowry Institute in Australia, while Song is conducting North Korea–related research at Melbourne University. Right after I defected, Graham published a long piece about me in a foreign media outlet. Later, my wife and I met with Graham and his wife in Seoul. We reminisced about that time more than ten years before when we had tried hard to figure out what the other person was thinking. Now that both of us are no longer diplomats, I think it has become easier to share what we really think.

CHINA TAKES A STEP BACK AFTER KANG SOK-JU HOLDS TALKS WITH CHINA'S FOREIGN MINISTER FOLLOWING THE DPRK'S FIRST NUCLEAR TEST

The country most angry with North Korea over its nuclear test was not the United States but China. China had led the Six-Party Talks and believed that it had control over the North Korea issue. The DPRK's nuclear test was like a slap in the face to the Chinese.

Three days after the test, on October 12, 2006, North Korean Ministry of Foreign Affairs First Vice Minister Kang Sok-ju and Chinese Minister of Foreign Affairs Li Zhao-xing met in secret in Shenyang, China. The Chinese had demanded a secret meeting with North Korea to impart its deep regret about the nuclear test. Kang and Li had studied together at the English Department in Beijing University's Foreign Languages College. They had even shared the same room in the school's dormitory.

Kang remembered Li to be a "very lazy person." While in college, the dormitory lights were turned on and off through the pull of a string; however, Li would tie a string around his foot and connect this string to the light's string a couple of hours before bedtime. He would then lie in bed reading and turn the light off with his foot when it was time to go to sleep—all because he found it troublesome just to get up and do it. Kang remembered that every time Li would shift his body while sleeping, the light would turn on and off. Kang said he had many sleepless nights as a result. At some point later in his life, Kang elicited laughter from those at a press conference by saying: "I couldn't study much because of the lack of sleep caused by Li Zhao-xing's way of turning off the lights. Look at us now. My friend Li is the head of the foreign ministry, while I'm still just a vice minister."

The two were thus familiar with each other, but inevitably, given the circumstances, the atmosphere of the secret meeting was a heavy one. According to records of the meeting held by the North Korean foreign ministry, Li told Kang the following:

> The Chinese people have a high level of respect for the great supreme leader of the people of the DPRK, Comrade Kim Il-sung. Comrade Kim Il-sung left a very strategic legacy of [ensuring] denuclearization of the Korean Peninsula. However, now the Korean comrades are violating his ideology and legacy. Comrade Kim Il-sung presented his vision of denuclearization of the Korean Peninsula because he predicted that the country could collapse due to excessive economic burdens in the event a small country like the DPRK engaged in a nuclear competition. Even a large country like the USSR ultimately collapsed following its entanglement in an excessive arms race with the United States. By conducting a nuclear test, the DPRK has crossed a line it shouldn't have. China hopes that the DPRK halts its nuclear development and focuses on economic

construction. China will increase its economic and military support to the DPRK if it stops its nuclear development. Nuclear weapons will not protect the DPRK's system. The country must quickly revive its economy first.

Kang responded to Li's remarks as follows:

I have no idea whether I am now in talks with Li Zhao-xing, the Chinese minister of foreign affairs, or Li Hong-zhang of the Qing Dynasty. You've raised the example of the USSR, but I am surprised that the foreign minister of China does not even know the reason why the USSR collapsed. The Soviet Union fell not because of an arms race with the United States, but because the [Soviet communist] party was lazy in conducting ideological training of its people and because the party itself was corrupted and degenerate. If the USSR had strengthened the party and ideological training like we have, it would not have collapsed no matter how much money it spent on an arms race.

You also mentioned the Supreme Leader Kim Il-sung's distinguished and great ideology of denuclearization of the Korean Peninsula. The denuclearization of the Korean Peninsula refers not just to our own denuclearization, but includes the entirety of the Korean Peninsula, including the South. The United States continues to conduct nuclear war–related military exercises on the peninsula, and could, at any time, deploy nuclear weapons there. Given this situation, the Korean Peninsula is in no way denuclearized. Only our own nuclear weapons can push away those held by America, and [denuclearization] can only happen when we receive assurance from the United States that it will not use nuclear weapons [against us]. We hope that China can mediate between the DPRK and the United States in ensuring that the Supreme Leader's vision of a denuclearized Korean Peninsula can be realized.

Kang used the North Korean logic that the DPRK would always use when involved in disputes with China about nuclear weapons. Li ultimately accepted Kang's demands. Despite North Korea's announcement that it would no longer engage in Six-Party Talks after the first session of the fifth round in November 2005, China again brought North Korea back to the negotiating table to take part in the second session of the fifth round in December 2006, two months after North Korea's nuclear test. In short, the second session of the fifth round of talks occurred one year and one month after the end of the first session.

At the third session of the fifth round of Six-Party Talks in February 2007, the participants reached the February 13 Agreement. Then, during the second session of the sixth round, held from late September to early October 2007, the participants reached the October 3 Agreement. The two agreements were aimed at implementing the details of the September 19 Joint Declaration agreed upon in 2005. In accordance with this agreement, North Korea promised to shut down and disable its nuclear facilities, while the five other participants promised energy and economic aid, including heavy oil. While the agreements seemed to signal another success, the reality was that China and Li Zhao-xing had taken a step back following North Korea's first nuclear test.

It was unclear in the agreements whether North Korea would have to report its stock of nuclear weapons and highly enriched uranium. Moreover, the agreements left it unclear whether North Korea would have to move forward with reporting on its nuclear facilities first, before receiving economic aid from the five countries, or the other way around. It was easy to predict what would happen: Ultimately, North Korea and the United States moved away from their agreements, each arguing that the other side had failed to live up to its commitments. The Six-Party Talks were no longer held after the second session of the sixth round. The talks were of no practical benefit, leaving only their name for perpetuity.

MY SON'S BRITISH TEACHER TELLS HIM, "YOUR COUNTRY HAS DONE SOMETHING WRONG"

The UN Security Council condemned North Korea's first nuclear test and demanded that it suspend any future nuclear weapons tests and ballistic missile launches. The council also adopted a resolution placing comprehensive sanctions on the DPRK. The vice minister of the British foreign ministry called in Ambassador Ri Yong-ho to lodge a strong protest about North Korea's actions. British society was in an uproar: Everywhere I went, everyone said they could not accept North Korea's possession of nuclear weapons. My younger son, upon his return from school one day, even told me his teacher had spoken to him angrily, saying, "Your country has done something wrong."

On hearing this, I got very upset. There was no excuse for his teacher to say that angrily to my nine-year-old son, regardless of him being the child of a diplomat. I couldn't accept what had happened. I told Ambassador Ri that I would go to the school and lodge a protest. He agreed with me.

Two days later, I met my son's teacher and told her, "The DPRK's nuclear test is a political issue. A teacher should not speak that way to a child no matter that he is the child of a DPRK diplomat." The teacher immediately apologized. When I returned home from the school, I told my son soothingly, "Your teacher has apologized, but don't get mad if you hear something like that again." Then he asked me this: "Dad, even BBC TV says that North Korea conducted a nuclear test and called our nation a bad country. Is our country not allowed to do a nuclear test?"

I had trouble finding the words to explain the situation in a way my son could understand, so I just told him, "Don't watch BBC. It's all lies." He then asked me again, "Dad, even BBC tells lies?" Feeling cornered, I just told him "Yes" to quiet him. He had watched BBC since early childhood and had believed that what came out of the BBC was the absolute truth.

Ri, who had been told by Kang before being sent to the UK as ambassador that he would be called back if "something big happened," was called back to Pyongyang right after the first nuclear test. His return signaled that the United States and the DPRK would enter full-fledged confrontation over the nuclear issue and that Ri would take a leading role in managing the face-off.

Ri returned home in October 2006, and his successor, Ja Song-nam, arrived in the UK in January 2007. As of this writing, Ja is North Korea's Permanent Representative to the United Nations in New York. One individual I worked with at the embassy in London was Ri Si-hong, who served as deputy ambassador and later served as the ambassador to Germany; Ri was replaced by Jung In-seong, who served as the embassy counselor. I also worked with Ha Sin-guk and Ri Ung-cheol, who served as embassy secretaries. Ha later retired from the foreign ministry and served as the head of the External Activities Department at the Kim-ilsungist-Kimjongilist League. Ri Ung-cheol worked at the World Agricultural Organization's office in Pyongyang until he was arrested by the

Ministry of State Security; he remained in prison until at least the time I defected to South Korea.

In early December 2005, the director of the North Korean affairs department at the British foreign ministry was replaced. The person in this position was replaced every two to three years. The British foreign ministry had a rule that an official could not stay in the same position for more than four years. By getting experience in various departments, officials were able to get a holistic understanding of the work of the foreign ministry. The rule appeared to be based on a philosophy that prioritized individual development rather than work efficiency.

In any case, I diligently met with the new department director to explain North Korea's policies. Sometime later, he said he would be posted to the British embassy in North Korea to see the country's realities for himself. The British foreign ministry typically had new department directors spend time in the countries they worked on for a certain period of time. During his time in Pyongyang, he met with officials in the North Korean foreign ministry's European Department to talk about the state of affairs and issues involving the improvement of bilateral relations. Then he returned to London.

THE HEAD OF THE BRITISH FOREIGN MINISTRY'S NORTH KOREAN AFFAIRS DEPARTMENT TELLS ME ANGRILY: "YOU HAVE NO RIGHT TO BE A FATHER"

Right before the head of the British foreign ministry's North Korean affairs department left North Korea to return to the UK, a message was sent to the North Korean embassy in London from Pyongyang telling us to investigate how he felt about his visit to North Korea. That was because he would have an impact on the UK's policy toward the DPRK. I asked to meet with him upon his return from Pyongyang. In contrast to the past, he proposed we meet at a bar near the British foreign ministry.

We chatted about this and that as he told me about his trip to Pyongyang. Suddenly his face grew serious, and he said, "I have a question I'd like to ask. Would you be willing to answer it honestly?" I answered: "What kind of question would need such a serious introduction? I will answer it as best I can." Then he proceeded:

North Korea and the UK have different systems and ideologies. They naturally will have different ways of thinking. However, while I was in North Korea, I couldn't wrap my head around one thing. In the cold winter, there were elementary and middle school students practicing for the mass games at the square in front of the Pyongyang Gymnasium. I came to tears when I saw eight-year-old children were wearing gloves and practicing tumbling on the concrete ground. No one walking by felt sorry for them. Why on earth would North Koreans not feel sorry for children trembling in the cold to prepare for the leader's birthday? Doesn't anyone take pity on them?

This is how I answered him: "As you said, the DPRK and the UK have different ideologies and systems. The DPRK places importance on collectivism. One person works for the benefit of all. Collectivism, however, isn't something created out of thin air. From childhood, collectivism is cultivated by having [children] conduct group activities such as constantly practicing a single dance routine. We consider the mass games to be education aimed at planting the seeds of collectivism [in children]."

He responded to this by refuting what I had to say: "I understand that your youngest eight-year-old child is attending an elementary school in London. Imagine if he was trembling in the cold and practicing tumbling on concrete. Would you accept that if only to prepare to celebrate the birthday of the leader?" I answered that I would have no problem accepting that. Then he told me: "You have no right to be a father. I don't have any interest in speaking to someone like you." Then he got up and walked out.

That left a bitter taste in my mouth. I fell into deep thought. I had frequently seen children in Pyongyang practicing for the mass games but had never thought that it was wrong. When I returned to the embassy, I told the ambassador about what the new department director had said. The ambassador told me to report what he had said verbatim back to Pyongyang. On his orders, I began writing up the telegram and included a line that said: "The new director's thinking in this regard seems to be due to bad influence by David Slinn, the British ambassador in Pyongyang." I cunningly added mention of the British ambassador in the telegram because I wanted to avoid blame falling on us in London that we had falsely promoted North Korean policy.

The telegram was sent to Kim Jong-il, and the North Korean leader called Kang Sok-ju to reprimand him. Kim seemed to have been uncomfortable with thousands of children suffering in the cold winter on the streets of Pyongyang in preparation for his birthday celebrations. The North Korean leader also told Kang that the "British ambassador in Pyongyang is an awful bastard" and ordered Kang to "create a plan to expel that bastard immediately." While I had not intended that, my telegram turned into a stray bullet, striking the British ambassador.

However, from that point on, the children's mass game practice was suspended. It was something no one could have predicted or even expected. Kim Jong-il himself may have given the order, though I do not really know. North Korean diplomats, who are aware of the irrationality of the DPRK's system, quietly try in various ways to bring even small changes to North Korea. My telegram may have been one part of such efforts; however, at the time I had no sense of joy. Yet, upon reflection, what happened was a huge deal. I dare say that it was my own meritorious action that made it so North Korean children no longer had to conduct mass games training in the winter. Indeed, the proudest thing I accomplished while working in the UK was putting a halt to these practices in Pyongyang to celebrate Kim Jong-il's birthday on February 16.

Kang Sok-ju, meanwhile, was in a dilemma after being ordered to find a way to chase David Slinn out of the country. Forcibly expelling him from North Korea could lead to Ambassador Ri Yong-ho's being expelled from the UK. After deep thought, Kang ordered his staff to refuse all meetings and requests to visit different locations emanating from Slinn's embassy. Kang planned to get the British ambassador so annoyed that he would decide to leave North Korea by himself. Over the next several months, all Slinn's meetings were refused, and North Korean officials were ordered not to meet with him. Eventually, Slinn requested to be posted somewhere else and left North Korea of his own accord.

I was actually very close with Slinn on a personal level. When I was the head of British affairs at the foreign ministry, I traveled with him to several areas in North Korea and frequently had drinking sessions with him. After leaving North Korea, he was posted in several other countries until he met a Canadian diplomat and settled down at the Centre for International Policy Studies at the University of Ottawa. I met him in November 2015 when he flew from Canada to London while I was working as the deputy ambassador in London. Even then, I did not tell him about why he had been "kicked out" of Pyongyang.

Slinn asked me when we met what I thought about Kim Jong-un. I answered I still didn't know what to think about the new leader, not wanting to call him the "Great Leader" as many North Korean diplomats did. After I defected to South Korea, he said the following in an interview with the *Dong-a Ilbo* in August 2016: "I met Thae Yong-ho in London in November 2015, and he was a completely different person to the one I had met while in Pyongyang around ten years ago. I can't confidently say why he chose to defect, but he clearly had doubts about the direction the North Korean system is going." Slinn had read into something in my demeanor that day we had met in London. I still share news with him by email from time to time.

A FUTURE SOUTH KOREAN LAWMAKER GIVES ME SOUTH KOREAN-MADE NAIL CLIPPERS

On March 26, 2007, an international conference entitled "The Results of the Six-Party Talks and the Cooperative Stability of Northeast Asia" was held in Como, Italy. The conference was called, in North Korean parlance, the "Como meeting." I was ordered to fly to Italy from London and join up with the North Korean delegation there. South Korean diplomats along with a researcher from the Korea Institute for Defense Analyses attended the conference. Many diplomats and North Korea experts from countries involved in the Six-Party Talks, including the United States, China, Japan, and Russia, also attended the conference.

The conference took place at a very important time for the North Korea nuclear issue. On February 13—one month before the conference was held—the countries involved in the Six-Party Talks adopted the February 13 Agreement. This agreement indicated that the countries were moving forward with the first stage of putting the September 19 Joint Declaration of 2005 into play, a year and five months after the declaration had been signed. The key part of the February 13 Agreement was that the United States would return the twenty-five million dollars that had been frozen in the BDA bank in Macao. The United States had promised to return the funds within sixty days but was delaying this.

The goal of the North Korean delegation at the Como conference was to get the United States to release the BDA funds. The delegation threatened to refuse to accept IAEA inspection teams if the BDA funds were not released. The South Korean and American delegations, meanwhile, tried to reconfirm the North Korean position that it would accurately report on its nuclear facilities and declare the end of its nuclear ambitions if the United States gave North Korea one hundred thousand tons of heavy oil and returned the BDA funds.

Some of the experts who attended the conference asked why North Korea was so hung up on the BDA funds, given that the United States had promised to return the money and there were only working-level issues left to resolve. The DPRK's reasoning on this front was unknown to them. At the time, Kim Jong-il had been pestering Kang Sok-ju incessantly about when the funds would be returned. There was a rumor in the foreign ministry that more than ten million dollars of those funds were owned by the Central Committee's Light Industry Department, which Kim Kyong-hui was heading, and she was badgering the North Korean leader about when they would be returned. The foreign ministry, which had promised that the funds would be returned within sixty days, was in a very difficult position. That is why the North Korean delegation had little choice but to press on with getting the BDA funds back as quickly as possible.

The United States tried to use a Chinese bank to release the BDA funds back to North Korea. However, China claimed that America's unilateral sanctions on the BDA had caused a fall in prestige of the Macao financial industry and demanded a U.S. apology. The start of a new back-and-forth between the United States and China shifted attention away from the BDA issue. The Como conference ended with the two sides just telling each other where they stood.

After the end of the conference, the North Korean delegation had dinner at a restaurant before going back to its hotel. We were sitting in the lobby when one member of the South Korean delegation headed toward us. It was the researcher from the Korea Institute for Defense Analyses. He proposed that we have a drink together. I was accompanied by two other members of the delegation, and he was alone, so we had no reason to decline. He went up to his room, grabbed a bottle of whiskey, and returned to the lobby. While he went up to the room, we told ourselves that he could be a National Intelligence Service (NIS) agent because he had approached us first, so we needed to be on our guard even if we had a drink with him.

It was raining that night. We talked about this and that as we passed around the whiskey bottle in the hotel lobby. We even asked about South Korea. When we parted, the South Korean researcher gave each of us a small parting gift: a set of nail clippers. There were cutters for fingernails and toenails, along with a nail file and even an ear wax remover.

I had a fungal infection on my toenails, so my toenails were quite thick. I went up to my room and tried the toenail clippers out—they were great! The clippers were a present from a "southern puppet," and I should have handed them over to the Ministry of State Security or thrown them out then and there, but I liked them too much to do so. My colleagues thought the same way. We agreed to take them along with us after etching off the "Korea Institute for Defense Analyses" lettering on the plastic cases.

The more I used the clippers, the more I liked them. The quality of a country's nail clippers can be an indicator of how developed its metal-works industry is. At the time, all the nail clippers in North Korea were made in China, and poorly made at that, so that their blades would dull very quickly. I used my new nail clippers until I defected to South Korea— for almost ten years!

One day in the spring of 2017, after my defection, I had the opportunity to have a meal with members of the Liberty Korea Party. When I got to the restaurant, one of the lawmakers took my hand in welcome and said, "It's been a really long time. Do you remember me?" His face seemed so familiar, but I could not for the life of me remember where I had met him. He laughed and told me: "You don't remember us drinking alcohol together in the lobby of that Italian hotel? As soon as I heard that you had defected, I knew that you were the person I had had that drink with. I have waited a long time for you to come out into the open."

His name was Baek Seung-ju, and he was a lawmaker with the Liberty Korea Party. I later had drinks with him again, ten years after our first meeting. I told him jokingly, "I actually thought you were a National Intelligence Agency agent at the time," and he responded: "In fact, I was the only person affiliated with the Ministry of Defense among the conference participants. All the rest were from the foreign ministry. At dinner time, they all left me hanging and went out with the embassy staff for a meal. I

198 AT THE HEART OF PYONGYANG'S LEADERSHIP

was so depressed that I wandered around the hotel lobby for a while, and then I saw the North Korean delegation come in. I told myself, 'What's the harm, let's have a meal with the North Koreans.' That's how it happened."

ONE PILLAR OF NORTH KOREA'S NUCLEAR DIPLOMACY WAS TO "PLACE A CHECK ON THE UNITED STATES THROUGH THE UNITED KINGDOM"

The British policy toward North Korea was expressed as "critical engagement." This has been, in short, an "English-style Sunshine Policy" that aims to bring about change in North Korea through dialogue and humanitarian exchanges. The North Korean embassy in London put in a lot of work until the British adopted this policy in 2005. When the United States was threatening military action along with dialogue during the second North Korea nuclear crisis, London's North Korean embassy ceaselessly lobbied the UK government until it agreed to adopt the policy of critical engagement.

The UK prioritizes dialogue to resolve North Korea's weapons of mass destruction and human rights issues. The country also places an emphasis on human exchanges and education and training for North Koreans. The UK's critical engagement policy is aimed at gradually bringing North Korea into the international community. As such, the UK has sent three English teachers to Pyongyang on its own dime and invites North Korean officials to England each year for English training. The country also proactively participates in various projects aimed at the North. The UK takes care of 18–20 percent of the costs associated with the EU's humanitarian aid for North Korea. A total of around two million British pounds is spent each year on aid to the country.

The central focus of British policy toward North Korea is on the study of English. North Korean officials who go to the UK to study can live with a British family for one month, although they must do this in twos. The program intends to have them learn about liberal democracy while living with a British family. During their time in the UK, North Korean officials learn about the British market economy, the two-party political system, the legal system, and the role of media in societal development.

This program poses a risk from North Korea's perspective because these officials come home filled with insight into the UK's liberal democratic system. Regardless, the reason North Korea continues to send its officials to the UK to learn English is clear: North Korea's leadership believes that because England is aiming to change North Korea through engagement and not force, the British can serve as a restraining force on America's military policies.

From the British perspective, North Korea must respond to its policy for it to speak up against American policies of military intervention toward North Korea. North Korean leaders believe that having the British, America's closest ally, oppose U.S. policies based on force is a good thing for them. The interests of the two countries dovetail, which has allowed the UK to maintain its critical engagement policy toward North Korea.

ERIC CLAPTON: "HOLDING A CONCERT IN PYONGYANG WILL BE DIFFICULT BECAUSE OF NORTH KOREA'S HUMAN RIGHTS RECORD"

The British policy of critical engagement toward North Korea can be viewed as a "success" of North Korean diplomacy. North Korea took advantage of the UK's policy to neutralize U.S. policy aimed at exerting military pressure on the country. After the first North Korean nuclear test, there was concern that the British could place diplomatic sanctions on the DPRK; however, all they did was condemn it without taking any measures. British policy toward North Korea has remained focused on critical engagement even though the DPRK has conducted a total of six nuclear tests.

Right around when I was about to end my time at the North Korean embassy in London, I received an order from Kim Jong-il instructing me to set up an Eric Clapton concert in Pyongyang. It was well known that Kim Jong-chul—one of the North Korean leader's sons—was a big fan of Eric Clapton. It was clear the son had pestered his father about holding the concert. That may explain why Kim Jong-il was so intent about it.

Later, when I returned to Pyongyang, I heard that Kim Jong-chul had frequently visited the foreign ministry to check up on progress regarding the Clapton concert in Pyongyang. That's because he knew that working-level contact with Clapton's representatives would be handled by the North Korean embassy in London, and the embassy's superiors were all in the foreign ministry.

Not many people in the foreign ministry knew Kim Jong-chul at the time. Ministry cadres and lower-ranking officials used different entrances to get into the building. Kim would wear an ordinary-looking sports training outfit and enter through the cadre entrance, heading straight up to Kang Sok-ju's office. After he left, cadres would ask themselves, "Who was that?" Kim was largely an unknown entity, but Kim Jong-un, his brother, was even less known. The two brothers were "crown princes living in seclusion."

In the UK, I met with one of Eric Clapton's representatives. The representative told me they would need a down payment of one million euros to go forward. That was equal to around KRW 1.4 to 1.5 billion at the time. When I reported this to Pyongyang, permission to transfer the payment was granted immediately. The representative told me he would put together a plan for the concert and get back to me.

Sometime later, I was informed by the representative that "[Clapton] can't go to Pyongyang now because of North Korea's human rights situation, but a decision will be made depending on the situation going forward." Even after I was posted back to Pyongyang, efforts continued to invite the British guitarist-singer to North Korea. Clapton never promised to hold a concert there, however.

5

FROM KIM JONG-IL TO KIM JONG-UN

AFTER THE DPRK'S FIRST NUCLEAR TEST, ALL DIPLOMATS ARE ORDERED TO SEND BACK ALL EXCEPT ONE OF THEIR CHILDREN

After my posting at the North Korean embassy in London ended, I returned to Pyongyang in January 2008 along with my family. We brought a big "gift" back with us on our return home: In 2007, my older son had miraculously been cured of a disease thanks to the help and attentive care of modern medicine. For three years starting in 2004, he received regular checkups at the Great Ormond Street Hospital in London.

When we heard from his doctor, "Your son is now completely cured, so there's no reason to come to the hospital anymore," I felt as though a huge weight had been lifted from my shoulders. Instinctively, we told the doctor that we must "meet again"; in response, he told us with a smile that the thing he hated to hear most as a doctor was "Let's meet again"; that, he explained, would mean that our son's disease had returned. The doctor assured us that our son's disease would not reappear. My wife and I bowed to him multiple times in a show of our gratitude.

In early 2007, the year before we left London, the embassy received a sudden order that concerned diplomats who were living abroad with two or more children. The order instructed parents to send one of their children back to North Korea. My family was pressured to send back our younger child, given that the older one was receiving medical care at the time.

The order had come as the international environment had grown more difficult for North Korea following the October 2006 nuclear test. International media outlets picked up news of the order, leading foreign embassies in Pyongyang to make official inquiries about whether it was genuine or not. In February 2007, the North Korean ambassador to the UK, Ja Song-nam, presented his credentials to the queen. John Everard, the British ambassador to Pyongyang, attended the ceremony and asked me "which child" I planned to send back. I told him that because I would be returning to a post at the foreign ministry later that year, I planned to take them both back with me. At that, he expressed concern, saying, "Counselor Tae, will [you] be alright?"

Almost all diplomats stationed abroad had to tearfully abide by the order; I, however, resisted it until the end. I was the only staff member at the embassy in London who did not adhere to the order. Ri Gwang-nam, a first secretary, sent his elementary school age child back to North Korea while his elder child, a middle schooler, remained in London.

My time as a diplomat abroad was coming to an end. While feeling that the authorities' order was very cold-hearted, I told my superiors, "Our entire family will return home soon, so just give us a couple of months." I knew that my love for my children was little different from the feelings all fathers felt toward their kids. While continuing to refuse to send either child back to Pyongyang, I readied myself for getting an earful at criticism sessions upon my return home.

After arriving in Pyongyang, I was immediately called to engage in criticism sessions. Surprisingly, however, I was not criticized; rather, I was given this consolation: "We understand how you felt. But what can be done? Revolution is a difficult thing, and sometimes you must bear difficult sacrifices. That's why Korea's revolution is said to be harder than revolution in India, where there a billion people of different races who speak different languages."

I was told this after I had said the following during my self-criticism: "I only felt sorry for my children and that's why I wanted to keep them with me. I've made a big mistake by failing to adhere to the party's instructions. I'm filled with remorse. Please forgive me." In fact, upon hearing the response to my self-criticism, it was I who felt ashamed. The Central Committee officials who managed my criticism session were all parents, so they seemed to understand why I had done what I did. I was grateful for that.

THE MINUTES I WRITE UP FOR PARTY MEETINGS ARE AKIN TO NOVELS

Sometime later, I was designated the vice director of the foreign ministry's European Department along with the department's branch party secretary.[1] In the foreign ministry, it is common for the department directors to handle administrative duties while department vice directors handle party-related activities. If, for example, a department is made up of fewer than thirty party members, the department vice director becomes the cell secretary; if there are more than thirty, the department becomes a branch party, and the department vice director becomes its secretary. There were more than thirty party members in the European Department, so there were three party cells. Each cell had a cell secretary, with the branch party secretary exerting control over these three cell secretaries.

As both the vice director of the European Department and the branch party secretary, I had a lot of work to do. A branch party secretary's daily routine would start by wiping off the dust from portraits of Kim Il-sung and Kim Jong-il. Other artwork featuring the two Kims hanging in the hallways also had to be cleaned. I didn't do any of this cleaning myself, but it was my job as the branch party secretary to make sure others in the department did so. In North Korea, these kinds of cleaning activities are called "work of devotion," and the members of all government agencies start their day with them.[2]

One thing I really hated as branch party secretary was collecting information about the "ideological trends" among my colleagues and reporting these trends to the foreign ministry's party committee. At 2 P.M. each day, I would have to go up to the committee's office on the fourth floor and report what had happened in the department that day along with any out-of-the-ordinary issues that had occurred among the department's staff. I had to report even trivial things such as fights between husband and wife and overdrinking. In order to make these reports, I had to walk around the office starting from 11 A.M. every day to ask everyone individually what had happened since the previous day. The WPK, Ministry of

State Security, and Ministry of Social Security are all involved in this kind of multilayered surveillance.

But the duty I hated the most as branch party secretary was writing up the records of criticism sessions and party meetings every Saturday.

Each party cell held criticism sessions every Saturday from 9:00 to 9:30 A.M. The sessions involved criticizing yourself and criticizing others. I was in charge of putting what was said into party meeting minutes and submitting the minutes to the foreign ministry's party committee. Writing up the minutes was not hard in itself; rather, it was tough to write them up in a way acceptable to the party committee.

I'm not sure when this started, but from some point party members just conducted self-criticism without criticizing others during the sessions. While each meeting would start with a warning for participants to criticize others, there was almost no one who did. Nobody would say it out loud, but everyone found it distasteful to get red in the face and raise their voices in criticism of others. The foreign ministry's party committee, however, thought it was a very serious problem that party members did not criticize others. The committee felt that the party's functions were being weakened by people's failure to participate actively in the criticism sessions.

The party committee conducted frequent checks of the meeting minutes as part of efforts to press the cell secretaries and branch party secretaries to do better. Because my colleagues did not criticize those around them, it was up to me to simply create many criticisms directed at others from thin air. In short, my meeting minutes were akin to novels. This exemplified the shrinking importance of the WPK.

"JOINT FUNDS" AND "SOLIDARITY"

As the branch party secretary, I managed the European Department's "joint funds." As North Korea's socialist welfare system and financial integrity collapsed, what grew up in its place was, ironically, joint funds. The funds were created by different foreign ministry departments to collect foreign currency from their staff members to use collectively. Department directors oversaw the joint funds. Members of the departments had to get permission from the department directors to use even a little bit of the funds.

People who returned from abroad were required to place one hundred dollars in the joint fund managed by their department. In the European Department, on average around seven to ten people returned from abroad each year, while a similar number of people were sent abroad annually. Even those who went on business trips abroad had to contribute twenty dollars on their return. Diplomats who went to places without North Korean embassies did not need to contribute to the funds. Over the course of a year, the joint fund in the European Department would total more than a thousand dollars.

Staff in the European Department found the joint fund to be very useful because it was not possible at the time to buy even one kilogram of rice with their salaries, which were paid in North Korean won. The fund would also be used in different ways. If someone was hospitalized, it was common for people in the same department to send several boxes of alcohol to the administering doctor. If Central Committee officials visited, staff would have to hand over cigarettes. Many Central Committee officials lived more poorly than even low-level foreign ministry officials, so when they visited the ministry, they expected to receive cigarettes.

Alcohol and cigarettes were typically purchased at foreign currency shops. People would use the joint funds to buy the goods because official salaries were insufficient. Apart from that, foreign currency was needed to purchase alcohol, meat, vegetables, and other items for various events. There were a lot of things that the money was spent on.

In departments such as the European Department, where staff members went abroad a lot, the staff was not burdened financially because there was always plenty of money in the joint funds. Departments whose staff never went abroad had a tough time because they had no money to put in their joint funds. The European Department, for its part, had joint funds for each of its teams. There was a severe divide between the "rich" and "poor" departments within the foreign ministry.

One other challenging thing I had to do as branch party secretary was drinking alcohol all the time. Being a party official in North Korea means you must "take care" of people in your department and take part in the various events held by your organization. The WPK demands that party officials take part in the "four ceremonial occasions of coming of age, wedding, funeral, and ancestral rites" that occur within their department if they are to become truly one with the people.

I managed around fifty members of the European Department (Department 12). There were weddings and funerals almost every month. Weddings were, relatively speaking, easier to handle. All I had to do was drink alcohol and celebrate together. Funerals, however, were a different matter. If, for example, a department staffer was the eldest son of the deceased, the department would have to manage the funeral. The department would first create a funeral committee and task a couple of staff members with creating the casket and reserving a spot at the Obongsan Crematorium. That was only the start, however; the funeral committee would have to manage all aspects of the funeral until it was over.

While South Koreans rarely hold funerals in their homes, North Koreans hold the ancestral rites conducted three days after the death at either the eldest son's house or the house of the deceased before the body is taken to be cremated. As branch party secretary, I had to receive condolences from the first day of the funeral and stay there until the corpse was placed in the coffin. Then, I would drink alcohol and play cards throughout the night.

Doing all of that was a pain for me, but I did not have a choice. I had to manage funerals almost twice a month. The European Department, however, was in good financial shape compared to other departments, which meant that each time we had to partake in the "four ceremonial occasions," the staff improved its ability to work in solidarity. One reason the European Department was able to win in volleyball and Ping-Pong games for two years in a row was our ability to work well together. I am still proud of this and believe it was an achievement of mine while acting as both the deputy department head and branch party secretary.

The foreign ministry held athletic events three times during the year: Kim Jong-il's birthday on February 16 (The Day of the Shining Star), Kim Il-sung's birthday on April 15 (The Day of the Sun), and the birthday of Kim Jong-il's birth mother, Kim Jong-suk, on December 24. On these occasions, the department head or deputy head had to participate in volleyball or Ping-Pong matches, because these two sports were considered the mainstays of the events. If a cadre did not play volleyball or Ping-Pong very well, they would be viewed as "damaged goods." I put in every effort I could to play volleyball and Ping-Pong after I became the vice director of the European Department.

The department placed first in the volleyball and Ping-Pong games in 2011 and 2012. However, the department's staff failed to maintain this position into 2013, after I had left for the UK. Since my defection to South Korea, I continue to play table tennis with my colleagues at the Institute for National Security Strategy, playing with them once a week on a regular basis. Sometimes, I casually think that if I had returned to North Korea, after having failed in my attempt at exile, the European Department might have been able to reclaim its first-place title.

FIRST VICE MINISTERS WIELD THE REAL AUTHORITY AND MUST BE ON ALERT ALL DAY FOR CALLS FROM KIM JONG-IL

All of North Korea's government agencies share the problem of conflict, or power struggles, between party committees and administrative organizations. Not understanding the role of party committees makes it almost impossible to understand North Korean society. The following are some questions I heard frequently after I arrived in South Korea: "How can an inhuman regime like North Korea survive for seventy-odd years? "What's its secret?" "What allowed a young Kim Jong-un to easily purge his uncle Jang Song-taek, who had been at the center of power for decades?" Where in the world is the center of power in North Korea?"

In North Korea, the party is always at the center of power. While central figures inside the WPK Central Committee's Organization and Guidance Department (OGD) can be executed, as seen during the *Simhwajo* Incident, it is impossible for North Korea's center of power to move to the left or to the right.

Many South Korean experts on North Korea believe that the center of power in the country moved from the party to the military after Kim Jong-il announced the start of *"songun* politics" during the late 1990s as the country was still in the midst of the Arduous March.[3] Now many believe that, following Kim Jong-un's rise to power, the center of power has shifted from the military back to the party. Some experts use power rankings alone to decide who is second or third in command. All of this is just empty conjecture because they do not know the role the WPK's Central Committee plays in the country.

The OGD is fundamentally tasked with establishing the monolithic leadership system of the supreme leader, while the Propaganda and Agitation Department (PAD) handles the establishment of the leader's One-Ideology System. The OGD is the country's most powerful institution, with authority to exert control over the entire society and manage personnel shifts, inspections, and punishments of the country's highest cadres. The OGD and the PAD have, from the beginning of the regime to this very day, formed the two major pillars of control in North Korean society.

Leadership power rankings in North Korea are meaningless. Even if Prime Minister Park Bong-ju were to be ranked third or fourth in the leadership, he would have no authority to appoint or fire members of the Cabinet. Who holds power in North Korea is decided by who has control over personnel matters, control over who gets commendations, and control over who gets punished in a particular organization. The person who has this kind of authority over Cabinet members is the vice director of Central Agency Affairs in the OGD. Ultimately, the OGD is the mover and shaker in North Korea, and this organization exerts control through party committees inside every organization. For example, the National Defense Commission cannot control the OGD, but the OGD can watch over and exert control over the National Defense Commission's activities through the General Political Bureau of the Korean People's Army.

To better help readers understand North Korean society, I will give an example here of a power struggle between the party secretary and administrative officials in the foreign ministry. Even within the foreign ministry, the center of power rests with the party committee. The party committee's party secretary exerts all-encompassing authority over what happens in the ministry.

In the mid-1970s, Kim Jong-il implemented the "first vice minister, first vice department head" system in government agencies over which he needed to exert direct control, which led to changes in the foreign ministry's power structure. In short, the first vice minister—an administrator—came to be directly controlled by Kim Jong-il. Kim implemented this system of exerting power in the foreign ministry and the Ministry of State Security. In the Ministry of the People's Armed Forces, the operations department director acted as first vice minister despite the existence of the General Staff Department.

Within this system, there is a first vice minister below the minister, and a first vice director below the department director. While lower in rank than a minister or department head, the first vice minister and first vice director are the people who directly implement Kim Jong-il's instructions. Power in North Korea was decided by how much contact you had with Kim Jong-il and how much power you had been given by the North Korean leader. The country's foreign minister leaves the office frequently for national events, diplomatic activities, and participation in various meetings; in contrast, the foreign ministry's first vice minister stays in the office from the morning until 11 P.M.

Kim Jong-il had such an impatient personality that he would immediately call the first vice minister if he needed to ask about a report or hand down an order. The first vice minister must have a very good idea of what has been reported to the North Korean leader. They must always be ready to respond to anything, so they have no rest days. Even when they go to the bathroom, they must have their secretary watch the phones for a call from Kim. That's why first vice ministers fall apart after around ten years in the position.

KANG SOK-JU ALMOST GETS PURGED FOR TRYING TO NUDGE THE FOREIGN MINISTRY'S PARTY COMMITTEE SECRETARY ASIDE

In the late 1970s, the foreign ministry's first vice minister was Ri Jong-mok. After Ri's death, Kim Chung-il occupied the position until the early 1980s, and when Kim moved up to the Third-Floor Secretariat, Kang Sok-ju, who had been serving as the head of the European Bureau of the International Department of the WPK's Central Committee, got the position. In the early 1990s, as U.S.-DPRK dialogue picked up steam, the foreign ministry's power structure began to center on Kang.

Kang's first move as first vice minister was to acquire control over personnel management within the ministry. Control over personnel management would normally have fallen to the party committee secretary, thus deeming it untouchable for an administrative official. At a secret party of

Kim Jong-il's that he attended, Kang told the North Korean leader, "We need to send skilled officials abroad to ensure the smooth implementation of party foreign policy. Right now, however, ambassadors lack ability, which has led to many difficulties in pushing things forward." The North Korean leader quickly caught on to what Kang was saying and gave him control over personnel matters at the foreign ministry.

From that time on, power began centering on Kang as opposed to the foreign ministry's party committee secretary. This development naturally increased the influence of administrative cadres within the ministry. While unthinkable in other government agencies, the party committee in the foreign ministry probed Kang's thinking rather than the opposite. The situation was such that if Kang complained about the party committee secretary in front of Kim Jong-il, that secretary would be out of a job.

Kang further tried to show off his authority by interrupting regular criticism sessions on Saturdays. In North Korea, Saturdays are under the thumb of party committee secretaries. The secretaries manage the entirety of the routine at the foreign ministry on those days, starting with criticism sessions, handing down instructions from the leadership, and leading study sessions. The period set aside from 10 A.M. on for handing down instructions from Kim Jong-il was particularly important. At this time, all the ministry's staff would gather in the lecture hall to hear what the party secretary had to say.

From some point, however, notes from Kang would start flying around among those seated in the lecture while the party secretary was handing down the latest instructions from the North Korean leader. Kang sent out the notes to request that some department director or team manager come to his office immediately as there was something to discuss. In North Korea, remarks made by Kim Il-sung and Kim Jong-il are considered as sacred as those found in the Bible. In other words, Kang's actions were akin to someone snatching away believers from a reverential reading of Christianity's holy book. Foreign ministry staff were concerned that Kang would "get in a lot of trouble" if he continued doing things like that.

And so it was that Kang got into hot water with the party. The OGD raised an issue about his actions and began an investigation. Kang could have been purged if he did not play his cards right. He was a smooth operator, however, and responded to the investigation as follows: "Everything we do is aimed at supporting the international activities of the Great

General Kim Jong-il. If Comrade Kim Jong-il were to call me and ask me about a certain issue, and I did not know what to say, what should happen? I should first call in someone who thoroughly knows about the issue to ask about it and then report to Comrade Kim Jong-il. Reports to the General should be done quickly. Must I make the General wait until the party secretary has finished his report on instructions [from the leadership]?"

Faced with this response, the investigation team—which had originally aimed to purge Kang—was put into a corner and quietly disbanded. The foreign ministry remained Kang's world until 2008. Of course, the WPK Central Committee, which had been stripped of its authority by Kang, would never let such a thing stand. Lee Jae-gang, the chief secretary of the Party Headquarters of the OGD, had a particular dislike for Kang. In late 2008, Lee posted Ahn Tae-gwang, his right-hand man and the chief party secretary of the Moranbong District of Pyongyang, to the foreign ministry with orders to reclaim the authority of the party committee. Lee was correct in doing this. There was no way in North Korea's system that a government official could be superior to a party official. It was from that point on that Kang and Ahn began a battle behind the scenes.

Ahn tried to put Kang in his place with the support of Ri Jae-gang, who also had Kim Jong-il's trust. Ahn was a rarity even in North Korea: a run-of-the-mill party official who viewed everything through the lens of party policy. He also had a sharp mind.

Kang was unable to meet with Kim Jong-il as frequently as before after the North Korean leader recovered from a stroke. Kim's health issues had led to a drastic cutback in the number of secret parties he held. Kang's monopoly over power in the foreign ministry collapsed as Ahn began his counteroffensive.

Ahn called in the branch party and cell secretaries from each department to inquire intensively about corruption on the part of vice ministers and department heads. Kang had reigned over the ministry for around twenty years, and naturally instances of corruption had occurred over that time. Ahn organized criticism sessions to place pressure on administrative officials, and a couple of department heads, along with Vice Minister Kim Chang-gyu, were accused of corruption and forced out of the ministry. Ministry officials moved to try to accommodate Ahn, and I, too, as a branch party secretary, could not cross him.

Ahn pestered the European Department to submit documents that showed evidence of the corruption committed by Department Director Kim Chung-guk and the vice minister with authority over the department. Nothing was more difficult than having to tattle on a direct superior I had long thought of as family. As Ahn investigated the ledger that showed the implementation of instructions from the leader, he indirectly criticized Kang, saying: "We must live with the belief in [only] one individual, General Kim Jong-il." Ahn also called in the vice ministers, leaving them waiting for one hour just to show off his authority. When one of the vice ministers left in anger, Ahn criticized him for "a wrongheaded attitude toward the party."

Ultimately, Kang was pushed out of the foreign ministry following his appointment as deputy premier of the Cabinet during a party conference in September 2010. While it may have seemed at first glance like a promotion, Kang had in fact been banished from the front lines of North Korean diplomacy. Ahn's abuse of his own authority, meanwhile, gradually grew worse. The entire foreign ministry bowed down to Ahn. Kim Gye-gwan, who was appointed first vice minister after Kang, did not have the same boldness that Kang had displayed. The foreign ministry's administrative officials had no choice but to come under the heel of the party committee: Elderly vice ministers and department heads had to bow their heads in greeting to members of the party committee, who were generally in their thirties.

This situation, however, did not last long. There were many children of WPK Central Committee cadres in the foreign ministry. They reported Ahn's abuse of power up the line, and the OGD posted Ahn to become the party secretary of the North Korean consulate in Shenyang, China. Ahn's replacement as party secretary was Ho Cheol, who was the son of Ho Dam.[4] Ho Cheol was part of the Kim Il-sung family and, like his father, was very skilled. He showed the proper respect to elderly administrative officials and put forward Kim Gye-gwan as the face of authority while exercising power behind the scenes.

North Korea's current foreign minister is Ri Yong-ho, who was appointed to that position at the Seventh Party Congress in 2016. Kim Gye-gwan, meanwhile, is not in a good state of health. I suspect that Ri Yong-ho and Ho Cheol have maintained a balance in leading the foreign ministry without the need for conflict.

KIM JONG-IL SUDDENLY STOPS HANDING DOWN SIGNOFFS; LATER, WE FIND OUT THAT IT WAS BECAUSE OF A STROKE

In late August 2008, I remember that Kim Jong-il suddenly stopped issuing sign-offs for proposals. At first, everybody thought that it was because he was conducting an unofficial visit to China. Something like that had happened before. The foreign ministry gave reports to Kim Jong-il about its activities in two different ways.

The first was a weekly report that went out every Wednesday. This report was more strategic and in-depth in nature and thus did not need immediate sign-offs from the leader. The daily reports were those that involved everyday issues and needed Kim's sign-off quickly.

The weekly and daily reports were all submitted to the Third-Floor Secretariat by email. After Kim read a report, he would either sign it or write a date on it, making it a "document personally signed and ratified." Reports that he had simply reviewed and then sent back down the line were called "documents viewed [by the leader]" or "Central Committee orders." The most important documents were those that Kim had personally signed or those where he had written specific instructions on their first pages.

There was no way to tell whether Kim had really read the reports himself, just skimmed the titles, or did not pay attention to the titles at all. The reports sent up to line from the foreign ministry every day numbered in the thousands of pages. Other government agencies would also send up a similar amount to the leader. Unless Kim was a god, it would have been impossible for him to read all of it. I think that most of the reports were first read by the staff of the Third-Floor Secretariat, who then sent up only the most important ones to the leader.

Sometimes, Kim would call Kang directly and inquire about a particular report or give out instructions. That suggested that Kim was given news of important developments. However, there were cases in which it was unclear whether Kim's view was reflected in decision making. Even if something bad had suddenly happened to Kim—and if the Third-Floor Secretariat chose not to alert anyone about it—everything would run as normal. That's just how North Korea's ruling system was set up.

In August 2008, Kim did in fact collapse due to a stroke, but the only people with knowledge of it were a very small minority in the Third-Floor Secretariat. When Kim's sign-offs stopped coming, the foreign ministry along with other central government departments fell into a state of confusion. There were many calls about whether the foreign ministry's proposals had received a sign-off from the leader. Not receiving a sign-off on a proposal meant that work on the project could not begin. That being said, the ministry couldn't just stop working. To keep things going, the ministry revised its proposals to read "We are preparing to do this or that" instead of "We hope we can do this or that." It submitted the revised proposals up the line and began preparations to start the projects.

Kim Jong-il did not attend the event on September 9 to celebrate the founding of the DPRK. This set off a buzz in the country, and every rumor you could think of began to proliferate. Kim returned to the public scene in October. Wearing sunglasses, he appeared at a soccer game between Kim Il-sung University and the Pyongyang University of Railways. He may have worn sunglasses to prevent anyone from seeing his glazed-over eyes. In the video of the event, he looks like he was having difficulty walking.

THE RYONGCHEON COUNTY STATION EXPLOSION COMES TO THE FORE AGAIN AFTER KIM JONG-IL'S RETURN

I think that Kim believed that his health was in bad shape and that he had little time left before his death. At around the same time, a series of unusual events occurred equal in scale to speculation about his poor health.

The first was the announcement of the arrest of Seo Nam-sik and some other Ministry of Railways officials. Seo was the general in charge of Room 8 and 9 (in charge of Kim Jong-il's train). Some of those arrested were executed. It is highly unusual in North Korea for the government to make official announcements of this nature. While the whole story behind the incident was never made public, there was a rumor that Seo and others had tried to assassinate Kim through the Ryongcheon County Station incident, along with a rumor of the discovery of a spy network that South Korea had set up during the Korean War. The Ryongcheon County Station explosion had happened four years earlier, whereas the

Korean War had broken out some sixty years in the past. It was clear that something unusual was happening.

Even the foreign ministry's European Department was caught up in the aftermath of the arrest of Seo and the others. One day in October 2008, the foreign ministry's party committee suddenly called in Seo Cheol, a member of the European Department. Seo had studied abroad at Beijing University's English Department before beginning work as an English teacher at the PUFS from 1979. He was the head of our class's English intensive reading courses when I entered the university the next year. Seo was special to me because I learned English from him.

Seo later gained recognition from Ri Su-yong for his English skills and began work in 1992 as the North Korean representative for UN agencies in Geneva. After returning to North Korea, he headed the British affairs team within the European Department at the foreign ministry and worked as the North Korean representative to the Swiss Agency for Development and Cooperation in Pyongyang.

After being called in by the party committee, Seo never returned and was taken somewhere in a black car. Several hours later, I was called in by the committee. I was told that Seo's family had been expelled from Pyongyang, so I was to take around ten people to pack up his family's bags at his home. The most physically strong staff in our department were selected for this task.

Seo's house was next to the Pyongyang Medical College Hospital. Security officials were already in the house's hallway preventing anyone from entering or leaving. Seo's entire family was sitting, crying. His elderly mother said, "I've lived so long that I've now witnessed something I shouldn't have." While we packed up their belongings, we learned that Seo was the cousin of Seo Nam-sik, the chief of the general staff of the Ministry of Railways who had been executed by firing squad some time before.

Seo's father had been a police officer during the Korean War, while his younger sibling was the head of the investigations department at the Ministry of Social Security office in Pyongyang's Moranbong District. They were a rarity even in North Korea: the "crème de la crème of communist families." I found it impossible that such a family could have been involved in an assassination attempt against the North Korean leader.

Seo's family was to be expelled to Sangwon County in South Pyongan Province before midnight that day. We had to make every effort to pack up everything in the house by that time. As we packed things up, Seo's wife quietly approached me, saying, "There's quite a bit of foreign currency in the house. What should we do with it?" The money appeared to be what Seo had saved up during his time as a diplomat in Switzerland for over almost six years.

Seo was still technically my colleague up until the morning hours of that day. I took the money and changed it into North Korean money at the local black market. Where Seo and his family was heading was so remote that they would not need American dollars. From Sangwon County, it was a distance of 200 *li* (around sixty-two miles) to the nearest railway station.

At the time, one dollar was equal to almost four thousand North Korean won. I bundled up the thousands of dollars I had changed into North Korean won inside a piece of cloth. When the security officers were not paying attention, I hid the bundle inside the family's packed-up belongings. I would have faced heavy punishment if the security officials had seen me do that, but I was able to pull it off because my entire staff wanted to help Seo's family. That night, five members of the European Department accompanied Seo's family to their new home in Sangwon County.

As I watched Seo's crying family leave Pyongyang, I thought that they would be able to endure life in their new home for at least a couple of years because they had a lot of cash on hand. Not even a year later, however, North Korea conducted a currency reform in November 2009. While witnessing all of the North Korean currency circulating in the country suddenly become worthless, I thought of Seo's family, who must have been suffering in the remote areas of Sangwon County.

I still have questions about the Ryongcheon County Station explosion. Was it really an assassination attempt as Kim Jong-il had thought? Or was it committed by the Ministry of State Security to alleviate the anxiety of a North Korean leader perennially afraid of being assassinated?

AT THE END OF HIS DAYS, KIM JONG-IL COULD BARELY CLAP

It was unusual for Ri Su-yong to be suddenly called back to Pyongyang after Kim Jong-il recovered from his stroke. I do not know exactly when Ri returned to Pyongyang from Switzerland. It may have been in late 2008 or early 2009.

Ri had long argued that North Korea must increase the number of "special economic zones," or SEZs, to revive the country's economy. Indeed, upon his rapid return to Pyongyang, Ri was ordered to form a joint investment committee with himself as the chairman. Why did Kim Jong-il do this? It may have been the North Korean leader's last move to do something—anything—to revive the economy, given that he knew he had only a short time left in the world.

There was a rumor that Ri was very close with Jang Song-taek. The rumor was based on the fact that Jang's Central Administrative Department, which had overall control over the North Korean economy, was managing the joint investment committee. After Ri became the committee's chairman, North Korea began efforts to prepare a new economic policy rooted in expanding SEZs. In 2012, right after Kim Jong-il's death, Ri played a central role in beginning a review of a detailed plan for this new policy. The plan called for the establishment of thirteen new SEZs.

The central tenant of the SEZs was to introduce capitalist economic methods to North Korea, just as the Gaesong Industrial Complex had done. The move to build more SEZs was so sensitive that those involved could be purged immediately if they failed to gain active support from (North Korea's new leader) Kim Jong-un. In late 2013, North Korean officials announced the construction of thirteen SEZs in areas outside of Pyongyang; however, this plan fizzled out once Ri Su-yong was appointed foreign minister in April 2014. The joint investment committee also fell by the wayside and was dismantled. This series of events suggests that Kim Jong-un seemed to continue his father's last attempt to revive the economy, but ultimately he failed. Upon gaining power, Kim Jong-un clearly showed an intention to move forward with economic reforms and open up the economy, but he abandoned those efforts due to several circumstances.

In October 2009, I saw Kim Jong-il up close. Wen Jia-bao, China's prime minister, was visiting North Korea at the time, and the elder Kim watched a North Korean operetta based on the ancient Chinese novel *Dream of the Red Chamber* with the high-ranking Chinese official. Kim looked as though he was having a very tough time and could barely walk. The left side of his body seemed to have been paralyzed, which made it difficult for him to clap. Nonetheless, his death soon after that took me by surprise.

FOLLOWING A STROKE, KIM JONG-IL INTRODUCES HIS TWO SONS JONG-CHUL AND JONG-UN TO HIS CLOSE CONFIDANTES FOR THE FIRST TIME

For a very long time in North Korea, it was believed that Kim Jong-il had no sons other than Kim Jong-nam. Even people in Kim Il-sung's family were said to have no idea about Kim Jong-un's existence.

A strange atmosphere began to pervade the country starting with the new year's address marking the start of 2009. During the Kim Il-sung era, the North Korean leader had read his new year's addresses out aloud. From 1995, after his father's death, Kim Jong-il took over the process of preparing the addresses—called New Year's Joint Editorials—in three newspapers, the *Rodong Sinmun*, *Korean People's Army*, and *Youth Avant-Garde*. These joint editorials took stock of the past year's activities and provided the policy directions for the new year in the spheres of politics, economics, inter-Korean relations, and international relations. The New Year's Joint Editorial in 2009 included an expression not seen before: "Today, we are standing at an important historical crossroads in the party's efforts to carry out the Revolution." Few people knew what this expression meant at the time.

Typically speaking, North Korean officials study the content of the joint editorials until mid-January. From that point on, officials then shift to preparing for Kim Jong-il's birthday, or the Day of the Shining Star. The foreign ministry's preparations for the birthday celebrations typically involved holding volleyball and table tennis matches between different departments along with a performance. In 2009, in contrast to other years, organizations were told to perform the song *Footsteps*. This came right after the song had been broadcast on North Korea's KCTV. The foreign ministry organized a troupe of the best singers among its staff to sing the song. The troupe met at 4 P.M. every day in the lecture hall to practice the song. Some lines from the song are as follows:

> "Tramp, tramp, tramp!" the footsteps go
> The footsteps of General Kim
> Wielding the spirit of February
> The footsteps go forward
> With each powerful footstep

The entire country follows along going
"Tramp, tramp, tramp"

The "spirit of February" mentioned in the song clearly referred to Kim Jong-il's spirit because he was born on February 16. It was also clear that the person wielding this spirit, "General Kim," was to be his successor. Despite singing the lyrics, we did not have any idea who "General Kim" or the "Comrade General" was.

Footsteps was distributed throughout the country in files made using "CNC technology." CNC, or computerized numerical control, was a slogan-like phrase that appeared amid Kim Jong-un's succession to power. Modernized countries were already familiar with the technology, yet North Korea spread propaganda about "converting industry to CNC." CNC refers to a manufacturing process that employs a computer micro-processor, and North Korean authorities placed the phrase "CNCization" on various slogans as Kim Jong-un came to the fore. For example, North Korean authorities would claim after building a small food factory that the production process had been "CNCized" with a view to maximize production.

KIM JONG-IL'S SUCCESSOR KIM JONG-UN EMERGES AS "COMRADE GENERAL"

On April 15, 2009, a fireworks display was held on the Daedong River to celebrate Kim Il-sung's birthday. The massive size of the fireworks display was unprecedented. The style of the event was very colorful and novel. Everyone heaped praise on what they saw. It appeared the authorities had spent at least a couple of million dollars on the event. Within the party, there was propaganda claiming that the "fireworks display was led directly by the Comrade General." People believed that the event was aimed at welcoming the entrance of the "Comrade General" onto the national stage.

I also wondered who this "General Kim" was. I was sure that he was one of Kim Jong-il's sons, but nobody was talking openly about this kind of thing. I had spent considerable time working in the foreign minis-try's European Department and knew that Kim Jong-il's sons had been studying in Switzerland. I did not know, however, how many children Kim had, and I had never heard any of their names.

The only son of Kim Jong-il I had seen was Kim Jong-nam. After completing his studies in Switzerland, Kim Jong-nam returned to North Korea in the early 1990s. He would frequently drive his luxury Mercedes-Benz to the Koryo Hotel at night. I even remember his car's license plate, 216–8888. Kim would park his car at the front of the hotel—where parking was normally prohibited—and head into the building. The hotel's managers would, of course, be there to receive him.

I also went to the Koryo Hotel quite often because most of the European delegations that I supported stayed at the hotel. Several times I saw Kim Jong-nam walking around the hotel from afar. I did not know initially that he was Kim Jong-nam; in fact, I thought he was a member of the Third-Floor Secretariat, so I found him a little strange. One time, I was watching him carefully when a superior working in my department nudged me, proposing that we just go. He then told me that the man I had been looking at was "The General's child."

Kim Jong-il ultimately lost confidence in his son because of an incident involving a counterfeit passport. The younger Kim was caught trying to enter Japan using a fake passport the day before the Swedish prime minister, Hans Göran Persson, was to arrive in Pyongyang on May 1, 2001. The incident was, naturally enough, heavily reported on in the Western press. At the time, the North Korean foreign ministry was giving Kim Jong-il almost real-time updates on worldwide press coverage of the Swedish prime minister's visit to Pyongyang. Persson was the first head of a Western nation to visit North Korea, and Kim Jong-nam's attempt to enter Japan illegally threw cold water on what should have been a joyous event. Strict instructions were given within the foreign ministry never to leak any news about Kim Jong-nam's attempt to enter Japan illegally.

It appears clear that Kim Jong-nam was removed from consideration as a successor following this incident. What's more, many people in North Korea already knew that his birth mother was a woman named Seong Hye-rim. Seong was a very famous actress in North Korea and was also the wife of the eldest son of Ri Gi-yong, a writer who chose North Korea over life in the South. When I was studying at the Pyongyang Foreign Language Institute in 1974 and 1975, I had a friend in my class who was named Ri Cha-dol. He was Ri Gi-yong's grandson.

Ri Cha-dol's father, Ri Jong-hyeok, was the North Korean represen-
tative for UNESCO in France. He is currently the vice chairman of the
Korea Asia-Pacific Peace Committee and the head of the South Joseon
(Korean) Issue Research Institute. Ri Cha-dol attended school while living in his grandfather's house, where Ri Ok-dol, an elder sister of Kim
Jong-nam who shared the same mother, also lived. Whenever I went to
Ri Cha-dol's place to study or play, Ok-dol would cut fruit for us and treat
me affectionately. When, at some point, I saw that she had disappeared, I
asked Cha-dol about it. He told me that she had entered the South Joseon
(Korean) Revolutionary Training Center. Given that Ok-dol was beautiful, I believed without a doubt what he told me about her entry into the
training center.

In 1997, I was working in the embassy in Denmark when I heard that
the nephew of Seong Hye-rim, Ri Han-yeong, had been assassinated.[5] It
was only then that I realized that Seong Hye-rim was Kim Jong-il's lover. I
was shocked no end by this. Sometime later, I also found out about where
Ok-dol had been. She had been following her husband, a diplomat, on his
postings to Finland, Italy, Austria, and Switzerland.

Taking all of this into account, I concluded that Kim Jong-nam would
not be Kim Jong-il's successor. The two remaining sons, Kim Jong-chul
and Kim Jong-un, were the only possibilities, but it was hard to know
which one would be chosen. Close confidantes of Kim Jong-il who had
met the two brothers knew that Kim Jong-chul was older than Kim
Jong-un. As a result, many people thought that Kim Jong-chul would be
selected.

Kim Jong-il's efforts to pick a successor were, as all this shows, done
secretly. Once the song *"Footsteps"* came out however, the succession
process moved into high gear. Toward the latter part of 2009, party
meetings began using expressions such as "Comrade General" and "Our
party is at an historic turning point." People grew much more curious about who "General Kim" or the "Comrade General" was. Then,
Kim Jong-un began to be mentioned by name. Throughout the country, posters were put up with the lyrics to Kim Jong-un's song of praise,
Footsteps, along with the phrase: "The glory of our nation that revels in
the fortune given by the General and General, the Young General who
continues the Mangyongdae Bloodline and Baekdu Bloodline: Comrade
Kim Jong-un."

NORTH KOREA ATTEMPTS TO BOLSTER THE SUCCESSION PROCESS BY CONDUCTING A CURRENCY REFORM RIGHT AFTER KIM JONG-UN COMES TO THE FORE

November 2009 brought a completely unexpected event: a large-scale currency reform. The currency reform came just three or four months after Kim Jong-un's name was released to the public. North Korea moved forward with three "tasks" to construct a strong and prosperous country by 2012, the one hundredth anniversary of Kim Il-sung's birth. These three tasks were constitutional reform, nuclear armament, and economic construction.

The constitutional reform was completed in April 2009, and the country's nuclear ambitions took a step forward with a second nuclear test in May 2009. However, North Korea's leaders failed to make groundbreaking progress in the country's economic construction. That's why the country's leaders moved to conduct a currency reform.

North Koreans did not put the money they earned in banks because they weren't allowed to take it out freely when needed. People would simply keep the money they earned from market commerce somewhere in their homes. The authorities thus had to ceaselessly create more and more currency to pay the monthly wages of millions of soldiers, public servants, and state-run enterprise workers. This led to increasingly severe inflation.

As the deputy director of the European Department in the foreign ministry, I earned a monthly salary of KPW 2,900. The cost of one kilogram of rice in the markets, however, was more than KPW 3,000. My salary was not enough to buy even a kilogram of rice in the markets. What allowed someone like me to survive was rations distributed by the state. Employees of central government agencies such as the foreign ministry could buy rice at the state-set price of KPW 40 per kilogram. As a result, no public servants simply took their monthly pay; the rice distribution day was the real payday for government workers. In the case of the foreign ministry, a female employee in each department would have the monthly salaries of all the department's staff in her possession, which she would then use to pay for the rice at state-set prices.

Kim Jong-il aimed to use the currency reform to prevent excessive inflation and entice people to bring out the money they were storing in their homes. He also planned to prevent the spread of the capitalist market economy through local marketplaces. Specifically, the currency reform forced people to exchange their old KPW 100 banknotes for new KPW 1 banknotes. There were limitations placed on how much money people could exchange, however. People who had too many old banknotes that went beyond the set limitations could not exchange all their old money, which became as worthless as toilet paper.

I remember that on the day the currency reform was announced, the authorities said that each household could exchange just KPW 100,000 of the old currency into the new currency. A couple of days later, however, a new measure was announced that said that one person from each family could exchange KPW 50,000 of the old currency into the new currency. The limitations placed on how much money people could exchange were too strict. People working in local markets felt the financial repercussions of all this particularly badly. Those in the elite or part of the *donju* had already been collecting foreign currency and making transactions in dollars, euros, and Chinese yuan, so they were not affected as much.[6]

THE PARTY'S ECONOMIC SECRETARY IS EXECUTED AFTER CITIZEN PROTESTS LEAD TO THE FAILURE OF THE CURRENCY REFORM

A massive protest erupted against the currency reform. Shops closed their doors, and products disappeared from markets. Kim Man-gil, the chief secretary of Pyongyang's municipal party committee, apologized in front of the city's residents and pleaded for businesspeople to restart their commercial activities. This had no effect, however. Kim Jong-il was greatly surprised by the people's outpouring of discontent toward the currency reform. He had failed to foresee that regular people, who had up until that time cowered at any word he uttered, would protest in such a collective fashion.

Once a person takes an interest in earning money, there is no turning back. People will fight to the death to continue earning money if someone tries to stop them. Moreover, North Koreans weren't just earning money for fun; they were doing it to survive. The country's citizens had long endured political control over their lives, but when the government took away their right to live, they risked their lives to protest their leaders. Kim Jong-il just did not understand that way of thinking.

Even in the foreign ministry, there was passive resistance against the currency reform. Initially, the currency reform turned the exchange from USD 1 equaling KPW 3,000 to USD 1 equaling just KPW 100. The cost of a kilogram of rice in the markets went from KPW 3,000 to just KPW 50. The problem was that the state-set price of one kilogram of rice distributed to workers in the central government remained at KPW 40.

Up until that point, government workers would buy one kilogram of rice for KPW 40 and then sell it for KPW 3,000 a kilogram in the markets. Foreign ministry employees lived in better economic conditions than many ordinary people, and they would either sell the rice they got at state-set prices into the markets or exchange the state-distributed rice for good-quality regular rice at a set rate. However, after the currency reform, nobody was interested in buying state-distributed rice at KPW 40 while rice was going for just KPW 50 in the markets. Most of the rice distributed to central government workers had been stored for many years in military granaries. The rice was moldy and of poor quality, so much so that it was called "rotten rice."[7] Foreign ministry workers naturally made efforts not to receive this rotten rice.

Following the currency reform, the foreign ministry's Financial Administration Accounting Department, which managed the distribution of state-held rice, was put in a difficult position. The foreign ministry's party committee warned me, "If the European Department staff does not accept their rations, (their actions) will be considered a direct challenge to General Kim Jong-il's currency reform policy and they could be punished for factionalism." At transition periods like these in North Korea, one can find oneself in big trouble if the right moves aren't made. After a discussion with the entire staff of the European Department, everyone ultimately decided to accept the rotten rice.

Following strong protest by regular people, however, the currency reform ended in terrible failure just one month after its implementation. It was unprecedented in North Korea's perfectly controlled society for a party policy to end in this way. Kim Jong-il placed all the blame on the director of the WPK's Planning and Finance Department, Park Nam-gi, and executed him as part of efforts to calm the people's discontent.

I believe that Kim Jong-un was behind the scenes in moving the currency reform forward. The currency reform was simply a failed attempt to strengthen his own rise to power. Following the debacle, North Korea has not been able to force its people this way or that on economic issues. Kim Jong-un learned the lesson that no matter how subservient North Koreans are, the regime can be rocked to its core if it violates their right to live.

YEONPYEONG ISLAND ATTACK LEADS TO THE DISSOLUTION OF PLANS TO ESTABLISH A NORTH KOREAN EMBASSY IN BELGIUM

On September 27, 2010, Kim Jong-un received the title of Korean People's Army general, and at a general party meeting the next day, he was appointed the vice chairman of the WPK's Central Military Commission and a Central Committee member. Kim Jong-un's status as successor to his father was now official.

North Koreans first saw the younger Kim's face on September 28. Most of them thought they were "looking at a spitting image of the Supreme Leader, Kim Il-sung." In contrast to Kim Jong-un's vigor, Kim Jong-il looked languid and could barely clap as he sat on the president's podium.

Bookending Kim Jong-un's official rise to power was the sinking of the South Korean naval ship, the *Cheonan*, in March 2010 and the shelling of Yeonpyeong Island in November 2011.[8] These two incidents were the most shocking to occur between the two Koreas in the past ten years. After I came to South Korea, many people asked me whether North Korea had indeed sunk ROK's *Cheonan*. I had only worked in the foreign ministry, so I do not know the truth; however, I do remember the following rumor circulating in North Korea at the time: "The DPRK's naval forces are incomparably weak compared to the South's, but with the *Cheonan* breaking apart [like that], we'll only know [for sure about South Korea's real naval strength] if the two navies fight each other." In short, the rumor suggested that North Korea had acquired confidence about its naval prowess from the sinking of the South Korean ship.

November 23, 2010, is a day I remember vividly because it was when North Korea shelled Yeonpyeong Island. On that day, a delegation led by the director of the Asia-Pacific department of the Belgian foreign ministry (Belgium was holding the presidency of the EU at the time) had arrived in Pyongyang. North Korea and the EU had been conducting political talks at the foreign ministry department director level every year. That evening, a welcome banquet was held by Vice Foreign Minister Gung Seok-ung at the Gobangsan Guesthouse, a hotel affiliated with the North Korean foreign ministry. By that time, the whole world was abuzz with the news of the shelling of Yeonpyeong Island, but within the North Korean foreign ministry, only Department No. 5 (the American Affairs Department) was aware of the shelling because they monitored CNN. A congenial atmosphere pervaded the evening banquet that night.

At 10 A.M. the next day, formal talks between the EU and North Korea were held at the People's Palace of Culture. Kim Chun-guk, who led the North Korean negotiating team, started off with some welcoming remarks, but the head of the EU delegation rose from his seat with a tense expression on his face. Before leaving the conference room, he told the North Koreans: "Yesterday, North Korea shelled Yeonpyeong Island, which is sovereign territory of South Korea. The EU, in protest against North Korea's attack, has decided to suspend political talks with the DPRK. This delegation will leave Pyongyang on the earliest flight out. That is the order we have received from our headquarters. This is a regretful situation."

North Korea had held a tremendous degree of expectations for the talks. The head of the EU delegation was the director of the Belgian foreign ministry's Asia-Pacific department, and a major issue on the table was whether North Korea could set up an embassy in Brussels. During the banquet the night before, the Belgians had hinted that things were going in a positive direction, saying, "There will be progress on the issue of setting up a North Korean embassy in Brussels depending on the results of the official talks." I had also gone to the conference venue with great hopes for success but was disappointed when the talks fell apart.

A couple of days later, I heard a rumor about the Yeonpyeong Island shelling. A long-range artillery unit in Gaemeo Village, Gangryeong County, South Hwanghae Province, had shelled Yeonpyeong Island before pulling out in expectation of a counterattack by South Korean forces, and the unit had consequently not suffered much damage.

THE GERMAN EMBASSY IN PYONGYANG ISSUES A DECLARATION CRITICIZING NORTH KOREA

The entire world condemned North Korea's shelling of Yeonpyeong Island. Even the EU released a statement of protest. The Germany embassy in Pyongyang, meanwhile, translated the EU statement into Korean and put it up on the bulletin board in front of the embassy building. The German embassy was in the foreign delegation quarters of Pyongyang's Daedong-gang District. The Ministry of State Security had checkpoints around the district to prevent ordinary people from entering.

The North Korean foreign ministry received news of the Germany embassy's posting of the statement from the Foreign Delegation General Bureau, which handles work related to foreign embassies. Foreign ministry officials moved to consider what options they had to respond. It was the first time a foreign embassy had ever displayed a statement criticizing North Korea directly in a public place. If North Korea allowed this to happen, other embassies could also post statements criticizing North Korea on their bulletin boards. The foreign ministry went into crisis mode. Foreign ministry leaders told Kim Jong-il that they would take immediate action and select someone to deal with the issue.

I was chosen to represent the foreign ministry as a whole, and I immediately tried calling in the German ambassador. He was abroad on business, so the chargé d'affaires came to the foreign ministry instead. I demanded that the embassy immediately take down the EU's statement of protest. He objected strongly, saying: "The German embassy's posting of the EU's statement of protest on its bulletin board is normal procedure to inform the people of the DPRK about our government's stance. If the DPRK's foreign ministry tries to exert control over what a foreign embassy puts up on its bulletin board, that would be a clear case of interference in the affairs of another country. The North Korean embassy in Berlin posts material criticizing Germany's ally the United States, but the German government has never interfered with that ever. We will not take down the statement."

All conversations happening in the interview rooms of the foreign ministry are listened in on by security officials. If I failed to respond properly during an interview, the Ministry of State Security could report the conversation to Kim Jong-il. I would have not been the only person to have been criticized for making a mistake during an interview. North Korean diplomats must never show weakness toward an opponent. I immediately began my counterattack:

> The reason countries establish embassies is to develop friendly relations with guest countries. That an embassy would directly criticize its guest country through posted materials cannot be seen as other than an intention to destroy bilateral ties. The DPRK embassy in Berlin may have posted materials criticizing the United States, but it has never criticized Germany directly. The provocateur in the Yeonpyeong Island shelling is the South. The South's military conducted artillery drills facing our territory first, and all we did is respond. We are the victims here. Why, then, is Germany turning us into the instigators? Do you not know the truth of what happened? Or do you know what happened, but are just taking the side of the South and the United States? I find this very suspicious.
>
> Currently, the situation on the Korean Peninsula has become a dangerous powder keg due to the Yeonpyeong Island shelling. Germany, which should be working to ensure peace and safety on the Korean Peninsula during this time, is instead just listening to one side of the story and has posted materials criticizing us on its embassy bulletin board. That is unacceptable. If you do not take measures about this, I am not sure what our angry people will do about the bulletin board. If you take no measures despite our warning, I don't know what will happen going forward. The German side must take responsibility for this.

The face of the chargé d'affaires reddened at my threats. He told me that he would report what I had said back to Germany before taking any next steps. I had quiet doubts about what could happen. If the German embassy decided to resist to the end, North Korea would be forced to take physical action. That would then lead to issues for the North Korean embassy in Berlin. Luckily, the next day, the German embassy took down the statement, and I received high praise from my superiors at the foreign ministry. I was lionized for "taking Germany down a peg."

NORTH KOREA PARTICIPATES IN THE LONDON SPECIAL OLYMPICS TO IMPROVE RELATIONS WITH THE UK

From early 2011, the British ambassador in Pyongyang took pains to persuade North Korea to participate in the London Paralympics, which would be held right after the London Summer Olympics the next year. He told the foreign ministry everything he thought it would like to hear: "For the DPRK to take part in the London Paralympics would greatly help the image of the DPRK's human rights situation and further develop UK-DPRK relations" and "The UK could immediately from this year increase aid to the DPRK if it decides to participate."

It was a time when North Korea's physically challenged people could not even dream of going abroad in a delegation, much less take part in the Paralympics. The WPK had long spread negative propaganda about disabled people doing athletics based on a Kim Il-sung teaching that "competitions involving disabled people are a pastime to satisfy the perverted interests of the rich."

Until the 1970s, North Korea did not allow families with congenital disabilities to live in apartments alongside the main roads of downtown Pyongyang. There were even cases in which North Korean authorities expelled families with disabled people to areas outside of Pyongyang.

Disabled people could not even enter universities unless their parents were anti-Japanese revolutionaries or high-level cadres. I am aware of two cases in which disabled people got into Kim Il-sung University: the son of Ryu Kyeong-su and Hwang Sun-hui, comrades-in-arms of Kim Il-sung during the fight against the Japanese; and the grandson of Ryang Sae-bong, a hero of Korea's Independence Army. When I was a child, I remember seeing a disabled student at an arts college who was a pro at *janggi* (Korean chess) during a performance at the Pyongyang Grand Theater. I found out later, however, that he was the son of a cadre.

For several years in the early 1980s, I lived in an apartment in Pyongyang's Seongbuk-dong neighborhood, in the city's Moranbong District, and two of the neighbor children were disabled. One had a slight limp in his left leg. His father was an official with the Ministry of State Security, yet the family was so afraid that they would be sent out of Pyongyang that the boy was sent to live with his aunt in Hamheung when he was young. The family even changed the boy's family registration to Hamheung, and it was only after he had become an adult that he returned to Pyongyang. The other child suffered from congenital childhood paralysis. It was almost impossible for the boy to go outside, but the authorities nonetheless moved them to another place because the apartment was located on a main road, otherwise known as a "No. 1 road." No. 1 roads were those frequently used by Kim Il-sung or Kim Jong-il. Disabled people or those with poor social status (*songbun*) were not allowed to live alongside these roads.

Nowadays, North Korea's policies regarding the disabled have liberalized quite a bit, and entire families with one disabled person are not sent out of Pyongyang anymore. I was excited about the British ambassador's proposal to send a North Korean team of disabled athletes to London on two accounts: my belief that North Korea needed to change its policies toward athletic events for the disabled, and my own personal experience with disabled people during childhood. In true North Korean style, I clung to my support for the idea.

I sent the UK's request for North Korea to participate in the Paralympics to the DPRK's Federation for the Protection of the Disabled with a request of my own for them to quickly create a proposal. If North Korea was to send a team of athletes to the Paralympics, the Federation for the Protection of the Disabled would have to create a proposal that would be signed off by the Ministry of Sport's Olympics Committee, the foreign ministry's International Agency Department, and the Central Committee's Science and Education Department, all before getting final approval from Kim Jong-il. The alliance, however, hesitated in writing up the proposal. They felt the risks were too great because the proposal would have to request fundamental changes to the country's policies toward disabled people.

The foreign ministry's International Agency Department provided this opinion on the matter: "Western countries have raised the disabled people's issue as part of their human rights offensive against the DPRK. If the DPRK participates in the London Paralympics, the country could face more questions about why it has not participated in past Paralympics. Moreover, disabled people with no experience abroad could make mistakes. There is a big risk that the DPRK's internal realities could be exposed. We think it best not to send [the athletes]." The Central

Committee's Science and Education Department also concluded that sending a group of disabled athletes to the Paralympics would be contrary to party policy. Only the Ministry of Sport's Olympics Committee argued to the Central Committee's Science and Education Department cadres that "athletic events for disabled people are not pastimes to satisfy the interests of the rich" and that "not going to the Paralympics will harm the image of the Republic." These arguments had no effect, however.

The issue of participating in the event could not be resolved through normal routes. The British embassy continued to press us on the question of participating. After racking my brains, I decided to completely change the starting point of the issue: I created a proposal that focused not on the Paralympics but on improving the political relationship between the UK and North Korea. The title of my proposal went from "Concerning the Participation of Our Delegation in the London Paralympics" to "Regarding the Issue Raised by the British Embassy in the DPRK." The logic I used in the new proposal went like this: "The British government has made all efforts possible to make the 2012 London Olympics a success. The British have placed great significance on the DPRK's participation in the Paralympics and continues to request that the Republic's delegation take part. The UK continues to adhere to its policy of critical engagement while opposing a military solution to the DPRK nuclear issue. If we accept their request, they will be indebted to us, and this will help in improving future relations with the UK. I recommend accepting the British proposal."

Rewriting the proposal like this turned the issue into one involving bilateral relations with the UK, and thus there was no need to receive permission from the foreign ministry's International Agency Department and the Central Committee's Science and Education Department. When they saw the proposal draft, foreign ministry cadres knew that I had used a "trick" to push forward North Korea's participation in the Paralympics. However, they also acknowledged the need for North Korea's participation in the athletic event, so none of them opposed my proposal.

Kim Jong-il gave permission to move ahead with the proposal the very day it was sent up to him. He had no reason to oppose it. For decades, the issue had never been proposed for fear that—despite it being a simple issue to resolve—proposing it in the wrong way could lead to trouble for the person who proposed it.

ONLY ONE SWIMMER PARTICIPATES IN THE QUICKLY-PUT-TOGETHER PARALYMPICS TEAM AND, DESPITE GETTING LAST PLACE, HE RECEIVES ENTHUSIASTIC CHEERS

Now that North Korea's participation in the Paralympics had been decided upon, the next problem presented itself: the DPRK had no one to participate in it. Apart from the foreign ministry, the Federation for the Protection of the Disabled, and high-level party officials, no other individuals or agencies in North Korea knew about the country's participation in the Paralympics. We first looked for someone among the children of foreign ministry staff. It appeared that the youngest son of Rim Yeong-chul, who was working as a counselor at the North Korean embassy in Beijing, could be trained up to swim. Rim was a childhood friend of mine. We had studied abroad together as children and attended PUFS and BFSU together.

Rim Ju-song, who was with his father in Beijing, practiced swimming every day at a nearby swimming pool. North Korea's first Paralympics athlete, he had no left arm or leg. There was a sad reason for this: When Ju-song was six years old, his father was posted to the North Korean consulate in Shenyang, China. Ju-song was not allowed to go because only one child could accompany the family abroad. He was taken care of by his grandmother. One day, Ju-song was playing at an apartment construction site near his home when he was hit by a crane that tore off his arm and leg.

At a loss about what to do, his grandmother reached out to me first about what had happened. My wife and I hurried to Kim Hyeong-jik Military University Hospital where Ju-song was hospitalized. I still remember vividly seeing the anesthetized boy lying on a hospital bed with his leg and arm torn off. My wife and I cried beside his bed. We grew even sadder thinking that if he had been sent abroad with his parents, Ju-song would never have suffered such an accident. His father and mother arrived in Pyongyang by train the next day. I cannot measure how deep the pain and suffering experienced by his parents and grandmother.

The London Paralympics was held from late August to early September 2012. The only North Korean athlete to participate was Ju-song. He was accompanied by twelve people. Most of them were the managers of companies who had been giving financial support to the Federation for the Protection of the Disabled.

The British government greatly welcomed the North Korean delegation. The vice minister of the UK's foreign office held a banquet at the foreign ministry building to welcome the North Korean athlete. This was the first time such an event had been held in the history of UK–North Korean relations. The British had, until that time, never held a banquet attended by a vice minister, even when the North Korean vice minister of foreign affairs visited the country. The event showed how much the British had wanted North Korea's participation in the games.

On the day of the swimming competition, Ju-song finished last in his freestyle heat. Naturally, he wasn't a great swimmer given his hasty preparation. At that moment, the announcer's voice echoed through the venue: "Ladies and gentlemen, for the first time, North Korea has participated in the Paralympics. The athlete coming in now to the finish line is North Korea's only Paralympics participant. He represents all disabled people in North Korea. Let's all stand up and cheer for him so he can make it to the finish line." Everyone stood up and started clapping while shouting out encouragement. There were a lot of overseas Koreans at the venue, and all of them stood up and cheered until Ju-song crossed the finish line. North Korea's participation in the Paralympics was a major success. However, on the day the North Korean delegation was to leave England, something unfortunate happened.

Overseas Koreans and journalists came to the airport to see the North Korean delegation off. The company cadres accompanying the delegation had purchased large amounts of products in London, and they were seen by the journalists and overseas Koreans checking bags with these items in at the airport. The next day, a local overseas Korean newspaper reported on this. North Korean foreign ministry cadres were very angry, complaining that the country had taken pains to send the delegation to London and all the company cadres had done was some shopping.

Despite that, North Korea's participation in the Paralympics led to major changes in North Korea's policies toward disabled people. From that time forward, international exchanges involving North Korean disabled people began. I took a special interest in helping North Korean disabled people find their footing abroad and took whatever effort necessary to help them.

KIM JONG-IL DIES; HIS DEATH IS ANNOUNCED TWO DAYS LATER BY ORDER OF KIM JONG-UN

After Kim Jong-un was officially designated his father's successor in September 2010, it did not take much time for all North Korea's power to land in his clutches. The younger Kim's rise to power contrasted with that of Kim Jong-il, who had to play, outwardly at least, second fiddle to Kim Il-sung despite holding the real power in North Korea. Kim Jong-il's death came abruptly.

At 11 A.M. on December 19, 2011, all foreign ministry staff were ordered to gather in the lecture hall at 12 P.M. for a "grave announcement" by the party committee. On that day, I had attended a morning assembly of the European Department at 9 A.M. before joining some colleagues to practice table tennis at the Federation for the Protection of the Disabled gym. We were training for a preliminary competition that was to be held before a foreign ministry athletics event to commemorate the birthday of Kim Jong-suk on December 24.[9]

Upon hearing there was a "grave announcement," I quickly returned to the foreign ministry. While grave announcements in North Korea can carry different meanings, it was the first time since Kim Il-sung's death that the entire staff of the foreign ministry had been called to gather in the lecture hall and watch an announcement. Everyone was tense as they gathered in the lecture hall, but we all wondered inside ourselves whether what we thought had happened had really occurred. At exact 12 P.M., the announcer Lee Chun-hee appeared on KCTV. She was wearing a black *hanbok* (a traditional Korean form of dress). Everyone in the lecture hall let out a collective sigh, knowing immediately what had happened. The last and only time Lee had worn mourning clothes was when Kim Il-sung had died.

Kim Jong-il had died at 8 A.M. on December 17. The announcement was made fifty-one hours, more than two days, after his death. North Korean state media explained that the authorities had originally wanted to announce the death on December 17, but it was a Saturday, and Kim Jong-un had ordered a delay in the announcement to give the North Korean people rest on the weekend. In my view, North Korea is probably the only country on Earth that can keep the death of its leader a secret for two days. The country, in fact, can roll along as usual for a time because all government-related work is done through computers, and only the few members of the Third-Floor Secretariat know what's really going on. The same thing would probably happen if Kim Jong-un were to suffer some misfortune in the future.

Following the grave announcement, the party committee secretary went up to the podium. "You may all return [to your offices]," he said simply, before disappearing behind the platform. Everyone got up from their seats and went back to their offices. Nobody was weeping or wailing in sadness. This response was in contrast to what happened when Kim Il-sung died. At that time, many people wiped away tears after hearing the grave announcement.

I returned with my team back to the office, but nobody took out their lunch boxes. Many people had suffered difficulties for not acting properly after Kim Il-sung's death. People who had gone to saunas, moved to a new house, or even played cards were hunted down after the memorial services for the leader had finished and expelled from Pyongyang. Having experienced such a thing in the past, everybody now knew how to act. There was, however, no place to show one's respects to the deceased. A statue of Kim Jong-il now stands on the hill in Pyongyang's Mansu Hill (Mansudae), but at the time, the only statue there was of Kim Il-sung.

My staff asked me, the branch party secretary, where they should go to pay their respects. When I asked the party committee, I was told to wait until orders were handed down. At around 3 P.M. that day, the party committee handed down an order: Set up a place to show respects in the interview room for foreign visitors by the evening.

In these kinds of situations, North Koreans must play their cards right. Everyone showed an excessive amount of loyalty to ensure they would not be accused of any lack thereof. The staff, not one of whom had shed a single tear after hearing about Kim Jong-il's death, began making white paper flowers as if locked in a trance. All these paper flowers were then combined to make a wreath. Everyone knew that clocking out of work would be impossible. The wreath was finally finished at 11 P.M. Only then could foreign ministry staff take their wreaths and head to the place set up to offer their condolences. Everyone then became a mourner, telling others that they would take care of things at the condolence center.

Each department of the foreign ministry was given a time to visit the condolence center. In rotation, each department went down to the center and spent one hour watching over Kim Jong-il's portrait. Other organizations did much the same. Throughout Pyongyang, including in Kim Il-sung Square, portraits of Kim Jong-il were put up and places to receive condolences were set up. Everyone, young and old, went to these makeshift places to give condolences, staying there for hours before returning home. Everyone was required to report to their party organizations the next day how many hours they had "protected" the condolence centers. Nobody knew what kind of trouble they would face if they failed to report their activities.

Kim Jong-il's body was placed in the Gumsusan Palace of the Sun, and a state funeral was held. That was the first time that Kim Jong-un's sister, Kim Yo-jong, made an appearance in state media outlets. Kim Jong-chul, meanwhile, was not on the funeral guest list nor was his name mentioned in the media. The funeral was held in a very organized manner as if going by a script. I believe that Jang Song-taek oversaw the event. Kim Jong-un would have been in a daze due to the sudden death of his father, and Jang was probably the only person at that time who could have coldly and rationally taken the reigns to move things forward.

KIM JONG-UN SHOWS SIGNS OF WANTING TO IMPLEMENT REFORMS EARLY ON WITH AN ORDER TO CREATE FOURTEEN MORE GAESONG INDUSTRIAL COMPLEXES

After Kim Jong-il's death, North Korea quickly consolidated under Kim Jong-un. The first thing that changed were the rules concerning how "No. 1 events" were to be protected. No. 1 events are those attended by the North Korean leader. In the past, the relevant party committees would send lists of participants to the Supreme Guard Command several days before an event. Then, on the day of the event, security officers and guards in civilian clothes would confirm the identities of participants. As Kim Jong-un took power, however, guards dressed in military uniforms began confirming the identities of participants. Machine-gun nests were placed on both sides of the entrance to Kim Il-sung Square, with heavily armed soldiers lined up beside them.

This new setup forced event participants to walk between the two machine-gun nests. I experienced this myself several times and felt chills go down my spine every time I walked by the guns. You would face certain death if one of the guns went off accidentally. Setting up machine guns aimed at people heading into the square to yell out "Long Live Kim Jong-un" was the same as declaring martial law. The authorities seemed to have nothing more in mind than to create a sense of fear to quash any thought of protest among the people.

In fact, an incident did occur that was akin to a declaration of martial law. Government agencies located near Kim Il-sung Square had to empty their offices of employees one day before a No. 1 event. These empty offices, which included the country's Cabinet, Ministry of Foreign Affairs, Ministry of Trade, Ministry of Agriculture, and Education Commission, were then occupied by fully armed soldiers. In short, the authorities deployed soldiers in advance to suppress an uprising if one were to occur. While people did talk about what happened, few people were able to predict at the time that Kim Jong-un would engage in a "politics of fear."

On April 11, 2012, Kim Jong-un was named the first secretary of the WPK. On April 13, he was designated the first chairman of the National Defense Commission, effectively taking over all his father's past positions. For the first time in world history, a republic made its third hereditary succession of power official. North Korea attempted to launch the Gwangmyeongseong 3 satellite on April 13, as well, but it failed due to technical issues. On July 18, the Supreme People's Assembly decided to give Kim Jong-un—already the supreme commander of the country's armed forces—a promotion to wonsu (marshal), a rank two steps higher than daejang (general).

North Korea's elite initially held a great deal of hope for Kim Jong-un's rule. The new North Korean leader had studied in Switzerland during his middle school years and, the thinking went, had experienced Western culture during a formative time in his life. The elites hoped that Kim was forward-thinking and would move ahead with the reforms and opening up that could keep the regime alive, something his father had failed to do. North Korea's elites shared the sentiment that North Korea needed to go down the same path as China, which had achieved rapid development through reforms and opening up following Mao Ze-dong's death.

Could Kim, with the open mind of someone who had studied abroad, modernize North Korea? People's expectations in this regard seemed to be right—initially at least. Everyone in North Korea participated in meetings held on Saturday mornings, whose name is roughly translated as "listening to instructions from the leader." These meetings had everyone listen to the remarks Kim Jong-un had made over the previous week. During the initial period after he gained power, the new North Korean leader's remarks made people think that North Korea would soon implement economic reforms: "The DPRK's current economic system is inadequate. Let's research the economic systems of other countries. Let's study all the economic theories that have been praised. Let's try doing that."

Kim said things that showed he had points of view completely opposite to his father's: "The DPRK must receive foreign investment to develop economically, but there are not many ways to do this because of American sanctions. The easiest way to earn foreign currency at this point is through tourism. We must dramatically increase the number of tourists to develop our tourism [industry]." He also emphasized the need for reforms and opening up while mentioning the example of the Gaesong Industrial Complex:

> Many people worried that the Gaesong Industrial Complex would become a long-term threat to the DPRK's system. However, we have gained much more. First, we have earned money that is essential for us to survive. Second, it has become easier to naturally control and manage the people of Gaesong. Other areas have had difficulties managing their people because of the markets. Fifty thousand Gaesong citizens work at a single complex every day, so there's no need for extra management. Overall, [the Gaesong Industrial Complex] has given us many more advantages. This kind of special economic zone must be replicated in the interior of the country. We must create fourteen more places like the Gaesong Industrial Complex.

Kim further remarked that "education is important" and that "No. 1 Higher Middle Schools must be constructed in every district and county to strengthen the cultivation of brilliant minds."

KIM JONG-UN WORKS HARD TO SHOW HIMSELF AS WARM-HEARTED WITH THE SUSPENSION OF THE ARIRANG MASS PERFORMANCES

The changes Kim tried to bring about were also felt in the foreign ministry. The North Korean leader ordered that the new year's banquet in 2012 would have everyone standing up and eating. The order flew in the face of traditions practiced since the Kim Il-sung era. A typical North Korean banquet would have everyone sitting down while eating. In the 1960s, Kim Il-sung held a standing-only banquet on a suggestion from Party International Secretary Park Yong-guk, who had recently returned from Europe. It was a one-time affair, however. At the time, party cadres complained: "Why do we have to eat while standing up at banquets we've always sat down at? Horses eat while standing. Are we horses? Our legs hurt while standing. Park Yong-guk, that bastard, he brought back something strange from Europe."

After that, Kim Il-sung never held any more standing-only banquets. In fact, North Korean officials typically avoid standing-only banquets, not because the events are uncomfortable but rather because they do not mesh well with North Korean culture. At standing-only banquets, people are free to choose whom they are going to approach for conversation and must choose the right topic of conversation to fit the situation. This kind of event is not at all welcome to North Korean officials who, when conducting diplomatic activities, must first receive permission before meeting and talking to anyone.

In any case, Kim Jong-un's order led to the 2012 new year's event being held as a standing-only banquet. While various ambassadors approached Kim Jong-un to wish him a happy new year, the atmosphere was very off-kilter. North Korean officials and the staff of foreign embassies gathered in groups among themselves here and there until the party ended. After the event, Kim expressed dismay to the officials who remained at the venue, saying, "Is this how you do diplomacy?" I got a good feeling while watching him say that, thinking that he was trying to instill in everyone a new way of doing things.

The Kim Jong-un who gained power in 2012 was much milder than the leader we see today. North Korean officials did not tremble in the presence of Kim as they do now. There are clear differences in Kim's demeanor when you compare videos from his early years with more recent ones. Cadres could approach the North Korean leader without difficulty, and Kim responded to them in an intimate way.

When Changjeon Street was completed in Pyongyang in June 2012, Kim did something that took people by surprise. The street, nicknamed the "North Korean New Town" and "Pyongyang's Gangnam," was the site of brand-new apartments. Kim took his wife to meet the families who had just moved into them. He even poured soju for elderly people as part of efforts to cultivate an image that he was a "leader of the people."

What caused the biggest sensation among North Koreans, however, was Kim's suspension of the Arirang mass games. Many North Koreans were discontented with the games, which mobilized students every year for six months of practice. Nobody, however, was able to raise an issue about it. While it's possible someone did suggest to Kim that the mass games should be suspended, his order to halt the mobilization of students for the event was enough to elicit praise from the people.

In August 2012, Kim created another sensation by taking an unarmed wooden fishing boat to inspect Mu Island and Jangjae Island, two islands across from Yeonpyeong Island. What he did was unimaginable during the lifetimes of his father or grandfather. North Koreans were excited to see Kim boldly inspect the country's frontline without any guards in tow. There were quite a few elderly people who wept as they saw the youthful and energetic North Korean leader braving the wind and waves on a small twenty-seven-horsepower wooden boat headed to a remote area of the country.

"TAKE OVER BBC IN EUROPE AND ABC IN AMERICA"

After Kim Jong-un came to power, certain changes began to emerge in North Korea's stance toward the international community. Kim was well aware of the impact of spreading propaganda through media outlets, given his time studying abroad since childhood, and he placed a priority on North Korea's interactions with the international media.

During the Kim Il-sung and Kim Jong-il periods, North Korea spent a considerable amount of effort cultivating the international media. Kim Il-sung held interviews with the world's top media outlets, such as the

New York Times, and knew how to handle foreign journalists. Kim Jong-il never conducted an interview with a foreign media outlet; however, he did order his officials to "dominate" the BBC in the UK and ABC in the United States.

It was understandable that Kim Jong-il wanted to exert influence over the BBC, as it had the most influence of any media outlet in Europe. In the United States, the outlet that showed the most interest in North Korea and whose journalists had visited North Korea the most was CNN. Kim Jong-il, however, ordered that efforts must focus on ABC, not CNN, if North Korea wanted to increase positive sentiments toward North Korea in the United States. I don't know why he thought this.

Regardless of how high a priority it put on improving their relationship with international media outlets, North Korea's leadership faced limitations. North Korea has no freedom of the press, which makes it hard to expect the country to have an effective media outreach program. This is a contradiction of North Korea, and a tragedy for the country. The DPRK's foreign ministry blocks criticism of North Korea by international media outlets and always deliberates about how to use those outlets to promote the country. The foreign ministry is perennially tasked with quickly transmitting North Korea's stances to the international community by way of foreign media outlets.

However, international media outlets place more importance on South Korean media than North Korean media. If a serious incident occurs, such as the shelling of Yeonpyeong Island or the sinking of ROK's *Cheonan*, South Korean media pounce on it faster than North Korean media. Moreover, the reports coming out of KCNA or *Rodong Sinmun* are brief and monotonous, with no special information. International news agencies have no choice but to cite or quote what South Korean media outlets have reported.

It is easy to guess why North Korean media reports and editorials are so slow to be published. The country exerts strict controls over news reporting. If North Korean media outlets are to report on the sinking of the Sewol ferry or the impeachment of South Korean President Park Geun-hye, they need to go through certain procedures: After consultations between the media team within the United Front Department and the South Joseon Affairs Media Team in the Central Committee's Propaganda and Agitation Department, a "South Joseon Affairs Report Plan" then has to be approved by Kim Jong-un.

North Korean coverage of international events such as the 9/11 attacks or the Iraq War must go through a similar process. The foreign ministry's media bureau is required to conduct consultations with the External Propaganda Team within the Central Committee's Propaganda and Agitation Department and then submit a "report plan for next week" to Kim Jong-un on Wednesdays for approval. Typically, North Korean coverage of international news goes out around a week after the events have happened.

North Korea's media environment is trapped in a contradictory situation in which journalists are told to talk but they can't say what they want. That's why Kim Jong-il and Kim Jong-un have shown duplicitous attitudes toward issues related to international media coverage of North Korea. One day, the leader would order diplomats to actively hold interviews and conduct briefings with foreign media outlets to promote North Korea's positions. On another day, however, the leader would arbitrarily tell diplomats that they must avoid contact with foreign media outlets and warn them that even trivial mistakes would not be tolerated.

NOBODY WANTS TO SERVE AS FOREIGN MINISTRY SPOKESPERSON, SO JUST A PRESS RELEASE IS HANDED OUT

Diplomats who make mistakes while meeting members of the international press face criticism during weekly and monthly party criticism sessions. It's not tremendously embarrassing for them because they only receive criticism from their colleagues. However, during quarterly criticism sessions, held every three months, a thousand party members in the foreign ministry gather in the lecture hall, and the session is led by the Organization and Guidance Department (OGD) deputy director in charge of the foreign ministry. Only a small number of people are placed on the podium and criticized, which makes it an embarrassing experience that can also lead to higher levels of punishment. The OGD deputy director for the foreign ministry will be faithful to Kim Jong-il's order that "criticism sessions must be held within an atmosphere of ideological struggle." The atmosphere pervading the quarterly criticism sessions are always brutal.

When I worked as the deputy director of the European Department, Chae Hwi—one of the North Korean officials who visited South Korea during the PyeongChang Winter Olympics—was the OGD deputy director in charge of the foreign ministry. Even Minister of Foreign Affairs Park Wui-chun was like a mouse in front of a cat when confronting Chae. If one did not want to conduct a self-criticism during quarterly criticism sessions, the best thing to do was to avoid recklessly interacting with the international press and just follow orders. With such a pervasive atmosphere of everyone trying to protect their own backs, it was not surprising that nobody wanted to hold an interview with international journalists.

Right before the hundredth anniversary of Kim Il-sung's birthday in April 2012, Kim Jong-un released information about the country's satellite launching site to the foreign media in a bid to shock the world. An order was handed down to ambassadors abroad to conduct interviews with foreign journalists to promote North Korea's policies. Most of the ambassadors, however, continued to avoid interviews with the international press.

The same year, I attended a meeting held at the foreign ministry regarding interactions with the foreign media. During that meeting, I made the following suggestion:

Currently, the foreign ministry releases the viewpoints of the Republic only through spokesperson dialogues or statements. All of these releases are in document form only. It would be no different if a broadcaster just read out the statements. No broadcaster in any country reads out the statements or conversations of the DPRK's foreign ministry verbatim. Starting now, we at the foreign ministry must also have a spokesperson to conduct briefings and answer questions from the media. That's the global trend. It doesn't make sense to only release press releases in Pyongyang while telling ambassadors throughout the globe to conduct interviews with the media. That way of doing things isn't speedy and lacks visual impact.

I had long been receiving requests from APTN to conduct interviews with a foreign ministry spokesperson or to hold press conferences. It was natural that they would request such things. The comments I made during the meeting were, in fact, an indirect request for the foreign ministry's media department to take on the role of spokesperson for the organization.

Everyone, however, sat silently at the meeting without expressing opposition or support to my suggestion. It was clear from people's faces that they were uncomfortable. The meeting ended without drawing any conclusions. After the meeting, Ambassador Song Il-ho, who had managed negotiations with Japan, quietly told me: "General Kim Jong-il has already made a final decision that a foreign ministry spokesperson should conduct briefings with domestic and international journalists. As you well know, the problem is that nobody in the foreign ministry has volunteered to become the spokesperson. Who would, given that any mistake would lead to trouble?" In short, Song told me that nothing I could say would change anything. Going forward, I continued to suggest at every opportunity the establishment of a system to transmit North Korea's stances to the world through interviews with APTN's Pyongyang bureau. Ultimately, however, these efforts went nowhere.

RI SOL-JU APPEARS AT A PERFORMANCE OF AN AMERICAN SONG PERFORMED BY THE MORANBONG BAND

Once, even I fell under the delusion that Kim Jong-un might be abandoning his father's nuclear development policies and leading North Korea to economic reforms. On the evening of July 6, 2012, a very special musical performance was held in Pyongyang. The performance featured the Moranbong Band, which had been created on orders from Kim Jong-un.[10]

Two things surprised me as I watched the performance. The first was that Ri Sol-ju, Kim Jong-un's wife, sat next to her husband while watching the show. Neither Ri's name nor any of her personal details had been released to the public at that time. The other thing that surprised me was that much of the foreign music that the Moranbong Band performed consisted of American pop songs. Of course, the songs were not referred to as American. For example, the band played one of the *Rocky* movie theme songs, "Gonna Fly Now," which was described in Korean on a screen atop the stage as "Light Music, Gonna Fly Now (Foreign Song)." The song plays when Rocky is running by himself and shadowboxing in the movie, and a scene from the movie was shown on a screen at the rear of the stage. The band also played Frank Sinatra's song, "My Way," which was described on the screen as "Light Music, My Way (Foreign Song)."

The highlight of the performance was a medley of theme songs from animated films, which were referred to as "A Collection of Famous Songs from World Animation." The collection included songs from Mickey Mouse, Pooh Bear, Snow White and the Seven Dwarves, Cinderella, Beauty and the Beast, and others from Disney animated films. People dressed up as Mickey Mouse, Minnie Mouse, and Pooh Bear came out on stage, and the stage's screen displayed a panorama of clips from movies in which these characters were featured. It would not have been wrong to call the collection of songs "A Collection of Famous Songs from American Animated Films."

Ordinary North Koreans who watched the performance on TV would not have known that the songs and animated characters were from the United States. I easily recognized them because I had watched many American movies while abroad. The performance was very shocking to me. I have heard that the performance caused quite a sensation in South Korea as well. A video of the performance can be found on YouTube.

For many years, North Korea had been trying to arrange a performance of its National Symphonic Orchestra in the United States. Kim Jong-un had clear intentions in having the Moranbong Band perform American pop songs and broadcasting the performance on TV. He likely wanted to send a message to the Americans that "the Moranbong Band is ready, so open your doors to North Korea."

On July 25, Ri Sol-ju officially appeared in North Korean media for the first time. KCTV reported on that day that "Kim Jong-un along with his wife Ri Sol-ju attended the completion ceremony for the Neungra People's Amusement Park." While many had suspected that the lady sitting next to Kim Jong-un during the Moranbong Band's first performance was his wife, people were completely taken aback by state media referring to her as "Comrade Ri Sol-ju."

What was even more surprising to North Koreans was that Ri was walking lovingly arm in arm with Kim. In North Korea it is very unnatural for couples to walk arm in arm in public. Ri and Kim were doing that at a national event in front of elderly officials. From the perspective of these officials, it could have been viewed as very disrespectful behavior.

POLITICS OF FEAR SOON RETURN WITH THE EXECUTION OF THE CHIEF OF STAFF OF THE KOREAN PEOPLE'S ARMY

What foreign ministry officials saw at the event was on everyone's lips the entire day. Even international media outlines headlined the completion ceremony. Some outlets even claimed that Kim Jong-un had intentionally appeared at the event arm in arm with his wife to show that he was open-minded and enlightened.

Ri became the center of an even more dramatic scene that day. Kim suggested to the diplomatic delegation accompanying him—including Liu Hong-cai, the Chinese ambassador to North Korea—that they get on one of the amusement rides called the Rotating Horse (a merry-go-around). When Kim got on the ride first, the diplomatic envoys had no choice but to sit next to him, but the rotating ride suddenly stopped. The officials did not know what to do, and amusement park managers furiously ran around here and there to fix the ride. Soon after, the Rotating Horse began circling around again.

While the incident was trivial, Kim abruptly yelled at one of the park managers as soon as he got off the ride. The manager trembled as he apologized. Liu and other members of the diplomatic delegation were also flustered by Kim's anger. Then, Ri Son-ju went over to Kim and quietly calmed him down. After Kim had calmed down, the North Korean leader and his entourage began looking at other areas of the amusement park, leading to sighs of relief from the people gathered there. Going forward, Ri would accompany Kim to his on-the-spot inspections and do a wonderful job of helping to exude the image of a loving couple.

The North Korean elite's hopes for Kim Jong-un, however, gradually began to collapse. In the second half of 2012, Kim intensified internal rules within the WPK as part of efforts to strengthen control over party officials. He ordered that all activities conducted by party cadres and party members be reported in detail in advance to party organizations. His specific instructions were: "Establish a reporting system where the Party Center can hear even the sound of a pin drop in Samsu and Gapsan counties."[11] In accordance with the order, all those ranked department director and above in the foreign ministry had to report their next day's schedule in advance to the ministry's party committee, and the party committee had to make a daily report on the specific activities of high-level foreign ministry officials, from the vice minister and above, to the OGD.

The first stage of Kim Jong-un's politics of fear was revealed around this time. Ri Yong-ho, the Korean People's Army's chief of staff, who was considered highly influential in the Kim regime, was reportedly executed after being caught saying something negative about the North Korean leader. Specifically, Ri allegedly said, with regard to Kim Jong-un's moves to conduct reforms and opening early in his administration, "Do you think the General [Kim Jong-il] didn't conduct reforms and opening because he believed they wouldn't improve the country's economy?" After his purge, Ri was reportedly revolutionized (punished) before being executed.

In the North Korea of today, if Kim Jong-un orders someone to be shot, they are put in front of a firing squad immediately. Kim executes at least one or two people whenever there is a large-scale construction project or national event commemorating something. The unlucky victims are killed during the start of the project so that everybody falls into line. The start of Kim's use of executions was during the massive remodeling of the Gumsusan Memorial Palace in late 2012.[12] The remodeling plan called for changing the square in front of the palace into a flower garden, and each government agency was allotted a piece of the square to work on. The job called for workers to dig out three meters of soil from the ground and then heat it before placing it back into the ground. They had to heat up the dirt to kill all the insects that lived inside. A work team from the Central Industrial Art Guidance Bureau found it difficult to meet the deadline to do this and just dug up 1.5 meters worth of soil before placing it back into the ground. The work team was caught in the act, and one department director from the organization was executed on Kim's order.

KIM JONG-UN HINTS AT JANG SONG-TAEK'S EXECUTION THROUGH A WARNING ABOUT "INTERNAL ENEMIES"

On April 14, 2012, Kim Jong-un held a meeting of the Supreme People's Assembly to explicitly place a mention in the constitution that North Korea was a nuclear-armed state. Plans to make official the country's status as a nuclear-armed nation had begun during the Kim Jong-il era. Kim Jong-il had wanted to declare 2012—the hundredth anniversary of Kim Il-sung's birth—as the year of the Strong and Prosperous Nation and strove to acquire nuclear-armed state status by that time. Kim Jong-il did not live to see 2012, but his obsession with nuclear weapons seemed to remain alive even after his death. Placing explicit mention of North Korea's status as a nuclear-armed state in the constitution was the first concrete example of this.

On December 12, 2012, North Korea fired off the *Eunha 3* and succeeded in placing a satellite in orbit. The satellite was launched in accordance with previous plans, and the launch seemed to be a signal that Kim Jong-un was returning to policies put in place by Kim Jong-il. Then, on February 12, 2013, Kim Jong-un conducted the country's third nuclear test and claimed that the country had acquired precision nuclear strike capabilities with a miniaturized and lighter device that boasted greater explosive force.

Finally, at the Central Committee's plenary session on March 31, 2013, North Korea made the Byeongjin (parallel development) policy of economy and nuclear weapons official party policy. The Byeongjin policy was aimed at spurring forward economic development while strengthening North Korea's military forces, particularly the asymmetrical weapons of nukes and intercontinental missiles. Following this decision, all of North Korea's resources were funneled into nuclear and missile weapons development.

North Korea's regime continuously changes its goals to meet the needs of certain periods. Without new goals, the country has almost no power to put its society into motion. For example, the DPRK proposed to complete a goal unconditionally by 2012, the year of the hundredth anniversary of Kim Il-sung's birth, and mobilized the entire country to meet that goal. If the leadership doesn't do this, the society will face instability.

When Kim Jong-un declared the start of the Byeongjin policy, however, he said something that was not in the report prepared by his underlings: "Completing nuclear weapons will not be an easy task. The United States, China, and other powerful countries will do anything in their power to stop us. We could get into a fight with the United States. However, we may face a war within our own country before there is a war with the United States. We must win the fight of ideology and of will before we can make nuclear weapons." We wondered who inside the country we were at war with but later saw, in retrospect, that Kim was hinting at a purge, although that wasn't clear at the time.

It was around this time that Kim abandoned his efforts to attempt reforms and opening up and turned to a hard-line position. Why did that happen at that particular moment? I would like to offer the following analysis.

Kim Il-sung returned to North Korea in 1945. He became North Korea's leader at the age of thirty-three and started the Korean War in his thirties. Kim Jong-un also wanted to achieve something while he was still young.

As Kim Jong-un gained power in 2012, he proposed that 2015 be the "Year of a Major Incident for Unification of the Motherland," and this phrase was frequently published in the *Rodong Sinmun*. During internal party and military meetings, decisions were made to finish preparations for war by 2015. Kim inspected military installations and checked up on progress to prepare for war. The realities he saw, however, were dismal.

Military equipment was old and dilapidated, so much oil had been siphoned off that there were inconsistencies in the records, and the soldiers were starving. Most decisively, North Korea's economy was not improving, and the country had no money or equipment to maintain its 1.2-million-strong army. Kim concluded that going to war with traditional weaponry was impossible. Thus, the only option left was to place all his cards on nuclear weapons, which his father had been working on since the Kim Il-sung era. Kim Jong-un believed that abandoning nuclear weapons would immediately make it hard for him to maintain power.

The key to success was money. Kim needed to devote all North Korea's financial resources to making nukes and missiles, but most of the country's economic interests were in the hands of Jang Song-taek. Jang had to decide whether to give up those interests or keep a hold on them. I think that one of the reasons Kim ruthlessly executed Jang was that his uncle couldn't abandon those interests. Of course, Kim's own deep-rooted hatred of Jang also played a decisive role in Kim's decision to eliminate Jang.

WHY CHINA CAN'T CONVINCE NORTH KOREA TO ABANDON ITS NUCLEAR WEAPONS PROGRAM

Kim Jong-un's turn to a hard-line stance may have been partially influenced by the Third-Floor Secretariat. At a basic level, the secretariat is tasked with deifying Kim Jong-il and Kim Jong-un and maintaining hereditary rule. The secretariat would collapse if the country turned to reforms and opening up and if ordinary people found out about the truth behind the two Kims. Kim Jong-un inherited the Third-Floor Secretariat from his father, and I think that he was unable to push back against their opposition to his plans for economic reform.

By placing explicit mention of North Korea as a nuclear-armed state in the constitution and adopting the Byeongjin policy, Kim had stipulated both in the constitution and in party policy that North Korea possessed nuclear weapons. Then, in the first half of 2013, the conditions of North Korea and China's debate over nuclear weapons started to change. North Korea changed the way it responded to China, and this shift was connected to the DPRK's making it explicit that it possessed nuclear weapons.

The North Korea nuclear issue became a frequent cause for serious debate between North Korea and China during high-level talks and exchanges. China's argument was as follows:

> We are not telling you to immediately stop developing nuclear weapons. It's alright to possess the weapons for a set amount of time. However, the DPRK must declare that the country's long-term goal is denuclearization and return to the negotiation table for talks on denuclearization. If the DPRK just returns to talks on denuclearization, China can increase aid to the country. We believe that the DPRK can gradually move to shut down its nuclear program once trust is developed between it and neighboring countries, including the United States, while maintaining possession of the weapons for a set amount of time.

China-DPRK exchanges are separated into communist party–led exchanges and government-led exchanges. Party-led exchanges involve the WPK's International Department and the Chinese Communist Party (CCP)'s International Liaison Department, while government-led exchanges involve the North Korean Ministry of Foreign Affairs and the Chinese Ministry of Foreign Affairs. During party-led exchanges, North Korea would counter the preceding Chinese argument like this:

> Fighting imperialism is the holy duty of communists. We must have nuclear weapons if we are to fight the American imperialists. When the

CCP developed nuclear weapons, it believed that there was no other way to fight against the United States other than nuclear weapons. Nuclear weapons protected socialism. When the world's communist parties opposed China's nuclear weapons development, only the WPK supported the CCP. While there may be large parties, small parties, parties with long histories, and those with short histories, there can never be higher and lower parties and parties that give orders while others receive them. All parties are equal. The policy of the WPK is to try and respond to U.S. nuclear weapons with nuclear weapons. Starting a dispute about this policy is interference in [the DPRK's] internal affairs and contradicts the international communist principles of conduct.

During government-led exchanges, however, North Korea's refutation would take a different tack: "The DPRK stipulates explicitly in its constitution that it possesses nuclear weapons. Telling us to abandon nuclear weapons is like demanding us to revise our constitution. While there may be large countries and small countries in the world, China is the only country that interferes in the affairs of other countries by telling them to revise their constitution. We are not in the era of the Qing Dynasty."

North Korea and China are both communist countries that place importance on theory and logic. There were many times when the outcome of a meeting was split because of battles over logic. The CCP, which has Marxism-Leninism as its guiding ideology, is intimidated by the North Koreans because it cannot oppose North Korea's nuclear weapons policy through existing ideology or theory. This is the reason China can't strongly push North Korea to denuclearize.

6

ON THE EVE OF MY DEFECTION

SEA OF TEARS UPON LEAVING FOR THE UK WITHOUT MY FIRSTBORN

I was appointed deputy ambassador to the North Korean embassy in the United Kingdom in March 2013. This was the month North Korea adopted a policy of pursuing nuclear weapons and economic development at the same time. I arrived in London on April 26 with my wife and second son. I could not bring my older son, who was in his fourth year at university. North Korea bans university students from residing overseas. I hadn't even considered bringing my older son along with us because he had completely recovered from his illness and was attending university at the time.

There were many twists and turns in bringing my second son with us to the UK. He was sixteen and a high school student. In principle, such students weren't allowed to live abroad either, but I resolved this problem, albeit with some difficulty.

On the day we departed Pyongyang Station, leaving behind my older son, who really wanted to go with us, I cried a lot. Needless to say, my wife and my younger son did, too. As the train pulled away and my older son slowly disappeared into the background, I wasn't able to see his face clearly because of the tears streaming down my face.

It is always a sea of tears when North Korean diplomats are forced to leave even one of their children behind upon leaving Pyongyang for an overseas posting. Parents cry because they feel sorry for their children left behind, while the children left behind cry because they don't want to be separated from their parents. It's no different from leaving for a battlefield. South Korean diplomats, even when they are stationed overseas, can return home on vacation. Alternatively, their children can come and visit them abroad. This is not even remotely possible in North Korea. Diplomats who leave their children behind in North Korea often cannot eat because they are thinking of their children.

All the news that came out of North Korea was bad. In August, the Unhasu Orchestra was purged. The head of the orchestra and seven others were executed, and the group was disbanded. The Unhasu Orchestra was famous, appearing on North Korean TV nearly every day. It was also the largest orchestra in North Korea. Kim Jong-un's wife, Ri Sol-ju, was a singer with the group. Ostensibly, the orchestra was purged because it had produced a porn video, but everyone knew it had something to do with Ri.

Ri was a very ordinary singer with the Unhasu Orchestra. Then one day, her luck suddenly changed when she became Kim's wife, leading inevitably to the spread of rumors. The Ministry of State Security got wind of what orchestra members were discreetly saying about Ri. The ministry reported to Kim that his prestige could be damaged if bad rumors about Ri spread. Kim ordered that the rumors be stopped at all costs.

THE "MOTHER COMPLEX" BEHIND KIM JONG-UN'S POLITICS OF FEAR

Kim has a complex that has led to his fixation on using "politics of fear." This is still true today. Even after he was designated as successor, the regime has not publicized Kim's birthday, academic background, or birth mother. These things are actually better known in South Korea. Based on the passport he used when he studied overseas, analysts have concluded that he was born in 1984, that he studied at a public middle school in Bern, Switzerland, and that his birth mother was either Ko Yeong-hui or Ko Yong-hui.

I don't know which name is correct. The Japanese newspaper *Sankei Shinbun* reported, "It is believed that North Korea's use of Ko Yong-hui instead of Ko Yeong-hui, her original name, is intended to cover up the fact that she is a Korean-Japanese, giving the impression that she is a different person from Ko Yeong-hui, who was born in Japan." Anyway, let's call her Ko Yeong-hui. But why can't Kim, despite wielding absolute power in the country, say her name in public? The reason is the impact his secret could have on the regime's stability.

Ko had three children with Kim Jong-il: Kim Jong-chol (born in 1981), Kim Jong-un, and Kim Yo-jong (born in 1987). Kim Jong-il had only three sons in all: Jong-chol, Jong-un, and Jong-nam (born in 1971) with Song Hye-rim. Ko gave Kim two of these sons and should have been able to hold her head high. But she was born in Japan. She came to North Korea in 1962 with her family during efforts to repatriate Japanese-Koreans back to the motherland. Ko was a Japanese-Korean who wasn't treated well in North Korea. Her career as a dancer with the Mansudae Art Troupe was not enough to give her the status of "Kim Jong-il's woman." Moreover, there were South Korean media reports that her father had worked with the Japanese military, meaning there may have been people aware of this fact in North Korea, too. Even if nobody did know about it, it was imperative that things stayed that way.

Another reason Kim Jong-un can't talk about Ko is that she was never recognized as Kim Il-sung's daughter-in-law or as Kim Jong-il's wife. Kim Jong-il's official wife, recognized by Kim Il-sung, was Kim Yong-suk. From what I heard in North Korea, up until the late 1980s, Kim Yong-suk and her daughters (Sol Song and Chun Song) would offer their respects to Kim Il-sung's family at Mangyongdae every holiday. But Ko endured the sadness of never receiving recognition as Kim Il-sung's daughter-in-law. That meant that Kim Jong-il could not honorably show her off in public.

Ko died of an illness in May 2004. After Kim Jong-il died in December 2011, Kim Jong-un in June the next year sanctified Ko's grave at Daesong-san Revolutionary Martyrs' Cemetery, making central government cadres pay their respects. Strangely, however, there is no name inscribed on the grave, just a phrase: "Mother of Songun Korea." The grave had no name as of the autumn of 2012, as far as I can remember, but the *Sankei Shinbun* article from August 2, 2012, mentioned earlier said the grave records her name as "Kim Yong-hui." I'm not sure if my memory is mistaken or if the Japanese newspaper got it wrong.

What's worth noting here is that the inscription on the grave was not just "Mother of Korea," but included the word *Songun*. *Songun* Korea refers to a North Korea that is led and centered on the military as announced by the WPK after the death of Kim Il-sung in 1994. The term "Mother of Songun Korea" acknowledges that Ko was recognized as a mother only in a very specific time and place; namely, the North Korea after the death of Kim Il-sung.

Along with sanctifying Ko's grave, Kim Jong-un also produced an archival film titled *Mother of Great Songun Korea* for use as propaganda, showing it to a tiny handful of cadres in March 2012. The cadres said that if the film was made public, it could cause a great stir in North Korean society. The film was never made public, but USBs with the movie eventually leaked out. The authorities demanded that people who saw the film turn themselves in, and several people within the Korean Central Broadcasting Committee were executed. The film even leaked overseas, and you can find it today on YouTube.

In March 2016, before I defected, North Korea forced cadres to study the revolutionary history of Kim Jong-un prior to a party congress. Yet even in the lecture materials on Kim's revolutionary history sent to embassies overseas, Ko's name was nowhere to be found. Even now, no one can safely publicize Ko's existence because Kim Jong-un is caught in a self-contradiction. The North Korean leader promotes his legitimacy and authenticity as a successor with pretensions concerning his place in the "Baekdu Blood Line." However, his birth mother was not Kim Jong-il's only woman; she was one of several women with whom Kim Jong-il had relationships.

LEARNING OF JANG SONG-TAEK'S EXECUTION IN LONDON

What would happen if North Koreans learned that Kim Jong-un had a half-brother named Kim Jong-nam, or that Kim Jong-il had children with several women, including Kim Yong-suk, Song Hye-rim, and Ko

Yong-hui? Kim Jong-un knows only too well that his family details are a source of instability for the North Korean regime. For that reason, I thought Kim Jong-un could not leave Kim Jong-nam alone, and I predicted as much during a lecture at South Korea's National Assembly in January 2017. Less than a month after the lecture, Kim Jong-nam was assassinated in Kuala Lumpur International Airport in Malaysia.

Kim Jong-un appears to suffer from psychological insecurity because his birth mother was not his father's official wife. Cadres who know this say the North Korean leader is worried about how others will perceive this, and thus he suffers from an inferiority complex. His family details are inevitably a big problem for Kim. This is because many cadres remember both Kim Yong-suk, Kim Jong-il's official wife, and Ko Yong-hui, who was no different from a concubine.

Kim Jong-il conducted many on-site inspections of the Mansudae Art Troupe in the late 1970s. Then, dancer Ko Yong-hui suddenly disappeared from the troupe, with even cadres unclear about where she had gone. If Ko's existence were to become known as Kim highlights his own birth mother, what would happen? People would think: "Ah, that's why Ko Yong-hui disappeared."

Kim Jong-il had to wait until Kim Il-sung died in 1994 before he started doing on-site guidance visits with Ko. Yet Ko was never mentioned in North Korean media reports. Thus, it was clear that Ko's sudden appearance after Kim Jong-un took power would present an even greater shock, her image a stark contrast with the shabby-looking Kim Yong-suk. Ko resembles Ri Sol-ju. Both are former members of performance groups who became partners of the country's supreme leaders. As such, the rumors about Ri that were whispered among members of the Unhasu Orchestra were akin to messing with Kim's "Achilles' heel."

Amid his efforts to strengthen control over his officials, Kim appears to have believed he needed to make an example of members of the orchestra. This is because cadres who stood at attention and wrote down notes when Kim Jong-il spoke showed Kim Jong-un a completely different attitude. It seems that Kim's sudden decision to execute members of the Unhasu Orchestra, after having treated cadres nicely, was calculated to improve cadre discipline.

In early December, before the shock caused by the purge of the Unhasu Orchestra had waned, South Korean media reported that Ri Ryong-ha, the first vice director of the WPK's Administrative Department, and Vice Director Chang Su-gil had been executed. They were close associates of Jang Song-taek. At the time, I thought it was an erroneous report.

Then, on December 9, Ambassador Hyeon Hak-bong called me into his office. He told me to look at an article in the online version of the *Rodong Sinmun*. It reported that "Jang and others had been purged as anti-party elements" during a meeting of the Central Committee on December 8. The article included a photo of Jang being arrested. It was unprecedented for a North Korean newspaper to run a photo of a high-ranking cadre being dragged off during a WPK meeting.

The paper explained the reason behind the purge, accusing elements who had attained positions within the party despite their lack of ability and temperament, as well as people who disagreed with the party from the inside, of attempting to castrate the party's unitary leadership at a critical historic moment in the passing on of the Juche Revolution, and of carrying out dangerous anti-party, anti-revolutionary factional activities by expanding their own power and boldly challenging the party through factional schemes.

Jang was relieved of all his duties, stripped of all his titles, and even expelled from the party. On December 12, the Ministry of State Security held a special military trial for him, and after the trial he was executed. The KCNA claimed that Jang had "stupidly" planned a military coup after "losing his senses in his desire for power." It was clear to anyone, however, that this story was fabricated. The bloody purge that followed was what Kim Jong-un had desired.

OTHER SITUATIONS THAT CAUSED THE PURGE

We need to examine the situation at around the time of Jang's purge. Even as Jang helped Kim Jong-un succeed his father into power, he could not cut off his relationship with Kim Jong-nam. If Kim Jong-nam asked for money from abroad, Jang would have his right-hand man send it to him secretly. The Ministry of State Security got wind of this and reported it to Kim Jong-un. The North Korean leader was furious that Jang was trying to sit on the fence between him and his half-brother, but he had no choice but to tough it out. He couldn't do away with Jang for something like that.

In the autumn of 2013, Kim visited Onchon Air Base in Onchon County, South Pyongan Province. Kim realized that not only weren't they ready for combat, but they also didn't even have side dishes to go with their rice. He asked the commanders of the air force whether they had plans to remedy this. The commanders asked that they be handed Department 54's Nampo Fishing Base, located near Onchon Air Base. They were angling for the dollars made by the fishing base to improve the air force's ability to buy food.

Some explanation of Department 54's Nampo Fishing Base is necessary here. In the late 2000s, Kim Jong-il hatched a plan to build one hundred thousand homes in Pyongyang by 2012. This plan called for evicting thousands of families from along the road leading from the Ryugyong Hotel to Pyongyang Airfield and building modern apartment complexes. The project was led by Jang's Administrative Department. Jang relied on Department 54 to carry out the project.

Launched in 1980, Department 54 operated under the Maebong General Trading Company, the leading foreign-currency-earning organization of the Ministry of the People's Armed Forces (MPAF). The department existed as a trading body within the Maebong General Trading Company, but Department 54 played a critical role. In 2008, the department began using the name Sungni Company, and from 2009 it gained almost a complete monopoly on major exports such as coal. When foreign currency earnings rose, the head of the department, Chang Su-gil, became closer to Jang Song-taek than he was to MPAF. With Jang's support, Chang turned sectors that earned foreign currency, such as exports of coal and seafood, into monopolies.

In order to build the one hundred thousand apartments in Pyongyang, Department 54 established a tile factory with investment from China. It agreed to repay the investment through exports of coal and seafood. The establishment of large-scale fishing bases in the seas off Nampo and Onchon was part of this effort. They earned more than one million dollars a year selling seafood such as clams to China. In South Korea, one million dollars would be nothing, but in North Korea, it was quite a feat for a single seafood company to earn that much.

Department 54 grew to hold a monopoly on fishing bases in the country. Military units near the fishing bases and ordinary seafood businesses naturally considered this unfair. That's why the commanders of Onchon Air Base asked Kim Jong-un to hand over the Department 54 fishing base closest to the air base to them. Unaware of the context of their request,

Kim, as supreme commander, ordered that the fishing base be turned over to the air force command.

Department 54's head, Chang Su-gil, was placed in a difficult position after he received a report about this turn of events in Pyongyang. If he were to turn over the fishing base to the air force, Department 54 would be unable to export seafood, and the contract with China would be canceled. The project to build one hundred thousand apartments would run into problems, too. Chang went to the base and received a detailed report from the manager. He told the manager, "Wait a bit. I'll head to Pyongyang and reverse things," and then left. Chang's words suggest he had no idea he was headed to his death.

Then, as now, Kim's instructions came down as "policies" or "orders." However, these policies and orders were based on "proposals" issued by each department. With interdepartmental rivalries ever present, a single proposal often led to winners and losers. The losing institution often went to Kim Jong-il or Kim Jong-un and reversed things by making frank complaints. Cadres called this "setting things right," "reversing things," or "receiving new instructions." Kim was unaware of this.

Chang's promise to "reverse things" didn't mean he would disobey Kim's order. It meant he would go through Jang to get Kim to issue another proposal to keep Nampo Fishing Base under Department 54's management. However, a security guidance officer dispatched by the Defense Security Command (DSC) who overheard this comment reported it back to his agency. The DSC apparently believed it had an incident it could use to look good in front of Kim. They made it look like a big deal, reporting to Kim that Chang had told his subordinates that he would reverse his order. At the time, Kim was sending out feelers to see whether cadres looked down on him. He ordered Chang's immediate arrest and an investigation into the truth of the matter.

With no knowledge of what was going on, Chang—with Ri Ryong-ha, first deputy director of the Administrative Department—went to Pyongyang and met Jang. After listening to what the two men proposed, Jang was in a double bind. Logically speaking, Chang and Ri were correct, but he couldn't "reverse" a decision by his nephew, the supreme commander, in front of his subordinates. Jang decided he would explain the situation to the North Korean leader when he got a chance to meet him face to face, and he sent the men away, telling them to drop their proposal for now.

Not long after, Chang was suddenly arrested by the DSC. The DSC tried to figure out who he was planning with to "reverse" an order by the supreme commander. Chang simply told them the facts. He had nothing to hide. Chang was simply trying to get new instructions, as he always had.

Many cases similar to this one occurred in the foreign ministry as well. One time, Kim Jong-il visited the port of Nampo for an on-the-spot inspection. A port official asked that they be allowed to receive charges for cargo storage in foreign currency rather than North Korean won. Kim acquiesced to the change, and relevant instructions went out to all government agencies. The change was difficult for the foreign ministry to accept, however. Foreign aid was flowing into North Korea through the port of Nampo, and the foreign ministry told Kim that to ask aid organizations to pay for cargo storage ran counter to international practices. Thus, Kim ordered that humanitarian assistance be excluded from storage charges.

With the foreign ministry getting an exclusion from the new charges, the military didn't just sit back. The military reported that charging foreign currency to store its supplies could hold up preparations for war. The military also got Kim to sign off on an exemption, and other departments got new instructions as well, conveying them to Nampo's port authority. Around a month later, Kim's initial order to "unconditionally" receive storage fees in foreign currency had essentially become null and void.

Reporting the Chang case to Kim Jong-un, the DSC exaggerated the situation, making it appear as if there were a conspiracy among Chang, Ri, and Jang to launch a coup. All of Kim's pent-up anger with Jang exploded. If Jang had gotten to Kim before the DSC and calmly explained everything, the "purge of the Jang Song-taek gang" might never have happened. Excessive loyalty on the part of Kim's subordinates and agitation on the part of Kim—who was ignorant of how cadre organizations did their reporting—served as the springboard for the purge.

KIM JONG-UN'S LONG-STANDING RESENTMENT OF HIS UNCLE

Jang Song-taek was the husband of Kim Jong-il's sister Kim Kyong-hui. Kim Jong-un apparently harbored a deep resentment of his uncle from the time he was young. Ko Yong-hui knew better than anyone that if one of her sons, Jong-chol or Jong-un, did not become successor, their whole family would be purged. While Kim Il-sung was alive, she wanted her children to be recognized and allowed to greet their grandfather. Who prevented this from happening? Kim Kyong-hui and Jang Song-taek.

While Kim Jong-il was alive, Kim Kyong-hui and Jang Song-taek were said to have found Ko Yong-hui's existence quite a burden. That Ko and her children could never appear before Kim Il-sung was partly due to Kim Jong-il's wanting to hide them; but Kim Kyong-hui strongly opposed this, too. It appears Ko Yong-hui and Kim Kyong-hui did not get along very well.

Kim Il-sung once got angry at Kim Jong-il for leaving his legitimate wife, Kim Yong-suk, and fathering Kim Jong-nam with Song Hye-rim, saying it disgraced the family. Song had a daughter named Ri Ok-deol with her former husband, Ri Pyong-gwa. Jang Song-taek reminded Kim Jong-il of this, telling him never to bring Ko and her children before the elder Kim. Ko harbored resentment at Jang, and this naturally got passed on to Kim Jong-un.

Kim Jong-un has expressed rage that he has no photos taken of him with his grandfather, Kim Il-sung. A single photo would have been much more effective in making his case than calling out "Baekdu Bloodline" a hundred times. The same went for Ko Yong-hui. The "Mother of Songun Korea" had no photos taken with Kim Il-sung. I think Kim Jong-un hated Jang Song-taek from the time he was a child.

When Kim Jong-un assumed absolute power in North Korea, Jang felt insecure. Having been closer to Kim Jong-nam than Kim Jong-un, Jang knew of Kim's resentment and felt the threat to his safety. Many relatives of Jang had critical positions in the party, military, and trade sectors. In 2012, he had already gathered his relatives together and told them to "wrap up their business and get out" because "we could be the target of an inspection." In North Korea, "business" means vested projects.

I have a friend named Cho Song-kyu, a classmate of mine at Beijing Foreign Studies University. His wife is named Jeon Un-yong. Her father is Jang Song-taek's brother-in-law, the former North Korean ambassador to Cuba, Jeon Yong-jin. Jeon Un-yong was running a teahouse on Changjeon Street, Pyongyang's new downtown area. She said she invested eighty thousand dollars in the teahouse. I remember she once worriedly told me that Jang had told her to pack up the teahouse.

Jang could sense that things had changed dramatically. Up until the day Kim Jong-il died, he was a powerful figure who could save people facing death. In fact, Jeon Yong-jin was nearly executed on Kim Jong-il's order but survived when Kang Sok-ju told the North Korean leader that he was Jang Song-taek's brother-in-law.[1]

In early 1992, as North Korea was facing diplomatic isolation, Kim Jong-il ordered all embassies abroad to report back "creative plans" to overcome the problem. Kim stressed that there were no bad ideas, but nobody should have believed that because it was a special technique Kim used to learn what his subordinates really thought.

Most of the diplomats abroad knew what Kim was up to and acted like radical leftists, saying: "We should protect the red flag until the end. China's and the Soviet Union's recognition of South Korea is an opportunity to highlight our independent diplomacy." Only Jeon, then the North Korean ambassador to Sweden, sent a bold plan back to Pyongyang:

> Since the collapse of the Soviet Union, anti-communist sentiment in Europe has grown much stronger. Just the use of the term *communism* creates hostility. They say if North Korea doesn't reform and open itself like China, it will collapse like the Soviet Union. Even if we fly the red flag forever inside our country, we need to pretend to be less hard-line and more open. I propose that we avoid use of the term *communism* with the outside world.
>
> Moreover, I understand that Pyongyang residents appear lethargic. This is what all foreigners who have visited North Korea say. Let's let Pyongyang residents use bicycles. It will help present an image of busy streets and lively people. Europeans believe our system is rigid and won't last long, but if we promote that we, too, are reforming and opening, we can make people recognize the everlasting nature of our system.

It was a very realistic plan, but Kim Jong-il was furious. Using hateful language, he told Kang Sok-ju, "There are bastards who want to lower the red flag when things get bad. Nobody must use the words *reform* and *opening up*. Ambassador Jeon Yeong-jin is a bastard who is ideologically rotten to the core and afraid of attacks by the imperialists." If Kim called for Jeon's execution, there would have been no stopping it. Kang summoned the courage and informed Kim that Jeon was Jang Song-taek's brother-in-law.

When Kim heard this, his anger subsided a bit. However, Jeon was nonetheless summoned back to North Korea immediately and put to work on a farm. Because he was Jang's brother-in-law, he avoided the political prison camps and suffered a couple of years in the countryside. Jeon was then restored as head of the Committee for Cultural Relations with Foreign Countries and appointed ambassador to Cuba. He was purged during Jang Song-taek's downfall, however. Interestingly, Jeon's proposal gradually became North Korea's reality from the second half of the 1990s. The party decided not to use the term *communism*, and it allowed the use of bicycles outside of downtown Pyongyang.

Kim Jong-un's hatred, built up over decades, ultimately resulted in the cruel way Jang was executed. After news of Jang's purge was reported in the *Rodong Sinmun*, North Koreans dropped work to talk about Jang. Nobody went to the markets for three days. That's how shocking it was for North Korean society. They weren't shocked just because of Kim's merciless purge. It was also because the ruling that ended Jang's life unveiled the unseemly side of the Kim family, which had long been hidden from public view.

What North Koreans were most angry about was Jang's alleged womanizing. They were furious that he lived such a dissolute life—he was living with the daughter of Kim Il-sung, so what could he possibly lack? Jang's ruling said he'd had affairs with several women, lost millions of dollars gambling overseas, and even took drugs.

Rumors suggested that Jang's children were just like him. Several entertainers were arrested and disappeared after being named "Jang's women," including an actress that appeared in the film *The Stem Grows from the Root*. The head of the Obongsan Political Prison Camp, who was named a Hero of Labor, was also detained. He was charged with incinerating the bodies of women Jang had killed after having his way with them. Even the schoolmaster of Gumsong Senior Middle School in Pyongyang's Mangyongdae District was arrested on charges that he supplied young female students chosen for "Section 5" of the Central Committee for Jang to use as sexual playthings.

AS NEWS OF THE LEADERSHIP'S DEBAUCHERY SPREADS, PEOPLE START TO PREVENT THEIR DAUGHTERS FROM JOINING THE *GIPPEUMJO*

The incident led to a new trend of parents' trying to prevent their daughters from being sent to Section 5. In fact, "subject for Section 5" is a well-known term in North Korea. If we liken it to the Joseon Dynasty period, it's a group of court ladies who work in the palace. The organization can select the court ladies, and it has a national system stretching from the Central Committee's Organization and Guidance Department to the provincial and city party organizations.

Section 5 selects female students ages fourteen to sixteen. The selection process is tough, with medical exams, document screenings, and interviews. Selected girls receive specialized training depending on their job. These range from cultivating skills with musical instruments, vocal music, and dance to nursing, security, household management, and phones and communication. After receiving this specialized training, they are enlisted in the military and sent to the Supreme Guard Command, Bonghwa Hospital, and elsewhere. Especially beautiful students are sent to the Kim household as phone operators, typists, bodyguards, members of the *Gippeumjo*, or nurses.

Women in Section 5 cannot go home, nor can they see their families. You might wonder what kind of parent would send their daughters to such a place, but prior to the fall of Jang Song-taek, ordinary people were happy to do so because they would be granted special privileges. They would receive presents on North Korean holidays such as the New Year and Kim Il-sung's birthday. However, many party cadres and other elites did worry that their daughters might be selected to join the organization. I even saw parents who prayed their daughters would not grow taller or prettier.

Women selected for Section 5 usually retire at age twenty-six or twenty-seven. After they leave the unit, husbands are selected for them, depending on how closely they served Kim Jong-il or Kim Jong-un. Those that worked most closely with the supreme leader cannot reenter society and are married to officers of the Kim family's bodyguard. Those with less contact with the leaders are married to people working in popular professions in North Korea, such as diplomats, party cadres, and trade officials. To keep the work they've done secret, most women who leave Section 5 are sent to party schools and work in party organizations after they graduate.

In North Korea, we often praised beautiful women by saying, "You'll get selected to Section 5" or "You're Section 5 material." It's like saying "You're Miss Korea material" in South Korea. However, after the fall of Jang Song-taek, North Koreans came to learn that female students selected for Section 5 were secretly being used as playthings by the most powerful. Section 5 began to take on an increasingly negative connotation among North Koreans, rapidly growing numbers of whom believed the state must not take their pretty daughters away.

North Korean people witnessed the rotten, corrupt nature of the "Baekdu Bloodline" through Jang's corruption and scandalous behavior. The Kim family used the husk of communism and the dictatorship of the proletariat but ultimately built a society of oppression that should never have existed. I think Jang's purge will be the Achilles' heel of Kim Jong-un's government going forward.

AROUND TEN THOUSAND OF JANG'S ASSOCIATES ARE PURGED

The purge wasn't limited to Jang's household. *Rodong Sinmun's* use of the term "Jang Song-taek gang" suggests this. The party's Administrative Department and all other departments Jang controlled became wastelands, including Department 54, Bureau 9, and the General Bureau of Engineering Troops under the Ministry of People's Security. All of his close associates were purged, too.

In the party's Administrative Department, a deputy department chief and fifteen officials at section chief and above were executed, while another four hundred people were purged. Officials below the rank of section chief were dragged off to political prison camps with their families. It was the first time ever that an entire department of the Central Committee was completely purged, with nobody left standing. Even young staffers who delivered documents were shown no mercy.

About three hundred people were kicked out of Department 54, too. When Jang's ruling talked of him "selling the nation's resources to foreign countries at a pittance," it was referring to Department 54's monopoly on coal exports. Chang Su-gil, the head of Department 54 and deputy chief of the Administrative Department, wielded numerous privileges over coal, seafood, construction, construction supply production, and other sectors; he met his tragic end before Jang.

When Chang and Ri Ryong-ha were shot, North Korean high officials were stunned. Senior cadres in the party and military leadership were gathered that day at the firing range of Kang Kon Military Academy on the outskirts of Pyongyang. This was where high-ranking officials were going to be shot to death. The cadres were shocked. Instead of the usual AK-47 used during firing range executions, eight four-barreled anti-aircraft guns of a type they'd never seen before were set up. In front, a white cloth was hung up, and it appeared somebody was behind it.

A short time later, a bus arrived, and Central Committee secretaries, department chiefs, and deputy chiefs got off. Then a bus arrived with Administrative Department officials. Surprisingly, Jang got off that bus. Everyone was surprised to see Jang get off the bus with the ordinary officials; normally, he should have taken the bus with the high-ranking cadres. Maybe Jang's fate was already sealed.

From the podium, somebody read out the list of crimes by the "anti-party, anti-revolutionary elements" Chang Su-gil and Ri Ryong-ha and sentenced them to be shot. The white cloth was lifted. Chang and Ri were tied to stakes. The anti-aircraft guns blazed at the two men, and the high-ranking cadres watching went still. I heard they couldn't eat for days after that.

The Ministry of State Security's Bureau No. 9, which also oversees foreign-currency-earning activities, lost about two hundred people in the Jang Song-taek incident. When the state-run Haedanghwa restaurant in China began generating lots of money, Jang put the restaurants under Bureau No. 9 and built the big Haedanghwa Service Complex in eastern Pyongyang. Cadres at many other agencies, such as the General Bureau of Engineering Troops, were purged. Jang had gained control of North Korea's economy thanks to the countless construction projects he had been put in charge of. He was tasked with building the one hundred thousand apartments in Pyongyang, building a waterway from Nampo to

Pyongyang, and building Mangyongdae Street. Under Kim Jong-un, he handled the construction of Changjon Street and Mansudae Street.

Even diplomats serving at overseas legations could not avoid the purge. Jeon Yeong-jin, the aforementioned ambassador to Cuba; Jang Yeong-cheol, the ambassador to Malaysia and Jang's nephew; Park Gwang-cheol, the ambassador to Sweden; and Hong Yeong, the head of North Korea's delegation to UNESCO were dragged back to North Korea. Park Gwang-cheol was an in-law of Park Chun-hong, the deputy chief of the Administrative Department, while Hong Yeong was the brother-in-law of Administrative Department Deputy Director Ryang Cheong-song.

Around ten family members of foreign ministry officials were dragged off to prison camps, too: Jeon Yeong-jin's family, Jang Yong-cheol's family, Park Gwang-cheol's daughter, Yun Yeong-il's daughter, Kim Gang-rim's father-in-law, Vice Foreign Minister Han Song-ryeol's daughter, the son of Ri Hui-chol, the head of the Situation Data Bureau, the daughter and son-in-law of Kim Jeong-ae, the head of the Gobangsan Guesthouse. An estimated ten thousand people were sent to political prison camps, mines, and provincial areas as part of the Jang Song-taek purge. Many more people fell victim during this purge than suffered during the *Simhwajo* Incident of the late 1990s.

NORTH KOREA'S AMBASSADOR TO UK MOBILIZED TO RECALL UNESCO AMBASSADOR

On December 8, 2013, KCNA reported the results of an expanded meeting of the Central Committee. Later, North Korea's embassies received a list of sixteen people accused of being "anti-party, anti-revolutionary elements." It came with an order to remove their photos and "accomplishments" as soon as possible. The list was as follows: Jang Song-taek, Ri Ryong-ha, Jang Su-gil, Park Chung-hong, Choe Gum-cheol, Kim Dong-yi, Ryang Cheong-seong, Han Ryeong-geol, Gil Gyeong-nam, Jeong Seong-il, Choe Byeong-hi, Ahn Jong-hwan, Jo Won-beum, Ri Cheol-ho, Kim Gyeong-su, and Jeon Eung-ryeol. Of these, Ri Ryong-ha, Jang Su-gil, and Ryang Cheong-seong had been executed before Jang, while the rest were punished with Jang. North Korea committed one mistake, though. The list included an in-law of Yun Yeong-il, then the head of North Korea's delegation to UNESCO.

North Korea should have recalled Yun first and then sent out the list. Since a number of high-ranking diplomats had already been recalled, Yun could have tried to defect.

North Korea held a meeting on January 5, 2014, ordering only the ambassadors to the UK, France (UNESCO), and Germany to return to Pyongyang. It was a smokescreen to drag Yun back. Yun returned to Pyongyang with ambassador to the UK Hyeon Hak-bong and ambassador to Germany Ri Si-hong, but Yun was the only one detained. When the South Korean media got hold of images of Hyeon Hak-bong returning to the UK, they reported that he had avoided the purge.

My memory of this is fresh. Before returning to Pyongyang, Hyeon was quite agitated. To be called back to discuss measures to achieve Kim's New Year's Address was unprecedented. He guessed foreign ministry officials and ambassadors in major countries were being called in for talks because the political situation was so tense. Hyeon bought a new suit and dress shirt, thinking he might have an audience with Kim. He bought dozens of cans of breath spray to give to foreign ministry cadres. At the time, North Korean cadres used to avoid speaking to Kim because the North Korean leader seemed to hate bad breath. Ultimately, though, having gone to Pyongyang prepared in this way, he found it was just a smokescreen to recall Yun Yong-il. Hyeon was quite despondent.

When Hyeon returned to London, South Korean ambassador Im Seong-nam was happy to see him again. Hyeon and Im were longtime partners. Im led the South Korean delegation during the inter-Korean talks over light-water reactors. Whenever another country held a diplomatic event in London, the two would meet. Im greeted the ambassador: "I worried a lot because I thought something bad would happen when you went back. I'm happy you've returned safely."

All Hyeon could do was issue empty words. "What are you talking about? Why would I have been purged? North Korea is not a nation that just kills people. What you've said doesn't make me feel good."

Hyeon's conversation with Im was reported in its entirety to Pyongyang. Later, when Im was recalled back to South Korea, Hyeon asked him if he was to be promoted, "since every South Korean ambassador to London had been promoted." Im said he would have to go to find out, but within a couple of months of his return, he was promoted to vice foreign minister.

Hyeon said North Korea didn't just kill people, but I knew many of the people who were executed in the course of the Jang Song-taek purge. As this was a painful thing even for me, I shall briefly introduce some of them one by one.

Ri Ryeong-nam, the younger brother of Administrative Department Deputy Director Ri Ryeong-ha, was a classmate of mine at Beijing Foreign Studies University. He was the secretary of propaganda in the provincial party committee of Jagang Province when he was put into a political prison camp with his family. Ri Ryeong-ha's in-law, the foreign ministry's Political Data Bureau Director Ri Hui-cheol, was exiled to the Grand People's Study House. Ri Hui-cheol had been ambassador to Sweden, and his son was Ri Ryeong-ha's son-in-law. Ri Hui-chol's son, daughter-in-law, and grandson were sent to a prison camp.

Park Chun-hong, the deputy chief of the Administrative Department, was an in-law of Park Gwang-cheol, the ambassador to Sweden. Park Gwang-cheol had been exiled from the foreign ministry and was working in the people's committee of Pyongyang's Seosong District. His daughter was Park Mi-hyang, the lead actress in the North Korean film *The Schoolgirl's Diary*. That film had been shown at international film festivals. After her father-in-law was executed, she and her husband and young son were sent to a prison camp.

Administrative Department Vice Director Ryang Cheong-song's brother-in-law is Hong Yeong, the head of North Korea's delegation to UNESCO. South Korean media published images of Hong being recalled to the North. Ryang's entire family was sent to prison camps, and Hong was kicked out of the foreign ministry. He now works in a people's committee in a district near Pyongyang.

Even among those who were fortunate to avoid execution, there was much suffering.

Ri Ung-gil, the head of the European Bureau of the WPK's International Department, spent decades as Kim Il-sung's and Kim Jong-il's Italian interpreter. He was also very close with Jang Song-taek. You can easily find his photo on the Internet. Ri, his wife, son, daughter-in-law, and grandson were sent to a prison camp. Later, only his daughter-in-law was released. This was because the daughter-in-law's mother was the daughter of Vice President Rim Chun-chu, the comrade of Kim Il-sung from his days as an anti-Japanese partisan.

The daughter-in-law I mentioned above is the daughter of Han Song-ryeol, the director-general of the U.S. affairs department in North Korea's foreign ministry. Kim Gang-rim, the son-in-law of Ri Ung-gil, was dismissed as head of the foreign ministry's UK desk. However, he was not kicked out of the foreign ministry and now works as a researcher in the ministry's Situation Data Bureau.

Cho Song-gyu and Jeon Un-yeong and his wife and family—whom I mentioned earlier—could not avoid the prison camps. Cho's last official position was deputy chief of North Korea's tourism bureau. The case of Jeon's sister, Jeon Hye-yeong, is even sadder. Jeon Hye-yong is the niece of Jang Song-taek and the wife of the youngest son of Hwang Jang-yup.[2] When Hwang's entire family was sent to the prison camps, Jeon was the only one Jang saved. She later remarried, but this time she was sent to a prison camp because she was Jang's niece. Jeon Hye-yeong's and Jeon Un-yeong's father is Jeong Yeong-jin, who was arrested after serving as ambassador to Cuba. The wife of Jang Yong-cheol, the ambassador to Malaysia, played the leading female role in the North Korean film *Hong Gil Dong*. Jang Yong-cheol and his family are living in a prison camp, too.

HOW FOREIGN MINISTRY OFFICIALS AVOID BEING PURGED

The foreign ministry suffered less harm in the purge compared to other organizations. The relatives of punished foreign ministry officials were kicked out of Pyongyang, but the officials themselves enjoyed the benefit of remaining in Pyongyang. This is because the foreign ministry exercised its "wits," mainly thanks to First Vice Foreign Minister Kim Gye-gwan. When the ambassadors and ministers were recalled to Pyongyang, Kim made the following report to Kim Jong-un: "After the Jang Song-taek incident, several ambassadors were recalled in accordance with party measures. When they were to depart for Pyongyang, intelligence agents of the countries where they were based encouraged them to defect, telling them they could help them just by saying they wouldn't go back to Pyongyang. However, all the comrades returned to the Motherland, staring only at the sky of Pyongyang where the esteemed Great Leader resides. They are highly loyal comrades. Even if you force them out of the foreign ministry, please let them remain in Pyongyang to live."

Kim Jong-un ordered the authorities to do as the foreign ministry proposed. The foreign ministry officials expected to be exiled to the countryside, but instead they cried tears of thanks, as if they'd been to the gates of Hell and back. Gradually over time, however, they began crying tears of blood as they thought about all their children, siblings, and in-laws who were taken to the camps.

Unlike other agencies, the foreign ministry has never been subject to a sweeping purge. After coming to South Korea, I've been frequently asked about this: "Purges happen all the time in every government body in North Korea, yet only the foreign ministry's staff has remained the same since the 1990s. What's its secret?" I've frequently heard the same question in North Korea, too, from officials of other organizations.

Of the North Korean cadres who took part in inter-Korean dialogue, the only ones who have survived from the adoption of the North-South Basic Agreement of 1991 to the present are those connected with Kim Yong-chol, who visited South Korea during the PyeongChangOlympics. Kim Yong-chol took part in inter-Korean talks as a representative of the military.

Of the United Front Department lineup, Ho Dam, Yun Gi-bok, and Kim Jung-rin have died, from disease or old age. Kim Yong-sun and Kim Yang-gon died in suspicious traffic accidents without a single witness. Choe Seung-cheol and Han Si-hae, the deputy chiefs of the United Front Department, were shot, as was the deputy trade minister Kim Jeong-woo and Ministry of State Security Deputy Director Ryu Gyeong. Meanwhile, the vice premier and trade minister Kim Dal-hyeon, an economic official, was kicked out to the countryside and died of a mental disorder due to stress.

In North Korea, working on projects with South Korea means already having one foot in the grave. However, uniquely at the foreign ministry— at least since I joined in 1988—there has been a smooth transition of foreign ministers from Kim Yong-nam, Baek Nam-sun, and Park Ui-chun to Ri Su-yong and Ri Yong-ho. The first vice foreign minister post smoothly transitioned from Kang Sok-ju to Kim Gye-gwan. Vice Foreign Minister Kim Song-gi, who handled relations with China, was arrested by the Ministry of State Security, so it's not as if the foreign ministry never experienced a purge. Yet the organization itself was never subject to a sweeping shake-up.

The foreign ministry's secret is due to the nature of diplomatic activities. If you work at the foreign ministry, you come to know relatively well how the world works. You learn to read the Kim family's thoughts faster than others, and you don't do anything that earns their distrust. Here is an example.

When cadres of the Chinese Communist Party visited North Korea, they used to advise Kim Il-sung and Kim Jong-il that North Korea should reform and open up. The Kims would claim outwardly that North Korea could learn things from Chinese policy, but inwardly, they believed North Korea would be ruined if it did what China was doing. They would use subtle methods to determine what party cadres thought of China's policies of reform and openness.

WHEN ASKED ABOUT ECONOMIC REFORM, ANSWER CAREFULLY

The Kims asked institutions like the People's Economy College or the Academy of Social Science to present plans to reform North Korea's current economic structure. Cadres who did not know what the Kims really thought would present plans similar to China's. Kim Jong-il would criticize the plans as "revisionist," and the cadres would be exiled to the countryside. However, because foreign ministry cadres already knew what Kim Jong-il thought, they could avoid his wrath.

The tolerant attitude of foreign ministry officials is another reason people in the agency have survived purges. Traveling and working overseas on three- to four-year cycles, foreign ministry officials know better than anyone the irrationality inherent in North Korean society. Even if a coworker expresses discontent with the North Korean system, people just laugh it off. Unlike in other organizations with their "loyal elements," foreign ministry officials rarely report their colleagues to the ministry's party committee or the Ministry of State Security. Even when criticizing each other, officials do so in a gentlemanly way. They do not engage in Red Guard–style attacks as in other organizations.

More than anything else, foreign ministry officials do not unconditionally carry out impromptu orders by Kim Jong-il or Kim Jong-un. The foreign ministry has a strict way of doing business, sending written reports
and receiving approval from the top leadership. Kang Sok-ju received
many impromptu orders from Kim Jong-il. Unlike in other organizations,
however, he did not unconditionally carry them out with a "Yes, sir!" If
he carried out an order after careful consideration, he would write the
following document to Kim to receive approval: "We held discussions on
measures to execute the order the General sent. Everyone said it was a
wise policy and presented many good opinions to do this and that."

When Kim issued an unrealistic order, he composed the following
document: "This will be good if we do things according to the General's
order, but it could also cause this problem. Some people believe it might
be better if we do this." After receiving such a report, Kim would have no
choice but to think it over once again and order either to drop the previous instructions or to continue as is. Whatever the decision, the burden
on the foreign ministry was lightened.

In other organizations, teachings and utterances by Kim Il-sung or
Kim Jong-il were regarded as "orders from on high" and carried out
unconditionally. If carrying out the order resulted in a bad turnout, they
would have to take responsibility. They would be removed from the party,
sacked, or even executed. Park Nam Ki, whom Kim Jong-il ordered to
"stop inflation by replacing the currency," was shot. He doused himself—
and himself alone—in public discontent when he pushed the currency
reform without considering the downsides of carrying out the order.

Kim Jong-il once ordered the construction of many small power plants
to solve the country's electricity shortages. He did not consider the local
geography, and with everyone building small power stations, there was
chaos. Despite a huge, almost wasteful, use of cement and other supplies,
some regions did not properly produce electricity. After a general review,
those responsible were sacked.

It's not easy to establish a management system such as the one that
exists in the foreign ministry. Such a thing is possible only if there is
unspoken consensus between cadres and officials as there is at the foreign
ministry. In other organizations, one side calls for absolute loyalty and
implementation of orders, while the other side puts their lives at risk by
trying to determine the pluses and minuses of carrying out the orders.

WHILE ENDURING THE COMMUNIST PARTY
OF BRITAIN'S CRITICISM OF NORTH KOREA'S
HEREDITARY SUCCESSION, I AM ORDERED BY
PYONGYANG TO "AVOID GETTING CAUGHT UP IN
PROVOCATIVE DEBATES"

Three diplomats were chosen to work at the North Korean embassy in the UK, including the ambassador. Leaving aside the ambassador for the moment, I handled British matters, including politics, economics, society, trade, and defense, while another secretary handled the EU, Ireland, Belgium, and Luxembourg. We were overworked. I never slept before midnight. We worked on the weekends, too. In South Korea, you'd call it a "Monday, Tuesday, Wednesday, Thursday, Friday, Friday, Friday workweek." In North Korea, we called it a "Monday, Tuesday, Wednesday, Thursday, Friday, Saturday, Saturday workweek."

However, we could put up with the overwork. The hardest part was working with British socialist and communist parties. Outwardly, they supported North Korea. But when you got to know them personally and they opened up with you, they actually criticized the North Korean regime. There is a YouTube video that South Korean media outlets repeatedly published immediately after I defected. It was a video of me speaking and signing at an event by the Communist Party of Britain (Marxist-Leninist). Actually, the person I had the most ideological debates with was the leader of this party, Harpal Brar.

During the event to mark the hundredth birthday of Kim Il-sung on April 15, 2012, the portraits of Marx and Lenin were removed from Kim Il-sung Square. Brar was especially upset and critical of this, saying: "The North Korean revolution has a special character. I understand to some extent the leadership succession within the Kim family. But removing the portraits of Marx and Lenin that had been hanging for decades in Kim Il-sung Square is too much, no? No matter how much times change, and the limits of Marxist-Leninism made apparent, the philosophical roots cannot change. The Workers' Party of Korea's decision to take down the portraits of Marx and Lenin have disappointed communists all over the world."

There were no orders or explanations from Pyongyang on how to respond to his criticism. I sent a message to the WPK's International

Department with what he said, but all I got in return was an order to "avoid getting caught up in provocative debates."

Marxist-Leninism, as a matter of principle, condemns hereditary succession as a feudal remnant. We might seem proud of it on the outside, but it is impossible for North Korea—which claims to be a socialist nation—to be proud of a hereditary succession. What's more, it has already happened twice.

The passing of power from Kim Il-sung to Kim Jong-il happened slowly over a long period of time. Even North Korean citizens accepted it naturally. Socialist nations and left-wing parties in the West took a dim view of it, but they let it go, saying that such things could happen. Nobody felt particularly awkward about it, even with portraits of Marx and Lenin hanging in Kim Il-sung Square.

However, the succession from Kim Jong-il to Kim Jong-un came as a sudden shock to North Koreans. Everyone knew this was not something you could brag about to the world. In this situation, it would have been extremely awkward to leave the portraits up as they were. You could not hold events to mark a hereditary succession—something Marx and Lenin opposed—with Marx and Lenin looking on from their portraits. I thought if they had carried out events with the portraits still up, the Western press would have mocked them. How could I have explained this to Brar?

I could not avoid the issue of the Kims' portraits just because I was in the UK. The North Korean embassy in the UK hosted celebratory events with British left-wing parties on major North Korean holidays, such as the birthdays of Kim Il-sung and Kim Jong-il. According to North Korean regulations, you must hang portraits of the Kims in the center of the venues of such events. To receive recognition for holding the event, you also need to take a photo with the portraits.

Problems arose when left-wing parties set up the venue. There was sometimes friction over the issue of the Kims' portraits. The North Korean embassy would try to put portraits of the Kims in the middle of the venue, but the British Communist Party and other parties would not allow it. They said if you're going to do that, put them up next to the portraits of Marx, Engels, Lenin, and Stalin at the side of the venue. No matter how great Kim Il-sung and Kim Jong-il might have been, they asked us to follow the basic rule that their portraits could not come before Marx's and Lenin's.

However, the North Korean embassy could not accept this. We would be sacked if we did. So North Koreans would show up in their suits at the venue an hour or two early to nail some portraits to the wall. Having done this once or twice, we developed a knack for it. To avoid having to argue with British communists every time, we bought a hanging board. There were nails in it already, and we kept it on the minibus when we went to each event. When we attached a red cloth to the portable hanging board, the portraits looked great.

Officials from the Central Committee's Propaganda and Agitation Department came to the UK in September 2015 to carry out an ideological inspection of diplomats at the embassy. We could not simply report the attitude of British communists regarding the portraits of the Kims. Unfamiliar with the local situation, the Central Committee officials appeared to get what I was doing and were "deeply impressed." They even ordered diplomats at other embassies to learn from the loyalty to the Leader shown by officials at the embassy in Britain. What they needed to learn was not my "loyalty" but my know-how.

THE DRUDGERY OF GETTING CONGRATULATORY MESSAGES FROM EUROPEAN LEFT-WING PARTIES

Getting messages of congratulations from leaders of British socialist parties on every major North Korean holiday also proved difficult. These messages are used as tools to promote the North Korean regime through KCNA or KCTV. The broadcasts are used to show that the nations of the world are loudly celebrating North Korean holidays and the people of the world send their respect and admiration to Kim Jong-il and Kim Jong-un.

North Korean diplomats receive reviews regarding these messages. If the number of congratulatory messages falls during your review, you're questioned about it. The problem is that North Korea has too many holidays, which annoys British leftists. This is the list of holidays on which we had to obtain and send congratulatory messages for Kim Jong-un:

The first day of the year, the day the New Year's Address is announced, Kim Jong-un's birthday, Kim Jong-il's birthday and the celebratory rally, Kim Il-sung's birthday and the celebratory rally, the day Kim Il-sung published his collective works, the day the North Korean army was founded, the day marking the signing of the June 15 inter-Korean declaration and solidarity rallies, the day marking the outbreak of the Korean War and the organization of demonstrations in front of the South Korean and U.S. embassies, the day marking when Kim Jong-il began his work in the Central Committee, events marking the "victory" in the Korean War, events marking Korea's liberation from colonial rule, events marking the foundation of the DPRK, events marking the foundation of the KWP, and events marking the birthday of Kim Jong Suk.

On these days, we had to gather a few people together for a celebratory event and send celebratory messages to Pyongyang. British leftists were inevitably annoyed by this. Several complained, asking if they might be able to send all their congratulatory messages at once. Every time, we used to say the following to calm them down: "The nature of the Korean revolution is that it has progressed through the heightening of the revolutionary atmosphere through memorial days and celebrations. The revolutionary conviction and passion of the Korean people grows through these events. If British comrades hold celebratory events and send celebratory messages, these will be reported in the media and the Korean people will battle on even stronger."

The British leftists got used to how North Korea worked, so they drafted letters ready for each month. All they would do is just change the year on the letters. They worried, though, that the Soviet Communist Party came to ruin prioritizing this kind of formalistic ideological propaganda and that something bad could befall the WPK as well.

That some communist parties criticized North Korea more actively than right-wing parties was also hard to deal with. In the UK, there are several left-wing parties. The biggest is the Communist Party of Britain, led by Robert Griffiths. Its newspaper, the *Morning Star*, is the only English daily in the world that espouses a communist ideology. Through the 1970s, students at Kim Il-sung University and Pyongyang University of Foreign Studies (PUFS) used to read the paper a lot. This was because it did not criticize North Korea or the Soviet Union. However, the *Morning*

Star turned anti-Soviet with the Soviet invasion of Afghanistan in 1979, and later it took the lead in criticizing North Korea's hereditary succession.

The paper said Marxist-Leninism was the truth but attacked the Soviet leaders and Kim family for dirtying Marxist-Leninism under the cloak of communism. It even published a long article claiming that the Jang Song-taek execution would be the spark that led to North Korea's collapse. It was natural to be attacked by right-wing parties, but to be openly slammed in the official newspaper of the Communist Party of Britain, which once wielded great influence over the global communist movement, was a lot to bear.

"PURE-HEARTED" DERMOT HUDSON CALLS ME A TRAITOR TO THE REVOLUTION

North Korean diplomats must constantly create and send back to Pyongyang fake materials that make it seem like the world revolves around North Korea and that Pyongyang is the center of the global revolution. In my case, I would send back exaggerated reports that dozens or hundreds of people gathered to celebrate the birthdays of Kim Il-sung or Kim Jong-il. The North Korean media would then report that there were large-scale celebratory rallies in the UK. In fact, it was seven or ten old British communists gathered in a tiny basement in London. Even my parents, who knew little of the outside world, said they were surprised that there were so many pro–North Korean groups and individuals in the UK, a U.S. ally. They believed North Korea was the center of a world revolution.

As the party secretary at the embassy, I would encourage embassy staff several times a year to donate their salaries to publish the works of the Kim family. North Korean authorities investigate how many volumes of the Kims' works are published and how many of them are distributed, while providing no cash support to do so. If you fail to match expectations, you are harshly criticized.

With the money donated by embassy staff, I went to the publishing house of the New Communist Party of Britain to print five hundred or a thousand volumes of Kim Jong-un's works. I had to report to Pyongyang who had donated how much and how many volumes were published. The problem is what happened next. There was nobody in the UK to whom to distribute a thousand or so copies of Kim's works. Even if you sent them to British left-wing groups, they'd all end up in the garbage within a few days. We'd keep publishing works with the precious salaries of the embassy staff to report to Pyongyang, and those works would keep ending up in the trash.

People like Dermot Hudson are treasures to North Korea. A foreigner who appears frequently in North Korean media, Hudson is the chairman of the British Group for the Study of the Juche Idea, chairman of United Kingdom Korean Friendship Association, and president of the Association for the Study of Songun Politics. He writes pro–North Korean articles every day on his website. Sometimes he announces a statement of support for North Korea and writes letters to Kim Jong-un. The North Korean media report on him nearly every week.

He believes that North Korean socialism can be victorious and that North Korea will unify the Korean Peninsula. At least he seems that way to me. He has engaged in "solidarity activities" for decades in support of North Korea, but as a person, he often appeared pitiful.

Hudson had been an ordinary civil servant who evaluated real estate prices. He was sacked from his job because he made pro–North Korean statements in a phone interview with the Sunday *Times*. He lived a tough life on his small pension, but he was willing to do anything for North Korea.

In 2015, his mother died. Knowing what his circumstances were like, I asked Pyongyang to provide three thousand euros for the funeral. Through the 1980s, North Korea provided financial support to pro–North Korean figures. That support completely stopped in the late 1990s, when the Arduous March began. After Kim Jong-un came to power, North Korea demanded that pro–North Korean figures send gifts to the country. The government demanded that they send books or even grass seeds.

Surprisingly, Pyongyang ordered that the three thousand euros be given to him. When I handed the envelope to Hudson, he said he could not accept the money because he needed to support the Korean revolution. I pressed the envelope into his hands. "You are somebody who was fired while supporting the Korean revolution. We have to look after you, but we, too, are in a difficult situation so we can't do much. So, just this time, please accept the money as a symbol of our sincerity."

He teared up. I felt an inexpressible affection for him as a colleague, maybe because we were roughly the same age. A day later, he came to me and said: "I inherited the house after my mother died. After selling the house, my brother and I decided to split the money with each getting four hundred thousand pounds. I want to use some of the money to spread the Juche ideology around the world. Please convey my wish to Pyongyang."

This was a big deal. He was living in a council house with an eight-year-old son. The house was not even properly lit. If I reported what he said to Pyongyang, when they were struggling with no money to spread the Juche ideology, it was clear that they would immediately ask for the money. I tried to reason with him: "More than the money, we want you to live comfortably in Britain without worries. Our hearts break that we cannot help a comrade who suffered fighting for the Korean revolution, so we cannot take the money from the sale of your mother's home. It's best that you take that money and quickly buy a home."

He cried again. That summer, he ended up going to North Korea. I caught him as he was heading to Pyongyang and implored him: "If you go to Pyongyang, I hope you make absolutely no mention of donations. If you mention it, they will tell you to give up your money. If North Korea receives your money, then that will be it, but you and I will have to keep working [together] in England. I can't see you poor. Please don't talk about money."

He agreed, but I was worried that he would promise to make a donation when he went to Pyongyang. Before he arrived in the city, I sent a very specific message to my superiors: "Hudson is living in very difficult economic circumstances. Even if he mentions a donation, do not take it." It turns out he did talk about a donation when he was in Pyongyang. Fortunately, even high-ranking officials read the message I sent ahead of time, and they did not accept his money.

After I defected, Hudson was said to have issued a critical statement calling me a "traitor to the revolution." But I believe even he knew how I felt, how I always sympathized with him and sincerely worried about him. I hope he is no longer fooled by the North Korean regime and lives a happy life.

I PUSH FOR A PERFORMANCE
BY YOUNG DISABLED PEOPLE IN THE UK

In early 2014, I received a message from North Korea's Federation for the Protection of the Disabled. It asked me to get support for the federation from British civic groups. The organization hoped for support for its facilities and to obtain medicine and asked me to set up exchanges with British civic groups working on disabled people–related issues.

A thought crossed my mind. When I was the deputy director of the European Department in the foreign ministry, I'd been to the headquarters of the Federation for the Protection of the Disabled while preparing for a European table tennis tournament. I happened upon a rehearsal by an arts group of disabled teens. They were quite good. I wondered if perhaps it might be a good idea for an arts troupe of disabled teens to visit the UK. I thought it would give hope to disabled teens and improve North Korea's image.

I also thought about an experience I had in pushing North Korea's participation in the London Paralympics. If I put together a good proposal, I thought I could make an overseas performance by the disabled art troupe a reality. This was a time when global opinion about North Korea was quite bad following the February 2014 release of a report on North Korean human rights by Michael Kirby, chairman of the UN Commission of Inquiry on Human Rights in the DPRK.[3] The mood was that North Korea's human rights situation was even worse than Nazi Germany's persecution of the Jews or South Africa's apartheid.

Some nations claimed that Kim Jong-un, the chief human rights violator, should be tried in the International Criminal Court. There were even charges that North Korea isolated and exterminated disabled people. I turned the situation to our advantage in my proposal: "If a North Korea arts troupe of disabled teenagers visits London and Paris, the centers of global human rights opinion, it would contribute greatly to blunting the Western human rights offensive. It could also be an opportunity to demonstrate to the world the superiority of North Korean socialism by showing that North Korean disabled people suffer no discrimination but are treated well. We must use a performance by an arts troupe of disabled people to ease the anti–North Korean human rights offensive, which worsens by the day." I sent this proposal to Pyongyang. Of course, I didn't make direct mention in the proposal about what I was aiming to do. What I had learned from the process of promoting North Korea's participation in the London Paralympics was to politicize the issues I raised as much as possible.

In fact, I had another reason for writing the proposal. There were disabled teens who spent years practicing because they wanted to go overseas. They played accordion, danced, and sang. There were also devoted teachers who taught them. I wanted to promote their efforts to the world. Moreover, if an overseas performance by the arts troupe got reported in the North Korean media, it could give hope to the tens of thousands of disabled young people who spend their days at home in depression.

Ambassador Hyeon Hak-bong lent active support to my proposal. Not long after, a message conveying Kim Jong-un's approval arrived. We had Kim's approval, but what to put in the performance weighed on my mind. In North Korea, all performances, from adults to kindergarten students, needed prior approval from the party's Propaganda and Agitation Department. To get approval, performances need material promoting the Kim family and the North Korean regime. If this is the case for domestic performances, for overseas performances, it goes without saying such things were also necessary.

However, if a bunch of middle school students with sight, hearing, and mental disabilities came to the UK and held a performance extolling the North Korean regime, it would be better that they just not come at all. After several days' struggling with this, I sent a message back to Pyongyang saying the performance needed to appeal to the tastes of British and French people to be effective, with content they could instantly recognize.

There was no response, so I was worried, but a bit later I got a message from Pyongyang saying: "Taking into consideration the opinion of the delegation, we decided to make the content of the performance apolitical."

It was the first time a North Korean performing group had put on such an apolitical show, with dances from *Snow White and the Seven Dwarfs*, a vocal performance of *You Raise Me Up*, and an accordion performance of songs from *Phantom of the Opera*.

Preparations for the troupe's departure proceeded at top speed. When the parents of the disabled students were told to prepare for an overseas visit, apparently nobody believed it. It was difficult enough for fully abled people to visit overseas, so who could believe these disabled students were visiting not even China or Russia, but Britain and France?

In February 2015, when the troupe departed, there was a huge crowd at Pyongyang Station. Parents, relatives, and even neighborhood elders saw them off, with tears in their eyes. The moment the train departed, they shouted the obligatory "Long Live the Great Leader, Kim Jong-un!" The departure of the arts troupe was immediately reported on North Korean radio and TV and in *Rodong Sinmun*.

THE TROUPE'S APOLITICAL PERFORMANCE IS LED BY RI BUN-HUI, WHOSE SON IS DISABLED

I met the arts troupe in London. There were about twenty people, including the students who suffered from visual, hearing, and intellectual disabilities; the deputy head of the Federation for the Protection of the Disabled, Kim Mun-cheol; and the head secretary of North Korea's Sports Association for the Disabled, Ri Bun-hui. Kim graduated from the English Department of Kim Il-sung University before being assigned to work at the Federation for the Protection of the Disabled. He contributed much to improving the treatment of disabled people in North Korea. Ri is a North Korean sports hero who won a gold medal in the 1991 World Table Tennis Championships, forming a unified team with South Korean table tennis player Hyeon Jeong-hwa. Ri's husband is the North Korean table tennis star Kim Seong-hui.

Ri has a disabled son. She turned down a job coaching table tennis with the Central Athletics Team to join the Sports Association for the Disabled. She did so to give hope and dreams to young disabled people. Leveraging her fame, she formed a disabled table tennis team and hosts table tennis tournaments for the disabled almost every year. Ri is largely to thank for disabled people being able to take part openly in sports. If she had come to South Korea during the PyeongChang Paralympics, I could have seen her, even if at a distance, but disappointingly, she didn't make it. In fact, I worry that something may have happened to her.

The troupe gave performances in London and Paris from the end of February to the start of March. In the UK, they gave three performances at the University of Oxford, the Royal Academy of Music, and the University of Cambridge. In France, they performed at the headquarters of the civic group Secours Populaire Français and Institut National de Jeunes Sourds de Paris.

The BBC and other British media widely reported the arrival of the North Korean arts troupe and news of their performances. Some anti–North Korean politicians appeared on TV and criticized the performances as aimed to deflect from the human rights abuses of the Kim Jong-un regime. The British government, however, was largely positive.

Senior British foreign ministry officials met with the students and talked to them about the employment situation for disabled people within their ministry. They encouraged the young athletes, telling them that disabled people, too, could become diplomats. One blind member of the House of Commons explained in detail about his situation, saying he was engaging in legislative activity with little trouble, even though he could not see.

Countless South Korean expats and even a few defectors went to the performances. One old woman who defected from North Korea and now lives in Britain clasped the hands of the students, who were wearing youth league neckties, and shed tears. Another elderly woman grabbed the hand of a deaf student and asked, "I'm from North Hamgyong Province. Are any of you from there?"

At the opening performance, the South Korean embassy said it wanted to go to congratulate the troupe, but the North Korean embassy had to respond that we felt "a bit uncomfortable with this." Inwardly, we wanted to tell them to come, but there was a Ministry of State Security agent in the delegation. If there was contact between the South Korean diplomats and the delegation, the agent would clearly ask for details of the conversation. This could have led to trouble. Yet the performances themselves allowed participants to collectively express hope for Korean unification. After the second performance, the South Korean community of New Malden invited the entire troupe to eat. They passed the evening singing "Our Wish Is Unification."

At the North Korean embassy, at Ambassador Hyeon's suggestion, we gathered a month's salary from all the staff. The embassy had a lot to do, too. We took charge of the flowers and food for each performance. The children of embassy staff served as interpreters, and even my own son slept and ate with the troupe, serving as their eyes, hands, and feet.

"WHY DOES THE PLANE TAKE OFF FROM INDOORS?"

One of the delegation members was a blind female professor who taught *gayageum* at the Pyongyang University of Music and Dance.[4] She was a famous disabled performer in North Korea. She was so talented that she performed in front of Kim Il-sung when she was younger. She was over sixty, but the way she plucked those strings evoked sighs of lament. Though her hands had appeared on TV for quite some time, she never had any rings. Even if she had just a single jade ring, she would have seemed less forlorn. Ambassador Hyeon seemed pained by this. With the money raised by the embassy, we bought her a gold ring. All the students received watches and bags as presents.

As we accompanied the arts troupe, we discovered something surprising. One of the deaf students didn't know how to read Korean. We couldn't even imagine there would be somebody who couldn't read since there are schools for the deaf even in North Korea, beginning with elementary school. According to a teacher who accompanied them, schools for the deaf have poor equipment and food, and what's more, they are found only in rural locations. Because of this, parents with deaf children avoid sending them to schools for the deaf. They bite the bullet and send their children to nearby schools without hope they can give their children specialized education. That's why this deaf middle school student was illiterate. We were told that the situation at schools for the blind was the same. It was heartbreaking.

A blind student who played the accordion asked me the following question. I'll never forget it: "When we return to Pyongyang, I will tell the comrades how we took the plane. I thought that planes fly outside. But the plane I was on took off and flew inside. Why was this?" I was a bit stunned, but soon understood what he meant. When the student entered the terminal of Beijing Airport, he moved around only inside. He looked forward to going outside to get on the plane, but he just moved around inside, sat down and the plane took off. I explained everything to him. But he looked concerned, not knowing how he was going to explain this once he returned to Pyongyang.

The North Korean disabled youth had the first foreign tour of their lives and returned to Pyongyang with unforgettable memories. The visit was also more successful than expected. The North Korean media reported the return of the troupe: "The performance was an important opportunity to burst the bubble of the enemy force's anti–North Korean human rights uproar. Seeing the high-quality performance, the audiences learned the high level of education the disabled receive in North Korea."

Regardless of how it was reported on by state media, the visit by the disabled arts troupe to the UK and France, which followed North Korea's participation in the London Paralympics, gave disabled teenagers new hope. One foreign ministry coworker with a daughter who cannot walk due to congenital paralysis said to me: "My daughter really wants to go overseas. Could you introduce my daughter to the Federation for the Protection of the Disabled? Her piano skills might not be up to par, but since you are friends with cadres at the federation, could they put my daughter in a team that goes overseas to perform?" His daughter had loved literature from an early age and wrote well. She wrote a novel that was known even in China's Yanbian Korean Autonomous Prefecture. One ethnic Korean woman from the prefecture even wrote her a fan letter after reading her book. The letter said the main character in the book, who struggles with a mental disability, gave her confidence that she could make it through life, too.

The coworker told me that his daughter had suddenly asked him to buy her a piano. She said that no matter how well she wrote novels, she wouldn't be able to go overseas, so she would learn the piano. Unable to overcome her pestering, he bought her the piano, and she practiced eight hours a day. As a father, I could fully understand my coworker's feelings of regret and pity. I introduced his daughter to the federation. Since the federation was quite indebted to the foreign ministry by that time, it said it would meet with her and decide what to do. I don't know what happened after that.

KIM YONG-CHUL, THE HEAD OF THE GENERAL RECONNAISSANCE BUREAU, CALLS IN THE ACTING BRITISH AMBASSADOR AND THREATENS A TERRORIST ATTACK

With the execution of Jang Song-taek, the international media refocused their attention on Kim Jong-un's barbaric style of "fear politics" starting around 2014. Even at the UN, there were growing calls to put Kim Jong-un before the International Criminal Court. For North Korea, the human rights issue—which inevitably focused attention on Kim Jong-un—was a bigger pain to deal with than the nuclear issue.

Thinking of how Kim Jong-il would order officials to aggravate the nuclear crisis to draw attention away from the human rights issue whenever it came up, I expected Kim Jong-un to likewise use the nuclear crisis to cover up the human rights issue. I was not mistaken in thinking that way.

The North Korean nuclear issue worsened from that year, drawing the attention of the world media and even movie companies. In June 2014, America's Columbia Pictures released the trailer for *The Interview*. In August of that year, there was a report that Channel 4 in the UK was producing a TV drama series called *Opposite Number*, which dealt with the North Korean nuclear issue. Of course, it was the job of the North Korean embassy in London to report this news immediately to Pyongyang.

I translated Channel 4's press release and sent it back to the Ministry of Foreign Affairs. According to the press release, the series had ten episodes of an hour each. The plot was as follows: "A British nuclear scientist on a secret mission is detained after entering North Korea. Under duress, he takes part in developing North Korea's nuclear weapons, leading to an international crisis. The British prime minister must work with a U.S. president with very different political views than him to rescue the nuclear scientist."

Channel 4 did not mention when the series would air or who would appear in it. However, a diplomatic dispute emerged, one that even the North Korean foreign ministry or North Korean embassy in London could not have predicted. The policy bureau of North Korea's National Defense Commission issued a statement for foreign consumption condemning Channel 4's plan to produce the show as a "political provocation and intentional hostile act." Claiming that the show's plot was "absurd and reckless" by making it seem that North Korea's nuclear deterrent was the result of illegally stolen British nuclear technology, the statement said the production was taking place "with the connivance, protection and encouragement of the British Prime Minister's Office," and called for British authorities to suspend the production and punish the producers.

First, I should explain the background as to how this statement got released without even the foreign ministry knowing. Since North Korea adopted the policy of pursuing nuclear development and economic development at the same time, interdepartmental enmity had intensified. In particular, the military leadership intervened in diplomatic issues under the guise of the National Defense Commission. North Korean diplomacy was in a state of chaos for a while as a result.

Whenever a U.S. politician criticized North Korea, or when South Korea and the United States held joint military exercises, the military's Reconnaissance General Bureau (RGB) would issue a flurry of statements. The bureau made no attempt to conduct discussions with the foreign ministry in advance. When Kim Jong-il was in power, at least there was some kind of order; when the General Staff Department or Naval Command issued a statement, they had to talk with the foreign ministry first. From 2013, however, the military skipped over what they needed to do with the foreign ministry and issued statements in the name of the National Defense Commission. Their actions were part of a competition to win loyalty from the leader.

Foreign ministry officials asked themselves why the military leadership was doing this, but Foreign Minister Park Ui-chun and First Vice Minister Kim Gye-gwan could do nothing but look on. Given that Kim Jong-un wasn't even giving orders by phone at the time, the foreign ministry wasn't in a position to report to the leader about its opinions. From what we heard, the head of the RGB, Kim Yong-chol, had recruited good writers and created within the bureau a specialized department for producing all sorts of documents for overseas consumption. Kim Yong-chol is a military hard-liner who was named the "chief criminal behind the sinking of the *Cheonan*" by the South Korean press and South Korean politicians when he visited South Korea for the PyeongChang Olympic Games.

Things didn't end with the National Defense Commission's statement on the Channel 4 series. Kim Yong-chol called in the British ambassador in Pyongyang for a talk. The actual ambassador was on vacation, so he met with a woman who was the acting ambassador at the time. Kim handed her a letter of protest from the policy bureau of the National Defense Commission to give to the British prime minister. The letter said if the British government did not stop the production of the anti–North Korean TV show, an "unimaginable act of retribution" would take place within the UK, the responsibility for which would rest with the prime minister. In other words, they threatened to blow up Channel 4's headquarters.

This threat took place the day after the National Defense Commission's statement was released. The situation had just gotten worse.

THE BRITISH FOREIGN MINISTRY EXPRESSES SHOCK: "IS THIS SOMETHING THE MILITARY SHOULD BE INVOLVED IN?"

The British government was baffled at what had unfolded. North Korea's military leadership had gotten directly involved in the Channel 4 issue, calling in the British ambassador to openly threaten an act of terrorism in defiance of the most basic diplomatic common sense and practice. The British government called in Ambassador Hyeon and me. In fact, the RGB didn't even bother to tell the North Korean embassy in London what had happened in Pyongyang. Knowing nothing, we could not hide our shock when we heard the explanation from the head of the British foreign ministry's Asia-Pacific desk.

The head of the Asia-Pacific department showed us a copy of the letter that had been given to the acting ambassador by Kim Yong-chol and asked for official positions from the North Korean embassy regarding the following issues:

1.   Relations between nations are generally under the purview of foreign ministries. The military steps in when the foreign ministry cannot exercise its authority; that is, when things must be resolved by force. This being the case, do you think the time has come for the military leadership to directly intervene in bilateral relations?

2.   Unlike North Korea, the UK guarantees freedom of the press. In the UK, the media are beyond government control, and media produce content based on their own judgments. Neither the British government nor the North Korean government may interfere in the activities of the British media. North Korea's demand that Channel 4 stop its production is a direct challenge to British values that guarantee freedom of the press.

3.   A North Korean four-star general, Kim Yong-chol, directly summoned the acting British ambassador in Pyongyang and demanded the suspension of the production of a TV program. Please clarify whether this

was an independent act by the military leadership or an act with the prior agreement of the foreign ministry.

4.   The North Korean military leadership declared that if the production of the Channel 4 drama wasn't suspended, it would carry out terrorism. We demand you reaffirm whether this is the exact position. Without a position statement from North Korea abandoning terrorism, the British government would have no choice but to show the Reconnaissance General Bureau's letter to the world. This could result in a very bad outcome, such as North Korea being redesignated a nation that supports terrorism.

5.   If North Korea forswears terrorism in the UK, the British government can quietly resolve this matter without revealing the letter.

Listening to what the British official was saying, we were so stunned we couldn't talk. We asked to meet again after reporting back to Pyongyang, and took our leave. The British official called for a quiet resolution to the matter, believing that the military leadership, unaware of how diplomacy works, had made the threats out of excitement. We reported to Pyongyang, and the next day an order arrived saying: "Just convey North Korea's position that it opposes all acts of terrorism. Don't say anything else and resolve the problem quietly."

Ambassador Hyeon could only meet with the head of the UK Asia-Pacific desk and parrot what he had been told. The British official asked if he could take the ambassador's statement as a refutation of terrorism against Channel 4, and whether he could take Kim Yong-chol's terrorism threat as the position of a single general, not that of the North Korean government. However, Ambassador Hyeon simply repeated that it was North Korea's consistent position to oppose all terrorism. The British official stopped pressing the matter, said he would take the ambassador's notice as a refutation of terrorism against Channel 4, and said he would bring the matter quietly to a conclusion. That's how this uproar came to a quiet conclusion.

WE MAKE A THREAT OF TERRORISM AGAINST A SALON MOCKING KIM JONG-UN'S HAIRSTYLE

With Kim Jong-un coming under global attention, another shocking incident occurred. On the afternoon of April 14, 2014, the North Korean embassy in London was somewhat busy because it was Kim Il-sung's birthday. We were rushing around participating in study groups and lectures about Kim Il-sung's greatness and selecting congratulatory messages to send to Kim Jong-un. Returning to the embassy after lunch, Choe Geun-song, the deputy chief of North Korea's delegation to the International Maritime Organization, told me that there was a photo of Kim Jong-un hanging at a beauty salon near his home. He said a photo that showed the country's "Greatest Dignity" was being used as an advertisement. With nobody in the embassy stepping forward, I—the party secretary—and Choe went to the salon together.

The salon was within three kilometers of the embassy. It was on a street corner Choe's children used when they went to school. The advertisement in the window had a picture of Kim Jong-un and the following ad copy: "Bad Hair Day? 15 percent off for male customers!"

A few months earlier, the global media reported that Kim Jong-un had ordered male university students in North Korea to wear their hair short on the sides like him. The owner of the salon took notice of the report and created an ad lampooning Kim's hairstyle to draw customers. In the UK, people use photos of the queen or prime minister in ads, but for a North Korean diplomat, this was intolerable. If we didn't take any action and this was found out, we'd get sacked.

I used a camera and a camcorder to record the exterior of the shop and Kim's photo, standing in the street within the shop owner's vision. This was to put psychological pressure on the owner. The owner was watching us even while cutting hair. After confirming the owner's disquiet, we entered the shop. When two men in suits and ties carrying a big camera walked in, the tension was obvious. I said in a threatening tone: "Are you the owner of this shop? Do you know who the person in that ad photo is? That's the Great Leader Kim Jong-un, the supreme leader of North Korea. We came from the embassy of the DPRK. North Korea is a nation that starts wars if you mess with the 'Greatest Dignity.' It seems you did this because you didn't know, so take down that photo immediately. If you don't, you'll be fully responsible for what happens. When we speak nicely, it's best to listen."

Trembling, the owner immediately took down the photo. We solved the problem quietly, and we walked out of the shop. We heard the owner scream at us to our backs: "This is a free democracy. Did you expect what you do in North Korea to work with me?" We pretended not to hear and returned to the embassy. The owner reported the matter to the police, perhaps because he felt a terrorist threat, and told the local press. That evening, the *Evening Standard* ran the first report of the incident. Within a few hours, the entire world's media—including South Korea's—were talking about how North Korean diplomats threatened a British hairstylist and that North Korea was a country that conducts nuclear tests if you mess with the "Greatest Dignity." The next day, British university students gathered in front of the North Korean embassy and shouted slogans: "Kim Jong-un, don't force your hairstyle on university students! North Korean embassy, respect British values!"

Instead of a celebratory parade for Kim Il-sung's birthday, we had sparked a protest. After giving interviews with the press, the proud owner of the salon rehung the photo of Kim Jong-un. A few days later, I went again to the shop. Perhaps because he was afraid he'd be a victim of North Korean terrorism, the owner appeared to have taken the photo down again. From Pyongyang, an order went out to all overseas legations to learn from the "loyalty of the staff of the North Korean embassy in the UK." Every time I think of the image of the hairdresser trembling at my threats, I really feel sorry for him.

THE MYSTERY MAN BEHIND THE "DANGEROUS" KIM JONG-UN–DENNIS RODMAN MEETING

In December 2014, an urgent message came from Pyongyang. It was like receiving an order to start an urgent operation: "Promptly meet with Colin Offland, the president of Chief Production, a British documentary film production company. He's producing a documentary about Dennis Rodman's visit to Pyongyang. Get from him the first cut and send it to Pyongyang by diplomatic package."

NBA bad boy Dennis Rodman was a famous U.S. basketball star known for his eccentricities and bad behavior. He visited North Korea several times between February 2013 and January 2014, meeting with Kim Jong-un. Before receiving the urgent message, I had no idea a British production company was filming a documentary about his visits to North Korea.

Who arranged the visits is still shrouded in secrecy. Some foreign news reports claimed they were set up by Kang Sok-ju, but this is groundless talk, little more than conjecture based on nothing except the fact that Kang was standing next to Kim when he met Rodman. Kim was reportedly a fan of Rodman, but inviting him to North Korea was something that shouldn't have happened, at least based on foreign ministry standards. Anybody would know that putting a "bad boy" next to the so-called "Greatest Dignity" was dangerous. This strongly suggests that the meetings weren't the foreign ministry's doing. In my view, it was the work of somebody who was close to Kim but had little experience working with the outside world. It seems this mysterious person knew that Kim was a fan of Rodman and wanted to make a news story of the "friendship" between the two to show the world Kim's human side. That Kim approved this proposal also provides a glimpse of his diplomatic perspective.

The Rodman invitation cannot be viewed separately from the December 12, 2012 launch of the *Unha 3* satellite and North Korea's third nuclear test two months later, on February 12, 2013. This was when the world was boiling over with criticism of North Korea and Kim. Rodman's first visit came at the end of February, right after the first nuclear test following Kim's rise to power, and was aimed at diluting the negative opinion of the North Korean leader resulting from the nuclear test.

Appearing laughing, clapping hands, and embracing with Rodman, Kim said athletic exchanges such as these "would contribute to promoting understanding between the DPRK and the United States." He tried to promote an image of himself as a very open leader, despite the fact that he had carried out a nuclear test. Kim's attempt was successful to a certain extent. The international media was confused, and a spokesperson for the U.S. State Department declined to even issue a statement about the visit.

Rodman visited North Korea twice more in 2013, and repeated that Kim was not a dictator but a "good man." From Kim's perspective, it was an advertisement that killed two birds with one stone: it dissipated world anger at the nuclear test, and it improved his image. Kim leveraged Rodman's usefulness as much as he wanted. In December 2013, when world opinion was again in an uproar over the Jang Song-taek execution, Rodman made his fourth visit to Pyongyang. Ostensibly, Rodman was invited to help celebrate Kim's birthday, but it's easy to understand what the hidden intention for the visit was. Rodman sang happy birthday in front of Kim and tens of thousands of Pyongyang residents.

When Rodman came under fire, the Irish gambling company that funded his trips to the North canceled their contract with him. I was quietly watching all this unfold in London when that urgent order suddenly came in from Pyongyang. I was a bit worried. I called Colin Offland of Chief Production and told him to "bring the first cut of the film to the North Korean embassy if it's completed." Offland came to the embassy the very next day and asked me: "It had been agreed for me to bring the first cut of the film to Pyongyang myself, so why am I not allowed to enter the country, and why am I being told to just send the film?" At the time, North Korea was forbidding all foreigners from visiting the country because of the Ebola virus. When I explained this to him, he didn't press the matter further and turned over the first cut of the film. There was no news from Pyongyang for several days after officials there had received the film. I didn't think there was a problem.

"IN THE SPIRIT OF PROTECTING THE SURYONG TO THE DEATH, PREVENT THE SHOWING OF THIS ANTI-DPRK FILM"

In January 2015, another order came from Pyongyang. It was a long order that said:

The first cut produced by Offland is entirely anti-DPRK. This runs counter to the agreement between us and Chief Production. In particular, there's a scene of Jang Song-taek being arrested at the beginning of the film. Rodman's visit to Pyongyang was not an ordinary foreigner's visit. It was an important visit related to the external prestige of Supreme Leader Kim Jong-un. The photo of Jang's purge is something that could damage Kim's external prestige. The film is scheduled to show at the Slamdance Film Festival in the United States, but it will be a major problem if the film is shown as it is. Meet with Offland at the embassy [in London] and make sure to get him to remove the photo of Jang. You must do this in the spirit of protecting the Suryong to the death. Use all means and methods if Offland doesn't listen, including threatening him with lawsuits.

I called Offland to the embassy and, when he arrived, an argument ensued:

Didn't you say you would consult with North Korea before releasing the film? Take the photo of Jang's purge out of the film. It can't go out that way to the Slamdance Film Festival.

It was North Korea that refused my visit due to the Ebola virus. If it hadn't been for that, I would have gone to North Korea and consulted [on this issue]. And now, world attention is on Jang's execution. If we don't deal with it, the film won't be recognized as reflecting reality. Moreover, the photo of Jang appears only for a second at the beginning of the film. It has nothing to do with the general flow of the movie. We've already submitted the film to the Slamdance Film Festival, and plan to show it at the end of January. There's no time now to edit the film.

You promised to consult with North Korea. If you don't keep your promise, we will have to take legal measures. Are you OK with getting sued?

I did agree to that, but I didn't give North Korea editorial rights. There is no such thing in the contract, either. If you're going to sue, do so. I will make these facts public through the press.

When Offland came out this high-handedly, I could respond no further. Whoever told Kim to invite Rodman appears to have had no experience dealing with foreigners. This mystery person trusted Offland too much, merely in the hope of making a film that praised Kim. This person didn't even draft a contract that gave North Korea the final editing rights. That's why he or she was trying to dump the responsibility for cleaning up the mess on the embassy.

I reported the conversation with Offland to Pyongyang. I added the following explanation, however, since I could not take entire responsibility for the matter: "When working with Western countries, you must make written contracts. This is especially true with films that deal with sensitive matters. It was a mistake from the very beginning to make a film without a contract that specified both sides' obligations. Even if you threaten a lawsuit in this situation, the other side won't budge."

Pyongyang came out swinging, too. They sent out another order, this one telling us to bring Michael Spavor, the head of Baekdu Cultural Exchange, to London to solve the problem. Spavor had visited North Korea with Offland to produce the film. Spavor ran Baekdu Cultural Exchange, a nonprofit operating in China's Yanji region. I called him to London, and he arrived several days later. Spavor, too, pleaded several times to solve this dispute: "I have nothing to do with the film production. Nor did I set up Rodman's visit to North Korea. I just participated in Rodman's visit to the North as a consultant. I asked Offland several times to remove the photo of Jang. I have to continue working with North Korea going forward, too. I must say this again: This film has nothing to do with me, so please leave me out of the dispute."

By this time, things were winding down. I reported what Spavor had said to the foreign ministry, and this time they ordered me to stop the film from showing at the festival "without fail," along with the phrase "in the spirit of protecting the leader to the death." We tried threatening Offland and getting the film edited, but in the end, the film was screened at the Slamdance Film Festival in January 2015 and won awards at several later film festivals.

In the end, I got away just with criticism that I couldn't achieve results through the "spirit of protecting the leader to the death"; however, somebody in Pyongyang was probably seriously punished over the incident. This ended Kim Jong-un's "basketball diplomacy" with Dennis Rodman. Kim didn't meet Rodman again until June 2017, when he was allowed to visit the North for the fifth time. Offland's film, titled *Dennis Rodman's Big Bang in Pyongyang*, ran on South Korea's TV Chosun the same month.

THREE JOURNALISTS DETAINED AMID NORTH KOREA'S EFFORTS TO STOP THE BBC FROM STARTING KOREAN-LANGUAGE RADIO PROGRAMMING

Having long had plans to open a bureau in Pyongyang, the BBC was looking for an opportunity to do so. The news agency couldn't just stand there watching as APTN, which had opened its Pyongyang bureau in

2002, kept broadcasting North Korean news. In 2015, the BBC earnestly began sounding out the North Korean embassy in London about opening a bureau in Pyongyang.

However, we got wind that the BBC also planned to start a Korean-language radio service from 2017 in tandem with opening a Pyongyang bureau. Korean-language broadcasts were, from North Korea's perspective, no different from a declaration of war against the country. Foreign media that put out Korean-language broadcasts included China Radio International, Voice of Russia, NHK, Voice of America, and Radio Free Asia. North Korea had little issue with Chinese and Russian broadcasts. The others, however, all carried programming critical toward the North Korean regime.

The BBC, as a public broadcaster, was quite different from APTN. APTN simply broadcast news with almost no commentary or editorials. The BBC was the opposite, and most of its programming was critical toward North Korean policies. We concluded that if the BBC began a Korean-language service, it was ultimately intended for a North Korean audience.

Following orders from Pyongyang, Ambassador Hyeon and I took turns visiting BBC headquarters to persuade the BBC to stop plans to start a Korean-language service. We told BBC officials, "All radio broadcasts aimed at North Korea thus far have been those that support America's hostile policy against the DPRK. If the BBC takes part in this, it will harm the authority, fairness, and objectivity of the BBC. Additionally, BBC journalists would forever be banned from visiting the DPRK."

In response, BBC officials told us, "Our broadcasts are not aimed at the DPRK, but rather for Korean-speaking people who reside on the Korean Peninsula and China's northeast. The programming will include news, culture, and sports, and we do not intend to run programming critical of the DPRK."

From North Korea's perspective, however, the act of informing its people about conditions in the outside world was itself a threat that would lead to collapse of the regime. The country could not accept the Korean-language service because it considered the BBC's soft power more lethal than physical weapons. To stop or at least delay the BBC from starting its Korean service, North Korea decided to leverage the BBC's desire for a bureau in Pyongyang. We told the BBC that North Korea would approve the opening of a bureau in Pyongyang if the news agency stopped plans to start the new Korean service. We also told them that they would have to use North Korean journalists, just as APTN did.

As these negotiations were happening, three BBC journalists visiting North Korea, including Rupert Wingfield-Hayes, were detained in late April 2016. They were accompanying officials from the International Peace Foundation and Nobel Prize laureates to promote exchanges of science and technology with North Korean universities and planned to cover the Seventh Party Congress set to convene in early March. Wingfield-Hayes provoked the North during his visit by describing Kim Jong-un as "corpulent and unpredictable."

The Seventh Party Congress was a major event, the first party congress in the thirty-six years since the Sixth Party Congress in 1980. Countless foreign journalists were either in Pyongyang or scheduled to arrive. If we permitted one journalist to "slander" Kim Jong-un, other journalists could follow suit. If that were to happen, things could spin out of control, throwing a wet blanket on the celebration the country had worked so hard to prepare for.

North Korea detained Wingfield-Hayes and the other two journalists, scaring them for a couple of days before sending them off on a plane. The BBC demanded an apology from North Korea for detaining its reporters, while I visited the British foreign ministry and BBC headquarters to issue protests to the British government and the broadcaster. A battle ensued, with both sides demanding an apology. Ultimately, the talks over the BBC opening a bureau in Pyongyang broke down. The BBC began a radio service aimed at North Korean listeners from August 2017. When the talks with the BBC ruptured, Stephan Evans, the BBC's Seoul correspondent, was very disappointed. He is also a friend of mine. We'll have to wait and see whether North Korea ever permits BBC journalists to visit the country, but it seems unlikely for the time being.

THE PASSWORD SENT FROM THE THIRD-FLOOR SECRETARIAT

In March 2015, I got a surprise phone call from a colleague at the North Korean representative office in France. Aware he might be bugged by intelligence agencies, he spoke in vague terms: "Comrade Thae, a request for something has come in from the father of a woman who works on the foreign ministry's fourth floor facing Kim Il-sung Square. I've sent an email with the request, so read it carefully. If you read it while thinking of your name and the official document you see every time you go abroad, you'll understand."

I thought about what he said for a while. I tried to put the puzzle together one word at a time. First, the "foreign ministry's fourth floor facing Kim Il-sung Square" meant the party committee. The foreign ministry headquarters is shaped like a square, and the party committee and cadre department were on the fourth floor, overlooking the podium of Kim Il-sung Square. When the party committee calls you in for a talk, bad things happen. On the other hand, when the cadre's department calls you in to discuss something, good things happen. In my experience, more bad things happen than good things. If someone makes a mistake and gets called by the party committee, they say "I need to go to the fourth floor." That's why the party committee was nicknamed "the fourth floor."

The "father of the female staffer" was Baek Sun-haeng of the Third-Floor Secretariat. At the time, there were only two female staffers in the foreign ministry's party committee. One of them was older than me. There was no way I'd know her father. The other one was a young staffer who'd just gotten married. She was the daughter of Baek Sun-haeng. Accordingly, Baek's "request" came from the Third-Floor Secretariat. In short, this request was an order from Kim Jong-un.

Baek graduated from the French Department of the PUFS. He entered the school seven years before I did. Proficient in French, he was sent to the North Korean trade delegation in Paris in the late 1970s. He came to Kim Il-sung's attention by arranging then Socialist Party chief François Mitterrand's visit to Pyongyang. After returning home, he entered the WPK's International Department, and from the late 1980s, he'd been tasked with taking care of Kim Jong-un and his family from the Third-Floor Secretariat. He oversaw everything when Ko Yong-hui went to Paris for medical treatment, too.

Meticulous and a known perfectionist, Baek continued to assist directly with Kim Jong-un's affairs from the Third-Floor Secretariat even after Kim assumed power. When Dennis Rodman visited North Korea, he was the figure who was standing right next to Kim. Between 2004 and

2008, when I was a counselor at the North Korean embassy in the UK, I had to work a lot with Baek. I contacted him when purchasing supplies in the UK to send to Pyongyang. One time, we tried to import a British horse, but failed.

With a racing heart, I opened my email, and there was a strange email there with an attached, password-protected Word file. Now it was time to unravel the meaning behind "my name and the official document I see every time I go abroad." It was a request to put together the English spelling of my name and my passport number. When I entered my name "thaeyongho" and my passport number as the password, the Word file opened.

The message was simple. It said to respond if I opened the message, and when sending documents, encode them using the English spelling of my name and the date. I responded, and another email arrived less than five minutes later. After exchanging messages like this several times, Baek, who was in Pyongyang, called my mobile phone directly. He also spoke in code. The code had grown more complicated. He said from the next email, I should use "the ambassador" first followed by "me." I won't divulge here the specific way I figured out how to do that.

This is how I communicated with the Third-Floor Secretariat—or, to put it another way, with Kim Jong-un's office in the Central Committee. The Third-Floor Secretariat didn't use the state-run telegram system because there was a matter that even foreign ministry cadres should know nothing about. If they used the state-run telegram system, not only would foreign ministry section chiefs, bureau chiefs, the vice minister, the first vice minister, and the minister know, but even the decoder who figured out the password would know. Baek's first order to me, sent by this highly secret and complicated process, is below.

THE BEST SEATS AT THE ERIC CLAPTON CONCERT

"This is a special matter pertaining to the personal safety of the Suryong. Neither the ambassador nor your own family must know about this. On May 20 and 21, there will be an Eric Clapton concern at the Royal Albert Hall in London. Prepurchase six tickets for the best seats. Four seats in the center, and two seats on the sides."

The only person who would come to the UK from North Korea to see an Eric Clapton performance was Kim Jong-chul. In the past, North Korea's leadership had pushed for a Clapton performance in Pyongyang, but this time was different. I had to carry out a mission direct from the Third-Floor Secretariat, a mission related to the "Baekdu Blood Line." I shall describe in detail my "sixty-one hours with Kim Jong-chul," as well the preparations that went into it, because I believe they provide an unobstructed view into the North Korean regime.

First, I let Ambassador Hyeon know that Kim Jong-chul was coming to the UK to see the Clapton concert. This ran counter to the order forbidding me from informing the ambassador, but if Kim came, Hyeon was bound to find out anyway. There were many instances in which North Korean diplomats clashed with their ambassadors when they carried out missions from the Third-Floor Secretariat independently, without reporting it to their bosses. To prepurchase the tickets, I would have to go to the concert venue, but since it was forbidden to go out alone according to embassy rules, I would have to tell the ambassador why I was going. This, too, allows one to catch a glimpse of how the North Korean regime works.

When I printed out a copy of the order from the Third-Floor Secretariat and showed it to the ambassador, he got extraordinarily nervous. I immediately raced to the concert venue. The best seats had already been turned over to middlemen. I returned to the embassy and purchased the best remaining seats I could find. But what did the Third-Floor Secretariat mean when they asked me to break up the seats between the center and the sides? I thought they were trying to ensure that Kim could move to one of the sides if the view from the center wasn't good. The meticulousness gave me a chill.

The second order I received from the Third-Floor Secretariat was to reserve two suites at London's Savoy Hotel. The Savoy is one of London's top hotels. The Third-Floor Secretariat wanted no ordinary suite, but one with two bedrooms separated by a living room. This meant that attendants were to wait in the living room in case Kim suddenly wanted something, ready to take care of his needs immediately.

I couldn't make a reservation based just on photos I found on the internet. I went to the Savoy to see the rooms with my own eyes. Suites with living rooms were more than two thousand euros a night, and they were booked out way in advance. I said I'd pay more, but the hotel said no. Two thousand euros was far more than two months' salary for me. I was stupefied and angered. I don't care how many rich people there are in the world, but over two thousand euros just for one night in a hotel?

When I reported to the Third-Floor Secretariat that the rooms were all booked, I got a new order to reserve a suite with a view of the Thames. Of course, there had to be a living room in the suite. I was easily able to find a suite with a living room and one bedroom. Yet it was almost impossible to find a suite with a living room and two attached bedrooms. I went to all the luxury hotels located a bit outside of downtown. I barely found a place, the five-star Chelsea Harbour Hotel, north of the Thames in central London. I reserved a suite along with two separate rooms. Suites at that hotel went for anywhere between KRW 2.5 million and KRW 4 million a night.

My third mission for the Third-Floor Secretariat was to select and report ten sightseeing destinations in London. I selected Trafalgar Square, the London Eye, Buckingham Palace, and other sights in London, squeezing in Parliament as well. I wanted to explain to Kim how British parliamentary democracy worked. At the time, the British ran an annual program to train twenty North Korean civil servants in the UK for a month. A visit to Parliament was a must. Upon seeing the prime minister and opposition lawmakers jeering and screaming at one another, North Korean civil servants couldn't understand at all what they were looking at: "If you attack the head of the government like that, what happens to the government's authority? Can Britain maintain its position as a major global power?" I hoped Kim didn't think this way.

When I sent photos and explanations of the sightseeing locations back to the Third-Floor Secretariat, I was then ordered to recommend some well-known restaurants. Making less than a thousand dollars a month, I had no way of knowing about such places. Searching on the internet, I selected a Japanese restaurant, a French restaurant, and an Italian restaurant, as well as a restaurant with nice scenery and a dinner cruise with views of the Thames. Apparently the Third-Floor Secretariat was dissatisfied with these, so I was ordered to reserve a table at the restaurant in The Shard and at a Spanish restaurant. The Shard is the tallest building in London.

"KIM JONG-UN SPECIFICALLY ASKS FOR COMRADE THAE YONG-HO"

Toward the end of April 2015, a "selection team" came to London. The three-person team consisted of Jang Ryong-sik, the deputy chief in charge of arts in the Third-Floor Secretariat; Kim Ju-seong, a staffer with the WPK's International Department; and the head of the Ministry of Culture's Bureau for Arts Exchanges.

Jang Ryong-sik, who served as an aide to Kim Jong-un on arts-related matters, performed the final screenings for all performances Kim saw. His name card said he was the head of the State Merited Chorus of the Korean People's Army, but in fact, he worked in the Third-Floor Secretariat. Most of his colleagues with whom he studied music in Moscow in the 1970s had been executed or sent to prison camps. The only one still surviving was Kim Il-jin, the head of the Mansudae Art Troupe.

Kim Ju-seong was a staffer with Section 8, a part of the WPK's International Department that managed Kim Jong-un's interpreters. A graduate of the English Department of PUFS, he went through the university's simultaneous interpretation center and worked as a section chief in the foreign ministry's translation bureau before entering Section 8. He'd done an embassy training program in London in August 2014. Less than a year later, he returned to London as part of the selection team.

The head of the Ministry of Culture's Bureau for Arts Exchanges was someone I had never met before and knew nothing about.

From the day after he arrived in London, Jang Ryong-sik began taking me around. In the day, we went to London's music shops, music schools, and music libraries, while in the evening, we took in musicals and orchestral concerts. Thanks to him, I got to see *Les Misérables*, *Miss Saigon*, and the BBC Symphony Orchestra.

Jang came with a list of albums to buy in London. It included concerts, music festivals, operas, and musicals, and he tried to buy them all. You had to order most of them through the internet, but there were also many you could get for free from YouTube. I gave him the notebook computer and USB I used and advised him to download things for free. He didn't understand what I meant. When I taught him how to download things from YouTube, he copied dozens of files while sleeping just two or three hours a day.

One day, he was smoking in the backyard of the embassy. He seemed deep in thought, so I asked him why. He expressed surprise at the power of the internet. "If I had the internet in my office, I could watch every world-famous performance," he said. I couldn't believe that the man who advised Kim Jong-un on arts-related matters had never used the internet before.

What this meant was that Kim Jong-un, who used the internet every day to access South Korean material, did not provide internet access even to his own "music teacher." Jang seemed to be in a really pitiful position. Yet the only thing he knew was music. After getting hooked on music through the internet, he didn't sleep properly. Jang told me that he happily spent all night listening to music. He visited South Korea during the PyeongChang Olympics as director of the Samjiyeon Band. I wonder what he must have thought when he saw Seoul's busy streets and South Korea's development.

One day Kim Ju-seong gave me a hint of what had happened. "You must perform this task well. Kim Jong-un has great faith in you. He specifically asked about your life." This meant that Kim Jong-un was looking into me. When I asked how this came to be, Kim Ju-seong shared the following with me. Allow me to dramatize what happened.

Kim Ju-seong was preparing for the London visit when a phone call came from an operator in the Central Committee. The operator said, "The Respected Comrade Kim Jong-un wants to talk with you."

To get a phone call directly from Kim Jong-un was a great privilege.

"This is Kim Jong-un."

Kim stood up and answered: "This is Kim Ju-seong, staff member of Section 8 of the WPK's International Department."

Kim Jong-un then asked: "Is this Kim Ju-seong? Have you been to London?"

"Yes, I have."

Kim Jong-un asked specific questions, such as how many foreign ministry officials worked at the North Korean embassy in London, what the ambassador and minister were like, how their English skills were, and how well they knew London. Then he asked for Kim Ju-seong's opinion: "I have an important task to give the London embassy. Who should I give it to?"

According to Kim Ju-seong, the North Korean leader seemed to be going through a list of people in an official document. Kim said, "I think it would be best to entrust it to Deputy Ambassador Thae Yong-ho." The North Korean leader then responded, "You think so, too? Understood." Then he ended the call.

Kim Jong-un had directly checked on me like this, but a year later, I defected from North Korea. Basically, I betrayed Baek Su-haeng and Kim Ju-seong, who vouched for me, as well as Kim Jong-un, who believed in me.

As the day of Kim Jong-chul's arrival approached, Ambassador Hyeon ordered that the embassy be cleaned. A thorough cleaning was carried out of the embassy grounds, the offices, and even the inside of the residences. Every corner. Even the wives of the embassy staff helped repaint the place. The plates and cups in the embassy cafeteria were inspected. We crafted specific plans for what to prepare if Kim wanted to come to the embassy and eat together. Up until this point, only Hyeon and I knew Kim was coming.

In early May, the Third-Floor Secretariat contacted me. Three people had applied for visas to the British embassy in Pyongyang, and I was ordered to negotiate with the British side to expedite those applications. The three applicants were Baek Su-haeng, the Moranbong Band guitarist Kang Pyeong-hui, and the head doctor of the Byeonghwa Clinic. All three were set to accompany Kim. Kim Jong-chul's entry into the country didn't present much of an issue. The British embassy in Pyongyang only issued a visa after a conducting a fingerprint and iris scan. Needing to use an assumed name while traveling abroad, I heard that Kim visited the embassy in person.

I went to the head of the Asia-Pacific desk of the British foreign ministry to discuss the visas of the other three. The British official already knew Kim was visiting. He said he would cooperate as much as possible, saying: "If you need something, let us know ahead of time. And if there is somebody from the British government he'd like to meet, we will prepare in advance." I reported this back to Pyongyang, adding my own comments as well: "The British side seems to have guessed who is coming and for what. Would it be better just to ask the British side for official protection? We asked for protection when Vice Foreign Minister Choe Su-hyeon's delegation visited London to open the embassy in 2003. They provided about ten security guards and two armored cars."

However, the Third-Floor Secretariat sent back this reply: "There will be no official meetings with the British government. If we request protection, the visit becomes official. Under no circumstances must it become official." The secretariat ordered us to use a rental car instead of the ambassador's car to take Kim around. It also ordered us to buy three analog-style mobile phones and several mobile Wi-Fi devices for Kim and his entourage to use. It seemed to me that this was aimed at ensuring that Kim Jong-un could communicate with Kim Jong-chul or his entourage at any time.

MY SIXTY-ONE HOURS WITH KIM JONG-CHUL

Kim Jong-chul and his three attendants arrived in London from Moscow on May 19. It was 9 P.M. The ambassador and I went to meet him at the plane door. Sitting in first class, Kim was the first to get off. We bowed at ninety-degree angles, along with the simple greeting of *sugohasipnida*.[5] He seemed very tired.

Everyone packed light, so there was no need to wait at baggage claim. We got right into our vehicle. Sitting in the car, Kim said, "Let's go to the HMV music shop on Oxford Street." It was close to 10 P.M., and it was about an hour away. It was already closed. Politely, I suggested that since it was already closed, it might be better to go the next morning. Nearly pleading, Kim made a request: "I thought of only that music store on the flight to London. If it's closed, can't you just knock on the door or call to open it? If a diplomat asks, won't the owner come? Don't you have that kind of network?"

I was in a pickle. London was not Pyongyang. If I banged on the door, the police would show up, but I couldn't say that to Kim. I said: "Understood. We shall go to the shop first." Kim's entourage all knew he was asking the impossible, but nobody told him.

It takes about two hours to go from Heathrow Airport to Oxford Street, which is in the city center. It would be 11 P.M. by the time we got there. Looking at his watch, Kim asked me again, "Will they open their doors?" This time I summoned the courage to say: "We can go and see, but it'll be impossible." Sighing, he asked to go to the hotel. Located on the Thames in West London, the Chelsea Harbour Hotel was in the opposite direction from Oxford Street. When I asked the British driver to take us to the hotel, he sighed as well and turned the car around.

We arrived at the hotel and put down our bags. Kim called me and asked that his pants be laundered immediately. He had spilled wine on them on the plane, and he had no extra pair. His hand luggage was completely empty. It was 1 A.M. I asked the hotel about laundering his clothes, but they said we'd have to wait until morning. In fact, I didn't even need to ask. I could have asked the hotel to name their price to do the laundering, and it would have made no difference.

Again, I offered some "polite" advice to Kim: "It's night time, and there is nowhere to get your pants washed. I think it would be best to buy a new pair of pants to wear in the morning and leave these pants for the laundry." When you report to Kim Jong-il or Kim Jong-un, you must never use the phrase "Let's do [something]." You always have to use expressions like "It seems," "I think," or "I thought."

Kim said, "Are you trying to say there are no twenty-four-hour laundromats in London? I love these pants. I don't want to wear another pair." I said I understood and took the pants with me. Outside the hotel, Ambassador Hyeon and Secretary Mun Myeong-sin were waiting. Choe Gun-seong and Yu Gwang-seong from the International Maritime Organization were standing on alert at the embassy.

Hyeon and Mun said they would visit every laundromat in London. At 4 A.M., Mun returned to the hotel. Fortunately, he had found a large laundromat and gotten the pants cleaned. Looking at the clean, stain-free pants, I thought to myself, "Well, things get done when the WPK makes up its mind." Now, when I recall this time, I feel only unhappiness and pity over the ridiculousness of it all.

Kim was wide-eyed when we handed the pants over to him in the morning. Though he had told us to launder them without fail, he was still surprised and asked, "You really got them cleaned?" When he asked if we searched all night for a laundromat, I said, "We found a laundromat after mobilizing all the comrades at the embassy." He was very thankful and put the pants on immediately. I had no idea he'd be so happy. He then asked us to gather around.

Pulling a bottle of whiskey from the minibar, he gave a shot to me and his entourage. He then told us to *Jjung naera*, a North Korean phrase similar to South Korea's "one-shot," or "bottom's up!"

His attendants did not refuse and drank, but I could not. Today was just like the first day of battle, and I couldn't get drunk. If I didn't keep my wits, it would be the end of the London embassy. Finding courage again, I told him: "If I get drunk, today won't go well. I won't drink this." Nonetheless, Kim told me to drink, saying, "Are there [really] diplomats who can't drink?" I pretended to drink a bit and put the glass down, thinking to myself, "You have to know how to drink well if you're to protect the leadership of the revolution."

I then told him I would pour him a drink but, unexpectedly, he refused. Apparently, the day before he left Pyongyang, he drank too much when he went to visit somebody. He then told me that the person suggested they have a drink when they weren't drinkers themselves.

Whom did Kim visit? And what kind of person would offer him a drink? I was curious. When cadres go overseas, they must visit their superiors to say goodbye. This is North Korean practice. The only person Kim Jong-chul would say goodbye to is Kim Jong-un. And the only person who could ask Kim Jong-chul to have a drink is also Kim Jong-un.

I couldn't put it all together. As far as I know, the entire Kim family likes to drink. Kim Il-sung and Kim Jong-il had said the entire family was born with "the DNA to drink." If Kim Jong-chul's "somebody" was Kim Jong-un, it meant that Kim Jong-un wasn't a drinker. While publishing photos of Kim Jong-un and Dennis Rodman drinking together, the foreign press said Kim drank lots of wine, whiskey, or cognac every evening to overcome his fears. To hear that the very same Kim Jong-un can't drink was hard to believe. It's still an unsolved mystery from that day.

TEARS COME TO KIM JONG-CHUL'S EYES AS WE SING "MY WAY"

While Kim Jong-chul's entourage was sitting around drinking and talking, Baek Sun-haeng had turned on the computer and was reporting something to Pyongyang. Baek was always writing reports in his small notebook. I think it was a random number chart with secret password combinations and jargon. Intelligence agencies could look at it every day and still not make out what it was saying.

A bit later, Baek reported to Kim, "I've finished making my report to Pyongyang. We've been ordered to proceed as scheduled." Kim said we should go to the music store. We spent the morning of May 20 buying music recordings. I suggested to Kim that we have lunch on the cruise boat on the Thames. It was a good choice when visiting London. However, Kim said he didn't want to do the cruise and suggested we have a simple bite to eat anywhere. I brought Kim and his party to the restaurant in The Shard. The restaurant served high-end cuisine, but Kim did not eat much.

Something awkward happened during the meal. After just a few bites, Kim said he would go out for a smoke. The restaurant is on the thirty-first floor. If Kim went down to the first floor to smoke, his entire entourage had to follow him. That was a tough thing to do, but nobody told him no. Again, I bit the bullet: "You have to go to the first floor, but I think it will take time to catch the elevator." Kim said he would take a few puffs in the bathroom and stood up. Embarrassed, I rushed after him. He entered a bathroom stall and lit up. I was scared a fire alarm would go off. A bit later, a non-Korean entered the bathroom. He could have informed the restaurant. I said to him, "I'm sorry. My friend is a chain smoker, and he lit up just to take a puff. Please forgive us this once." He laughed and said OK, just like a British gentleman.

Kim was true to his word. After a few puffs, he tossed the cigarette in the toilet. At that moment, I thought of Kim Jong-un, who smoked everywhere, even in hospitals and kindergartens. Kim Jong-chul said he would smoke everywhere in his four days and three nights in London, regardless of time and place. Before he got in the car, he would need to smoke. Even after he got in the car, he would need to smoke every 30 minutes. I asked the driver if he could let him smoke in the car. The driver said smoking was banned, and he would need a special car wash to remove the smell, but that was expensive. I said I'd provide the money he needed, and the driver happily agreed.

After Kim was allowed to smoke in the car, he was very happy. Without thinking, I began to hum. I didn't know which song. Then Kim asked me to sing a song. After pondering a bit, I sang a song I liked, Frank Sinatra's "My Way." When I started, Kim was so excited he started singing along. I couldn't remember the words, but he sang the first and second verses. But his eyes teared up a bit as he sang "My Way." At that moment, I felt compassion for him.

The car arrived at Parliament. I had been determined to include this on the itinerary. In front of Parliament are statues of Churchill and Gandhi side by side. I explained their worldviews to Kim, including the tolerance of the British that allowed them to put a statue of Gandhi in front of Parliament. I enthusiastically explained the British political structure and how Parliament worked. Kim didn't seem to care much, however. Oh no, I thought, was he displeased with what I said? I was a bit frightened as this thought crossed my mind.

The next stop was the London Eye. When I said we would go there, Kim suddenly asked if there were any neighborhoods with music shops in London. Mentioning some guitar brand, he said he wanted to see if the shops carried it. This was something I hadn't realized ahead of time. He'd come to see a guitarist's concert, and I regretted I hadn't guessed he would be interested in this ahead of time. I asked the driver, and he said there was a world-famous street of music shops in London. He said it was called Denmark Street and laughed that he didn't know why it was called that.

As soon as we entered Denmark Street, Kim was ecstatic, as if he'd gotten everything he'd wanted from the world. He went into a guitar shop, picked up a guitar he liked and did some impromptu playing. He was quite good. He was so good the shop owner—who appeared to be in his thirties—asked Kim what his name was and if he'd ever released an album. The two then played together. Most of the shop owners on the street were in their thirties and forties. Many of them were professional guitarists who ran shops during the day and played in pubs in the evening.

Unfortunately, they didn't have the guitar he was looking for. The owner suggested a small village about a hundred kilometers from London. He said they had the guitar he was looking for. Kim was very disappointed and had to satisfy himself with buying lots of guitar accessories. Kim talked with the owner for a while about Eric Clapton. Knowing nothing about guitars, I understood nothing. I asked Kang Pyeong-hui if Kim played in Pyongyang, too. She said he formed a band and often put on shows.

It was already getting close to 5 P.M. To see the Clapton concert, we needed to arrive at the venue one hour ahead of time. It was time for dinner. Since he was so dour at lunch, we didn't bring him to a high-end restaurant. Instead, we asked him what he wanted to eat. Unexpectedly, he said he wanted to have a McDonald's hamburger. When I said I'd order from McDonald's, he said he'd do it himself. Watching how much he enjoyed that burger, I could only think, "If I'd known, I'd have brought him to McDonald's before."

At around 6 P.M., we arrived at the Royal Albert Hall. At the shop at the entrance to the venue, Kim bought Clapton memorabilia, including T-shirts, cups, key rings, and albums. He bought a lot of it. I was looking through this and that at the shop when Baek approached me. "Let's quickly enter the concert hall," he said. "Somebody is snapping photos from behind a column." I thought he was overreacting. I looked around, and it didn't seem like anyone was paying attention to us.

Kim sat in the middle of the hall, while I took a seat on the side. I paid attention to ensure I could respond immediately if Kim asked to change seats in the middle of the concert. The concert began, but I couldn't concentrate even one moment. With binoculars, I kept an eye on the surroundings, worried that somebody might approach Kim. He seemed entranced by the concert. He didn't leave his seat and clapped enthusiastically. Kim was so excited he raised his fists, too.

His excitement didn't seem to abate when he returned to the hotel. He also wanted to drink. It was no different from an order. We emptied the minibars in each room of their liquor and beer, bringing them into my room. We drank all the alcohol in the minibars that night.

KIM CLUTCHES A GUITAR HE BOUGHT IN A SMALL TOWN

I passed out after drinking all night, but got a phone call in the early morning of May 21 from Ambassador Hyeon. In an upset voice, he urged me to look quickly online: "The Japanese media sighted Kim Jong-chul. They photographed him buying souvenirs at the entrance and him cheering during the concert. The global press is talking about Kim's attendance at the Eric Clapton concert, not to mention the South Korean and British press."

When I looked online, I found he wasn't wrong. The gist of the reporting was that Kim, having lived a secluded life for years after the death of Kim Jong-il, was now freely traveling the world. His entire entourage was nervous. Kim Jong-un had clearly seen the reports. There were no orders from Pyongyang. I don't think Kim Jong-chul got any calls to his mobile phone, either.

He would have to return if he was told to go back. It was important for Kim to make a decision. Baek asked him in a roundabout way about whether it was a good idea to see the other concert that day, but Kim was defiant: "I've come this far, so am I going to return without seeing the [next] concert just because of those petty journalists? I'll definitely see the show."

Baek fired off a report to Pyongyang. With no new orders, we decided to begin the itinerary for the third day. That morning we were to head to a small town the shop owner on Denmark Street had said would have the guitar Kim wanted. It seemed a bit strange that such a small town would have a guitar shop. Kim worried that we were wasting our time, but when I checked the internet, I found there was no reason for doubt.

We left immediately after breakfast. It was a tiny town, but it had a massive two-story guitar shop. According to the owner, many professionals came there to buy guitars. Having found the guitar he wanted so badly, Kim held it close. It was a U.S.-made electric guitar, but I don't remember the name. As far as I could see, it didn't seem to be that rare a guitar.

Kim complained to me, "I sent messages to several embassies about buying this guitar, so I wonder why nobody could find it." He strapped on the guitar and played for about forty minutes. Kang Pyeong-hui joined in, too. I didn't know much about guitars, but it seemed like a pro-level performance. Baek said he would pay for the guitar, but Kim paid for it himself. It seemed there was some delineation in how money was spent. The food and concert costs were paid by the Third-Floor Secretariat, but Kim appeared to pay for his own private items, despite it all being money from the same coffers.

The guitar cost about GPB 2,400. It didn't seem too expensive, yet it seemed just right for Kim's particular tastes. I offered to carry it for him, but Kim strapped it to his shoulder and held it to his chest even in the car. It was like a father hugging his young child. He really loved it. He kept telling me thank you. I also felt happy for no particular reason.

Baek seemed to have received a new order from Pyongyang. "Go to today's concert as planned," he said. "There's no doubt reporters will be camped out at the venue, so you must go in a disguise. Buy sunglasses and hats." I suggested then that we should ask the British government for official protection, but Baek didn't budge. We mustn't do this, he said, because if we asked the British side for protection, this would make Kim's visit official.

After buying sunglasses in a glasses shop, Kim asked to go to a children's clothing shop. He'd be a "bad dad," Kim said, if he came all the way to London and didn't buy children's clothing. We took him to the Selfridges Department Store on Oxford Street. Kim's entourage also had things to buy. I took care of Kim, while Mun Myeong-sin took care of the entourage. Baek advised that I not stick too closely to Kim when he selected items. He said Kim didn't like other people to know what he was buying. Taking this advice, I showed Kim where the children's clothing shop was and watched from a distance. Baek, meanwhile, went down to the basement and purchased several bottles of high-end liquor such as vodka and scotch.

After a quick bite to eat at the hotel, we all went again to the Royal Albert Hall. There were reporters camped out at every entrance. We had to force our way in. We parked our car at the entrance with the fewest reporters. We tried to get out quickly and enter the venue, but journalists immediately swarmed around. That night, the sight of Kim and me entering the performance hall was broadcast to the entire world.

Even the performance hall was filled with reporters. Flashes went off everywhere. The star of the show wasn't Eric Clapton, but Kim. I couldn't concentrate on the concert this time either, but Kim was just as relaxed as before. He enjoyed the concert without any expression of concern. When the concert ended, reporters gathered around him. Outside the venue, crowds began to gather.

We were surrounded by reporters in the hallway of the venue. We were helpless, but then some burly British bodyguards appeared. They created a path through the reporters and guided us through. The British authorities, which had been watching quietly, had rushed security personnel to the scene, thinking people could get hurt if things continued this way.

KIM JONG-CHUL IS A MAN WITHOUT A TITLE, JUST KIM JONG-UN'S MUSIC-LOVING BROTHER

We did as the security guards instructed. We went to an underground parking lot where ordinary cars were forbidden to enter. We got in our car, and as soon as we left the underground parking lot, reporters began snapping away. We made it to the hotel, but we were equally exposed to reporters there, too. There were even broadcast cameras at the entrance of the hotel. Now we couldn't even enter the hotel.

After a discussion, we decided that the embassy staff would remove the luggage left in the hotel and we would relocate to the outskirts of London. We got rooms at the Holiday Inn near Heathrow Airport. Perhaps because things had again become relaxed, Kim collapsed on his bed as soon as he entered his room.

Getting out of the UK was also tricky. Knowing that Kim had arrived in London through Moscow, reporters were waiting at the airport exits for planes to Moscow. I negotiated with the airport to use the VIP lounge early in the morning. The airport allowed us to use the VIP lounge and agreed to let Kim and his entourage board later than anyone else, forty minutes prior to takeoff.

Kim and his entourage got on an Aeroflot flight that departed at 10:40 A.M. on May 22. Before getting on the flight, Kim grabbed my hand. "Comrade Deputy Ambassador, you really did a great job. When you return home, I'll definitely treat you to a grand meal. Make sure to find me." I parted with him, saying, "Let's meet again." This was the last moment of the sixty-one hours I spent with him.

Kim did not speak to me in *banmal*.[6] He always used the respectful title "Comrade Deputy Ambassador." Yet I never called him "Comrade Kim Jong-chul" or "Comrade General." Nor did his entourage tell us to call him by those titles. Whenever I needed to say his name, I would instead first start with "Um . . ." before saying what I was going to say.

We had to call Jang Song-taek's daughter Jang geum-song "Comrade General" or "General Elder Sister." But Kim Jong-chul was a person without a title. Even his entourage didn't use a particular title toward him. There might be many people who think Kim Jong-chul helps Kim Jong-un, but if this were so, he would need to have a job title and a form of address. The Kim Jong-chul I saw was just a person obsessed with music and guitars. He was just the son of Kim Jong-il and the elder brother of Kim Jong-un.

When we returned to the embassy, there were reporters camped out in front of the building, too. They didn't know Kim Jong-chul had already left for Moscow. With all the fatigue building up, I could only think of sleep. I hadn't told anyone Kim was coming except for the ambassador, but now even the children of embassy staff knew that Kim had come and gone from London. It's an unwritten rule of North Korean society that you don't talk about or ask about the Kim family. The embassy people were waiting for me to talk about Kim. When I got home, my children said coldly: "They said Dad went somewhere, and it turns out you went to show Kim Jong-chul around."

In North Korea, if someone completed a major task like what I did on Kim Jong-un's direct orders, it was cause for praise. Nobody would blame you for being proud. I thought my children would think their father was a great person and would be curious about this and that. But my children were more perceptive, saying: "Ordinary people cannot listen to rotten capitalist music, and if you listen to foreign songs, you even get expelled from university. While forcing the people to endure the Arduous March, the Kim family does whatever it wants. Does it make sense that he would waste thousands of dollars a night while listening to decadent Western music?"

My children couldn't repress their outrage. A new generation was forming, one completely different from our generation that viewed the Kim family as "god." I was suddenly ashamed that I had assisted Kim Jong-chul for several days. In the end, it turns out it wasn't anything to be proud of. It was like a prisoner taking care of a prison warden. My wife didn't praise what I'd done, either. I think the people at the embassy thought more or less like my wife and children.

A few days later, an official message arrived from the North Korean foreign ministry. It said the embassy in London had successfully carried out an important task. I think Kim Jong-un praised the embassy's work. Yet I felt as though I shouldn't walk around proudly because of it.

I HELP A REUTERS JOURNALIST BANNED FROM VISITING NORTH KOREA ENTER THE COUNTRY

Ahead of the Seventh Party Congress in May 2016, I got a call from Reuters' Seoul correspondent James Pearson. He had applied for permission to enter North Korea with Beijing-based Reuters photojournalist Damir Sagolj; however, only Pearson was allowed to enter, while Sagolj was denied permission. Pearson asked me to help Sagolj enter the country. In short, a Reuters reporter in Seoul had asked the deputy ambassador of the

North Korean embassy in London for help. It might seem a bit strange, but Reuters is a British news agency, and I'm friends with many British journalists, so it was natural that such requests would come my way.

Sagolj was a world-famous photojournalist. It was clear that if he were denied entry to North Korea, many journalists around the world would criticize the measure. North Korea had never approved a visit by a reporter after initially turning it down, but I asked why he was on the blacklist. Pyongyang responded by saying Sagolj's photos taken in North Korea were all over the internet, but they were very hostile to the North Korean regime.

I looked at his photos on the internet. There were photos of North Korea's backward farms and children in rags. Yet those were the kind of photos even tourists to North Korea could take. You couldn't call them "hostile." I sent the following opinion to Pyongyang: "After considering Sagolj's photos, they cannot be considered hostile. They might be slightly negative, but the internet is full of photos of that kind. You need a more persuasive reason to block a journalist from Reuters, a globally reputable agency, from entering the country. If we stop a reporter from entering without presenting such a reason, we'll end up turning our backs on Reuters."

Though he made the request, Pearson wasn't optimistic about Sagolj being allowed into North Korea. He hung his hopes on me, a friend of his, on the off chance that I could get him in. A day after I made my report, Sagolj's entry permit was issued. After I defected, I met Pearson in Seoul. He said when he told Reuters' headquarters that Sagolj was allowed in, they couldn't believe it. Pearson is the husband of *Korea Times* journalist Kim Hyo-jin.

The miracle Reuters couldn't believe happened was actually quite simple. North Korea found and saved articles and photographs of journalists who visited the North through its embassies. If that journalist reapplied to enter the DPRK, the authorities would open his or her file and if they found anything even remotely unseemly, they would deny them entry. In principle, if the local embassy vouches for the journalist, DPRK authorities would allow him or her entry into the country.

However, almost no North Korean diplomats were willing to do this. They didn't want to take on the responsibility. I helped several British journalists who could not enter North Korea enter the country, but Sagolj was my last.

NORTH KOREA SELECTS 2018 AS THE YEAR TO GENERATE A PEACEFUL ENVIRONMENT TO FIRM UP THE COUNTRY'S STATUS AS A NUCLEAR POWER

The Seventh Party Congress, which was never held during the Kim Jong-il era, was meaningful not just because it was the first party congress to be held in thirty-six years but also because it served as a starting point for when North Korea accelerated its "dangerous nuclear race." During the party congress, North Korea reaffirmed that it was a nuclear power and declared the perpetuation of Kim Jong-un's policy, announced in March 2013, of simultaneously pushing nuclear weapons and economic development. Kim was also "named" party committee chief, and a shake-up of party organizations and figures ensued.

After the party congress, workplaces throughout the country held meetings to discuss next steps. The foreign ministry was no exception. All ambassadors serving in embassies abroad returned to the DPRK to take part in the party congress and to hold the Forty-Fourth Ambassadors' Meeting in Pyongyang. The meeting discussed "efforts by warriors in the diplomatic sector to complete the country's nuclear armament as presented in the Seventh Party Congress." The meeting, led by Ri Yong-ho, who was named foreign minister during the party congress, had three major agenda items:

Establishing the period for completing North Korea's nuclear armament
Predicting how bad international sanctions would get
Determining what things North Korea would have to do to become a nuclear
   power

The ambassadors concluded that since protracted sanctions would cause massive damage to the North Korean economy, the country should complete its nuclear armament in a short period of time. The appropriate time to do this would be from the second half of 2016 to the end of 2017. The basis for this was as follows:

The U.S. presidential election is at the end of 2016. It will take until mid-2017 before the new U.S. administration can complete its policy review and make new appointments. Also, the South Korean presidential election is in the second half of the year. Prior to early 2018, when the new South Korean government comes to power, South Korea and the United States will have difficulties during their policy consultations. Ultimately, we can say there will be a U.S.-South Korean policy vacuum from late 2016 to the end of 2017. Until that time, the United States will not be able to launch military attacks against North Korea.

As for sanctions, North Korea had been enduring them and could endure them for the time being. Even if sanctions did worsen, there was nothing really to fear. All that remained was for North Korea to become recognized as a nuclear power. What the ambassadors concluded is that they should creatively apply the Indian and Pakistani models to North Korea: "From early 2018, when the new South Korean government comes to power, the DPRK must also begin creating a peaceful environment to firm up its status as a nuclear power. At this time, the DPRK—like India and Pakistan—should declare a freeze on nuclear testing and generate 'immunity' in South Korea and the United States toward the DPRK's nuclear weapons."

India and Pakistan had conducted a series of nuclear tests over a short period of time but then suddenly declared an end to testing. The world's five nuclear powers, including the United States and Russia, initially said they could not recognize India and Pakistan as nuclear states, but the September 11, 2001 terrorist attacks suddenly changed all that. Fighting a war against the Taliban in Afghanistan, the United States needed cooperation from Pakistan and India. In these circumstances, both nations naturally became recognized as nuclear powers.

However, the North Korean ambassadors' conclusions were based on failed predictions. At the May 2016 party congress, North Korea predicted that the Democratic Party candidate would win the U.S. election that year and the progressive forces would win in the South Korean presidential election in 2017. Based on these predictions, North Korea conducted its fifth nuclear test in September 2016.

North Korea's predictions were off the mark. Republican Donald Trump won the U.S. presidential election, while in South Korea, the conservative government was driven out nine months early after the "Choe Soon-sil scandal" with the Moon Jae-in government taking power in May 2017. North Korea, which had been planning to complete its nuclear arsenal by 2017, had no choice but to accelerate things further. This is why North Korea carried out its sixth nuclear test that year and, after conducting two ICBM tests, declared it could hit the U.S. mainland.

A few months after my defection to South Korea, in December 2016, I held a press conference with reporters who covered the Ministry of Unification.[7] I unveiled North Korea's plan to complete its nuclear development, calling it a "nuclear race plan." North Korea's nuclear test and ICBM launches in 2017 were fully predictable, even for me. According to the plan, 2018 was the time North Korea would use to create a peaceful environment to make its status as a nuclear power an established fact. We can understand North Korea's active gestures toward reconciliation around the time of the PyeongChang Olympics along these lines. I wish even more people understood just how desperately North Korea is clinging to nuclear weapons.

WATCHING THE PURGES AND EXECUTIONS IN NORTH KOREA FROM THE UK, I FEEL SHAME AND ANGER

In March 2016, a couple of months before I defected to South Korea, I received a cable from Pyongyang: "As part of efforts to cleanse the remaining poison of the anti-party, anti-revolutionary factionalist element Jang Song-taek gang, we are demolishing Pyongyang Folklore Park, which was established in Pyongyang's Daesong District. Photos related to the park should be removed from all published material, and promotional publications related to the park that have been distributed to British people should be confiscated and incinerated."

I had nothing to say, it was so absurd. Pyongyang Folklore Park, the construction of which had been led by Jang, was built over several years with the mobilization of Pyongyang residents and soldiers. The construction cost hundreds of millions of dollars. Envious of foreign tourists flooding to Seoul's Gyeongbokgung and Changdeokgung palaces, North Korea built Pyongyang Folklore Park and widely promoted it at home and overseas as a site where visitors could experience Korean folk culture. At that time, even the North Korean embassy in London distributed a lot of promotional materials about the park. On wedding days, it was a must for the newlyweds and their friends to visit Pyongyang Folklore Park. There was only one reason why it was being demolished just three years after its completion: "When I see Pyongyang Folklore Park, I think of Jang Song-taek."

That a park bigger than ten football fields was demolished based on this one statement from Kim Jong-un is something reminiscent of the era of the Roman tyrant Nero. If you look at where the park was in Google Earth, you can see it has been completely destroyed. Though Kim executed his hated uncle and cruelly purged tens of thousands, the North Korean leader was apparently unsatisfied. The demolition of Pyongyang Folklore Park clearly demonstrated Kim's propensity to hold grudges.

When I look back, my life as the deputy ambassador at the North Korean embassy in London was a time of regret. Just a few weeks after coming to London, members of the Unhasu Orchestra were executed, then the appalling Jang Song-taek purge took place. I was deeply wounded. I was ashamed of working for such a government. At the same time, my fury surged. It was stinging, too, to watch older and younger colleagues of mine executed or dragged off to camps.

While I was working as deputy ambassador in the UK, relations between Pyongyang and London were never that good. There was one piece of progress, though. The two countries exchanged nonresident defense attachés. The exchange of defense attachés was first proposed by the British. London, believing that it was time to exchange attachés, as ten years had passed since the establishment of diplomatic relations with North Korea, sounded out Pyongyang. It suggested making the British defense attaché in Beijing the nonresident defense attaché in Pyongyang.

This was a delicate issue for North Korea. British officers and small units with the UN Command had been taking part in the U.S.-South Korean "Key Resolve" joint military exercises every March. Each year, I would visit the British defense ministry and demand that the UK not participate in the joint exercises. When I did, I received a formal response:

The UK takes part in military training with not only South Korea, but also other allied nations. British participation in joint U.S.-South Korean exercises is not a hostile act aimed at North Korea. Key Resolve is a defensive drill that takes place every year. All nations conduct military exercises, but the joint U.S.-South Korean ones are at a very high level. The

UK, too, learns a lot by participating in them. Even the UK, a military power with a special relationship with the United States, cannot give up participating in Key Resolve, given that it does not conduct such exercises with the U.S. military.

Every time South Korea and the United States conduct joint exercises, the North Korean military leadership has to conduct response drills. Every time, they use up so much war material that it's difficult to bear. The very existence of the drills weakens North Korea's military strength. The military leadership, complaining of such difficulties, used to ask the foreign ministry whenever it got the chance to get the joint drills suspended.

Though it happened every year, the UK's participation in Key Resolve was uncomfortable for North Korea. Accordingly, North Korea's acceptance of a British defense attaché could suggest that it was tacitly accepting the situation. However, from the North Korean military's perspective, strengthening exchanges with a foreign military was a good opportunity to boost its own status. It could also lead to cooperation, such as receiving British training for army doctors. In August 2015, North Korea and the UK signed a deal to exchange defense attachés, with the North Korean defense attaché in Moscow covering the UK and the British one in China covering North Korea.

NORTH KOREAN TROOPS SUFFER IN CAVES DURING EVERY JOINT EXERCISE

I've long known just how hard North Korea's responsive drills to joint South Korea-U.S. military exercises are to endure. That's because I had the following experience.

Kim Jong-il once called on a team of experts to learn tunnel-building techniques from Sweden, the European nation best prepared for a nuclear war. A delegation of about ten North Korean military tunnel experts then visited Sweden. Accompanying the delegation, I found myself surprised as I looked around Swedish tunnels built for nuclear war.

Sweden has underground shelters for its entire population, though it faces little threat of war. The tunnels have not only food and medicines, but also schools, hospitals, nurseries, and other welfare facilities. The fans were working so well that there was no moisture. After ten days of looking around Swedish tunnels, the delegation grew ashen-faced. This is what they said:

> North Korea and Sweden's ways of building tunnels for war are completely different. North Korea builds them in a straight line from the entrance to the center. This is because we believed that if you did so, many people could flood into them and they wouldn't fall into chaos or crush themselves to death. Swedish tunnels, on the other hand, turn ninety degrees just after the entrance and zig-zag to the center. In a nuclear war, damage from nuclear blasts is most severe. To minimize the damage from the blast, it's better to reduce the pressure of the blast by zigzagging the tunnel corridor.

It was a simple difference, but the North Korean experts were shocked. North Korea, which suffered enormously from U.S. bombing during the Korean War, constructed countless tunnels after the war in accordance with the party's nationwide fortification policy. Key defense industries, major equipment, military command facilities, and communication facilities were all placed in tunnels. After the delegation returned home, North Korea switched to Sweden's method of tunnel construction.

However, a problem arose from elsewhere. In wartime, a tunnel strategy could be effective. However, with North Korea's economic level and energy situation, it was difficult to keep tunnels functioning normally. If power goes out, the fans stop working, so major facilities like communication equipment rusts away and soldiers suffer from various ailments. When North Korea declares a state of semi-war or South Korea and the United States conduct joint drills, most of the North Korean army has to live in tunnels. The burden and pain are enormous.

A North Korean military official used to worry that if the fans in the tunnels didn't work, all the equipment would rust away over the long term. He didn't say it outright, but it was clear that there was a serious problem with the North Korean military's strategy of relying on tunnels. Some twenty years later, North Korea's energy situation hasn't improved much. You can easily imagine the extent to which North Korean military equipment has rusted away in that time.

BRINGING MY ELDER SON TO THE UK PROVIDES OPPORTUNITY TO DEFECT

The happiest moment in my life in the UK was in February 2014, when an unexpected opportunity arose to bring my older son to the UK. I considered it an opportunity from heaven.

As Kim Jong-un conducted on-site guidance, he felt the thing North Korean society lacked most was a high-quality workforce that could realize his vision. Most of his closest cadres were in their seventies and eighties. They couldn't understand what Kim was saying. Even cadres in their sixties were ignorant of the ways of the world. They didn't listen to what he asked for. Angered, Kim ordered that more students be sent overseas. However, he just ordered that they be sent overseas. He didn't resolve the issue of providing funds for that to happen.

North Korea's education ministry used to pester overseas embassies all the time to put together scholarships to let students study at leading universities because the country had no funds to make this happen. I met with several groups and universities in the UK to negotiate potential opportunities, but got nowhere. To put together a scholarship, you first need to select the target students and decide which universities and which departments they will enter.

For North Korean students to enter British universities, they must submit an admission application and an IELTS score online. In North Korea, where neither internet access nor British testing centers exist, this is very difficult. You also have to submit a medical exam showing you are free of TB, but the UK does not recognize documents from North Korean hospitals. The closest medical examination centers to North Korea are in Beijing. Given the fact that North Koreans were not free to travel overseas, it was almost impossible to go to Beijing to get a health exam. And even if you managed to get all this done, you wouldn't be able to take the interview though an online video call.

Through the end of 2013, North Korean authorities tried to enable students to study overseas, but there was no way to do this. At the time, it appears somebody suggested to Kim Jong-un the following: The children of diplomatic staff residing overseas could be sent to universities in the countries where they were based.

In January 2014, Kim Jong-un ordered that the university-age children of diplomats be sent overseas to study and improve the talent pool. Diplomats enthusiastically welcomed this. I, too, was very pleased.

With this measure, I could go to Pyongyang in March and bring my older son to London. In short, the minimal conditions for me to defect to South Korea had been met.

II

EMANCIPATION

7

STUDYING ABROAD

I AM SELECTED TO STUDY ABROAD AS A TEENAGER

In January 1976, when I was fourteen years old, I was given a golden opportunity. Starting several months earlier, Central Committee officials had been visiting the school I was attending, the Pyongyang Foreign Language Institute, to examine the school register of second- and third-year students studying English, French, and Arabic and to give them tests. The students were also taken to a hospital and given physical examinations. While by no means a common occurrence, the Central Committee would sometimes use these methods to identify potential agents for a government agency that conducted espionage activities in South Korea. A rumor emerged among the students that some of them could be selected as espionage agents.

When I told my father about what was happening, his face tensed slightly. People thought that being selected as an espionage agent was the same as heading to one's death. That being said, nobody could reject an order from the party. There were even people who thought that sacrificing one's life for the revolution was the honorable thing to do.

However, most of the students who received physical examinations were the children of cadres. I was feeling a bit of relief at the thought that cadres would be unlikely to send their own children to almost certain death. One day, my teacher quietly called for me. She told me to tell my father to attend an urgent meeting of parents that was to be held that evening. I called my father, and he asked whether I had done anything wrong at school. I told him no, and later returned home. I waited with some anxiety for my father to return from the parents' meeting.

My father came back home late that night, and my mother asked him what had happened. He told her to set up a table for drinks and snacks because the family had met with good fortune. According to him, a Central Committee cadre at the meeting had told the assembled parents: "The children of the parents gathered here have all been selected to go to Syria and China for study thanks to the consideration of the party. They will depart in late January, so we must now begin preparing to send them abroad. The party will take care of all preparations including their suits [to wear], so all you must do is prepare them ideologically." My father told us that while cadre families had sent only the mothers to the meeting, the households of ordinary people had sent only the fathers.

Starting the next day, all the students selected to study abroad were sent to the Nampo Revolutionary Institute to receive ideological education over the course of several weeks. The sons and daughters of high-level cadres who were selected included Kim Dong-ho, the son of Kim Yong-nam, the president of the Presidium of the Supreme People's Assembly; Choe Son-hee, the daughter of Choe Yong-rim, chief secretary of the Secretaries Office of the Gumsusan Assembly Hall under Kim Il-sung; and Ho Yeong-hui, the daughter of Ho Dam, a former minister of foreign affairs. The children of mid-level Central Committee officials were also selected, including Ri Yeong-suk, the daughter of the vice director of the Cadre Department, and Jeon Jae-gwang, the son of a section chief in the Central Committee's Science and Education Department.

I found it wonderfully curious how I—without membership in an influential family—had been selected. Later, after I joined the foreign ministry, I couldn't shake off my curiosity and read Kim Jong-il's "Collection of Remarks on International Activities." The book was top secret and held in the foreign ministry's library. The next section provides a summary of the background to my own selection to study abroad.

THE SYRIAN PRESIDENT INVITES NORTH KOREAN
STUDENTS AS PAYMENT FOR MILITARY AID

In October 1974, the Syrian President Hafez al-Assad visited North Korea and requested military aid from Kim Il-sung. Kim, who was a rising leader in the Third World in the 1970s and espoused an independent foreign policy, promised to accept all of al-Assad's requests. The North Korean leader aimed to create a strong base of support for North Korea in the Middle East through Syria. The Syrian leader told Kim, "Syria can't give the DPRK much back in return. However, as the DPRK may need Arabic specialists, we will educate students that you send to us."

After al-Assad left, Kim Il-sung gave Kim Jong-il the following instructions: "Based on my experience, foreign languages must be learned during childhood. I learned Chinese and Russian when I was young, and I still remember them. We can't just send children, however, so send a good mix of middle school and university students."

Kim Jong-il decided to show his gratitude to the confidantes who had helped him become his father's successor. Kim Yong-nam, the party's international secretary, and Ho Dam, the foreign minister, had completed all the necessary behind-the-scenes preparations to ensure that Kim Jong-il was designated official successor at the Central Committee's plenary session of February 1974. Kim Jong-il asked the two men which school their kids attended and what grades they were in; that was the moment when Kim Yong-nam's son and Ho Dam's daughter—both of whom attended the Pyongyang Foreign Language Institute's English Department—were selected to be sent abroad for foreign language study.

Kim Jong-il ordered the selection of students to learn Arabic along with those majoring in English and French. This was because he had more cadres he needed to make happy. Students selected for English and French study would be sent to China, but only because there was nowhere else to send them. Kim Jong-il also ordered that "an appropriate number of children from ordinary families be selected because just sending the children of cadre families could lead to negative sentiment." Kim reported his plan in writing to his father. Choe Yong-rim, who handled all the reports sent up to the elder statesman, then found out about the plan. That is how his daughter, Choe Son-hee, was selected to go abroad for foreign language study.

The children of cadre families attending the French Department of the Pyongyang Foreign Language Institute were also selected to go abroad, including An Gyeong-ae, the daughter of the vice director of the Central Committee's OGD, and Choe Hwa-seon, the daughter of the vice director of the Central Committee's Finance and Accounting Department. All of them occupy behind-the-scenes yet powerful roles in North Korea.

WHILE STUDYING IN CHINA, I PRETEND TO BE A MEMBER OF AN EMBASSY FAMILY

Ultimately, I was selected to study abroad with the children of cadres because I had done well in school. The team I joined was made up of twenty-four students from Hamheung, Chongjin, and Sinuiju. Hyeon Yong-il, the son of North Korea's ambassador to China, Hyeon Jun-geuk, along with Seo Geum-cheol, the son of the embassy's deputy ambassador, joined the team in China.

Students selected to study Arabic were sent to Syria, while students selected to study English and French were sent to China. Choe Gwang-su and Eom Cheol-ho, who had suffered in the Frunze Military Academy incident, left for Syria at this time as well. As mentioned previously, the two were later colleagues of mine at the foreign ministry.

On January 21, 1976, our team left Pyongyang by train and crossed the Yalu River. I, along with the rest of the students in my team, were fourteen years old, which in the South Korean system would have had us in the second year of middle school. We needed people to look after us, likely because of pressure from the cadre parents. The party provided the team with Choe Gwang-bae, a teacher at the Pyongyang Foreign Language Institute and his wife; a cook from Changgwangsan Hotel and his wife; and a driver affiliated with the Ministry of Social Security and his wife. They all joined the team under the guise of being embassy employees.

Upon our arrival at the North Korean embassy in China, we unpacked our bags. I was selected as the head student of the team; there were a lot of cadre kids in the team, and I still don't know why the embassy chose me as the leader. As team leader, I managed negotiations with the Chinese school and watched over the activities of other students. Despite a month's having passed since our arrival in China, however, we were still unable to go to school. I wasn't sure why that was. Sometime later, each student in the team was given a guardian. We were all trained to treat these guardians as family, calling them various iterations of "uncle" used to describe an uncle on the mother's or father's side of the family. The guardian I was assigned was my "uncle" on my mother's side; he was a counselor at the embassy named Seo Jae-pil.

North Korea had failed to tell the Chinese that they were going to send students to study in the country. The whole thing was put together quickly to reward Kim Jong-il's supporters. The downside of this was that there were already dozens of North Korean university students studying in China in accordance with an agreement on cultural exchanges signed by the two countries. The costs associated with the existing study abroad program was being covered by the Chinese, which meant that the North Koreans would not have been able to tell China that they would be sending middle school students not included in the agreement. It was quite unlikely that the Chinese would have accepted us. North Korea therefore turned to a "guerilla tactic" to move forward with the study abroad program. The authorities simply sent the students into the country, calling them the children or relatives of diplomats. That's why my designated guardian (Seo Jae-pil) was supposed to be my "uncle on my mother's side"; there were few people with the last name Thae.

Our team entered the Beijing No. 55 Middle School disguised as children of diplomats studying Chinese. We had been selected to study English and French but found ourselves in the ridiculous position of studying at a school taught in Chinese. It was no better than studying in North Korea.

I AM SHOCKED BY THE CRITICISM DIRECTED TOWARD MAO ZE-DONG BY CHINESE STUDENTS

I was still attending the Beijing No. 55 Middle School when Mao Ze-dong died on September 9, 1976. I will never forget this date because it is the same day that commemorates the founding of North Korea (the Day of the Foundation of the Republic). Each year on that day, China would hold a luncheon at the Great Hall of the People for North Korean embassy staff and students studying in the country.

On September 9, North Korean embassy staff were murmuring among themselves that the atmosphere at the luncheon was strange. Most Chinese cadres did not attend the event. As the food was brought out, all that the lower-level officials told us was "Today eat as much as you want among yourselves." Everybody thought that something unusual had happened and ate very little before leaving. When we asked the Chinese about what had happened, they avoided giving a direct answer and simply told us that we would "know soon." The faces of the Chinese officials looked very serious.

Everyone returned to the embassy. It was only that evening that China began releasing the news that Mao had died. The streets were filled with crying people. I still vividly remember Chinese people on the streets and in the school wailing. The No. 55 Middle School suspended classes for several days and held memorial services daily. Many Chinese children would stand for hours at a time listening to the memorial services before they collapsed and were taken away.

Extraordinary things began happening in China right after Mao's death. A power struggle ensued, and the "Gang of Four" were removed from power. Deng Xiao-ping, who had been languishing in the provinces, returned to Beijing. Fellow Chinese students who, just a couple of months before, would shed tears at even the mention of Mao, now said without hesitation, "Comrade Mao Ze-dong had achievements but also made mistakes." In the Chinese press, there emerged the claim that Mao was 70 percent right and 30 percent wrong in how he had managed the country. Hearing this was a major shock to us North Korean teenagers studying abroad.

We attended No. 55 Middle School for more than two years. The students progressed little in building their English proficiency, and our fake parents and uncles participated in parent meetings at the school. The performance put on by North Korea had reached its limits. For some time, Kim Yong-nam and Ho Dam had been demanding that the North Korean embassy take measures to ensure the students could properly learn English. Then, North Korea's ambassadorship to China shifted from Hyeon Jun-geuk to Jeon Myeong-su. Jeon had worked as a vice minister in the foreign ministry until March 1977, when he was appointed ambassador. He arrived in Beijing after receiving a direct order from Ho Dam to take measures regarding our studies.

At the time, China and North Korea had similar systems regarding how to cultivate foreign language experts. The Beijing Foreign Studies University (BFSU), for example, would establish an affiliated middle school that would teach students foreign languages from that age. Most of the graduates from this middle school would then enter BFSU. North Korea did foreign language training in the same way.

In the beginning, Jeon did not have any special plan to solve the issue. Time passed without a resolution until he decided to take a drastic step. Jeon invited Huang Hua to a banquet put on by the North Korean embassy. After the right amount of alcohol had entered everyone's system, Jeon told Huang, "I have a personal favor from Foreign Minister Ho Dam I would like to ask of you." Then he called in Ho Yeong-hui, Ho Dam's daughter, who had been waiting outside the banquet venue.

"This is Foreign Minister Ho Dam's daughter," Jeon said, which greatly surprised Huang.

"Why is she in Beijing?" Huang asked, which opened the door for Jeon to explain: "Our country is trying to cultivate foreign language experts from among our gifted [students]. However, we have no place to send them. The only country we can send our children to study is China, but we didn't think that our Chinese comrades would accept young students. Without any other option, we pretended they were the children of embassy staff and placed them in the Beijing No. 55 Middle School. However, their English education is not going well. We would be grateful if you could have them study in the middle school attached to the Beijing Foreign Studies University."

The Chinese foreign ministry held administrative control over both the Beijing Foreign Studies University and its middle school. Huang could not reject the request, given it involved Ho Dam's daughter. The Chinese foreign minister ordered all of us to transfer from the No. 55 Middle School to the English department in the middle school under the Beijing Foreign Studies University starting in April 1978. That happened two years and three months after we had first arrived in China.

I TAKE A COMMEMORATIVE PHOTO WITH KIM IL-SUNG

Kim Il-sung made an unofficial visit to China the same month that we transferred to the new middle school. I am not sure exactly why he visited China at that time, although preparations were made before he arrived. An advance party made up of dozens of people arrived at the North Korean embassy. Everybody—even we teenagers—had to clean up embassy. We swept and wiped down the inside of the embassy building along with the embassy's living quarters. We prepared for a performance involving the entire embassy staff and students, and we even conducted a rehearsal of shouting "Manse" (Long live!) in preparation for the North Korean leader's entrance into the embassy. Preparing for the performance and conducting rehearsal did not last just a day or two. The embassy windows were shut every evening before the rehearsals began. Shutting the windows was a security precaution: Kim's visit to China was an unofficial one.

Whenever the North Korean leader made official visits to other countries, he would frequently stop by the local North Korean embassy to take commemorative photographs. There remained a large possibility that Kim would not stop by the embassy this time because of the unofficial nature of his visit; however, the embassy had to prepare for any possibility and did so in the best way it could. All its efforts, however, were for naught.

In the end, Kim did not stop by embassy because he was on an unofficial visit to the country. However, embassy officials and the students were ordered to come to Beijing's Diaoyutai State Guesthouse, where Kim was staying during his visit. When we arrived at the guesthouse, Chinese officials were already setting up a place for a photograph to be taken. We waited a long while at the photo spot. Then, we saw Kim Il-sung and his entourage walking toward us from the garden area.

I had only seen Kim in propaganda films, and as the North Korean leader gradually came into view, it felt like I was in a dream. Everybody in the group yelled out "Manse" as loudly as they could. Kim was waving his hand as he approached the photo platform. With just about five meters separating us, I saw Kim Il-sung up close for the first time in my life. I even heard Kim ask the North Korean ambassador whether we were the "students studying abroad." Responding to his question, the ambassador said, "There are students along with children of embassy staff." Kim then said, "Make sure they study well," before sitting down at the center where all of us were standing. We were instructed to stop yelling out "Manse," and then the commemorative photo was taken.

We again yelled out "Manse" after the photo was taken. Kim waved his hand and said something either to us or to the ambassador; it wasn't clear because the yells of "Manse" were too loud. Soon after that, the North Korean leader started to move slowly away from us, still waving his hand.

The whole experience lasted less than ten minutes. Even after Kim disappeared, everybody just stood absentmindedly in the same spot. The embassy's party secretary came down from the platform and yelled at us to get on the bus again. It was only then that everyone fell out of their daze and started moving toward the bus. Everyone felt as if they had met God. That night, I couldn't fall asleep because I couldn't get the image of Kim waving his hand and walking toward me out of my mind.

Several months later, a ceremony to present the commemorative photograph was held in Pyongyang. It was a color photograph, which was unheard of. It was a period in North Korea's history that commemorative photographs with Kim Il-sung or even color photographs were nonexistent in the country. Everybody was really happy about it.

Taking a commemorative photo with the country's supreme leader gives power to the people in the image. Such photos are used as measuring sticks to show to what degree a family is part of the country's "core class." Households that have a lot of commemorative photographs with Kim Il-sung or Kim Jong-il can live proudly. North Koreans who are pessimistic about their chances of entering the core class believe that they have escaped the "wavering class" if, by chance, they are in a commemorative photograph with the supreme leader. There's a reason why Kim Jong-un continues to take commemorative photographs every time he goes out to conduct "on-the-spot inspections." The Kim family's political use of photographs is one of the key pillars of North Korean society.

My photograph with Kim Il-sung allowed my family to escape trouble a couple of times. North Korean authorities in Pyongyang engage in nighttime crackdowns on visitors to the city staying in other people's houses, referred to as "night accommodation inspections." Not just anyone is allowed to enter Pyongyang. People living outside the capital city must receive travel passes to enter the city. Parents and other relatives who obtain the passes and enter Pyongyang to see their kin are not allowed to sleep wherever they like. People who intend to provide sleeping arrangements for visitors must go to their local *inminban* leader to register.[1] On a special form to be signed by the head of the *inminban*, they must provide the name of the person for whom they intend to provide sleeping arrangements, the travel pass serial number, and their relationship with the person. The registration process is finalized only after they have taken the signed form to their district office to be recorded in a ledger. In South Korea, this would be akin to getting a form signed by a neighborhood leader and then taking it to a local police office to get it approved.

The night accommodation inspections occur when a local police official selects *inminban* leaders at random to conduct inspections of all households in a particular district. The inspections seek to identify households providing sleeping arrangements for unregistered people. The inspections are typically conducted at around 2–3 A.M. Nowadays, people caught in an inspection can bribe their way out of trouble with money or valuables; at that time, however, we had no other choice than to beg for forgiveness.

My father was once caught up in an inspection of this kind. He was found to have provided sleeping arrangements for one of my uncles. My father told the police officer he had committed an error and didn't expect to be let off lightly. However, the police officer saw the color photograph of me with Kim Il-sung on the wall and asked him: "Comrade, why do you have this photo? Do you know someone in it?" My father said in response, "My son is studying in China. The photo was taken when the Supreme Leader visited China."

"It's not right that such a family as yours would violate the rules pertaining to the registering of sleeping arrangements," the police officer said before returning my uncle's citizen registration card and quietly leaving the house. The officer was surprised at seeing a color photograph for the first time, and was probably even more amazed to see that it was a commemorative photograph taken with Kim Il-sung. He likely concluded that a family with such a photograph on its wall had a high-level cadre among its relatives.

Another time, our house was searched by local prosecutors because of an issue concerning the waste of materials while my father was working as an engineer at a construction site. The prosecutors saw the photo on the wall and asked my father who I was. They then halted their house search and left.

North Korean authorities conduct inspections on all sorts of things, including on electricity usage. Given the country's poor electricity situation, people are not allowed to waste electricity. There are frequent cases in which people are caught by "electricity inspection teams" who stage raids on homes that secretly use electric rice cookers.

NORTH KOREA CALLS ITS STUDENTS BACK HOME OVER CONCERNS OF NEGATIVE INFLUENCE FROM CHINA'S CAMPAIGN TO "DOWNGRADE MAO"

Mao died soon after I arrived in China, and sometime after I left the country, South Korean President Park Chung-hee was killed. North Korean students studying abroad were really pleased to hear about Park's death, saying: "Now unification will happen. [Another] figure like Park Chung-hee will never emerge from the South." North Koreans were aware that Kim Il-sung really hated Park. Newspapers, radio, and TV outlets spewed criticism and insults toward the South Korean leader on an almost daily basis. I also believed unification would soon occur now that Park had died.

I didn't know this at the time, but around the time that Park died, North Korean leaders were discussing the return of the students studying in China. The leadership was concerned about the unusual events unfolding in that country. In December 1978, two years after Mao's death, the Chinese Communist Party (CCP) held a general plenary. During that meeting, the CCP declared that it acknowledged the failure and damage done by the Cultural Revolution and that it would lead China to reforms and opening up. Following the CCP's official acknowledgment of Mao's mistakes, Chinese intellectuals and media outlets competed with each other to criticize Mao's Cultural Revolution.

This turn of events sent shock waves through Kim Il-sung and Kim Jong-il. If anything, Kim Il-sung had put even more effort than Mao into mercilessly executing his political rivals through factional purges within the WPK. As he watched Deng Xiao-ping go over the achievements and mistakes Mao had made, Kim Il-sung deepened his determination to never turn over power to just anyone. For the North Korean leader, the only person he could trust was his son, Kim Jong-il.

The younger Kim, for his part, was concerned about the stability of the North Korean system as he watched China degrade Mao's legacy. Worried that the young students studying in China could drink "bad water," he went into action, handing down an order to quietly extract the students from China without causing concern among Chinese officials.[2] Ultimately, I, along with the other students, left for North Korea in February 1980 without graduating from the middle school.

In order to attend a university in Pyongyang, you have to be part of the "wavering class" or higher. The bar to enter universities affiliated with the WPK is even higher, requiring one to be part of the core class.

North Korean universities are divided into two categories. There are general higher-level educational institutions run by the Education Commission, along with educational institutions managed directly by the WPK. The former includes Kim Il-sung University, the Pyongyang Foreign Language Institute, and Kim Chaek University of Technology, while the latter include the Kim Il-sung Higher Party School, the People's Economy University, PUFS, and engineering universities located in each city.

In April 1980, I entered the PUFS as an eighteen-year-old. The university was a four-year school aimed at cultivating diplomats copied from the universities of foreign studies in the Soviet Union and the Eastern Bloc. The school taught the history of international relations, international law, how to conduct oneself abroad, how to write diplomatic documents, world history, world geography, and the history of Kim Il-sung's and Kim Jong-il's activities abroad. The school also taught English, Russian, French, Spanish, Chinese, and Arabic. There were around a hundred students in each grade while each class had around thirty students. Each grade was made up of three classes.

Most of the students were discharged soldiers who had spent around ten years in the military. There were also twenty students who had studied in China during their childhood and around ten students who had entered the school from foreign language institutes in Pyongyang and other parts of the country. Most of the student body was made up of students from outside Pyongyang who lived in the dormitories. Only about 30 percent of the students in each grade lived at home in Pyongyang while attending school.

There was a massive farm inside the university. The students had to work on the farm, even on Sundays. The university gave students who lived at their homes in Pyongyang—and who participated in the farmwork— a bag of potatoes or one kilogram of pork each month. I always took part in the farmwork. My mother would always praise the school as a good one whenever I brought back potatoes or pork, saying, "What other school would give students things to eat?"

WITH THE ERUPTION OF THE MAY 18 GWANGJU DEMOCRATIZATION MOVEMENT, WE THINK "UNIFICATION WILL HAPPEN NOW"

In 1980, the same year I entered PUFS, the May 18 Gwangju Democratization Movement occurred in South Korea. North Korean TV reported on the movement daily. North Korean university students were shocked to see scenes of armed Gwangju citizens riding trucks speeding through the downtown area of the city. It was yet another shocking event that came after President Park Chung-hee's death. We believed that "unification will happen now."

In North Korea, the Gwangju Democratization Movement is called the "Gwangju People's Revolt." "People's revolt" is a very common term within the context of North Korea's "united front tactics." These united front tactics posit that a people's revolt will lead to the overthrow of the dictatorship, which will then lead to the establishment of a pro-North government and, eventually, the unification of the two Koreas. As university students, we expected the two Koreas to be unified soon upon hearing the phrase "people's revolt." That, of course, was a misreading of the situation at the time.

Kim Il-sung and Kim Jong-il also misread what was going on. The North Korean leadership falsely believed that simply "eliminating the South's dictator will lead the South's people to stage a revolt, leading to the unification of the two Koreas." Kim Il-sung had believed that a similar thing would happen through his attempt to eliminate Park Chung-hee in 1968 by sending Kim Sin-jo and other North Korean operatives to South Korea.

After the end of the Gwangju Democratization Movement, Kim Jong-il made a misjudgment, believing that killing Chun Doo-hwan would allow the establishment of a pro-North government in the South. That's why Kim engineered the attempt to end the South Korean president's life through the terror incident in 1983 at Aung San's mausoleum. South Korea's political system was engineered to survive the elimination of its top leader. Meanwhile, North Korea fell into self-contradictions when the Kim Dae-jung administration came to power because the regime relied blindly on the logic of united front tactics.

This logic demanded that the Kim Dae-jung government be a "pro-North administration." In short, this pro-North government would have to either give up control of South Korea to the North or join hands with the DPRK to achieve unification. That would never happen, however. After the Kim Dae-jung administration came to power, North Korea abandoned its preexisting united front tactics. It had realized that establishing a pro-North government in the South through a "people's revolt" led by *jusapa* or anti-government forces would be impossible.[3]

In the past, North Korea had spread propaganda to its people about how unification would be achieved in this or that way. After Kim Dae-jung became president, however, North Korean authorities stopped spreading propaganda about the country's strategy of unifying the two Koreas under the "red flag." North Korean officials focused on a "fake peace campaign" using phrases such as *urriminjokgirri*, the "spirit of June 15," and the "spirit of October 4," or the unification of the two Koreas through a federal system. North Korean leaders determined that the South Korean *minjung*, or people, were no longer a group the DPRK could embrace on the road to unification. Kim Jong-il concluded that North Korea could continue to exist only when South Korea, including its people, was eliminated as a state through nuclear weapons or other kinds of weapons of mass destruction. In other words, North Korea's new unification strategy centered on developing nuclear weapons.

THE KIM SONG-AE WATCH AFFAIR AND THE START OF KIM JONG-IL'S ELIMINATION OF THE "OUTER BRANCHES"

The same year the Gwangju Democratization Movement happened, an incident with symbolic significance occurred at PUFS—the so-called "Kim Song-ae watch affair."

In North Korea, students manage university campus security, and those keeping watch have to sleep at school. A fellow student of mine who was two years senior to me was the younger brother of Kim Gwang-seop. Kim was a son-in-law to Kim Il-sung. He had married Kim Gyeong-jin, who was the daughter of Kim Il-sung and Kim Song-ae. Kim Gwang-seop is currently the North Korean ambassador to Austria.

I don't remember the name of Kim Gwang-seop's younger brother. One day, the younger brother stood guard at school, but when he woke up the next morning, he couldn't find his gold watch, which he had taken off before going to bed. It was clear that someone had stolen it. He went to the head student of his class and the party cell secretary to complain: "I lost my gold watch last night. My older brother is Supreme Leader Kim Il-sung's son-in-law, and the watch is very special to me because Comrade Kim Song-ae put it on my wrist during the marriage ceremony [between Kim Kyeong-jin and Kim Gwang-seop]. Please find it for me."

When they heard the names Kim Il-sung and Kim Song-ae, the head of the class and the party cell secretary were intrigued. They seemed to believe that they would be rewarded if they found the watch. The two proceeded to interrogate students in my class, and Choe Gwang-il, who was two years my senior, was one of them. A party meeting was held at which the party cell secretary accused Choe of stealing the watch until he confessed. The atmosphere was akin to a people's court. An older student even went as far as to hit Choe in the face. Choe's father, however, was a department director in the OGD. The father heard about what had transpired from his son, who returned home with a bloody face. That's when the whole affair took a serious turn. While ordinary North Koreans were unaware of what was going on, Kim Jong-il was establishing a monolithic leadership system at around that time. Kim Jong-il and Kim Kyong-hui, birthed by Kim Il-sung's first wife Kim Jong-suk, were considered the "mother branches," while the children of Kim Il-sung's later wife Kim Song-ae—Kim Gyeong-jin, Kim Pyong-il, and Kim Yong-il—were considered the "outer branches." The building of the monolithic leadership system was essentially the elimination of the "outer branches."

Choe's father, upon going to work the next day at the Central Committee, submitted a report about the furor over Kim Song-ae's lost watch. Even Kim Jong-il saw the report. Soon after, Kim Yong-nam, the Central Committee's international secretary and a close confidante of Kim Jong-il, quickly made his way to the school. He gathered all the students together and told them, "Stop this nonsense in finding the watch." Then he stripped the head of the class and the party cell secretary of their party membership and expelled them from the school right then and there.

The students were dumbfounded. They had no idea that the establishment of Kim Jong-il's monolithic leadership system signified the elimination of the "outer branches." That being said, Kim Yong-nam was not in the position to explain this to them. The Kim Song-ae watch affair was symbolic in the sense it showed that Kim Jong-il was taking over the levers that would allow him to succeed his father. Kim Gwang-seop's younger brother, who was essentially the "outermost branch among the outer branches," did not suffer immediate disadvantages because of the affair. However, he failed to obtain a job in a central government agency after graduation. He was still the younger brother of Kim Il-sung's son-in-law and thus could have been given such a position; that he wasn't was just a sign of how cold-hearted Kim Jong-il was.

THE PYONGYANG UNIVERSITY OF FOREIGN STUDIES TEACHES ME NEGOTIATION SKILLS TO TACKLE OPPONENTS

While at PUFS, I learned the ropes of diplomatic negotiations. With the passage of time, I have come to realize that the fundamental reason North Korean diplomacy is strong may in fact rest in such education. PUFS taught me in detail the basics of diplomatic negotiations, including how to physically prepare before negotiations, how to achieve success in negotiations, how to break negotiations, and how to occupy the high ground during negotiations.

For example, courses at the school taught us never to eat any unusual food three days before conducting an important negotiation. We were even told to avoid drinking a lot of water during negotiations because that could lead to a bathroom trip during talks. These points were emphasized as being especially important during negotiations with enemy countries such as South Korea or the United States. We were also taught that sometimes the first side to stand up from the negotiating table was considered to have lost in the negotiations.

Courses at the school taught us about specific cases of negotiations, such as the back-and-forth between North Korean and American negotiators during a meeting of the Military Armistice Commission in

Panmunjeom.[4] Trying to prevent their own side from being the first to stand up from the table, the Americans and North Koreans sat across from each other for thirteen hours before the head of the American negotiating team finally stood up in defeat. I imagine it would have been very frustrating to have sat for thirteen hours before standing up.

The school also taught us that there are certain ways to break negotiations when required. One way was to provoke anger on the other side by turning the opponent's words against them. In fact, this method was used by North Korea during inter-Korean talks. In this instance, the U.S.-ROK Team Spirit military exercises had begun before a meeting of the two sides. The North Korean side planned to rupture the meeting and blame the South Koreans for the failure of the talks.

The South Korean head negotiator, who had no idea of the North's plans, started the meeting with a greeting: "This morning, as I came to the conference building, I heard the sound of frogs. It's not yet *gyeongchip*, but it seems that spring has come early this year given the frogs are up and about.[5] I think [this means] our meeting will go well."

The head of the North Korean delegation responded with words aimed at drawing the ire of the South Koreans: "Do you really think that the frogs came out of the ground because spring came early? They more likely came out because of the sound of tanks in the Team Spirit exercises. How loud do you think the Team Spirit exercises are to have woken up frogs before the start of spring?" This exchange happened as journalists were taking pictures of the two sides before the start of negotiations. The South Koreans couldn't stay silent after hearing that. The talks, which began with a war of words between the two sides, ended up breaking down.

When negotiators needed to break negotiations while only informing the other side of North Korea's position, they used another tactic. In the 1970s, the two Koreas held meetings between their respective Red Cross organizations. Generally speaking, journalists would leave the negotiation room after taking pictures as the two sides shared greetings with each other and before full-fledged negotiations began. In this case, the North Korean side decided to maximize the opportunity they had by letting the other side know North Korea's position while journalists took pictures.

The head of the North's negotiating team, Kim Tae-hui, walked into the negotiation room and instead of shaking hands and saying hello to the head of South Korea's negotiating team, Lee Beom-seok, Kim simply told

Lee to "Please speak first." Lee instinctively refused to accept Kim's unusual and sudden proposal and said, "The North should start first." Kim sat down, and if as on cue, he said, "OK. I will start speaking first." And without waiting for Lee's approval, Kim took out a document from his pocket and began reading. Lee was flustered at this and protested, "How can you do this without first deciding who will speak first?" Kim, however, did not respond and continued to read out his prepared remarks.

I VOLUNTEER FOR THE NIGHT LABOR BRIGADE IN MY SECOND YEAR OF UNIVERSITY AND BECOME A PARTY MEMBER

While PUFS may have been teaching students manipulative and deceptive methods to use in their future diplomatic activities, doing this was somewhat understandable given that the school aimed to cultivate warriors who would be deployed into the frontlines of diplomacy—otherwise known as "war without the sounds of gunfire." Even Kim Jong-il put significant effort into the development of PUFS's educational curriculum, and it was not hard to guess where his interests lay upon a review of the books he gave to the school. Generally, the books talked about the activities of foreign intelligence agencies and intelligence agents. I still remember two books from that time: a book about the Soviet spy Richard Sorge's activities in Japan, and another about the Imperial Japanese Army Nakano School, which was a training center for the Japanese military's secret agents.

The university's teachers taught students that they needed to "sacrifice their lives as if they were worthless for the motherland, just like the graduates of Japan's Nakano School." It was enormously ironic that North Korea—a communist country whose hatred of Japan tops all other nations—taught students at PUFS to imitate the graduates of a Japanese school for training spies. In any case, I was greatly impressed by the "military exploits" of graduates of that Japanese school.

PUFS was run by the WPK, which meant students enjoyed certain benefits not available at ordinary universities. Students with good grades during their graduating year would be given party membership.

Becoming a party member in North Korea is a tremendously difficult thing to accomplish. Young people generally join the military first to ease the path to party membership. After becoming a party member, they then go to university or join society. Someone like me, who had studied abroad and then matriculated into university, would have had to work for almost ten years out in general society before being able to gain party membership. That means I would have been in my late thirties before I could become a party member.

Without party membership, it is difficult to receive promotions and impossible to attend meetings for party members. Party members are promoted faster and become high-status members of society more quickly than non–party members. In short, non–party members hold a lower status than party members even if they are doing the same work in the same organization, and they must always obey what party members say. This causes non–party members frequent bouts of shame. When I was young, I witnessed my father succeed in the difficult process of becoming a party member. Only after he had volunteered to work at construction sites for many years was he able to become a member of the WPK. Seeing that, I made my own decision to first become a party member before getting married.

A PUFS tradition was to make almost all its students party members before they entered their graduating class. However, this tradition changed right around the time I entered my final school year. North Korea's leadership tightened party membership requirements over concerns about the quality of new recruits. The school moved from making all students with outstanding grades into party members to reviewing both grades and unique characteristics that set students apart from each other.

The only non–party members in my class were those who had studied abroad when they were young and students who had matriculated directly from other foreign language schools. All our grades were about the same. It was thus challenging to know who would become a party member based on grades alone. Everyone had to distinguish themselves from each other to become party members; this meant, in essence, that we had to do something special to set ourselves apart.

An opportunity for me to do that came in early 1982, the year North Korea celebrated the seventieth birthday of Kim Il-sung. Kim Jong-il handed down an order to construct the Juche Tower, Kim Il-sung Stadium, and the Pyongyang Arch of Triumph by April 15, the elder statesman's birthday. The authorities called on all party members and the entire population to participate in the building of these structures.

I was at the end of my second year at PUFS and was determined not to miss the opportunity. North Korea has a unique way of mobilizing people to take part in projects: The party announces plans to construct a building of some kind and calls on people to participate in the construction. When the construction is complete, party membership is granted to all those who participated. Those working on the projects do not get paid at all; however, people who want to raise their social status (*songbun*) happily take part in the project. North Korea used this method whenever it required labor for large-scale construction projects.

In early 1982, North Korean authorities called on all party members, office workers, and university students to take part in the construction projects. Outwardly, the authorities made an appeal for people to participate; in reality, however, people were mobilized for the construction work. That was because party members living outside of Pyongyang were deployed to the construction sites as part of labor brigades, while Pyongyangites were forced to join "nighttime labor brigades." There were many people who would do anything to obtain party membership. While existing party members joined labor brigades and construction work teams, Pyongyang residents seeking party membership volunteered for nighttime labor brigades. Those who joined the nighttime labor brigades had to work at the construction sites from 8 P.M. to 12 A.M.

The nighttime labor brigades were divided into regiments, battalions, companies, and platoons, just like the military. Members of the brigades had to confirm their attendance every day and complete assigned work quotas. The results of everyone's work were then sent to either their places of work or their universities. I joined a nighttime labor brigade and worked on the construction of the Kim Il-sung Stadium from early January to April 1982. After school, I ate dinner and then worked from 8 P.M. to midnight. I found myself dozing off a lot during class, but my university teachers did not raise an issue. In fact, they were happy to see how much I wanted to become a party member.

Thanks to my several months of work on the construction site, I was the first person in my class to become a party member during the party member recruitment period in February 1984. Since childhood I had always had a strong desire to win, and I was happy to have obtained party membership before my peers. Later in life, I came across colleagues at the foreign ministry who had suffered for almost ten years because they had failed to become party members. I felt sorry for them, yet was also proud of myself for having eased my path to party membership by joining a nighttime labor brigade at age twenty.

WHILE STUDYING ABROAD, I MEET CHINESE STUDENTS WHO YEARN FOR PARK CHUNG-HEE

I graduated from PUFS in March 1984. Other graduates were placed in jobs related to international trade and diplomacy, such as the foreign ministry, the trade ministry, and the Committee for Cultural Relations with Foreign Countries. However, students who had studied abroad while young were ordered to "wait." The reason for this was unclear until a Central Committee cadre came and explained. He told the group of us, "Thanks to the consideration of the Dear Leader Kim Jong-il, you have again been given the opportunity to study abroad." Then he told each of us where we would be going.

We all thought that we'd be sent to China again. Some, however, were sent to various African and Asian countries. Han Dong-cheol, who was part of the same English cohort as I, was sent to Sierra Leone (a republic on the western coast of Africa with a population of 6.16 million), while Ri Cheol-seok was sent to Zaire (now Congo), and Ri Ho-jun to Vietnam. After Han Dong-cheol returned from study in Sierra Leone, he was placed in a government agency that was involved in conducting espionage activities in South Korea. Later, we met once or twice in China, but I lost touch with him. I found it strange that he was sent to a small country in Africa whose name was unfamiliar to most North Koreans. Ri Ho-jun is currently a counselor at the North Korean embassy in Vietnam, while Ri Cheol-seok was, until recently, the vice chairman of North Korea's National Economic Development Committee. All three of them were born into ordinary families.

The rest of us were sent to China's Beijing Foreign Studies University (BFSU). We departed for China and matriculated into the school in September 1984.

BFSU was like an alma mater to us because we had attended the middle school attached to it around five or six years earlier. As such, returning to the school should have felt normal, but changes that had happened in China in the intervening years gave us a shock.

Everything in China had changed completely. The whole country was in the midst of serious efforts to reform and open up its economy. It didn't feel like a communist country. The movies and dramas playing in theaters and on TV were all American or Japanese productions. The focus of our university lectures was completely on the realities of the United States, and American professors taught classes on American-style democracy and the two-party system. I found these changes completely unexpected. Chinese students also had very different views of Mao Ze-dong. While positive renditions of Mao's historical legacy have recently made a comeback, there was more focus on the Chinese leader's mistakes at the time.

Chinese students we met would tell us: "South Korea has achieved a tremendous economic miracle. However, what is North Korea doing now? It is impossible to head to communism through existing socialist planned economy theory. [North Korea] must improve its economic power through the socialist market economy like China before heading to communism." North Korean students would counter this argument with: "The achievements of the revolution will be lost if we do things like China. China's current path is making people think that money is most important. The DPRK will protect the red flag until the very end."

Chinese students showed a great deal of support for the state-led industrialization economic policies of South Korea's Park Chung-hee and Singapore's Lee Kuan-yew. Whenever I heard them compare Park Chung-hee and Kim Il-sung, I felt my anger level rise inside. North Korean students at BFSU inevitably fell into depression whenever they got into disputes with Chinese students during discussions held within our department.

In fact, China was moving forward rapidly with economic growth, but North Korea's economy was continuing to fall into stagnation. There were only around sixty North Korean students living in the foreigner dormitories at BFSU. The majority of the other foreign students at the dorms came from the United States, Japan, and the UK. There was not one South Korean student, although there was a small number of South Koreans studying at the Beijing Language and Culture University.

During the evenings, we would drink beer with other foreign students in the garden near the dorms. At first, discussions focused on the students talking about their homelands, but they would always end with people saying, "North Korea has absolutely no freedom." Physical fights broke out frequently because of the ridicule we faced from other foreign students.

At the time, there were around four hundred North Korean students studying throughout China, including in the major cities of Shanghai, Nanjing, Tianjin, and Guangzhou. Most of these students were studying English and French, while some were learning Cambodian, the official languages of Sri Lanka, and Indonesian.[6] Our lives in the dorms were akin to being in the military. It wasn't so much that we had learned to live like that in North Korea; rather, we genuinely believed that's how we should live. That being said, this style of living wasn't completely voluntary. We faced restrictions.

Everyone had to wake up at 6 A.M. before starting morning calisthenics and jogging. It didn't matter what time of year it was. Foreign students would ridicule us for this, too: "Does North Korea even have rules about when to wake up?" At 10:00 each night, all North Korean students would gather in the reading room of their dorms for a roll call. Everyone had to participate in the roll call by 10 P.M., even if you had just gone to the library to study. It was considered a crisis if even one student didn't show up for roll call. I remember suggesting the following to the deputy secretary in charge of the students in the North Korean embassy's party committee: "The foreign students are making so much fun of us, why don't we stop the group wake-up calls in the mornings? We can wake up by ourselves. Please give it some thought because it has an impact on our country's reputation." The deputy secretary, however, told me that it would be difficult to change the rules. The foreign students continued to make fun of our lifestyle, calling it a "military dictatorship," but we had no choice but to live our lives by the rules. Interestingly, female foreign students showed a considerable degree of interest toward us North Korean students. I found it interesting that, despite the very bad perceptions of North Korea in their countries, young women from the United States and Japan were the first to approach male North Korean students.

LIVING IN A COLLECTIVE FASHION, NORTH KOREAN STUDENTS FACE CONTEMPT YET ARE ALSO OBJECTS OF CURIOSITY

Every Sunday morning, North Korean students would gather to play in sports events, and female foreign students would come in droves to watch. We would frequently separate into two teams to play soccer or volleyball, and the female students would watch, clapping and cheering us on. The young women would come over after the game and quietly try to start conversations with us. Their curiosity had evidently been sparked partly by the rumor that the male North Korean students were all virgins.

I think I had a tinge of responsibility for the spread of that rumor. We would talk about personal things every time we drank beer with other foreign students. Some of them asked about our sexual experiences, and it would have been ridiculous to claim to have had an experience that hadn't in fact happened. When we said we had no sexual experiences, however, most of the students thought we were lying.

A French exchange student I was on friendly terms with asked me, "You're twenty-three, but you really never have had sex?" I told him, "I swear. I have never done it." It wasn't the type of thing I needed to swear to, but I answered him that way because he just didn't believe me. After that, a rumor was started that claimed that North Korean students had almost no experience with sex. Some foreign students even continued to ask me, "How do you live without any sex in college?" With a serious look on my face, I answered them like this:

The DPRK is very strongly influenced by Confucian culture. You can face criticism if you have untoward relations with the other sex before marriage. That's of course true for men, but for women it is fatal: if they have relations with even one man that doesn't lead to marriage, they will face bad rumors. That can make it difficult for them to get married. If rumors emerge about a love affair between male and female students, they can even face expulsion from school. Universities in the DPRK really crack down on offenses against public decency. Honestly speaking, I can't image having sex with a woman out of curiosity before marriage.

The foreign students gradually began to understand our country's sex culture. They told us they could never live in such a society, yet followed us around while calling us "innocent." When we were about to head back to North Korea, a French student along with a female American student named Chris pestered us, saying, "We want to spend time with you. We want to go to North Korea." With our help, the two did end up coming to North Korea after being hired as foreign language teachers.

Chris and the French student, however, were enormously disappointed by what awaited the them in North Korea.[7] They thought they could have a good time with their North Korean friends in Pyongyang, but on arrival in the country they suddenly found themselves outcasts. Their North Korean friends avoided meeting them because all foreigners in the country were targets of surveillance by the Ministry of State Security. I reckon it was difficult for the two women to understand that they couldn't continue living a real life abroad after their arrival in Pyongyang.

The French student would call out the names of their North Korean friends each time she passed the headquarters of the foreign ministry, before screaming out: "Hey, come out quickly to Kim Il-sung Square! Where have all the scoundrels gone hiding who said we could have fun and drink beer in Pyongyang?!" I heard what the French student had said from Park Gyeong-nam, who was in charge of watching over her. Park was a fellow alumnus of PFLI. I felt sorry for no reason when I thought of the French student calling out my name as she passed by the foreign ministry headquarters. I did secretly meet with her a couple of times at the Koryo Hotel to drink beer. Chris, meanwhile, went back to the United States by herself. She's probably a housewife in her early fifties by now.

While many female foreign students tried to interact with us, most of the North Korean students rebuffed their approaches as nicely as possible. We would have faced being returned to North Korea if it was discovered that we were in a relationship with a foreign female student. It would have destroyed our lives. Reminiscing about it now, I think the female students who remained at the dorms on Sunday mornings probably enjoyed watching our sports competitions. Other students watched movies or went out on dates off campus. For passionate North Korean male students in their early twenties, it would have been a good opportunity to gain experience in romance. Alas, there's no way to turn back to clock.

I FIND SIMILARITIES BETWEEN NORTH KOREA'S REALITIES AND THE MOVIE *ANIMAL FARM*

At Chinese universities in the late 1980s, research and discussions were taking place in earnest about the United States, Japan, and South Korea. The country was seeking new ways to succeed economically. Many Chinese students showed support for the state-led economic development model espoused by South Korea's Park Chung-hee and Singapore's Lee Kuan-yew.

One day, BFSU put on a screening of the American film *Animal Farm*. The movie was an animated version of George Orwell's novel of the same name, and Chinese students greatly praised it. The North Korean students, however, were very depressed after seeing the film. The message of the movie—"All animals are equal. But some animals are more equal"— seemed to be a painful reflection of the changing realities of North Korea.

From the early 1980s, foreign currency shops sprang up throughout Pyongyang. This development signified the start of an era in which "*donpyo* exchanged for foreign currency" reigned.[8] People began to judge how much someone was worth by how much *donpyo* they had. North Korean students who watched *Animal Farm* gained a new consciousness of a society in which "having money could make things more equal." Many students were shocked by this idea, while some expressed quiet admiration at how Orwell had been able to vividly portray changes and developments in communism.

Indeed, North Korean students studying in China ended up drinking the "bad water," as a concerned Kim Jong-il had predicted. It was easy to see why, given the talk in China about reforms and opening, the screening of American films, the holding of American-style lectures, the debates over the future of communism, and the spreading concept of "free love."

Some of the North Korean students began to have doubts about North Korea's system. There was even a student who, while drinking alcohol, said, "I think that China's reforms and opening-up policy are the right way to go. Our party should revise its policies." Normally, someone saying such a thing should have been reported to the embassy's party committee and repatriated back to North Korea. Upon hearing what the student said, however, most of the students did not respond and simply avoided contact with him. I found myself doing much the same: generally speaking, I would quietly go somewhere else whenever I heard some of the students talk about North Korea's system.

It is impossible to forget freedom once you've tasted it, and once the seeds of doubt have been planted, they are hard to destroy. My cohort of students returned to North Korea in July 1988, but the impact of our time abroad began to appear soon enough: one student older than I was arrested, while another was taken away by the authorities a little less than a year later after our return home.

THE "KIM IL-SUNG UNIVERSITY READING CLUB AFFAIR" LEADS TO PURGES OF STUDENTS WHO HAD STUDIED ABROAD

After my return from China, I joined the European Department at the foreign ministry. Ri Ui-seong entered the foreign ministry's Treaties Department, while Seo Geum-cheol had been working at the then-named State General Bureau of Tourism.

Seo was a friend of mine from childhood. We had attended PUFS and BFSU together. Ri had been sent to China for language study after having been deemed an "outstanding talent" at the Gaesong Foreign Languages Institute. After these two were arrested, I along with their colleagues were called in by a Ministry of State Security (MSS) official assigned to the foreign ministry. The security official asked me whether Ri had made any good American friends during his time in China.

Ri did hang around with American students to practice his English conversation skills, but I had never heard him talking badly about North Korea. I was released from the interrogation without any trouble after testifying, "I never witnessed anything unusual regarding Ri Ui-seong."

Later, I found out that Ri was accused of being recruited by America's Central Intelligence Agency. Even now, I do not believe that he was an American spy. However, Ri did express a lot of concern about the future of North Korea, and after his return from China, he made statements that were at odds with what would have been accepted by the authorities. I suspect that the Ministry of State Security put all of this together to make him out to be a spy.

Seo Geum-cheol's case was a bit different. When he was arrested, his father was the head of the North Korean consulate in Nakhodka, a city in the Soviet Union. Seo's father was known as a veteran diplomat within the foreign ministry. He had previously served as the deputy ambassador at the North Korean embassy in Beijing and as a department director in the WPK's International Department. In fact, he was the North Korean embassy's deputy ambassador when I was in Beijing in the late 1970s.

Seo Geum-cheol, meanwhile, had strong doubts about North Korea's system. I even heard him once say: "The Kim Il-sung and Kim Jong-il system will not last that long. There are already rumblings among young university students and the intellectuals. If these rumblings explode, their impact will be felt widely very quickly." When I heard this, I did not respond at all because I thought he was thinking about things without a real basis in reality. I also had my own doubts about whether what he was saying was even possible. When I didn't show support for his thinking, Seo didn't say anything further—perhaps because he felt what I was thinking. I still don't understand why he tried to sound out what I thought.

Seo was a year older than I at BFSU. He returned to North Korea one year before me and was given a position in the International Affairs Department of the State General Bureau of Tourism. When I returned to Pyongyang, he had already been arrested. I was given advice by a lot of people right after my return: "Be really careful about what you say, because Seo Geum-cheol and some other students who studied abroad have been arrested."

Ultimately, Seo and his entire family were expelled to an area outside Pyongyang. What I heard later about what happened was as follows.

In 1988, the MSS had an informer who reported that students at Kim Il-sung University were holding a secret reading club. At first, the agency thought that immature university students were gathering to discuss their own political debates, but an investigation showed that what they were doing was something else completely.

First, the students participating in the reading club were all excellent students. All of them, in fact, were considered the smartest students in their departments. Moreover, the issues being discussed in the club were tremendously sensitive and serious ones. One example of what was discussed can be summarized as: "The Kim Il-sung dictatorship can no longer develop the DPRK. A caste system, a legacy of feudal society, is still alive and well in the DPRK. This system is in complete contradiction to the ideology of communism, which promotes a classless society."

The MSS immediately arrested and tortured the students involved in the reading club. The agency's investigation found evidence that both Kim Il-sung University students along with students who had studied abroad but had already entered society were involved in the club. Kim Jong-il ordered all students who had studied abroad to be investigated because foreign intelligence agencies could be involved in the affair.

At first, a couple of students who had studied in China were arrested. Then, the arrests were expanded nationwide. As noted earlier in this book, students who had studied in Kazan were particularly affected by the investigation. The purge of students who had studied abroad did not stop there. After the affair, a new trend emerged in North Korea. Students with study abroad experience were once considered excellent candidates to be wedded to the daughters of party cadres; now they were considered worthless. Cadres who had been eager to send their children abroad suddenly decided otherwise.

Kim Jong-il handed down instructions: "Kim Il-sung University, where the pillars that will protect the system should be cultivated, could [instead] become a hotbed for anti-state forces." A MSS branch was established inside the school campus. Generally speaking, universities had one or two of the agency's officials on campus, but it was the first time that a university had an entire branch established on its premises. If North Korea collapses, there will be various reasons given for why it happened. I'm certain that one of the major reasons will be the roles played by people who graduated from Kim Il-sung University.

8

THE THAES OF MYEONGCHEON

THE MYEONGCHEON THAE FAMILY: FROM TENANT FARMERS TO BENEFICIARIES OF LAND REFORM

I'm not too thrilled talking about my birth, family, childhood, and marriage. I'm still only fifty-six years old, and my life has been very ordinary. I doubt there will be many people who will be interested in my life. But I've tried seeing it another way. I realized I could describe changes in North Korean society and life over the years, and how they all inevitably permeate my own life, so that South Koreans can better understand the DPRK and even their own country better.

What I'm suggesting here is to overlay a new image of North Korean society on top of the image South Koreans have about their own society. There will be overlapping parts and parts that stick out. One bit may seem similar, while another bit may be different. I believe that new realizations can be gained by contrasting with North Korean society the realities of South Korean society that South Korean people themselves are unaware of, and vice versa.

I was born on July 25, 1962, in the neighborhood of Jongno, Central District, Pyongyang. Like Seoul, Pyongyang has a Jongno, too. Seoul Jongno starts at Dongdaemun, the Great East Gate, while Pyongyang's Jongno also starts at the city's Daedongmun. Daedongmun Gate is the name for the Great East Gate of Pyongyang. When I was born, my house was located in a residential area of single-story buildings between the Mansudae Art Theater and the Pyongyang Student Youth Palace (a place that offers after-school activities in art, sports, and science education for teenagers). It was a small, one-story, twenty-square-meter house. I grew up there with a sister a year older than I and a brother five years younger than I.

My father, Thae Hyeong-gil, was born in 1935 in Hwanggok Village, which is in the Agan Township of Myeongcheon County, North Hamgyong Province. In other words, my father's family is part of the Myeongcheon Thae clan, which became the source of the word *myeongtae*, the Korean word for pollack. It is said that the word *myeongtae* originated from the fact that the Thaes of Myeongcheon caught that fish for the king. My mother, Kim Myong-dok, was born in 1937 and was from Myeonggan County, North Hamgyong Province. The counties of Myeongcheon and Myeonggan lie adjacent to each other.

When I was born, my father was a lecturer of construction at Pyongyang University of Construction and Building Materials, and my mother was a teacher at Seomun People's School (an elementary school). I spent my early years at my grandfather's house in Myeongcheon County until I entered elementary school. This is because my mother's health was poor.

I recall that my grandfather, Thae Dong-sik, was born in 1918. He was illiterate, but as a poor farmer, he took up left-wing ideology during the Japanese colonial era and joined the Myeongcheon Farmers' Union. From a very young age, I heard that he was caught by the Japanese police and beaten for his farmers' union activities. But there was no way that my grandfather had a deep knowledge of socialist and communist theory.

After I came to South Korea, I scoured popular magazines from the Japanese colonial era to find traces of my grandfather. When I entered his name as a search term, there were no results, but when I looked for "Myeongcheon Farmers' Union," several articles turned up. For example, the *Dong-a Ilbo* daily newspaper reported on March 2, 1935, that Myeongcheon Police Station had detained 130 rural youths with the support of Gilju Police Station, adding, "It seems that farmers' union activities in rural villages have been exposed." It may have been around this time that my grandfather was arrested by the Japanese police.

In 1935, when the *Dong-a Ilbo* article appeared, my grandfather was seventeen years old. He was already a married man who had set up a house with my grandmother, Ri Sun-hyang, who was two years older than he, and in that year she gave birth to their first son (my father). After that, one daughter (Juk-sun) and two sons (Jong-gil and Jung-gil) were born, making three sons and one daughter in total. Their family wasn't big by the era's standards, but they still benefited considerably from Kim Il-sung's land reform thanks to having four children.

On August 15, 1945, after liberation, Soviet troops led by Kim Il-sung entered Korea. On March 5, 1946, Kim Il-sung carried out a land reform under the principles of expropriation without compensation and the free distribution of land. Kim divided farmers into four classes during this process. Those who owned more than five *jongbo* of land (roughly five hectares) were landlords, followed by wealthy farmers, middle-class farmers, and tenant farmers.

My grandfather belonged to the class of tenant farmers. On the other hand, my grandfather's older brother, my great-uncle Thae Tong-chan, was classified as a middle-class farmer. The reason was simple. My grandfather had inherited from his father a rocky piece of land with walls built of stones piled up on one another. Meanwhile, my great-uncle had inherited good land because he was the eldest son and had to perform ancestor veneration rituals.

During the land reform, the fortunes of the two men were reversed. The good land was allocated to my tenant farmer grandfather, and because he had several dependents, he received a fairly large plot of land. On the other hand, my great-uncle, the middle-class farmer, was in a disadvantageous position. Middle-class farmers were regarded as a destabilizing force in the progress of North Korea's socialist revolution. In short, two brothers from the same family were designated a tenant farmer and a middle-class farmer; one received good land while the other got bad land. It seemed like a tragedy, but really it wasn't. Now that I think about it, even middle-class farmers and wealthy farmers were barely getting by, eating rice mixed with various grains. Regardless, Kim Il-sung had laid the foundations for his rule by strictly classifying farmers into different classes.

Kim Il-sung gave land to all poor tenant farmers and demanded that they join the WPK. My grandfather was not familiar with communist ideology, but he was so happy to suddenly have some land that he was the first in the village to join the party. My great-uncle also joined the party, but he faced a different situation. My great-uncle's eldest son, Thae Se-gil, had gone to Shenyang in Manchuria during the Japanese colonial period and had even graduated from middle school, so he was one of the few intellectuals in Myeongcheon County at the time. My great-uncle reluctantly joined the party at the request of his son.

I completely understand why my grandfather took the lead in joining the party. He had raised enough money during 1946 to buy a calf just by farming the land he'd been given by the Communist Party. He would not have been able to earn that much money even if he had worked very hard for years on that rocky patch he had inherited. My grandfather went to the market proudly announcing he would buy a calf with the money, but he returned home in shame empty-handed. The root of the trouble was that he had sat down to a Hanafuda (literally, "flower cards," a style of Japanese playing cards) game with dreams of turning his calf into an ox, but he lost all the money in the gamble. He regretted it greatly and threw himself into farming again the following year, eventually buying a calf. It was a time when anyone could work as hard as they wanted and be rewarded for it. Grandpa believed that his good fortune was thanks to the WPK. He would have done anything the party told him to.

Speaking of which, my grandmother often made two requests of me as a young child. The first was that as a man I should eat up all my food, leaving no leftovers. The second was to never gamble. She said if I kept these two things in mind, I would never fail. I am proud that I have lived up to my grandmother's requests. After liberation, gambling was permitted in North Korea for a while, and I understand that many people were addicted to this vice. Kim Il-sung had a lot of faults, but I think it was a good thing that he eliminated the system of concubinage and severely punished those who gambled and did drugs.

The five years between Korea's liberation from Japanese rule and the Korean War could be considered the heyday in the developmental stage of North Korea's social history. The implementation of land reform and the country's Nationalization of Industries Act purged the nation of the land-owning and capitalist classes who had owned land and factories. Most of them went to South Korea full of resentment, yet there was an improvement in the overall atmosphere of North Korean society. I've heard that people at the time burned with zeal to develop the country under the slogan "Constructing a Democratic Korea."

MY FATHER WONDERS WHETHER TO FOLLOW PARTY COMMITTEE ORDERS OR JOIN THE *CHIANDAE*

The Korean War changed the fates of many Koreans just as Kim Il-sung's land reform had done right after liberation from the Japanese. My grandfather, who lived in a remote area of North Hamgyong Province, was no exception.

On October 17, 1950, the Korean People's Army (KPA) beat a full-scale retreat after the Republic of Korea's (ROK) Army occupied Pyongyang. When the KPA withdrawal began, a cold wind blew in the quiet mountainous area of Myeongcheon County. Myeongcheon County's party committee issued a retreat order to all party organizations at the village level. When the order to retreat came, the chairman of Hwanggok Village's party committee gathered twelve party members and ordered them to meet at the county party committee's headquarters at 9 P.M. My grandfather was one of these twelve people.

He returned home and told my grandmother to pack, but she tried to stop him.

"It's going to become cold soon. Where are we going to escape to?"

"The party has ordered us to retreat, so we must follow orders."

"If you really want to go, take Hyeong-gil [my father] with you. The ROK army will come after him for being a [Socialist] Korean Children's Union leader."

"The ROK army won't hurt a child. It's hard enough for me to walk alone, let alone if I'm going with a child!"

The argument went back and forth, and my grandfather put a lump of opium in a sack. Farmers were still allowed to plant opium back then and it was used to treat diarrhea and colds. My grandfather had been weak since he was young and intended to rely on opium to endure what would be an arduous retreat.

Eventually, Grandpa headed off in retreat by himself. I heard this story from his own lips. He said that when he got to the county party committee's headquarters at the appointed time, only my grandfather and the chairman of Hwanggok Village's party committee ended up gathering there out of the thirteen party members in the village. The party committee chairman ordered them to set off, and from that moment, the two began marching in the direction of Chongjin. Grampa said that he just headed north without knowing why or where he was going. They walked for ten days and arrived in Musan, North Hamgyong Province. Rumors were circulating that an order might be issued to fall back across the border to China.

On October 25, the Chinese army crossed the Yalu River. Then, an unexpected order came down from the leadership: Because the U.S. military was now in retreat, party members were to follow the advancing Chinese People's Volunteers and KPA back to their own hometowns. They marched in formation all the way to Myeongcheon County. Whenever my grandfather got behind in the march, he quietly fell out of the ranks and chewed some opium. Each time he did that he felt his energy rise again and eventually— thanks to the opium—Grampa wasn't left behind in "enemy occupied territory." I felt my grandfather's pride in what he had accomplished from his tone of voice and facial expression as he told the story.

All in all, my grandfather had made a trip from Myeongcheon to Musan and back, a distance of around 142 kilometers. He traveled for a month on foot across a distance that one could travel in half a day by car. That one month changed the fate of my grandfather and many others.

When Myeongcheon County's party committee retreated, the ROK Army occupied Myeongcheon County's seat of government. While the ROK Army force was small, it ordered the creation of a *chiandae* (low-level civilian militia) in Myeongcheon County. I understand there was even an order given to shoot those who would not join the *chiandae*. Most residents of Myeongcheon County, who either did not or could not retreat, joined up. My great-uncle also joined the corps at that time. Most WPK members had no choice but to join, too. Even Thae Se-gil, the eldest son of my great-uncle and a party member, joined the new force.

Although he wasn't pressured at gunpoint, my father, who was fifteen years old at the time, was also pushed to join the *chiandae*. The head of the village *chiandae* came and told him, "Agan Middle School will open again soon, so you, the former [Socialist] Korean Children's Union leader, must come to school so that other children will come, too," before emphasizing again, "Make sure to come to school." The man was a close friend of my grandfather.

My father was selected as leader of the local chapter of the children's union a year before the Korean War broke out. Kim Il-sung had created the union on June 6, 1946. It was akin to Boy Scout troops affiliated with schools. In 1949, a national meeting of the children's union was held. Agan Middle School, which my father attended, had to send a representative to the meeting. My father was the best student, so he was elected as leader of the local union chapter. Even on ordinary days, the leader would wear an insignia on his arm that had three red stars and three red stripes. Being a local leader was a source of great pride for him, given the atmosphere of the society at the time.

He found, however, that he had no proper suit or shoes to wear upon his sudden selection to attend the national meeting. He went to borrow money from my great-uncle, who was reasonably well off. "The Thae family has cause for great celebration," my great-uncle said as he went to take out some shoes, but my great aunt stopped him, saying, "How can you give adult shoes to a child?" She had long treated my family with cold-ness because of what had happened during the land reform. Ultimately, my father returned home without shoes or a suit. With tears in her eyes, my grandmother tore up the only blanket in the house, stitched a suit, and dressed my father in it the next day. Later, my father proudly told me, "I was Korean Children's Union local leader number 74. When you grow up, make sure to become a children's union leader, too."

I did not become a children's union leader like my father, but now that I am getting older, I often remember how proud my late father was during his lifetime.

My father hesitated when the local *chiandae* leader ordered him to go to school. Grampa had retreated northward with the WPK, and the village elders including my uncle (Thae Se-gil) had joined the *chiandae*. My father must have struggled to decide which side to take. He had no political leanings at all and didn't want to go to school, so he ultimately decided to just play around for a month. That month played a decisive role in shaping my destiny. Neither my grandfather nor my father could have imagined that the choices they made then would later play a major role in helping my career as a diplomat.

Less than a month after occupying Myeongcheon County, it was the ROK Army's turn to retreat toward Hamheung. My father said he did not see a single South Korean soldier despite everything going on. As the WPK officials returned home, they carried out a large-scale investigation. Those who had joined the *chiandae* were the first targets. However, there was no rush to carry out cycles of reprisal killings as there was everywhere else. Since they had all lived together in the same small village for many years, they were all tied together by blood and marriage.

The head of Hwanggok Village's party committee, who had retreated together with my grandfather, quietly visited him and suggested that they get their stories straight: "When we left, we deliberately left party members behind. If everyone had retreated, there would have been no one to take care of the remaining families. As the village party chief had instructed, some party members joined the *chiandae* and protected the villagers."

The village party chief suggested they create an investigation document and submit it to the county party authorities. He wrote a false account of what had happened and turned it in to the county party committee to save everyone. Besides, it was true that they had joined the *chiandae* and protected party members and families of KPA soldiers. There was not a single massacre. It isn't possible to know whether the county party authorities believed the report, but party members who had joined the *chiandae* like my uncle Thae Se-gil were not expelled from the party. Instead, they were forgiven. A list of names of students who attended school at the instructions of the ROK Army and the *chiandae* was also written up, but at the time no one could have known the eventual significance of that list.

My father graduated from Agan High School in 1954, the year after the Armistice put the Korean War on hold, and sat the entrance examination for Pyongyang University of Construction and Building Materials. As an aside, I've heard that universities in Seoul are called "in Seoul*dae*,"[1] but in North Korea, universities in Pyongyang are collectively called "Pyongyang Central Universities." Other students from Myeongcheon County with excellent grades also applied to Pyongyang Central Universities such as Kim Il-sung University, but only my father was accepted. This is because recommendations for entry into such schools were rejected for students who had gone to school during the period of the ROK Army's occupation.

My father was the first student from Myeongcheon County to enroll in one of the Pyongyang Central University schools. He told me that when it was vacation time, he would get off the train at Gocham Station and walk the almost fifteen kilometers to Hwanggok Village wearing his university cap. Everyone he passed stared at him with envy. When he arrived at the village, the people working in the fields rushed out and welcomed him.

That evening, the whole village came by with eggs or a bag of wild vegetables, and sometimes even a basket of rice. It was a time when there was no radio, no electricity, and no newspapers, so my father's Pyongyang stories were riveting. They would stoke a fire late into the night to keep away the mosquitoes, and adults and children would gather round smiling as they listened to his stories. My father was also excited to share his experiences.

"In Pyongyang, one apartment building is put together every fourteen minutes to heal the wounds of war."

"Is that true?"

"Of course it is."

"Wow, the world has gotten so much better."

"In a little while, we'll have electricity in Hwanggok Village, too."

My father said that conversations went like this, and the whole village cheered when they heard that there would be electricity.

However, my father's hometown was still poor even years after the Korean War ended. My own family didn't experience any significant changes, either. My grandfather's health was not good, and my father was a student with no income. For a time, it seemed impossible to escape poverty, but in just a few years, North Korea's rural communities would experience major changes.

COLLECTIVIZATION HITS REMOTE HWANGGOK VILLAGE

Kim Il-sung was convinced that in order to increase agricultural production, a socialist form of farming had to be created through collective farms. Since it was still a time when free debate was allowed within the WPK, Choi Chang-ik and others opposed Kim's idea, arguing that it was too early to collectivize. They pointed out that North Korea had not yet been industrialized, and collectivization required large agricultural equipment such as tractors.

Kim waved away this counterargument and implemented a policy of organizing collectives in several regions on a trial basis and then gradually expanding them. First, tenant farmers, discharged soldiers, and their children went to remote regions to organize collectives with farmers who were short on labor, and the government supported them through preferential loans and provisions of fertilizer. This led to an acceleration in the country's rural collectivization. In the late 1950s, the wind of agricultural collectivization blew through Hwanggok Village, too. The village party committee chairman visited my grandfather. There are two reasons why the local party chairman consulted with my grandfather whenever there was an important issue on the table. One is that my grandfather was a key party member, and the other is that the Thae family was one of the village's most influential. Members of the Thae and Dong clans had lived side by side for generations, and they were considered powerful families.

The village party chairman was a Dong. He told my grandfather: "We have been instructed by the party to collectivize. This method involves bringing together all the land that was distributed and merging it together in a collective. Cows and farm equipment will be shared. Soon we will hold a meeting to organize a collective farm, so please let everyone know you will actively participate." Grandpa did not understand what a collective farm was, or even why the land that had once been distributed had to be merged together again, but he said he would be happy to step forward because it was what the party had told him to do. Later, when the meeting was held, my grandfather read off the script he had been given and, with that, the Hwanggok Village Collective came to be.

Villagers who owned good-quality land, cattle, and agricultural equipment were somewhat sour on the idea of forming a collective. Some wealthy farmers even secretly sold their livestock before joining it. They were criticized in criticism sessions held in the village, and party officials took measures to prevent livestock from being disposed of. In general, people complied without much resistance. If they didn't join the collective, they would be labeled reactionaries. Although it was not compulsory, the majority of farmers joined collectives because the state focused all its aid on making the farms work. Kim Il-sung had yet to reveal his true colors as a dictator, so there were farmers who hesitated to join until the end, and they faced no penalties such as being sent to prison or labor camps.

There wasn't enough farmland in the country although it was densely populated, so it made sense that agricultural production would increase if farmland was merged together and the labor force was used efficiently. Collectivization was a great success in the early stages of its implementation. North Korea announced in August 1958 that the socialist stage of farming had ended, signifying that all farmers had become members of collectives.

My grandfather was in charge of raising cattle in his collective. Rather than raising them, however, he was really taking the cattle to graze on grass in nearby mountains and fields. It was a life much easier than the hard work of farming. My grandmother also said she liked the collective farm. My grandmother had previously farmed together with my frail grandfather, my young uncles who didn't want to work, and my aunt. It was hard work and boring. However, once they joined the collective, she became a member of an agriculture-livestock team and raised pigs. The job seems to have suited her.

Aunt Thae Juk-sun became a clerk at a village store, a job that all the other young unmarried women in the village coveted. Instead of farming, she dressed up nicely every morning and sold goods at the store. There weren't many customers, so all she had to do was work alone all day and organize the bookkeeping from time to time. My uncles Thae Jong-gil and Thae Jung-gil no longer had to help with the farming after school. Sometimes all they had to do was chop some wood.

Collectivization worked in a way that was exceptionally good, at least for our family. This may be because the WPK classified my grandfather, who had retreated during the Korean War in accordance with party orders, a member of the core class. However, collectivization did not work well for everyone. It goes without saying that the non–core classes suffered relative disadvantages.

Similar to the country's administrative areas, collectives were organized at the *ri* (village) level, so the party's political activities and the collectives' economic work closely overlapped. The party's establishment of shops, day-care centers, kindergartens, and elementary schools on the village level was the result of the simultaneous pursuit of political legitimacy and economic efficiency. In addition, the authorities had the same person serve as both the village people's committee chair and the chair of the collective management committee in order to fuse the management of politics and the economy in an organic way. Looking back on it now, it was a major revolution in how things were done.

Yet calling this move to organically fuse politics with economy "a major revolution" shows how backward the current makeup of North Korean people's consciousness is. In South Korea, who would say, "fifty or sixty years ago was better?"

IN THE 1960S, FARMING VILLAGES WERE AS GOOD AS PYONGYANG, BUT LATER, GOING TO THE COUNTRYSIDE MEANT ENTERING THE ABYSS

Collectivization changed the way villages were run, too. In the past, the local party committee chairman wielded great power, but traditional authority centered on the elderly, wealthy farmers, and men. That's why people like my great-uncle exerted considerable influence. However, as collective farms were created, power shifted to cadres in the collectives. In this new era, the instructions that came from the collective farm management committee chairman, the head of the work teams, and the heads of sub-work teams, became more important than those given by village leaders, elders, and even one's father. It was a great resetting of relationships. I can provide an example of this. Previously, the seat of honor at wedding ceremonies and sixtieth birthday parties (called *hwangap* in Korean) was reserved for the family elders or village leaders. However, after collectivization, cadres such as the village party chairman or the farm management committee chairman sat in the seat of honor.

A similar thing happened within families, too. My grandfather had been poor and weak, so he would receive a cold reception at family gatherings. He had to eat humbly in another room instead of sitting with the other adults at the main table where the meal was served. However, as the situation and times changed, Grampa proudly came to sit in the seat of honor. No matter what anyone said, my grandfather was an important party member. Moreover, he was a respected individual who had raised his children so well that one attended a Pyongyang Central University and the other was a salesclerk at a store. In North Korean parlance, the farmhand had become one of the rulers.

Women's growing right to speak was also a clear change brought by collectivization. My grandmother had always been quite sensible and a good speaker, much better than my grandfather in fact. Nevertheless, it was difficult for her to tell even another person's housekeeper what to do. However, after joining the collective farm, she became the head of a sub–work team, received positive work evaluations, and became a female boss doling out instructions and criticism to men. A sub–work team includes around twenty people; above that is the work group, followed by the collective.

Many men had died in the Korean War, and the strong young and middle-aged men were still serving in the military. That made the role of women important. Data suggest that 40 percent of the work-group heads at North Korean agricultural collectives in the late 1950s were women. The chairman of Hwanggok's party committee had died in the war, and when a female village party chair was appointed, it seemed to reflect the trend of the times. The new chairwoman was a young widow. Her husband had been in the army and was killed in action in the Korean War. Party officials had kept an eye on her for a while, sending her to a cadre school in North Hamgyong Province to study for about a year. After that, she was given all authority in the village. This widow became the village's most powerful person, controlling everything.

After collectivization was completed, North Korea embarked on a massive rural cultural revolution. Villages throughout the country were connected to the power grid. After initially laying electrical cables to households scattered here and there, the authorities came up with a new idea. They decided to gather households in rural parts of the country into collective residential areas to make it easier to connect them to the power grid. Doing this also made it easier for the government to exert control over and surveil its citizens.

From 1959, the Socialist Modern Housing Construction project found its way into Hwanggok Village. The local people's committee selected a site to build a collective village. That the new was replacing the old was demonstrated right from the selection of the site. At first, the village elders tried to decide on a good location based on the principles of feng shui. However, the local management committee criticized the idea of using such principles to decide on a site as a remnant of feudalism; even the *jangseung* (a traditional Korean-style totem pole) at the entrance of the village was done away with because party authorities claimed it was based on "superstition." Instead, the management committee selected a site where groundwater came to the surface and then earnestly began constructing modern-style housing.

All the houses built were based on the same design. Even today, North Korea does not recognize personal ownership of real estate; instead, it grants people only the right to use a house. My grandfather was one of those assigned a new house. He abandoned his old thatched-roof cottage and moved to the new house, which was large and had a tiled roof. The house was a two-room building with a large kitchen, storeroom, shed, chicken coop, and pigsty, along with a toilet and even a grinding mill. Having a mill was unusual. A thirty-*pyeong* (hundred-square-meter) yard also stretched out in front of the house.

When I was in kindergarten, I lived in my grandfather's house. Later, when I was in elementary school, I used to go there during summer vacations. It was twice as big as our house in Pyongyang. Now that I think about it, the interior was about eighteen *pyeong* (sixty square meters). Our house in Pyongyang was a single-story house that had no running water. We used the neighborhood water system. My grandfather's house, on the other hand, had a manual water pump with a pipe that led to the kitchen. All you had to do was put a bucket of water in it, pump it up and down, and water would come out of the faucet in the kitchen.

There was no television at the time. We could listen to the radio and watch movies because there was electricity. When they were building modern-style houses in the village, a propaganda office was built, and every Saturday a projector was brought from the administrative center of the county to show movies. On movie day, children flocked to the propaganda room hours before the start time and played around. I was one of those kids. When the movie started, I recall going back behind the screen up on stage and marveling at the view.

My father told me that every time he went back to his hometown, he could see drastic change had taken place in the village. I also remember that when I went to my grandfather's house during vacation, my grandmother boiled eggs every morning and killed a chicken to eat in the evening. In my house in Pyongyang, we couldn't eat eggs every day, and it was rare to eat chicken even once a week. I think this shows that living standards of Pyongyang and rural areas at the time were at least similar; rural areas may even have been better off economically.

As part of efforts to promote agricultural production, the WPK continued to supply fertilizer to farming areas. Gradually, tractors were allocated, further increasing crop yields. Rural areas had electricity, and the construction of socialist modern houses had been completed, all part of efforts to completely modernize North Korea's rural villages. The idea gradually spread throughout the country that anything would be possible under the rule of Kim Il-sung and the WPK.

All this was how things looked in rural areas from the late 1950s to the 1960s. When Kim Jong-il came to lead the country, however, most of North Korea's resources became concentrated in Pyongyang. Kim Jong-un has now virtually given up on modernizing the DPRK's rural areas. The gap between Pyongyang and the rest of the country is so wide that people divorce each other if one person has to leave the capital city. For Pyongyangites, being sent to the provinces is a nightmarish plunge into the abyss. This is the tragedy caused by the empty fiction of communism and the dictatorship of the Kim dynasty.

THE AUTHORITIES FIND OUT MY GRANDMOTHER'S FAMILY FLED SOUTH DURING THE KOREAN WAR, LEADING TO MY FATHER'S DEMOTION

My father graduated from university in 1959 and became a lecturer at Pyongyang University of Construction and Building Materials. He married my mother that same year. In North Korea, weddings are held at the houses of both the bride and the groom. At that time, my father's house was in Myeongcheon County, North Hamgyong Province, and my mother's house was in the city of Hyesan, Yanggang Province. They first held a wedding ceremony at my father's house, and the next day, they took a train to Hyesan and did it all over again.

My parents first met in Myeongcheon. My mother came to Myeongcheon from her birthplace of Myeonggan County to attend high school because there was no high school in Myeonggan County. Since my mother's uncle lived in Myeongcheon, she went to high school there and got to know my father. They said that my father's classmate Ri Jin-kyu brought them together. Jin-kyu was my father's "study rival." He was a good student, and his family was wealthy. Jin-kyu's father was a doctor at Agan County Hospital in Myeongcheon County. Basically, he was the son of a well-known village leader in the county, and his younger cousin was my mother.

My father had grown up in a poor household and didn't seem fond of Jin-kyu at the beginning because of his wealthy upbringing. Nevertheless, Jin-gyu must have liked him enough to introduce his cousin to my father. One day he came to my father and said, "Hey, why don't you go out with my cousin? She's pretty enough."

My father already knew who she was, so he said yes. In fact, Jin-kyu had already asked my future mother, "One of the guys in my class, Hyeong-gil, is a good student and a good person. Do you want to go out with him?" My mother didn't say no either. That's how my father and mother met for the first time in the mountains behind the school, and their relationship grew from there. Even after graduating from high school and entering Hyesan Normal School in Yanggang Province, my mother continued to date my father.

My father and mother then got married, but they weren't able to move into a house. In North Korea, the state allocates houses to the people free of charge. At the time, however, it took a long time to get a house because so many had been destroyed during the Korean War. As a first step, my father brought my mother to Pyongyang. My father's first cousin once removed, a man named Thae Eul-hyeok, lived near Pyongyang Station. He had six children living in a one-room house. My father took my mother to that cramped house and asked his cousin to let her stay for just a month.

My father visited the people's committee for Pyongyang's Central District and asked the officials there to give him a piece of land to build a house himself. It was a reasonable request because my father was an expert on construction, not to mention North Korea was a socialist society. The people's committee gave him about nine *pyeong* (thirty square meters) of land near the Pyongyang Student Youth Palace. The site was right near the foreign ministry, my future place of work.

When they heard that my father was building a house, his fellow teachers and students all offered to pitch in. At that time, it was the height of the "socialist construction" period. Colleagues who were managing construction work at building sites and their students brought bricks, cement, and other construction materials. There was no one to guard the construction site, so any materials lying around could be carried off. The only reason that didn't happen was that people at the time generally accepted the tenets of communism.

The house was completed in a month. Even though my father worked on it only after clocking off and on weekends, the house was completed quickly because he and his construction expert colleagues worked together. With the house finished, my father brought my mother there, and they started their lives as newlyweds. Although it did not last long, North Korea was once again enjoying a heyday after overcoming the scars of war. It was at this time that people started saying that the country was a "socialist paradise." North Koreans were feeling a sense of confidence and pride toward their country, and they were tasting the small joys and happiness of everyday life.

I was born in that atmosphere. Nobody locked their doors because there was no need to worry about thieves, and the neighbors were full of generosity. Local elderly women used to switch out the coal in our fireplace because my mother, who worked as a teacher, didn't have time to go home from school during lunchtime. In those days, the whole neighborhood was like a family.

After I turned seven years old, my mother woke me up early every morning. She left me with the job of dumping the burnt coal at the only trash dump in the neighborhood. Even now, I tend to wake up early in the morning. It must be a habit I developed then. Starting when I was nine years old, I changed the coal myself. Our house was in the center of Pyongyang, yet it wasn't as nice as my grandfather's house in Myeongcheon County. We had to use a common water supply and common toilets; however, at the time, I thought everyone lived like that. We weren't rich, but it was a happy time. I don't have any memories of being cold or hungry.

Yet amid such happiness, the tragedy of the North Korean regime was being conceived. On May 25, 1967, when I was five years old, the Fifteenth Plenary Session of the Fourth Central Committee of the WPK was held. That was the day when Kim Il-sung's so-called May 25th Instructions were released. With this meeting, Kim's power became absolute, and the work to establish the party's monolithic ideological system became official. The North Korean leader purged his political opponents and carried out a nationwide effort to register everyone with the government. It was the so-called Project for the Maintenance of Party Ranks. The intention of the authorities was likely to establish a dictatorship by once again sorting out everyone's *songbun*, or social status.

Everybody again had to record all their family relationships, which had changed in the wake of the Korean War. During this process, we found that the whereabouts of my father's aunt (the older sister of his mother Ri Sun-hyang) and her family were unknown. Her son had joined the North Korean military and then gone missing, and the rest of the family disappeared around the time ROK forces retreated. The party believed they had defected to the South, which led to a change in my father's status from "core class" to "wavering class."

I remember something from my childhood about this. One day, I was looking around my father's bookshelf and found something strange. While he was working as a teacher at the construction university, he wrote several textbooks and other works. However, in one book, it said that he worked as a reporter at the Construction Editorial Department at the Central Information Agency for Science and Technology (CIAST). CIAST is an important organization that brings advanced technologies from foreign countries into North Korea. Being a reporter was also a respectable job, but I was so curious about why my father was listed as a reporter I asked him about it.

It turned out he had become a reporter because my aunt's family had gone to South Korea. The Party Committee at the Pyongyang University of Construction and Building Materials deemed it inappropriate for a faculty member with a defector in his family to teach students and transferred him to CIAST. Nowadays, university instructor is not a very popular job in North Korea, so people work hard to avoid becoming one. However, at the time, the status of a university lecturer was higher than that of people working for central government agencies. My father had suffered a demotion, and he was very upset about it.

Nevertheless, he did not work against or complain about the party. He accepted his fate as an inevitable step taken on the path of the revolution. After that, my father worked as a reporter and tried to obtain membership in the party, but the matter of my aunt and her family's defection to South Korea repeatedly held him back. Seeing my father struggle like that, my grandmother asked the Myeongcheon County Party committee chair if she could give him the party membership card of my grandfather, since he was sick and of no use to the party. I can still remember seeing her do that. Soon after, my father volunteered to be sent to work on construction sites in Pyongyang, and only after working as an on-site engineer for a number of years was he able to join the party.

THE FALL OF A MATH GENIUS WHO MISSPELLED
MANGYEONGDAE AS *MANGGYEONGDAE*

Around the time my father was forced out of his university instructor job, my uncle had also stopped teaching mathematics in the Department of Architecture and Design at the same university and became an instructor at the Ministry of Agriculture's Bureau of Orchard Planning. He had also been demoted, but like my father, my uncle did not show antipathy nor did he complain.

The husband of my mother's sister, Kim Se-kwon, had graduated from the same university and class as my father. His nickname was "math genius." He was such a good student that people said he could just sit and solve math problems all day long. My uncle was a typical mathematician who looked kind of nerdy and didn't care about his clothes at all. Around that time, my aunt was majoring in dance at Hyesan Normal University in Yanggang Province. They say that she was well known in Hyesan for her skills at dancing, and when she left home in the mornings she caught the eyes of many bachelors on the street.

My father introduced my uncle to my aunt. He told my mother: "Skills make a person. Kim Se-kwon has a brilliant mind and is a good man. There is no man who'll make as good a husband as him." But when she saw my uncle for the first time, my mother said she worried that her sister would reject him because he looked like such a nerd. Yet my aunt, good looking and coy as she was, liked him at first sight: "My brother-in-law already figured him out when they went to college together, so how could I think any differently? If my brother-in-law says he's a good person, I'm sure that's true."

My aunt and uncle got married in a hurry that year. After that, my uncle graduated from Pyongyang University of Construction and Building Materials and lectured in mathematics at the Department of Architecture and Design, but he was demoted to the Ministry of Agriculture's Bureau of Orchard Planning after Kim Il-sung issued his May 25th Instructions in 1967. He was considered a competent designer, however, so he was given an apartment in the Jongno neighborhood of Pyongyang's Central District, a place where everyone in North Korea wanted (and still wants) to live. The apartment was in a building with corridors lining its exterior. I remember that was around 1970.

At the time, we lived in a single-story house in the same neighborhood. My aunt's house was ten minutes away, and our family stopped by almost every day. I think we were very envious of my aunt for living in an apartment. She was then a teacher at Changjeon Elementary School, which is where I went to school. I remember my father severely criticizing my uncle in his own home once. Looking back on it now, I believe this is what happened that day.

There was a test on people's knowledge of Kim Il-sung's revolutionary activities at the Ministry of Agriculture. In answering the question "Where is Kim Il-sung's childhood home?" my uncle wrote "Mang-gyong-dae," instead of the correct spelling, "Man-gyong-dae." The party committee told him to prepare for a criticism session, but my uncle protested, saying, "I only got one letter wrong; what's the problem?" At that time, the country was in the process of establishing Kim Il-sung's monolithic ideological system, so it was possible that my uncle didn't realize what a terrible sin it was to misspell "Mangyongdae" as "Manggyongdae."

My uncle seemed to have expected my father's support as he told the story of taking the test at the Ministry of Agriculture. On the contrary, my father told him off, saying, "Are you out of your mind? You'll be in big trouble because you couldn't even write the Suryong's hometown properly." Later, when my uncle joined the party, I heard he suffered criticism because of this incident.

FEAR OF A U.S. ATTACK ON NORTH KOREA

While living in North Korea, there were two times when I believed that the United States would actually attack North Korea.

The first came shortly after North Korea seized the U.S. Navy spy ship, the USS *Pueblo*, in January 1968. It happened when I was six years old and living in Pyongyang, and I remember my mother wiping away tears as she packed some of my clothes and snacks into a backpack. There seems to have been an order from the top to evacuate children to areas outside of the capital city.

The second time came after the Korean Axe Murder Incident of August 18, 1976. On that day in Panmunjeom, about thirty North Korean soldiers used axes to kill two U.S. military officers who had been overseeing the pruning of two poplar trees. Following the incident, Kim Pyong-il, then a student at Kim Il-sung University, entered the military. Kim Pyong-il is Kim Jong-il's half-brother, born to Kim Sung-ae, Kim Il-sung's second wife. When Kim Il-sung sent his son to the army, senior party cadres could not sit idly by. Most of the children of these cadres and college students joined the army, too. Air raid warnings sounded every day in downtown Pyongyang, and residents of the city conducted evacuation drills.

North Korea sent members of the "hostile classes" numbering in the tens of thousands to the provinces, as part of efforts to defend Pyongyang from a U.S. attack. The forced evacuations were aimed at ensuring that wavering or hostile forces would not join up with the enemy if there was a battle to defend the capital city. Only those considered "communists to the bone" were left in Pyongyang.

My aunt and her family were ordered to leave for Heukgyo in Hwangju County, North Hwanghae Province. My aunt wailed loudly upon hearing of the order. My uncle hurriedly packed some luggage, saying, "The party has ordered me to go out there and prepare for war, so what good is fussing?" My aunt complained to my father, "Why did you marry me off to a man like him?" My father, for his part, consoled her and told her not to say useless things like that.

My aunt's young son and two daughters were paralyzed with shock, not understanding what was going on. My aunt forced a smile as she wiped away her tears when a car arrived to take her and her luggage. Still smiling, she bravely climbed aboard, saying, "I'll work hard and come back up to Pyongyang. Let's live happily when we meet again."

My uncle worked very hard after arriving in Heukgyo. There were orchard construction sites all over North Korea. He went on many business trips throughout his career to enable his family to live in Pyongyang again. He never obtained a house in the center of Pyongyang, but he did become a planner at the Agriculture Ministry's Orchard Planning Office in the Nunggum-dong neighborhood, in Pyongyang's Yokpo District. Still, that small joy didn't last long either. My uncle died of a brain hemorrhage. He had said his dream was to let his children live in central Pyongyang before he died, but he never realized that dream.

Still, my aunt and her family said things were alright because they could visit our house whenever they wanted to. Travel passes were required to enter Pyongyang from the provinces, and obtaining one was quite difficult. However, residents of Yokpo District, located on the outskirts of Pyongyang, could obtain a travel pass with just their registration card. My cousins used to take the bus on Sundays and then walk for hours to get to my house.

My cousins had spent their childhood in Pyongyang, so they had memories of the city and pined for it. I think they felt satisfied just walking through Pyongyang, seeing its high-rise buildings, paved roads, neon signs, and streetlights. South Koreans may not understand how much of an honor it is for people from the provinces to have visited Pyongyang at least once.

Women who live in the provinces have a strong desire to meet "Pyongyang bachelors." Such a man is worth his weight in gold. As part of efforts to prevent such women from using marriage to settle down in Pyongyang, the North Korean government rarely allows them to live in the capital city. However, if a couple gets married while living in a rural village and then are assigned to jobs in Pyongyang on the party's orders, they will be allowed to live in the city. The reasoning? The government can't break up families.

I asked my father once why my aunt and her family were forced out of Pyongyang to the provinces. My father said that my uncle's father (my aunt's father-in-law) had served as a village leader during the Japanese colonial era. When my aunt's family was still living in Pyongyang, my uncle's father came to live with them. He was respected by the neighbors in Jongno and was called a party member. He also participated in local meetings and discussions about the process of mobilizing work groups, sharing his experience and insight.

My uncle's father was first to join the party after liberation and retreated with the party during the Korean War. He could have been grouped into the core class, but after the May 25th Instructions were issued, his history of being a village leader during the Japanese colonial period became a problem, and he was excluded from becoming a member of the core class. The reason my aunt was temporarily evacuated rather than permanently exiled to the provinces was that my uncle's father had worked faithfully for the party after liberation.

Once exiled, people cannot return to Pyongyang or its surrounding areas. It is possible, however, that if an exiled person works hard in the provinces and the party recognizes their achievements, they can return to live in the outskirts of the capital city. They still face the restriction that their children can't attend a Pyongyang Central University. When I told my cousins to study math hard like their father and go to college, they told me this: "If we go to a university in the provinces rather than one in Pyongyang, we will not be assigned [a job] in an area around Pyongyang and will have to return to the provinces. If that's going to be the case, we'd rather just not go to college. We prefer to live near Pyongyang like we do now."

In the end, my cousins did not go to college and worked as farm laborers at an orchard farm in Yokpo District.

MY FRIEND AND HIS FAMILY MEET MISFORTUNE AFTER MAKING A *TTAKJI* OUT OF A PHOTO OF KIM IL-SUNG

I entered Changjeon People's School on September 1, 1970, after attending Jongro Kindergarten. At that time, elementary schools were called "people's schools" in North Korea, but now they are just called elementary schools. Children from kindergarten to high school are assigned classes strictly based on where they live. So, my friends from kindergarten studied with me through elementary school until we graduated from high school. Basically, there was no distinction between neighborhood friends and classmates.

In April of the year after I entered elementary school, one or two students from each class were selected to join the Korean Children's Union, which was customary practice at the time. I was selected that April, and after swearing the oath at Kim Il-sung's hometown of Mangyongdae on April 15—his birthday and a national holiday—I joined the children's union. The reason I was selected was that I had continually been class president since kindergarten. Those who join the children's union receive a red scarf to wear around their neck. I was the only one in the class wearing a red scarf, and even at that young age I felt a sense of pride.

The first children's union welcoming ceremony is held on April 15, the second on June 6, the union's founding day, and the third on July 27. The fourth round follows on September 9. It is done this way to have the top of the class enter the children's union first, followed by everyone else until reaching the student at the bottom of the class. Eventually, all the children in the class get to join the organization. The reason for not letting them in the children's union all at once is simple. This is to thoroughly divide and rule the students by establishing an order of who's first and who's last in rank. North Korea's party and labor organizations all use the same process to bring people into their ranks.

When I was young, my dream was to be an astronaut. I very much admired Yuri Gagarin, the Soviet astronaut who was the first human to make a trip into space and return to Earth. At that time, *Rodong Sinmun* often reported on the economic achievements of the Soviet Union, and I probably learned of Yuri Gagarin from its pages. At that time, I had a habit of gazing at the sky and the stars every night. It was unbelievable to me that Yuri Gagarin had circled that sky several times. When my father noticed my interest in the stars, he said, "Grow up to become an astronaut like Yuri Gagarin."

Two things that I experienced during my time at Changjeon People's School are particularly memorable. There was a big free-standing house near the school. A Korean-Japanese family who had returned from Japan lived there. The father of the household drove a Toyota. Children in the neighborhood usually saw only Soviet-made Volga vehicles, so they followed the fancy Toyota closely whenever it passed by. Everyone peeped into the car windows when it was parked anywhere.

One day, my father was on his way home when he saw me following that Toyota car with the other children. He dragged me home and severely rebuked me, saying, "Don't envy other people's cars. When you grow up, you'll have a car at your house, too." Then he went on: "Our country is now developing rapidly. At the Fifth Party Congress, the Suryong presented a Six-Year Plan, and when that is completed, we will get a television in our house. And we'll be moving to an apartment. And there's a bus route that'll go to Myeongcheon County where your grandmother lives. When you visit her house, you won't have to walk from Myeongcheon to Hwanggok anymore. You'll be able to take a bus. When you reach my age, there'll be cars at every house like in Japan, so we can go swimming at Nampo, Wonsan, and Hamheung on weekends." Listening to him in a small single-story house where we had to burn coal briquettes for heat, I felt like what he was saying was a fairytale. Just hearing that we would also live in an apartment and have our own car overwhelmed me. After that, I never followed a car belonging to a *jaepo* ever again. In North Korea, ethnic Koreans who come over from Japan are called *jaepo*.[2]

I was also no longer envious of the television of the rich family next door, where the neighborhood children used to crowd in the evenings. That's because I remembered my father's words that my house would also have a TV. That my father's conviction could be passed on to me at the young age of around ten shows that people strongly believed in North Korea's system at the time. It was the period when we all lived on wages alongside government rations. No one was particularly well off, but no one was poor either. The years stretching from the mid-1960s to the mid-1970s seem to have been the best time in North Korea's history. This period overlaps with my childhood and youth.

Another thing I remember from that time is something sad. I had a childhood friend named Sun-cheol. He was an incorrigible prankster who was good at soccer. Sun-cheol was also great at the *ttakji* flip game.[3] He carried more *ttakji* than anyone else and won them away from his playmates in the neighborhood or at school. I loved playing the *ttakji* flip game too.

One day, Sun-cheol and a few others were playing a game of flip the *ttakji*, and a policeman passing by suddenly asked to take a look. The officer picked up some *ttakji* and asked who they belonged to. One made of white vellum paper was Sun-cheol's. When that *ttakji* was unfolded, it was a photo page of Kim Il-sung from the front of a volume of *Kim Il-sung, Selected Works*.

Even at that young age, everyone knew not to make a *ttakji* ticket with the portrait of the "Father-General." Except for Sun-cheol, all the children shouted, "You're in trouble!" We never dreamed that Sun-cheol would make a *ttakji* with the portrait of Kim Il-sung. The police officer asked where Sun-cheol's house was, disappeared somewhere for a while, and then returned with several more people. They entered Sun-cheol's house and stayed in there a long time. I heard Sun-cheol's mother giving him a beating. Sun-cheol cried pathetically. We were frightened, and everyone scattered to their own homes.

A few days later, I heard that Sun-cheol's family was going to be exiled to the provinces. Nobody knew what that meant, and I didn't know at the time that being sent to the countryside was such a big deal. On the day Sun-cheol's family left the neighborhood with all their possessions, no adults came out to see them off. Only the children gathered around him to say goodbye, and I can still see Sun-cheol sobbing in the car. Later, my father urged me never to touch the portrait of Kim Il-sung or we'd be exiled like Sun-cheol's family.

IN THE BELIEF THAT "TO LIVE WELL, SPEAKING ENGLISH WELL IS A MUST," THE CHILDREN OF PARTY CADRES ARE SENT TO FOREIGN LANGUAGE SCHOOLS

In July 1974, I graduated from elementary school. Unlike in South Korea, North Korean elementary school lasts only four years. During those years, my grades seemed to fluctuate from first to third place in my class. Before entering middle school, I never thought about my future in any detail. I had the vague idea that I could go to Seomun Middle School after Changjeon People's School, just as boys before me did. Seomun Middle School was just over the wall from Seomun People's School, where my mother taught.

I remember the day when my father and mother quarreled over my future career path. My mother said, "We must send him to Pyongyang Foreign Language Institute [PFLI]." In response, my father said: "Do you want your eldest son to become an interpreter? We have to raise him to be a construction engineer like me, a doctor of mechanical engineering, or an astronaut." My mother's argument went like this: "Scientists and engineers have no prospects. From now on, if you want to live well you have to be a high-level cadre or a diplomat. Nowadays, the children of senior cadres graduating from Seomun People's School are preparing to sit the entrance exam for foreign language institutes. Cadres see the future of the country better, so how could you know more than they?"

My father seemed taken aback at her insistence that cadres saw the future of the country better. At that time, there were many families of Central Committee workers and doctors, such as Kim Il-sung's personal physician, who were living around Seomun School. This is because of the proximity of Namsan Hospital, which was for the exclusive use of party cadres. Many of them sent their children to Seomun People's School. My mother was asked numerous times by parents to recommend their children for entry into PFLI.

With that experience, my mother reasoned with my father, "To live well now you must be good at English. All the children of powerful families are applying to study English." But he countered, "Even if he must learn a foreign language, it's Russian you have to speak to go to the Soviet Union. What good would it do if he learned the language of the American bastards?" Yet he couldn't break my mother's stubbornness. My future had been decided.

At that time, each elementary school severely limited the number of applicants to the PFLI. If there had been a lot of Central Committee cadres or Namsan Hospital doctors among the parents of kids attending Changjeon People's School, I wouldn't have had a chance to take the entrance exam. Fortunately, there lived many senior officials of the Ministry of the People's Armed Forces around my school. At that time, military cadres did not know the advantages of having their children learn a foreign language.

In my class, only four people including me applied to PFLI, and three passed the entrance exam. Choe Yong-hak, the son of Choe Yong-gon, a vice president of North Korea, and Jeon In-cheol, a childhood friend, passed together with me, while the son of a driver for Central Committee officials failed. In-cheol and I entered the English Department as we had hoped, and Choe Yong-hak entered the French Department. In the whole of Changjeon People's School, a total of eleven children passed the exam, including Han Cheol-beom, who had been the Korean Children's Union leader.

There is a story worth adding here about Han Chol-bom. He also entered the French Department, worked for the Ministry of Trade after graduation, and was sent to France in the early 1990s as a secretary at the North Korean Trade Representative Office. In the late 2000s, he joined a special government organization and worked in China. He had been responsible for providing financial support to Kim Jong-nam, but when Kim Jong-un took power, he was summoned to Pyongyang and executed by firing squad. This was just because he was close to Kim Jong-nam. His wife and children were taken away to a camp. She was the second daughter of the famous North Korean voice actor Ju Chang-hyeok. Park Myeong-ho, Han Cheol-beom's brother-in-law, managed to escape demotion and is currently the deputy ambassador at the North Korean embassy in

China. I've heard it was only thanks to Kim Jong-un's "special consideration" that he was able to continue working at the embassy.

On September 1, 1974, I entered Class No. 2 of the first grade of the Pyongyang Foreign Language Institute's English Department. I had walked to my elementary school, but now that I went to school by subway, I felt like I was making a round trip all the way through Pyongyang every day. I also had to bring a lunch box, which we called a *bento* at the time. But this was no more than a minor change. At the Pyongyang Foreign Language Institute, I witnessed the new realities of North Korea for the first time. The children of cadres made up 25 percent of enrollments.

The first year of the English Department was divided into three classes. Just looking at the offspring of top leaders among them, there was Ho Yong-hui, daughter of Foreign Minister Ho Dam; Choe Son-hui, daughter of Kim Il-sung's chief secretary; and Kim Tong-ho, son of the president of the Presidium of the Supreme People's Assembly Kim Yong-nam. Later they were joined by transfer students Oh Son-hwa, daughter of Minister of People's Armed Forces Oh Jin-u; and the daughter of Ri Myong-je, head of the Third-Floor Secretariat. Choe Son-hui is currently vice minister of foreign affairs in charge of the North America Department, and Kim Tong-ho is currently a counselor at North Korea's embassy in China. By comparison, Sok Yong-hui, daughter of the deputy head of the Central Committee's Organization and Guidance Department, an organization that exerts a powerful influence inside the WPK, was not even elite enough to put her name on the list of children of senior cadres.

At the Changjeon People's School, I never saw any cadre children. I never even heard that so-and-so's father drove such-and-such a car. At that time, North Korea educated the children of elite families at Namsan People's School and Namsan Middle School. They were supposed to be isolated from the children of ordinary people. Kim Il-sung's own children, Kim Jong-il, Kim Pyong-il, Kim Kyeong-jin, and Kim Yong-il all graduated from the Namsan schools. I was shocked to see the children of senior leaders at the Pyongyang Foreign Language Institute. I thought they would simply put their trust in the influence of their fathers and not bother to study, but they were even more enthusiastic than the children of ordinary citizens. I don't know what they heard from their parents, but they studied English particularly hard. Watching them, I realized that I had to study hard if I wanted become a cadre in the future.

Every country, indeed every society, has education for its elites. North Korea is no exception. In the DPRK, the training of elites begins at the middle school level. Until the 1960s, there were only two elite training bases at the secondary education level. One was Mangyongdae Revolutionary School, established by Kim Il-sung in Mangyongdae district of Pyongyang after liberation from the Japanese, and the other was Pyongyang Foreign Language Revolutionary School. It should be noted that the word *revolutionary* is attached to both schools.

After Korea's liberation from Japanese rule, Kim Il-sung established a boarding school at Mangyongdae to raise the children of his comrades who had died during the anti-Japanese armed struggle in Manchuria. It was initially named the Mangyongdae School for the Bereaved Children of Revolutionaries, and it became customary to add the modifier *revolution/revolutionary* before the word *school*. Kim Il-sung took the children of his comrades buried in Manchuria and enrolled them at Mangyongdae Revolutionary School. He intended to raise them into pillars that would support his regime.

During the Korean War, Kim Il-sung placed graduates of the Mangyongdae Revolutionary School in charge of security for the military leadership. It was called the Leadership Protection Squad. Kim Il-sung said, "Their parents died fighting Japanese colonial rule; we can't make warriors of them, too," so instead of sending them to the battlefield, he made them security guards. At the end of the war, Kim sent them to study in the Soviet Union and Eastern European countries. In fact, they did serve as pillars of North Korea's postwar restoration and construction period, and in the 1970s they played an important role in the efforts to make Kim Jong-il a successor to Kim Il-sung. Among the Mangyongdae Revolutionary School graduates who have risen to senior party positions are Kang Song-san, Yon Hyeong-muk (premier of the Cabinet from 1988 to 1992), and Kim Hwan (deputy premier), as well as Oh Kuk-ryol and Kim Yong-chun, who both served as chiefs of general staff of the Korean People's Army.

Many Korean War orphans entered the Pyongyang Foreign Language Revolutionary School. In the beginning, they were sent to the Soviet Union and Eastern Europe to study, but it was not possible to send them all. As orphanages were set up nationwide and the government raised the orphans, only certain children considered particularly intelligent were admitted to the Pyongyang Foreign Language Revolutionary School to learn foreign languages. Until the 1960s, almost all graduates of this school and PUFS were war orphans. Having lost their parents during the war, they had a strong hostility toward South Korea and the United States, and they became a group of diplomats that faithfully served as "diplomat-warriors" working first and foremost to fulfill Kim Il-sung's wishes.

The number of war orphans had shrunk each year, and by the 1970s, the children of senior cadres began to enter Pyongyang Foreign Language Revolutionary School. Cadres had already foreseen that the society would undergo a new division into social classes and predicted that foreign language experts would be at an advantage economically going forward.

Having experienced the Sino-Soviet split in the 1960s, Kim Il-sung began to shift his foreign policy direction to strengthen relations with Third World countries through the WPK's Fifth Congress in 1970. This, in short, led to a significant increase in the demand for foreign language experts. The general public couldn't tell what was going on, but the cadres could. That was why children from elite families began flowing into the Pyongyang Foreign Language Revolutionary School from the early 1970s. Meanwhile, the popularity of the Mangyongdae Revolutionary School, whose graduates had gone on to become military or party officials, gradually declined. As the enrolment of war orphans fell in the early 1970s, the word *revolutionary* was removed from the school's name, and it became simply the Pyongyang Foreign Language Institute.

MANY NORTH KOREAN DEFECTORS ARE GRADUATES OF THE PYONGYANG FOREIGN LANGUAGE INSTITUTE

There are two paths available if you want to train to become a foreign language expert in North Korea. One is to graduate from the Pyongyang Foreign Language Institute and go to PUFS or a department of foreign literature at Kim Il-sung University. If you go to PFLI, you will continue on to PUFS, if you're good enough. PFLI actually serves as a springboard to get into PUFS. From the early 1970s, some students came to PUFS from foreign language schools that were established in North Korea's cities and provinces. Among the high school graduates who majored in English and Russian, if they studied well and had good social status (*songbun*), they would go on to Pyongyang Foreign Language University or a department of foreign literature at Kim Il-sung University.

Once I was there, I could see that PFLI provided strictly elite education that could not be found in other middle schools. Every month, they held academic contests and posted the results from top to bottom on the bulletin board. It was aimed at making everyone judge their own performance against all the others. First place in my grade was often taken by Hwang Seong-pil, who now works at the Ministry of State Security, and Cha Cheol-ho, who now serves as the vice dean of school affairs at PUFS. They were competitors I could not beat. I went up and down between first and fifth places.

PFLI was unique in many ways. First, the school used foreign textbooks. In class, we recited texts from the BBC's Linguaphone textbook series (an English conversation teaching program). I played the tape and tried hard to imitate the sounds of the Englishman I heard. Later, I encountered a lot of South Korean diplomats and noticed that North Korean diplomats were more accurate in their pronunciation of English. This gap may be due to the differences in how listening practice was conducted in the two Koreas. These kinds of textbooks were not available among ordinary people, who were banned from even trying to purchase them. They were not allowed to be shown or leaked to outsiders.

The Linguaphone textbook contained a wide variety of pictures. There were scenes of British people at home, eating breakfast, and going shopping. There was a sofa and a pet dog in the living room, and they were shown taking a car to go shopping. Bread, butter, cheese, and bacon were all new words, and I learned for the first time that English people drink tea or milk every morning. It was a whole new world to me. I was shocked. When I was younger, my dream had been to go to the moon, but now, after looking at English books, I wanted to go to this country called England.

My father also admired the pictures, saying, "People in Europe really live well." At that time, North Korea was using all sorts of propaganda tools to spread the song called "Nothing to Envy" in the country. The lyrics said that North Korea was the best country in the world to live in. People sang that song every day, but the PFLI showed a different world that students really envied.

Sometimes foreign films were screened at school. The English Department showed American and British films, while the Russian and French departments showed Soviet and French films, respectively. Movies like *The Sound of Music* and *Mary Poppins* are still fresh in my memory. I also learned famous songs from these foreign movies. We were told that after graduation we would have to be able to sing at least a couple foreign songs when meeting foreigners. The education at the school was designed to show us that North Korea was not closed off from the world. Yet we were also taught never to sing the songs in front of ordinary North Koreans.

It is a serious crime in North Korea for ordinary people to secretly watch foreign movies. There are even cases in which people have been executed for doing so. When I told my father that American movies were being screened at school, he wasn't sure whether to believe me. Watching these movies as part of an elite education, however, is permitted by the regime. That's what separates elite education and ordinary education in the DPRK.

Another unique part of life at PFLI was the respect that had to be shown toward older students. Even if a student is just one year older, their juniors must obey what they say. Older students sometimes beat up students in the lower grades, but in most cases, teachers turned a blind eye to this. These kinds of junior-senior student relationships continued even into adulthood. Even within the Ministry of Foreign Affairs, I used honorific language to people who had graduated before me from PFLI even if I was in a higher position within the ministry.

Another unique part of life at the school was sports. PFLI had a swimming pool when even Kim Il-sung University didn't have one. Our pool was large enough to hold Olympic swimming events. PFLI graduates who weren't good at sports were treated badly. To be popular, you had to be good at sports rather than at studying. We played hard during sports matches against other middle schools or vocational schools. During lunchtime, we had to go out to the playground to play soccer, table tennis, and basketball. When we played soccer against students in other departments, it was like war. If we lost a match, older students in the English Department came up and showered us with curses.

To this day, the fastest way to become a diplomat or trade official in North Korea is to enroll in PFLI. Graduating from the school opens the door to entering PUFS or Kim Il-sung University. Many talented people and famous people graduated from PFLI, including the current vice chairman of the Seventh Central Committee of the Workers' Party of

Korea, Ri Su-yong; Foreign Minister Ri Yong-ho; and Baek Sun-haeng, the vice director of the Third-Floor Secretariat. There's also Ryu Gyeong, a powerful official who served as deputy head of the Ministry of State Security until his execution a few years ago; Kim Gye-gwan, the country's first vice foreign minister; and Choe Son-hui, the vice minister of foreign affairs in charge of the North American portfolio.

A considerable number of graduates of PFLI and PUFS have defected to South Korea. The first to come to Seoul was Kim Hyeon-hui, who blew up a Korean Air (KAL) aircraft in 1987. I know that she is the same age as I (born in 1962), but if so, she would have been in the same grade or one year ahead. I don't remember seeing her at school. However, after the KAL bombing, rumors circulated in North Korea that Kim Hyeon-hui had studied Japanese at PFLI and that her father, who worked for the Committee on External Economic Relations, had disappeared along with their whole family.

The next to defect was Ko Yong-hwan, former deputy director of South Korea's Institute for National Security Strategy, followed by PFLI French Department graduate Kang Myong-do, English major Kim Gwang-jin, and German major Choe Se-ung. These are people I can name because they are already well known, but there are many others whose defections have not even been disclosed yet and who are working to unify the two Koreas. I think it's time a South Korean chapter of the Pyongyang Foreign Language Institute Alumni Association is formed. When that day comes, my wife, my two sons, and I will join as full members. All of my family went to that school. Unfortunately, there are many alumni who have already been purged or whose whereabouts are unknown. In my wife's case, she doesn't know where around half of her classmates are. They may have been purged with their husbands or exiled to the countryside.

THE PARTY'S SECRET: KIM HYEON-HUI'S BOMBING OF KAL FLIGHT 858

Kim Hyeon-hui's bombing of KAL flight 858 left a deep impression on me because it was something I had to deal with from the moment I entered the Ministry of Foreign Affairs.[4] Initially, I accepted without a doubt all of the party's policies and propaganda. However, in the wake of the KAL bombing, it surprised me to learn that WPK policy was split between parts that were disclosed and undisclosed.

At the time, the North Korean media criticized South Korea and the United States every day, claiming that the bombing of KAL flight 858 was a false flag operation perpetrated by South Korea, but discussion in the European Department of the foreign ministry moved in the opposite direction. The North Korean espionage team behind the bombing had conducted training in Europe, specifically in Austria and Yugoslavia. After the incident, the two nations protested strongly to North Korea, and the foreign ministry's European Department was eager to cover it up. Austria and Yugoslavia cooperated with Interpol to fully investigate the North Korean team's stay in the region.

The Eastern Bloc countries did not make any public statement against North Korea because they shared the same communist systems, but Austria took steps to drastically reduce the number of diplomats at the North Korean embassy in Vienna. The embassy there served as a base for overseas missions in Western countries. A considerable number of professional diplomats as well as agents from North Korea's special agencies, including the WPK's Investigation Department, were stationed there under diplomatic cover.

North Korea protested that it had nothing to do with the bombing of the KAL aircraft and demanded that the order to deport diplomats be rescinded. However, Austria threatened that if Pyongyang continued to deny its involvement, it would have no choice but to disclose the details of the North Korean espionage team's stay in Vienna. North Korea was forced to back down and respond with silence. Austria quietly moved on without disclosing to the media the details of the North Korean espionage team that had trained in Vienna. That was fortunate for North Korea.

As I watched this all play out, I realized that the party's policy of "opposition to all forms of terrorism" was not true. The international media had reported that North Korea was responsible for the Aung San Mausoleum bombing of October 1983 that occurred while I was studying in China, but I firmly believed the party's insistence that it was part of an "anti–North Korean propaganda offensive." However, after the downing of the KAL passenger jet, I saw what was happening at the Ministry of Foreign Affairs, and I found myself having somewhat mixed feelings. I wondered to myself: "No matter how much you hate South Korea and dislike that Seoul is hosting the Olympics next year, how can you kill innocent people?"

While I felt there was a gap in how I thought and what the regime was doing, I nonetheless believed in the North Korean theory of violent revolution, which taught that "sacrifice is inevitable in the course of the revolution." I rationalized the party's actions, telling myself: "There was no other way to wreck the Seoul Olympics." This is a bitter memory for me.

I MARRY INTO A FAMILY RELATED TO IMPORTANT GUERILLAS WHO FOUGHT AGAINST THE JAPANESE

North Korea does not allow its people to freely choose their careers. This is true for people who have studied overseas, too. The WPK's Cadre Department considers the academic performance and *songbun* (social status) of those returning from overseas studies and deploys them to agencies such as the Ministry of Foreign Affairs, the Ministry of State Security, the Ministry of People's Armed Forces, the Ministry of Trade, and the Committee for Cultural Relations with Foreign Countries.

North Koreans who have studied abroad hate being assigned to university teaching positions, scientific research institutes, foreign literature publishing houses, and the Korean Central News Agency, because there's not much to be gained financially from working at these places. Instead, they prefer being assigned to places where they can accumulate foreign currency, such as the Ministry of Trade, the Korea National Insurance Corporation, and Office 99, which handles the import and export of weapons.

Although things have changed a little now, the Ministry of Foreign Affairs was a preferred place to be assigned among those who had studied abroad. I began working there in October 1988, and I was often the target for introductions and blind dates with the daughters of cadre families. I don't remember whose daughter it was, but I was once promised that if we only got married, we would be sent to a good country like Sweden or Switzerland, with the sky as the limit career-wise. I was twenty-six years old when I joined the foreign ministry. At the time, that was considered the right age to start a family. I received some introductions before then, too, but rarely with daughters of cadres.

My parents wanted a wife who would be a good match for me, but their conditions were very specific. They said that since she was going to be a diplomat's wife, they'd like her to have majored in English at PUFS or Kim Il-sung University, and they wanted her to be younger than me but older than my younger brother (who was born in 1967). This meant finding a single woman born between 1963 and 1966 who had studied English at a one of the two top schools. There were not many women in Pyongyang who checked all those boxes. I went on blind dates with a few, but they didn't go well.

One of the matchmakers was Kim Dong-ho, who had been dating a girl named Ri Myeong-hui for quite a while. She was studying English at PUFS, and the girl Tong-ho wanted to introduce to me was Oh Hye-seon, Myeong-hui's classmate. But there was a lot of drama in her home environment, so I didn't think she'd fit in with my family.

Hye-seon's father was Oh Gi-su, a lieutenant general in the Korean People's Army. At that time, he was serving as president of Kim Il-sung University of Politics. Their home was a free-standing house on the grounds of the school with armed guards posted around the clock. This was already drama enough, but Oh Gi-su was also the nephew of Oh Baek-ryeong, a partisan who had fought in the anti-Japanese struggle with Kim Il-sung. Oh Baek-ryeong's eldest son, Oh Geum-cheol, was commander of the air force, and his second son, Oh Cheol-san, was a naval commissar. In other words, Oh Gi-su's cousins were leaders in both the Air Force and the Navy. It was as if the wider Oh Baek-ryeong family held the entire North Korean armed forces in their hands.

At first I turned down Dong-ho's offer for an introduction to Hye-seon because I was not that interested. My parents also said that a more ordinary woman would make a better choice. But Dong-ho said all kinds of things praising her, remarking that she had a good and pleasant personality despite being the daughter of a cadre. In fact, what really caught my attention was that she had been part of the welcoming party representing the Korean Children's Union when Tanzania's President Julius Nyerere visited North Korea in 1981.

The Korean Children's Union would organize a welcoming party whenever a foreign leader visited North Korea. Usually, Kim Il-sung would go out to meet them at the airport and drive around downtown Pyongyang in an open-topped car with the foreign leader. Then, upon arriving at the venue for a welcoming event—such as the square in front of the April 25 House of Culture or the one facing the Arch of Triumph—one male student and one female student leader of the Korean Children's Union would step forward. After the male student gave a greeting in Korean and the female student in English ("Welcome to our country, Your Excellency"), Kim Il-sung and the visiting foreign dignitary would join hands with the two children, walk through the welcoming crowd, and climb back into the open-topped car. Being chosen to be in the welcoming party to present a greeting to a guest of the state meant that her physical appearance had to be exceptional.

I pretended I had been won over and accepted Dong-ho's offer of an introduction. My parents also said they'd like to meet her. Then the thought occurred to me that I could get in trouble if I recklessly met a girl from an elite household. If the girl said she liked me but I said no, pressure could be applied on me through foreign ministry cadres.

I went to visit Choe Geum-seon, an English teacher at PUFS. Choe had been my teacher and was now Oh Hye-seon's homeroom teacher. Choe had once lived in the same neighborhood as my family, so my parents knew her well. When I asked Choe what kind of student Oh Hye-seon was, she said right off the bat that she was good and that I wouldn't regret marrying her.

I first met Oh Hye-seon, the woman who is now my wife, one day in April 1989 on the spring blossom–filled road going up to Moranbong. After just a few words, I knew enough. There was no need to say more. I was brimming with confidence at the time because I met all the conditions of being the perfect catch by North Korean standards: I had graduated from college, studied in China twice, was working in a good job, and was a party member. In fact, I had been set up on blind dates with several women before I met my future wife, but none of them moved my heart. With Hye-seon, however, it was love at first sight, so it must have been a match made in heaven.

I took her home to meet my family the same day we met for the first time. My parents liked her very much. At her suggestion, we also visited her home on the same day. My future father-in-law rushed over in his car. My in-laws seemed to have already heard a lot about me from Dong-ho's girlfriend. The arrangements were made in a flash.

My future wife was still in her senior year of college at the time. The parents of both families suggested we have an engagement ceremony first.

We got engaged a month after our first meeting and married on October 17 of that year. We both participated as members of the Korean Youth and Student Delegation at the World Festival of Youth and Students held in Pyongyang in July before our wedding. This was the festival that the South Korean student Im Su-gyeong secretly traveled to North Korea to participate in.[5] At the festival, we received countless messages of congratulations from other members of the delegation. That, too, is an unforgettable memory.

OUR LIVES AS NEWLYWEDS

My wife's grandfather, Oh Do-hyeon, was the eldest of six and, as a result, was the only one among his siblings who went to middle school. The next younger brother was Oh Baek-ryong, but his birth name had been Oh Su-hyeon. It is said that he was given the name Baek-ryong by Kim Il-sung as an exhortation to fight like five hundred dragons.

Her grandmother, Sin Il, had been a cook in Kim Il-sung's guerilla army. In Kim's memoir, *With the Century*, she features as a female partisan. Her grandfather had been killed by Japanese troops sent out to suppress the guerillas, but her grandmother died the year after we got married. Whenever I visited my in-laws, my wife's grandmother sat me down and told me her story of life in Manchuria. These were historical tales that my wife's family had heard a million times and were not interested in hearing again, but I found them fascinating. Sometimes, female guerrilla fighters who were still alive visited my grandmother-in-law. I share below what she told me.

Kim Il-sung sometimes visited the village where Oh Do-hyeon and his wife lived and held meetings with young people on the issue of organizing armed struggle. He was able to communicate well with Do-hyeon, who had graduated from middle school in a village where most were illiterate. One day, he had lunch at Do-hyeon's house. My father-in-law was then a toddler and kept climbing over Kim Il-sung. She said that Kim took a bullet out of his bandolier and gave it to my future father-in-law to play with. After that, Do-hyeon was killed in battle against a Japanese force tasked with hunting down the guerillas. Now that the eldest had died, the second brother, Baek-ryong, joined Kim Il-sung's guerrilla band, followed by the third and fourth brothers. The brothers followed Kim to eastern Manchuria, where the third and fourth brothers were killed and only Baek-ryong survived.

After Korea's liberation from the Japanese, Kim Il-sung established the Mangyongdae School for the Bereaved Children of Revolutionaries and sent my father-in-law and other children of partisans who had died in Manchuria there to study. Afterward, my father-in-law served in the Leader Protection Squad that guarded the military leadership during the Korean War before going to study in Moscow. It was the typical path taken by the children of fallen revolutionaries. After studying abroad, my father-in-law was put in charge of Soviet matters at the Ministry of Foreign Affairs, but when Kim Il-sung packed the Ministry of People's Armed Forces with the children of his comrades-in-arms, he went back to the military as director of the Cadre Department in the General Political Bureau of the Ministry of the People's Armed Forces. After that, his star kept rising, and later he went on to serve as political commissar of the 105th Tank Division, second in command of the North Korean delegation to the Panmunjeom Military Armistice Commission, and then president of Kim Il-sung University of Politics.

Having grown up in such a family and living comfortably all her life in a free-standing house, my wife suffered a lot when she married into my humble family. Back then, my house was a small three-room apartment in the Gaeseon-dong neighborhood of Moranbong District. My wife, who had been used to cooking with a gas stove that was found only in the houses of the elite, didn't know how to handle our butane stove, so I had to help her a few times. At first, my mother was very worried, but my wife quickly adapted. She also received generous praise from my father for her excellent cooking.

My father-in-law liked me very much, too. On weekends, my wife and I spent time at her family's house, and her father knew that I liked beer, so he would serve beer that even my brothers-in-law weren't allowed to drink. Having once worked as an official at the foreign ministry in charge of Soviet affairs, my father-in-law asked me a lot about the international situation. In a closed society like North Korea, even the president of a military-affiliated university was cut off from outside information. He listened to my stories with great relish and showed particular interest in the progress of U.S.–North Korean talks.

My wife graduated from university in September 1989 and entered the Ministry of Trade. The Ministry of Foreign Affairs and the Ministry of Trade were on either side of Kim Il-sung Square. My wife and I went to work together every morning, and sometimes we would meet at an arranged time in front of Victory Station on the subway and go home together. These were happy days for us. Later, I hung a picture on the living room wall showing my wife as a child, standing before Kim Il-sung and the president of Tanzania in her role as one of the official greeters. A few times when colleagues visited my house I boasted about her, and they would call me a "first-class fool." In North Korea, that is what men who boast about their wives are called.

Our first son was born in 1990. My father had the right to name him because he was the firstborn of his grandchildren. My father wrote two Chinese characters that meant my son would be responsible for his own destiny and should one day attain fame for himself. However, North Korea was a society in which no individual could become master of their own destiny except, of course, for the three generations of the Kim family. Now that my son has escaped North Korea and lives in a free country, it seems that my father had some foresight after all.

9

FOR UNIFICATION AND FREEDOM

"WHO IS YI SUN-SIN?"

Watching my children grow up has made me realize anew how quickly time flies. My older son was born in 1990, the year Germany was unified, and he has already lived a life of many ups and downs. Born in Pyongyang, he went to elementary school in Denmark and Sweden, returned to North Korea, and then went to England to attend middle school.

I remember the time when my son attended an international Catholic primary school near our embassy in Denmark. There was a South Korean girl in the same class. Since all classes at this school were conducted in English, the children knew enough to realize that there was some kind of difference between North Korea and South Korea. Perhaps that's why my son said he and the South Korean girl barely spoke to each other. It is a sad reality, but it shows that even young children are conscious of Korean division.

One day, my son returned from school and asked who Yi Sun-sin was.[1] Although children are taught about Yi Sun-sin in North Korea, he had never attended elementary school there because he was too young at the time. How he heard about Yi Sun-sin is a funny story. My son said that the students all had to give a talk about who the greatest person of their home country was and why that person was so great.

Of course, my son said, "The Great General Kim Il-sung is the greatest in our country," adding, "He drove out the Japanese who had stolen our land." The South Korean child, when it was her turn to give a talk, said, "Admiral Yi Sun-sin is the greatest in our country. He drove out the Japanese who had invaded our land." The class teacher knew about Kim Il-sung, but did not seem to know about Yi Sun-sin. The teacher called on my son and the South Korean girl and asked them, "Why do North Korea and South Korea say something different about who drove out the Japanese?" But the two children had no answer to give. If a Japanese child had been present, it would have been even more awkward.

I don't know if my son remembers that incident, but I don't feel good when I think about the identity confusion that he must have experienced at the time. He later went on to middle school in London, returned to North Korea, and attended PUFS before coming back to England. My son spent his childhood—a time so formative for one's personality traits and character—and his twenties—a time of young adulthood when one should be studying and enjoying life—in a way that was very different from many other people.

Still, unlike the families of most North Korean diplomats, there was only a short time when we parents lived apart from our children. When I came from Pyongyang to Great Britain as consul in April 2013, we were separated from our first son for only about a year. During this time, our younger child lived with us. Fortunately, his older brother came to England in March the following year.

Both boys studied quite hard in England. While studying public health management in London, the older one developed a considerable interest in the United Kingdom's public health and welfare system. He might have thought it was his last chance to learn something. During his practicum, he took care of local patients very attentively.

My second son loved soccer. When we had just arrived in England, he dreamt of becoming a professional soccer player. When he was in his fourth year of studying Chinese language at PUFS, he was a striker on the Korean language department's team that beat the team from the English department. It was the first time the Korean language team had won in the decades since the school's opening. When he left Pyongyang, the teachers jokingly said, "Now that you're going, the Korean language department soccer team is ruined."

Even after arriving in London, he played soccer every day, but after about a month he suddenly said, "There's no hope for me to go professional, so I'd better just study." He said he couldn't keep up with the soccer skills of British players. After that, my son began to concentrate on his studies. I can't forget the pride I felt when I went to an all-parents' meeting a year later. The teacher in charge of English language teaching said that my younger son's English composition had been selected as an excellent piece of work and that he had wanted to meet the parents. The mathematics teacher, who was also the homeroom teacher, praised my boy, saying he had a bright future. He vied for first and second place in his entire grade level in mathematics grades.

Nevertheless, my sons were changing a lot from when they were young. In short, they were waking up to the realities of North Korea. It was hard to compare what they were going through with my time growing up. Looking back, I think my mother bought me books and tried to give me philosophical training. The first books that my elementary school teacher mother bought were Soviet novels such as *How the Steel Was Tempered*, *The Iron Flood*, and *Mother*. They were so interesting that I read them over and over again.

In later years, I watched movie and drama adaptations of *How the Steel Was Tempered* several times, but it was still enjoyable every time. The words and actions of protagonist Pavel Korchagin, who gives his all for the proletarian revolution and to build a proletarian society without inequality, are still vivid in my memory. The scene in which Pavel hugs his love interest, Tonya, and confesses his love, saying, "If you're really serious and not just playing with me, I'll be a good husband to you. I'll never beat you, never do anything to hurt you, I swear it," made my young heart flutter.

After that, my mother bought me several more foreign novels, and whenever I finished reading one, she would ask me my impressions of it. Then she would say, "Yong-ho, just like the main characters in this novel, you should grow up and fight for the liberation and freedom of humankind."

My father felt the same way as my mother. He bought me *Recollection of Anti-Japanese Partisans*, which tells the true story of Kim Il-sung's anti-Japanese armed struggle. I tore through it in just a few days. My heart leaped at the story of communist fighters who fought for the liberation of mankind and the independence of Korea.

Immersed in such memories and sentiments, I once forced my children to re-create my own experiences. Every evening, I gave them the task of reading Kim Il-sung's memoir, *With the Century*, for hours on end and then delivering an oral book report. I thought that since my children grew up in European countries, they lacked unconditional obedience to the North Korean regime. That's not to say that such a spirit was right, but I was concerned about the dangers and hardships my sons might face without it.

I couldn't get my boys to finish reading *With the Century*. They could not find any enjoyment in it because the content of the memoir and the reality of North Korea were so different. Even now, North Korea forces its students to read *With the Century* and *Recollection of Anti-Japanese Partisans* and write book reports. In contrast, almost no students in North Korea voluntarily read communist books or novels. I believe this reflects the realities of the younger generation, and their sentiment will become the foundation for the unification of the two Koreas.

No matter what anyone says, I was born and raised during North Korea's golden age. It was a time when the role of the socialist state to solve food, clothing, medical, and welfare problems for its people functioned to some extent. I felt a sense of pride in and loyalty toward my country, and I am not ashamed of that now. But my children are completely different. Far from a golden age, they were born and raised during the so-called Arduous March. Not only did they not receive any benefits from the state, they even experienced instances in which the state degraded their own personal sense of pride and patriotism.

My children were made fun of at their schools abroad. If you say you're from North Korea, people respond differently than if you come from another country. It's not "Oh, I see"; rather, it's "Really?" or "Are you serious?" And as they became more friendly with the other kids, the teasing continued.

"I heard that there is no internet in North Korea. How do you survive?"

"Do all young people have to cut their hair short like Kim Jong-un?"

"Is it true that Jang Song-taek's body was made into dog food after he was executed?"

There were constant questions that were difficult to answer, embarrassing, and sometimes even insulting. My children also experienced the same hardships that I had to go through every day.

They began to hold critical and pessimistic views of North Korea from reading books, watching movies, and using the internet. They also lamented the human rights situation in North Korea. Still, they have never asked me plaintively, "Why were we born as [North] Koreans?" It was difficult for me to see them hold such critical views of their home country.

WE CAN'T LIVE LIKE THIS

It had been a little over two years since our elder son came to London. In March 2016, a group of North Korean restaurant waitresses in China defected en masse to South Korea. It was a shocking incident. Of course, there had been many cases of families or relatives who escaped from North Korea together, but this was the first example of group defection from a single organization. A strong castle doesn't collapse all at once; it starts with small stones falling out of a wall and collapses when large rocks are removed. I believe that this group of waitresses will be the beginning of the collapse of the North Korean regime.

North Korean society was turned upside down by the incident. The rest of the waitresses who did not defect were immediately recalled to Pyongyang for interrogation. It was found that the waitresses had developed a yearning for South Korea by enjoying its movies and dramas.

The North Korean embassy in Britain received instructions after the incident. It was to investigate all the computers in the embassy chancery and residences and detect any members who were watching South Korean movies and dramas. In May, new instructions were issued. My heart sank. The orders said: "The reason the female employees defected in a collective fashion was because they were watching too much South Korean content on the internet and went mad. You are to send all embassy children over the age of twenty-five back to the motherland by the end of July." This meant that our older son would have to go back to Pyongyang. Kim Jong-un's plan to solve the shortage of talent in North Korea by sending diplomats' children abroad to study was now scrapped after less than two years.

Working as a diplomat, I had knowledge about the North Korean regime. I knew there were quite a few cases in which problems had arisen after young people who had returned from abroad in the middle of their studies had then transferred to North Korean universities. I had warned my sons many times that they should never talk about what happened in England. However, I couldn't help but feel rage now that I had to send my son, who had been doing well in his studies in the UK, back to North Korea.

Many North Korean diplomats worry about their children. They miss them terribly and worry about them whenever they are separated from them. When parents are stationed overseas and their children live alone in Pyongyang, educational problems arise. To put it simply, there are many cases in which their children go off the rails. They are easily exposed to wrongdoing such as drinking and gambling, as well as inviting friends of the opposite sex to their home while their parents are abroad. It is not difficult to find cases of depression among diplomatic spouses who have had to leave their children behind in Pyongyang.

I think the worst thing in the world is to take advantage of the love between parents and children and use it for some other goal. Whatever the excuse may be, the children left behind in Pyongyang end up being seen as hostages by their parents working outside the country.

I asked Ambassador Hyeon Hak-bong, "My older son's semester ends in July, so please allow him to keep going to school until then." My request went up the chain to Pyongyang, and a few days later I received an order from the top that my son was to go back during the month of July no matter the circumstances. Pyongyang continued to press me on the issue after that. As July approached, my son's face clouded over. My wife also spoke up less and less. I made up my mind: "We can't live like this. Don't parents have the right to live with their children? Let's not live like this anymore. What kind of life is this?"

I had served the North Korean system all my life. I had also received many privileges and benefits. However, I didn't want to have to weigh up my boys' future anymore. I was tired of a system in which parents couldn't live with their children as they wanted. I had fought with the authorities several times over the issue of having our sons live with us. I would do anything if it meant that I could live with my children. Raising my off-spring well was one of my lifelong goals. I couldn't take it any longer.

I thought, "Let's find freedom, which is a particularly precious com-modity for our children. Let's break the chains of slavery and seek out our dreams." I made up my mind that it was time to leave North Korea. Shortly before my older son was to return to Pyongyang, we went for a walk as a family in a park near the embassy. I had already discussed the issue of defecting from North Korea with my wife. Even though they were my children, when it came to actually talking about the decision to defect and escape from North Korea, my heart beat and the words wouldn't come out. Unsure of what signs they might have picked up, I finally calmed my overworked heart in front of my nervous sons and began to speak.

As a father, I can't just send my older son to Pyongyang. It is regrettable that in past times we had to comply with the instructions of the authorities. Now I've decided to pursue my human rights as a human being. I can't live like a slave anymore. It is enough that I have lived like a slave until now. I have made up my mind to defect. If we defect from North Korea, our siblings and family members will suffer great disadvantages, but let's find freedom first. All you have to do is live a good life for their sake. As a father, the legacy I can give you is freedom. Even if we go to South Korea, it won't work out as we hope, but at least you two will be free to live as you choose.

My wife and two sons also gave me their opinions. I don't think it's appropriate to share all of what they said, so I'll just quote one thing from each of them. My wife told my sons: "If we take you back to North Korea despite this opportunity [to defect], we will regret it, and you'll be stuck there and you will blame us, too. If we defect, your grandmother and relatives would suffer unbearable pain because of me, and my heart would break when I think about that. But I will bear all that blame. I believe that the day will come when we will be proud of ourselves for leaving first in search of freedom. Let's do our best for them."

Our sons told us: "It's heartbreaking to think about our relatives, but we also want to live in freedom. Let's do well in life, and on the day [the two Koreas] are unified, we will return to the North and take good care of our cousins. Thank you, Mom and Dad."

When our family decided to defect, Ambassador Hyeon Hak-bong, who had been like a brother to me, was on my mind. I felt so sorry for him. Hyeon, six years my senior at PUFS, had been a close colleague and friend since I joined the Ministry of Foreign Affairs. He had been the ministry's deputy director for the American Department (Department 5), when I was deputy director of the European Department (Department 12). We had also both been branch party secretaries. We knew each other's difficulties and shared the joys and sorrows of working at the foreign ministry. In 1990, he and I had been conscripted into a Ministry of Foreign Affairs labor brigade to take part in building houses for six months on Pyongyang's Unification Street. In that year, when my wife gave birth to our firstborn but could not lactate well, Hyeon himself went to a fisherman and bought some carp. In North Korea, it is customary to feed carp's blood to women who are not lactating.

In the UK, Hyeon and I sometimes worked all night long. He was a man of frank disposition. He hid nothing from me. However, I couldn't tell my colleagues, not even him, about my plans to defect. When Korea is unified, I would like to ask for their forgiveness for not even leaving them a message saying that I was defecting.

My family set a date and carefully planned our escape. No one in the embassy noticed. At last, the day came. We walked about four hundred meters out of the embassy. I had to look back at the embassy one last time. It was my moment to say a final goodbye to the North Korean regime, to which I had devoted my life. Had I lived fifty years only to leave like this? Tears flowed down like a river on my face. The embassy gradually faded out of view. It broke my heart to think of my comrades who were laughing and chatting at the embassy without knowing of my escape. I wanted them to be safe; I just wanted them to be safe.

THE KIM JONG-IL ERA TURNS NORTH KOREA INTO A FEUDAL SOCIETY

Just before our defection, I said to my family, "Kim Jong-un won't last long. However, if we do nothing, the North Korean regime may last longer than we thought. When we go to South Korea, I'm going to work for unification. I will struggle harder than before to free my relatives stuck in the depths of oppression."

Even after coming to South Korea, I've never forgotten that promise for a minute. Fortunately, I have been given a place to work for unification, and I dare say that I am spending every waking minute on that task. One of the things that surprised me when I came to South Korea was that the younger generation is not very interested in unification. This is a complete contrast to North Korean students, who regard Korea's unification as an urgent national task.

But I am not disappointed. If we quietly put one foot in front of the other toward unification, I believe that the time will come when South Korea's younger generation will desperately want it, too. The important thing is that we must prepare in advance how to lead the process of unification. This is where I can help, and this is my mission.

My decision to write a book that is almost an autobiography, something hardly suitable for a man in his late fifties, comes from my goal of giving a correct understanding of the current state of North Korean society. In South Korea, the way people look at North Korean society is tied closely to the ideology of socialism and communism. Given that, it is inevitable that North Korea policy is divided into left and right, conservative and progressive camps, and that there is a broad spectrum of debate on North Korea policy in South Korea. So, is North Korea a socialist society or a communist nation?

A socialist society refers to a society in which equality in people's social and economic status has been achieved. If mankind could really build a utopian socialist society, there would be nothing better.

My own relatives and my wife's parents believed that if they only did as Kim Il-sung told them to, they could build an ideal socialist society on the Korean Peninsula. However, they died without understanding how North Korea's socialist society changed into a socialist feudal society and then regressed from a feudal society to a society of oppression again. That was how secretly the regression process of North Korea's socialism proceeded.

The Korean War ended with the tragic deaths of millions of people, but the enthusiasm of North Korean communists for unifying the Korean Peninsula was not curbed even after the war. By taking advantage of the ideals and enthusiasm of these communists, Kim Il-sung purged all factions in the party by the end of the 1960s and succeeded in establishing a monolithic leadership system. He also established East Asia's first socialist welfare system.

I remember all of that with clarity. There were no burglaries, even though people didn't lock their homes. When my parents came home late from work, the old lady next door came to stoke the fire and make dinner for me. When I was six or seven years old, I took a train alone from Pyongyang to my grandfather's house in Myeongcheon County or my maternal grandfather's house in Hyesan. It took almost ten hours. This was possible not because I was smart. At Pyongyang Station, my father would find passengers going to Myeongcheon County or Cheongjin and ask them, "Please make sure this boy gets off at Gocham Station in Myeongcheon County." Then he would telegraph my grandmother in Myeongcheon County, saying, "I'm sending Yong-ho," and my uncle would come out to Gocham Station at dawn, find me getting off the train, and give me a ride on his back to my grandmother's house.

On Sundays, my father would buy draft beer in a "bucket." In our small single room, he would burn a mosquito-repellant candle and drink beer all night with the locals. It was not much, but it was a time when he laughed with his neighbors and envisioned the future. Until the early 1970s, there weren't many differences between Pyongyang and the provinces.

When did socialist North Korea begin to tilt? I think it was when Kim Jong-il joined the WPK after graduating from college and established an ideological and theoretical system to ensure hereditary rule. On May 25, 1967, Kim Jong-il, under his father's name, announced the so-called May 25 Instructions. The instructions said that in order for North Korea's socialist society to progress further, the class struggle and proletarian dictatorship had to be further intensified.

It was the proverbial bolt out of the blue when it suddenly struck in peaceful and happy villages. From the late 1960s, a North Korean–style "cultural revolution" took place. It ran contrary to the basic flow of history. Looked at theoretically, it seemed as if Kim Jong-il had inherited Lenin's and Stalin's dictatorship of the proletariat. The instructions could also be seen as a measure to take into account the specific situation of the divided Korean Peninsula. However, it was a historical regression to divide North Korean society into different classes once again. The intention was to make Kim Il-sung not a human leader but a superhuman one, one that we could worship absolutely.

Following the May 25 Instructions, North Koreans were divided into the core class, the wavering class, and the remnant elements of the hostile class. Citizens not lucky enough to be ranked among the core class were unable to get their status raised. Even if they lacked ability, they could automatically go up a level if they belonged to the core class. As in the Joseon Dynasty, the practice of dividing people into aristocrats (*yangban*), bureaucrats, commoners, and the untouchables was revived.

Those who fought in the KPA during the Korean War or who retreated following WPK became part of the core class. Those who—through no fault of their own—stayed in their hometowns and greeted U.S. and South Korean soldiers were classified as part of the wavering class. Children of landlords and capitalists, families with members who lived in the South, and families of the "South Korean rebel forces" were branded as members of the hostile class.

Even more ridiculous was the case of the people who were originally members of the Workers' Party of South Korea who had fought in the Korean War for North Korea, or those who returned from Japan to their "socialist Motherland." Both groups were bumped down from the core class to the wavering one. Even if someone had been an anti-Japanese partisan, if they didn't come from Kim Il-sung's group, they would be branded an "anti-Party traitor trying to widen the revolutionary tradition in all directions." Accordingly, they, along with their children, were expelled from the party and all official positions.

If you weren't in the core class, you could not enter the basic offices of the party and the state, such as the party itself, or become a diplomat, security official, policeman, prosecutor, or military officer. For example, PUFS, the university I attended, was a training institution for party cadres, so admission was not possible except for children from the core class. In 1976, Kim Jong-il expelled non-core-class residents from Pyongyang to the provinces, in the wake of the Panmunjeom Axe Murder Incident the same year. My aunt was one of those expelled from the capital to the countryside at that time. Among the hostile classes, residents who resisted or protested against aspects of North Korean society were either executed or dragged away to prison camps. The whole country gradually became a giant prison and garrison state.

TAKE IT FROM ME: NORTH KOREA IS LIKE A PRISON

After the May 25 Instructions, Kim Jong-il proclaimed the "Ten Principles for the Establishment of a Monolithic Ideological System" and began to turn his father into a god. Kim Il-sung no longer served as a leader to unite and guide the party and society as one; this new system established an absolute supremacy of the leader, under which everything in the country, including the party, the state, the military, and the economy, served the needs of Kim Il-sung. The history of the struggle of North Korea's true communists, who numbered in the hundreds of thousands, was completely erased. The revisionist view was that the only Korean history was the revolutionary history of Kim Il-sung and the history of his Mangyongdae Clan.

Since the early 1970s, North Korea has preached the feudal morality of "loyalty and piety" towards Kim Il-sung. From that time on, not only did Kim Jong-il fabricate history to deify his father, but he also carried out activities everywhere to glorify the leader. In 1972, the year Kim Il-sung turned sixty, he was elevated from the status of Prime Minister of the Cabinet to President of the Nation. The justification was that Kim "must be properly respected," but the ulterior motive was to turn him into a figurehead. In fact, from then on Kim Jong-il only allowed Kim Il-sung to engage in activities related to foreign policy.

When Kim Il-sung was prime minister, the Cabinet controlled the economy. In line with the nature of socialism, the economy worked according to the plan set by the National Planning Committee. When Kim Jong-il gained control, he removed the military economy from the Cabinet and turned it into a party economy. Within the party, he set up bureaus and offices to guarantee the luxury lifestyle to which he and the Kim family had become accustomed, including Room 39 and the Gumsusan Accounting Department.

The socialist planned economy system began to collapse. Cadres asked Kim Jong-il to take charge of the Cabinet's work to prevent the economy from fracturing, but he said, "Kim Il-sung told me not to get involved in economic business," adding that he would only take charge of the party and the army. The nation's economy has therefore degenerated into an economy run solely for the Kim family's pleasure.

In emphasizing loyalty and filial piety toward Kim Il-sung, Kim Jong-il turned the direction of all artistic activities toward praising his father. No movie or song was allowed past the censors unless it was in praise of the elder Kim. The son wished his father could live a long and happy life, and in doing so he established Department 5 to select and summon young and pretty women from around the nation, while building special villas and guesthouses in scenic spots.

Kim Jong-il paralyzed even the party's normal functions. Before he got involved in party-related business, it had a collective decision-making system. Although there was already a monolithic dictatorship led by Kim Il-sung, policy was decided after collective discussion and debate. Kim Jong-il, on the other hand, established a "written proposal system," on the pretext that he had built a strong leadership system for the party that reported all issues to the Supreme Leader, received decisions, and then carried them out. Since he was secretary of the Workers' Party, when Kim Jong-il said, "I will report all proposals to Kim Il-sung and receive his decisions," in effect it meant that from then on everything had to be reported to him. This system also turned Kim Il-sung into a straw man and resulted in his son's monopolizing all information and power in the country. In short, an entire system had been formed that allowed Kim Jong-il to be the sole decision maker.

Since the 1980s, North Korea had been living in an era of rule through proposals (sent up the line to the leadership) and policies (handed down by the leader). Those that came from Kim Jong-il trumped party policy and even national law. Horizontal discussions and consultations on a departmental level almost disappeared, leaving only a vertical work system. Everyone had to report only to Kim Jong-il, who then handed down instructions for what to do next.

It was around this time that the North Korean leadership began cultivating the idea among the people that they were serfs serving only Kim Jong-il. A slogan such as "Let's defend with our lives the Workers' Party's Central Committee headed by Comrade Kim Il-sung" was turned into "a spirit of eight million guns and bombs ready to sacrifice their lives for Kim Jong-il." All adolescents had to learn the spirit of "the General is the marksman, and I am the bullet."

North Korea was already a de facto feudal society or dynastic state. A superstitious idea of the absolute supremacy of the Supreme Leader dominated society as a whole. Kim Jong-il, who had actually been born in Russia, suddenly transformed into the lodestar born on Mt. Baekdu. The whole country was blanketed in frauds and falsehoods. North Korea declared that it had produced four million tons of food and harvested eight million tons of grain and that it had reached the threshold of a complete socialist victory in the 1980s, despite the fact that people were starving and the economy was on the verge of collapse. All sectors had to demonstrate extreme loyalty to transform North Korea into a successful socialist state and ensure that the Supreme Leader was treated like a divine being. Otherwise, one could be branded an anti-party, counterrevolutionary element.

As if being a feudal society wasn't bad enough, North Korea then regressed into a society akin to a prison. I see that as having happened during the period after 1994, when Kim Il-sung died. After his passing, Kim Jong-il's *songun* politics went beyond turning North Korea into a military dictatorship. Everyone's life was determined by the feelings and emotional state of the prison warden, Kim Jong-il. It was Kim who engineered the Frunze Military Academy Incident, the Kazan Overseas Student Incident, the Germany Overseas Student Incident, and the *Simhwajo* Incident, causing ruthless executions and purges and eventually putting all the blame on his subordinates. Even when inflation reached its peak because of the sale of large amounts of North Korea's bank bills to Europe, and North Koreans rebelled for the first time in the country's history in response to the 2009 currency reform, Kim Jong-il avoided responsibility, taking the lives of his underlings instead.

A prisoner must serve at the beck and call of others and is deprived of all rights and means of production. North Koreans have no basic human rights such as freedom of expression, freedom of movement, freedom to own the means of production, and freedom to raise their own children as they see fit. To be sure, today's North Korea serves as a prison for its people.

KIM JONG-UN IS BRUTISH AND SPONTANEOUS, YET ALSO INTELLIGENT AND LOGICAL

Still, it took Kim Jong-il more than fifteen years to complete his path to succeed his father. He joined the WPK's Central Committee in 1964 and got anti-Japanese revolutionary fighters to help him emerge as successor at a party plenary session in 1974. Kim confirmed his path as successor at the Sixth Party Congress in 1980.

Kim Jong-il threw his heart and soul into becoming the chosen successor of the North Korean kingdom. That's why when he was formally nominated as successor, the WPK explained that "Comrade Kim Jong-il has proven his ability as successor while working in the party's Central Committee for ten years." During this period, he made the party and the Kim family his support base. At the same time, he pushed his uncle Kim Yong-ju, his stepmother Kim Song-ae, her older brother Kim Gwang-hyeop, and her son and his own half-brother Kim Pyong-il out of major positions.

In the process, Kim Jong-il highlighted his identity through his lineage, with his father a partisan general and his mother an anti-Japanese heroine. It was an attempt to gain support from Kim Il-sung's partisan comrades and from within his wider family. Kim Jong-il was able to remove Kim Yong-ju and Kim Pyong-il from becoming Kim Il-sung's successor because he was his father's eldest son and the child of his father's first wife. North Korea has a special social structure that fuses concepts from communism and neo-Confucianism. The basis of neo-Confucianism is legitimacy and rationality. It may seem that everything happens in a reckless manner, but in fact North Korea puts great value on these two things. Confucianism, which remains deeply rooted in North Korean society, granted Kim Jong-il legitimacy and justification as a successor.

As a result, Kim Jong-il became the de facto ruler of North Korea from the early 1980s, while Kim Il-sung was still very much active. The younger Kim got rid of his political rivals and secured the position of successor. Kim Jong-il, in effect, conducted a bottom-up succession process to become the successor to his father.

Kim Jong-un is the same as Kim Jong-il in that the latter inherited the North Korean regime built by his father. However, the difference between the two men is that Kim Jong-un conducted a top-down succession process. In other words, Kim Jong-un took power from his father without having to exert any effort of his own.

In addition to his failure to build any charisma in the process of gaining power, Kim Jong-un also has an inherent complex about himself. While he asserts himself as part of the Mt. Baekdu lineage, he popped up out of nowhere to assert his legitimacy and failed to receive acknowledgment from Kim Il-sung. Moreover, Kim Jong-un took over the reins of power in North Korea at a very young age. It is therefore natural that he feels anxious about whether cadres and ordinary North Korean citizens accept him as their ruler.

Far from godlike, Kim Jong-un lacks even the legitimacy and justification required to be a leader, so he ultimately had to choose nuclear weapons, intercontinental ballistic missiles (ICBMs), and the politics of fear to cement his status. If this fails to create the necessary charisma and godlike status he craves, not only will Kim Jong-un's regime collapse, but the whole system will, too. This is why Kim is so obsessed with nuclear weapons, ICBMs, and the politics of fear, exemplified by the purge of Jang Song-taek. Jang's fate has already been discussed in great detail earlier in the book.

Kim Jong-un is very impatient, spontaneous, and brutish. Yet, at the same time, he has brains and the capacity to reason. This means that there are both personality and strategic aspects to his radical behavior, and sometimes these two may appear blended together. First, I will give two examples that show aspects of his personality.

The armistice that ended the Korean War was signed on July 27, but this day is celebrated as the Day of Victory in the Great Fatherland Liberation War in North Korea. Before the scheduled reopening in July 2014 of the Victorious Fatherland Liberation War Museum, a fire broke out in the building. Hearing the news, Kim Jong-un rushed down into the basement, which had become a sea of water. Hundreds of people were working hard extinguishing the blaze and salvaging exhibits, but Kim shouted and cursed, saying, "I told you to watch out for fires, so why the hell weren't you paying attention?"

The whole atmosphere turned icy because everyone had heard what he said. Then Kim found a photo of Kim Il-sung that had escaped the fire. It was a famous photo in North Korea. Calming down, Kim said, "But this picture is safe. It's a good thing that this at least survived." His words lightened the mood.

In May 2015, Kim conducted an on-site inspection of a turtle farm. The factory was not in good shape. The baby turtles were almost dead. The factory manager cited a lack of electricity and feed, but the North Korean leader reprimanded him harshly, saying, "It is absurd to say that production cannot be normalized because of electricity, feed, and equipment problems." High-ranking officials who were accompanying Kim kept their heads down and were busy writing down his instructions. Getting back in the car, the leader ordered the execution of the manager, which was carried out immediately.

In some cases, Kim can be calculating and logical even while behaving violently. I want to share an incident that occurred when the U.S. presidential election was in full swing in May 2016. Republican presidential candidate Donald Trump made headlines around the world by saying that he would be happy to talk with the North Korean leader over a hamburger. In March of that year, North Korea had sentenced Otto Warmbier, an American college student, to fifteen years in prison with hard labor and in April, Korean-American Kim Dong-cheol received a ten-year sentence. As a result, U.S. public opinion toward North Korea and its young leader was very negative at the time.

On May 18, shortly after Trump's remarks, a British delegation from Associated Press Television News (APTN) visiting North Korea interviewed Yang Hyeong-seop, the vice president of the Presidium of the Supreme People's Assembly. APTN is a British video news agency with a permanent office in Pyongyang. Asked what he thought of Trump's remarks, Yang said, "We are not opposed to dialogue itself. Talks can be held during wartime. There's no reason why we can't talk." He said this based on the script written in advance by the Ministry of Foreign Affairs, which had essentially made clear that North Korea is "always ready to engage in dialogue."

APTN assumed from the remarks that Kim Jong-un wanted to have a meeting with Trump. It reported the same day that North Korea welcomed Trump's proposal for dialogue. Kim, who was watching major international media channels in real-time in his office, heard this news. Late that night, he called First Vice Minister of Foreign Affairs Kim Gye-gwan and scolded him: "Hey, how can that old guy [Yang Hyeong-seop] say I'll talk to Trump without getting my approval first? Who gave him the authority to speak on my behalf? I'm the leader of [North] Korea and Trump is just a presidential candidate; he's not even president, so we're not on the same level. Did the foreign ministry tell that old man to say that?" Yang Hyeong-sop is believed to have been born in 1925 and was the husband of one of Kim Il-sung's cousins. Calling him "that old guy" clearly shows Kim Jong-un's rough, unrefined character. However, I think it should not be overlooked that there is a certain kind of logic and calculation to what he says.

Since APTN is a British-based news agency, the North Korean embassy in the UK was ordered to deal with the matter. Ambassador Hyeon

Hak-bong defused the situation by saying it would not be appropriate for a mere presidential candidate to talk to the Supreme Leader.

In Pyongyang, foreign ministry officials who had written the script for Yang Hyeong-sop received a stern warning from the Central Committee's Organization and Guidance Department (OGD). The officials all fumed inside from the injustice of it. North Korea's consistent policy was to respond to dialogue with dialogue and to military attacks with retaliation. If Yang Hyeong-sop had known more about Kim Jong-un's personality in advance, he would have answered APTN's question by saying, "Such a matter will be decided by our Comrade Supreme Leader." In the wake of this incident, anyone who is asked a question about Kim Jong-un now answers, "That is a matter for the Comrade Supreme Leader to decide."

On September 20, 2017, President Trump made a very strong statement in a speech given at the UN General Assembly, saying, "The United States has great strength and patience, but if it is forced to defend itself or its allies, we will have no choice but to totally destroy North Korea." The next day, Kim Jong-un issued a retaliatory statement and referred to Trump as a "dotard." At the time, I recalled Kim calling Yang Hyeong-sop an old man and had the gut feeling that "dotard" was an expression that the North Korean leader himself had put in the statement.

WHY THE NORTH KOREAN REGIME CANNOT LAST

There is a photo of North Korea that is quite well known in South Korea. It shows Kim Jong-il and Kim Jong-un side by side at a military parade commemorating the sixty-fifth anniversary of the founding of the WPK on October 10, 2010. At first glance, Kim Jong-il looks very sick, or to put it more harshly, it seems that his death is just lurking around the corner. Kim Jong-il is looking at his son, Kim Jong-un, and looks very worried. He seems to be more concerned about his son's future than his own health. I think this picture symbolizes the future of the Kim Jong-un regime following the death of Kim Jong-il.

Having tried to build charisma through nuclear weapons, ICBMs, and the politics of fear, Kim Jong-un is becoming a greater and greater failure. Since taking power, he has conducted four nuclear tests, and fired off plenty of ICBMs. Now that his uncle Jang Song-taek and his half-brother Kim Jong-nam have been killed, no matter who gets killed now, it can't make the North Korean people fear him more. The only direction his charisma will go is down. It's pointless to imagine now, but if Kim had instead tried to build charisma by highlighting the youth, vigor, openness, and international perspective of his own experience studying abroad, things might have turned out differently.

If Kim fails to build his charisma, it will lead to the downfall of both him and the regime. In the days of Kim Il-sung and Kim Jong-il, even if the leader's charisma had been damaged, it was possible to maintain the system by blocking the inflow of any external information, controlling the movement of people, using brainwashing in education, and placing emphasis on people's political and organizational lives. All these things, however, have collapsed in the era of Kim Jong-un.

Nowadays, popular South Korean dramas and movies are entering the North Korean market on DVDs or USB sticks within weeks of their original airing. This is not because the lives of North Koreans have become prosperous, but rather because the deterioration of the country's power grid over the past ten years or so prevents people from watching TV whenever they want. North Koreans turned to videos to replace broadcast television. Chinese companies stepped up to fill the gap. They manufactured what is called a Notel, a media player that plays DVDs or USB media running off a twelve-volt battery, and pumped it into the North Korean market.

The Notel battery can be charged with only one or two hours of electricity a day. Even with continuous power outages, people can buy spare batteries at local markets. The price for the device was so low—around thirty to seventy U.S. dollars—that almost all households in North Korea acquired a Notel. This is why South Korean content stored on DVDs and USBs has spread like wildfire throughout North Korea.

In addition, with the introduction of cell phones, information sharing on prices and demand is taking place in real time throughout North Korea. The time has come when North Korean defectors risk their lives and the rest of their families in the country to talk to their family members on their cell phones near the North Korea–China border.

There have also been improvements in the country's freedom of movement. When general markets were formed nationwide, a bus system connecting major cities was created with the tacit approval of the authorities. Now, people from even small and medium-sized cities and counties can access major cities. Basically, it is possible to travel anywhere in North Korea except for the Demilitarized Zone and the border with China.

Growing up, North Korean children no longer look up to Kim Il-sung and his feats. The brainwashing education just doesn't work anymore.

Self-criticism and mutual criticism, the basis of political organizational life, have long been relics of the old days. In rural areas, that's even more so. Even within central government agencies such as the Ministry of Foreign Affairs, very few people participate in criticism sessions. Everyone brings cigarettes or money to members of the local party committee to make deals to remove them from the roll call for mutual criticisms. I mentioned this earlier in the book, but party meeting minutes require one to just write fiction.

Many people doze off during party meetings. Warnings are continually issued during break times, telling people not to fall asleep. Nowadays, even the chairs of the meetings pretend not to notice and just read out lecture notes. At the May 2016 Party Convention, delegates kept dozing off even though Kim Jong-un was seated on the podium. Then, the authorities lowered the temperature of the conference hall to 14°C [57°F] through air-conditioning, leading countless people to catch colds.

At the party convention, the head of the Pyongyang City Railway Bureau's political department and the director general were dismissed as party delegates for being anti-party elements, and one of them committed suicide. This fact was reported in the South Korean media. This is what happens at party conventions, where the highest officials of the land gather to deliberate.

That the North Korean regime is unstable can also be determined through the sentiments of the elite. Elites are turning their backs on the North Korean regime and on Kim Jong-un. This is because even in the communist world, North Korea is the only country that has not been able to throw off its economic troubles for the past twenty years. The Arduous March was the first economic crisis North Korea experienced after the Korean War. It was thus possible to offer excuses for it and to rationalize it. Kim Jong-il remarked: "Socialism is science. The Arduous March is not due to the policies of the WPK failing, but due to the difficulties faced by all of the Eastern Bloc." North Korea continued to broadcast the realities of life in the Soviet Union and Eastern Europe on television. The country's people also came to believe that their country, which had risen from the ashes of war, could soon overcome the Arduous March.

Years later, all other Eastern Bloc countries had overcome their own economic crises and gotten back on track, but North Korea had stagnated, and its situation worsened over time. Vietnam, Laos, Cambodia, and Angola—all countries North Korea had sent aid to in the past—now became destinations where North Korean laborers were dispatched in order to earn hard currency. At this stage, even party cadres are asking whether the country really underwent a revolution "just for this." Moreover, when they think that this oppressive existence might continue for another thirty to forty years, they shudder even more.

Under Kim Jong-un's reign of terror, North Korean cadres are trying to maintain an appropriate distance from him, recalling the saying, "Those who get too close to the sun will burn and those who stray too far will freeze to death."

Cadres believe that North Korea has no future. Everyone is bent on secretly stashing some dollars for themselves. Once they have the necessary power, they send their children to work in foreign currency-earning organizations to earn cash.

Besides all this, the biggest threat to the Kim Jong-un regime is the country's markets. In fact, there were marketplaces (*jangmadang*) in the 1960s when I was a child. Back then, they were not called *jangmadang*, but farmers' markets. They were places where farmers sold what they produced in their own garden plots, and market days were held monthly or every ten days. These markets did not exist in cities like Pyongyang, however.

It was in the late 1990s that marketplaces as we know them today were formed in North Korea. Illegal vendors emerged not only in the provinces but also in streets and alleys of Pyongyang. At first, garlic, vegetables, and potatoes produced in private kitchen gardens, along with beer, bread, or shoes secretly taken out of the factories were traded. Then, food that the state strictly rationed, such as rice, began to appear in markets.

I left for Denmark in June 1996 and returned to North Korea via Sweden in July 2000. When I left for Denmark, there was no official marketplace in Pyongyang. Four years later, I returned and visited Inheung Market in Moranbong District near my house and felt that a tremendous change had taken place. The state-run store shelves were empty, but the marketplace and foreign currency store were both full of goods. The gulf between rich and poor was enormous. People were busy running around trying to make money.

Since Kim Jong-un came to power, the number of North Korean markets has increased significantly. Even during the Kim Jong-il era, there were markets, but the state ignored their existence. In the era of Kim Jong-un, however, the authorities decided not to crack down on the marketplaces. North Koreans still do not enjoy the rights of citizens, but economic rights such as the right to buy and sell are gradually expanding.

Once your right to open your eyes to view reality is violated, you will risk your very life to fight. In these marketplaces, there are frequent disputes between merchants and police officers. Merchants, who had once hopped around like grasshoppers to avoid the police, now stay put like ticks and stare down the law. Once, when asked at a press conference by a foreign journalist, "Don't North Korean citizens show any resistance?" I answered, "The grasshoppers have turned into ticks."

In fact, the resistance shown by the North Korean people when the 2009 currency reform failed was unprecedented in the country's history. That shows how dangerous markets are to Kim Jong-un.

IF NORTH KOREANS WERE TO REALLY BELIEVE IN GOD

There is one other thing that threatens the North Korean regime and Kim Jong-un, although it is of a different nature from what I've talked about above: religion. No matter how deified Kim Jong-un becomes, he is only a mortal human in the eyes of a devout believer who believes in a real god. Of course, the religious beliefs and religious activities of the North Korean people are very weak. However, it should not be forgotten that North Korea has religious believers and religious activities do exist. This is not the same as saying that North Korea has freedom of religion.

After coming to South Korea, I met quite a few religious figures who had visited North Korea. Although they had been there many times, these are the most common questions they asked me:

"Is there really freedom of faith in North Korea?"

"I've been to Bongsu Church and Changchung Cathedral. Are the people there really believers?"

"It is said that there are hundreds of home churches in North Korea; is that true?"

When South Korean religious people visit North Korea, the country's religious representatives show them around places of worship and talk as if the country has freedom of worship. If you go to a place of worship and observe a religious service or ceremony in North Korea, you may get the wrong idea that the country allows freedom of religion. That couldn't be further from the truth.

North Korea's socialist constitution stipulates freedom of religion, but there are laws in the country that are higher than the constitution. These include the words of the three Kims, the Ten Principles for the Establishment of a Monolithic Ideological System, the rules of the WPK, and policies of the party or the Suryong. Since party policy stipulates that one should only believe in Juche ideology or Kimilsungism and Kimjongilism, having a religion in North Korea is an act that runs contrary to party policy.[2]

After the Korean War, North Korea turned its hostility toward the United States into a religion and thoroughly suppressed all other faiths. Church members were classified as part of the hostile class and were subject to surveillance and control. North Korea attacked religion as a "tool to oppress and exploit the people" and "a tool or front for the ideological and cultural penetration of imperialism." It also defined a church as a "base for propagating and spreading ideas that paralyze the people's class consciousness." North Korea's view of religion goes beyond the standard communist bromide that it is the "opiate of the masses."

In the 1970s, Kim Il-sung declared that the problem of religion had been solved because the people had trust only in the WPK. At the same time, he ordered the resumption of activities by nominally religious organizations. The aim was to establish a united front as part of his strategy to achieve Korean unification. It should be noted that this is precisely the time when inter-Korean dialogue began.

In the 1980s, South Korean religious organizations became more active than ever before in the struggle for that nation's democratization. In doing so, they tried to put forward the claim that Christianity existed in North Korea, too. From that time on, North Korea began deleting the words "Christianity is a front for the spread of imperialist ideology and culture" from its texts and described churches more objectively as "places where various religious ceremonies are held."

In 1988, the Bongsu Church and Changchung Cathedral were built in Pyongyang. Putting it gently, the building of these churches was intended to expand exchanges with anti-government religious organizations in South Korea; to put it more negatively, North Korea intended to coopt members of these organizations. However, there is a reason why the churches were built only in Pyongyang and not in the provinces. Originally, there were plans to build worship facilities in major local cities such as Wonsan and Ganggye, but in the end there was no choice but to scrap them. This is because it was impossible to exert control over them over long distances.

There are some minimal preconditions to getting a church up and running in North Korea. There must be a pastor and fake congregants. The pastor might be someone who is selected by and sent from the party. However, the fake congregants had to be selected from locals living around the churches. This is because buses did not run on Sundays in the late 1980s.

Therefore, "communist women" living near Bongsu Church or Changchung Catholic Cathedral were selected. The danger of any real church members appearing had been eliminated in advance. At first, it was really difficult to get them to come to church or mass. That's why the church managers even made an attendance register. Those who had poor attendance had to engage in self-criticisms and receive mutual criticism during struggle sessions. They were also forced to attend special lectures that told them: "Church attendance is not just an activity to sing hymns and participate in religious ceremonies. It is a struggle that shows the superiority of the socialist system. In our holy war against imperialism and America, it is a noble struggle for the winning over of South Korean religious figures and for the unification of the Motherland." Such education did not improve attendance. Many women often didn't show up at church, saying that they were sick or that something had suddenly come up at home. But at some point, changes began to emerge. Despite laxer control over attendance, the number of women attending church actually increased.

The women seem to have felt they could benefit from engaging in religious activities, despite the potential disadvantages. Listening to a pastor's sermon and singing helped them relax and become more social. Everything changed when actual faith developed in those who had only pretended to be worshipping and praising. More and more people came to church even before the start of service or mass. Even when sick with a high fever, people did not skip weekly church attendance. These were the same people who previously would stay home if they had so much as a sniffle.

Seeing that these people were volunteering to go to church, the party recognized that they had developed real faith. When "risk factors" emerged, the party had people with binoculars placed in apartments around Bongsu Church to monitor people walking toward the place of worship. In other words, the authorities tried to identify people who were keeping their faith a secret.

Something extraordinary happened. When the sound of hymn singing was heard coming from the church, some youngsters appeared and leaned against the church wall. They appeared to be furiously scribbling something down. Officers from the State Security Department (now the Ministry of State Security) arrested them. They were composition students in a local music college. In the 1980s, North Korean music colleges did not teach well-known masterpieces from liberal democratic countries. One day, a music student who heard a hymn told his classmates about it. The classmates wanted to collect hymns, but they couldn't enter the church. They were caught by the SSD while secretly listening and taking notes outside the wall surrounding the church. The students were released only after receiving a stern warning from the security agency.

Another case came as a shock to party authorities. During church services, there were people who appeared without fail and hung around in the side streets nearby. When they were arrested and interrogated, it was found that they had once been believers. Kim Il-sung had declared that there were no more believers in North Korea and that the problem of religion had been resolved, but here was proof that the faith of church members had remained unchanged. They had only said that they had abandoned their faith for fear of oppression by the authorities.

The party decided not to build any more churches or cathedrals. It was clear that if any were built in the provinces to show off to the outside world, they could become a threat to the regime. The religious community in South Korea needs to keep this in mind. If any new places of worship were created in North Korea, then fake believers would have to be selected, and if those counterfeit churchgoers found God, what would happen? The results are obvious.

KIM YONG-NAM'S TEARS AND KIM YO-JONG'S SMILE

The Juche idea and communist ideology that supported North Korean society have long left the hearts of North Koreans. Even now, North Korea produces propaganda saying that its people can rely on the Suryong for everything and leave their fate and future in his hands; in reality, however, North Koreans believe only in their own brains and brawn. The biggest change currently taking place in North Korean society is that people want to know the facts and the truth.

What Kim Jong-un is most afraid of is the power of truth. He is desperately preventing the truth from entering North Korean society, but in the end it will be of little use. North Koreans' desire for reality is getting stronger by the day. When all North Koreans know the truth and reach a consensus, the Kim Jong-un regime will collapse with barely a whimper.

Truth in itself is nothing special. But in North Korea, where information is blocked, the reality of the outside world is the truth. We must use every possible means to show North Koreans this reality of the outside world, including South Korea, and prompt their minds to start making comparisons. If North Koreans compare their country with South Korea, and even with the world, the results are obvious.

I was shocked to watch the opening ceremony of the PyeongChang Winter Olympics in February 2018. I thought it would be great because these were the winter Olympic Games hosted by South Korea, a world-renowned IT powerhouse. However, I never imagined such a fantastic opening ceremony. I remember thinking it was fortunate that about four hundred people from North Korea, including Kim Yong-nam and Kim Yo-jong, visited the South to attend the opening ceremony of the games.

During the PyeongChang Olympics, I watched North Korea's KCTV every day. My expectations were high that Kim Jong-un would show the opening ceremony to North Koreans, at least as a prerecorded broadcast. However, KCTV only showed a few photographs. It also twisted the facts to make it sound as if the Olympics were going well because of the participation of the North Korean delegation. That's how afraid Kim Jong-un is of the truth.

While in South Korea, Kim Yong-nam wept several times, and Kim Yo-jong mysteriously smiled several times. These scenes were shown countless times through South Korean media. What was the meaning of those tears and smiles?

Kim Yong-nam had visited many countries in his life as a diplomat, but it was his first time in South Korea. After Korea's liberation from Japan, he entered a Marxist-Leninist school established by the Soviet army in North Korea and learned about communist ideology. During the Korean War, he went to the Soviet Union to study. It is no exaggeration to say that he devoted his entire ninety-plus years to building a true communist and socialist society in North Korea.

As far as I know, Kim Yong-nam is a cool-headed person who does not cry easily. In North Korea, influential people are judged by the presence or absence of authority over personnel, commendations, and disciplinary matters. Kim Yong-nam has had the opportunity to exercise all three of these types of authority through the various high-ranking positions that he has held, including as secretary for international affairs in the Central Committee, foreign minister, and president of the Presidium of the Supreme People's Assembly. But he never used his authority. The moment you use your authority, people gather around and flatter you. That is when you know all too well that you could be checked by Kim Jong-il or Kim Jong-un, and it could be off with your head in an instant. He avoided no small number of executions and purges, nor has he ever been sent to a camp for "revolutionizing."

In other words, Kim Yong-nam is a cool-headed and well-behaved communist. Why then did he shed tears in South Korea? I can guess, but I won't try to explain what I think.

Kim Yo-jong must have been very concerned about whether the members of the North Korean cheer squad and artistic troupe, having seen South Korea's development, would continue to remain faithful to the North Korean regime. It must have strengthened her determination not to give up nuclear weapons or missiles but to hold onto them for the sake of maintaining the North Korean system. I think that such a confluence of emotions is what brought about that hard-to-read expression on her face, like the smile of the Mona Lisa, as some media outlets described it.

As I watched the North Korean art troupe and cheer squad leave South Korea, not all of them looked happy. The time they spent in South Korea will remain in their heads for the rest of their lives.

UNIFICATION IS A REVOLUTION TO FREE NORTH KOREA'S PRISONERS

The American Civil War was a war to end slavery. This is why it is remembered as a just war in human history. Recently, I met some South Korean college students. Many students are not interested in Korea's unification and do not think it is necessary, but most of them look favorably upon the American Civil War. According to the students, although countless lives were sacrificed in the war, their deaths were not in vain because it was a war to free the enslaved.

We need to consider the unification of the Korean Peninsula through a moral lens and look at it from the point of view of restoring the universal rights and dignity of human beings. The characteristics of North Korea's oppressive society have deepened in the Kim Jong-un era. Unlike his father, Kim Jong-un quickly became the official successor without any formal procedures, and he reigns more brutally than his father. Examples include the Department 54 Fishing Base Incident, the execution of Jang Song-taek, the shooting of members of the Unhasu Orchestra, and the demolition of Pyongyang Folklore Park. Kim kills people for saying one word wrong and executed his uncle because of his personal dislike for the man. The Pyongyang Folklore Park, a perfectly fine amusement park that opened in 2012, reminded the North Korean leader of Jang Song-taek, and that's why he had it turned into rubble. These are things that would have happened in an ancient slave society where deceased rulers were buried with slaves who were still alive, or in countries run by the Taliban or Islamic extremists.

To restate the case, North Korea is an oppressive state in which the entire country exists only to serve Kim Jong-un and his family. Therefore, the unification of the Korean Peninsula is a revolution to free North Koreans from their bondage. Korean unification will restore the inherent rights of North Koreans as human beings. Unifying the two Korean systems and ideologies and fusing the national culture and homogeneity are values that will emerge after unification.

We cannot leave the North Koreans to languish amid oppression. Although armed methods cannot be used as they were in the American Civil War, the fight for the liberation of the people in North Korea must begin. To this end, the main focus of unification should be seen as the North Korean people. North Koreans have their own strength and consciousness, and a tremendous amount of outside information is already entering North Korea.

Changes within North Korea are already underway. It's just a question of how these changes will look and how fast they will come. More than ten years ago, something hitherto unimaginable happened: Who could have predicted that the number of marketplaces in North Korea would grow to be in the hundreds and that people would watch South Korean movies or dramas? However, South Korea should not just sit back and watch. The country needs to take the lead in continuing sanctions on North Korea to speed up such changes.

The impact of sanctions targeting North Korea should not be measured simply through economic numbers. We should understand sanctions to be a device that promotes growth in North Korea's markets, which in turn promotes the flow of capitalist elements into the country. For example, if North Korea's coal exports are blocked by sanctions, coal will be diverted to meet domestic demand. Export prices are based on international markets, but domestic prices are determined by the North Korean authorities. That being said, the prices set by the authorities are as low as one-hundredth or one-thousandth of international prices.

Under these circumstances, the authorities have no choice but to distribute the coal back into the country's marketplaces. That's because the product can be sold in the markets at hundreds of times the prices set by the state. Coal is just an example I'm using here, but if all supplies flock to markets in this way, the country's market economy will inevitably grow. If the government tries to control this, conflict between the government and the markets will be inevitable, leading to assured victory for the markets.

What's more, North Korea's biggest economic player is the military. Soldiers are mobilized to construction sites and various other sites of production. If sanctions against North Korea continue, the government will have no choice but to open its military stockpiles of rice. In effect, this would be the same thing as the country giving up on getting involved in a war.

What needs to come next is the ceaseless dissemination of South Korean cultural content, or soft power, into North Korea. I think this is what Kim Jong-un is most afraid of. In November 2017, *Rodong Sinmun* published a long article that said young people are sensitive to novelties and that if the work to educate them ideologically is unsuccessful, it could be a great misfortune for North Korean society. Until now, North Korea has never said that the regime could be brought down by a U.S. military attack. However, seeing that the regime considers the penetration of outside ideas and culture to be threat factors plainly shows that the North Korean regime fears these things.

That North Korean society is dying can also be seen from the fact that new North Korean movies and dramas have not been released recently. Movies and dramas currently being broadcast were produced more than ten years ago. In the past, dozens of films were produced every year. Kim Jong-un still urges the production of movies or dramas, but this hasn't had much effect. The country's writers and directors know well that nobody wants to watch whatever they make.

Kim Jong-il was a fan of movies and, after much consideration, the North Korean authorities even opened his movie warehouse. Among the thousands of movies stored there, some interesting ones were selected and distributed on DVD. As YouTube will show you, there are several stores in Pyongyang that sell such DVDs. However, South Korea's soft power cannot be beaten by socialist movies that inspire war, espionage, and patriotism. North Korea even distributes American cartoons such as *Tom and Jerry* and *The Lion King* to its people. If the authorities don't distribute this kind of content, people will watch South Korean movies and dramas. In short, what the authorities are saying is that everything is permitted as long as it is not from South Korea.

If South Korean media content produced in the 1970s or 1980s, to say nothing of the 1960s, had been disseminated in North Korea, the films or dramas from that era would not have been very popular in the

North. Indeed, during those decades, North Korea arguably had a similar, if not better, standard of living than South Korea. However, through the smuggling of South Korean films and dramas produced in the early 2000s, North Koreans learned that South Korea's realities were different from what their country's official propaganda told them. In particular, it shocked them that the standard of living of South Koreans was incomparably higher than that of North Koreans: "Why are we so poor when the South is so well off?"

According to North Korea's Suryong leadership ideology, the Suryong plays a decisive role in the process of revolution and construction. It also attributes the development of North Korea to the wise leadership of the Suryong. Following this theory to its conclusion, North Korea is living in poverty incomparable to South Korea because of its Suryong. This is why the North Korean leadership is extremely wary of any realistic image of South Korea being shown in the North.

North Koreans can be forgiven somewhat by the authorities if they watch Chinese or even American dramas. However, the consumption of South Korean films or dramas is subject to heavy punishment. When they go abroad, North Koreans must watch out the most for South Koreans, not Americans or Japanese people. When a North Korean returns from abroad, they will be vetted and debriefed by the Ministry of State Security; at the root of this investigation is the question of whether they met any South Koreans while abroad. In the same vein, even if they can receive money from relatives living in the United States or Japan, North Koreans are not permitted to receive money from South Korean relatives.

All this being said, North Koreans have already succumbed to South Korea's soft power. After Kim Jong-un took over, he established a permanent crackdown squad called Group 109 that declared war on "impure recordings" and specialized in preventing people from accessing elements of the Korean Wave. Group 109, however, now just focuses on earning money: How much do you have to pay if you are caught watching South Korean content? How much if South Korean games or e-books are found on your cell phone? How much if you are caught using a South Korean word or phrase? That's what it comes down to. For college students, parent meetings are held every six months to check how well access is being restricted to this impure content; however, these efforts have not eliminated interest among young people toward South Korean culture.

There are too many South Korean expressions, such as *jagiya* ("darling" or "babe"), *oppa* (used by a woman to address her boyfriend or older brother), or the informal verb ending *geoya*, that are used by young North Koreans, so there's not much the North Korean authorities can do.

Every North Korean I know has watched South Korean films or dramas. What the country's authorities cannot control is the influx of drugs and the Korean Wave, which basically means that South Korean cultural products are as powerful as drugs. People will watch Korean movies and dramas at the risk of receiving death threats or even execution.

We possess and can employ sufficient means and tools to change the consciousness of North Koreans. Tailored content that reveals North Koreans' oppressed lives and the irrationality of the country's hereditary leadership should be produced and sent into North Korea. If we produce and send enough tailored content in a range of fields such as politics, economy, society, and education as well as entertainment and culture that North Koreans can watch twenty-four hours a day, this content will promote peace and unification on the Korean Peninsula, as well as democracy, reform, and the opening of North Korea. To this end, it is imperative that the internet and Wi-Fi be made available in the country, along with infrastructure that supports the consumption of radio and satellite TV.

Germany was unified because East German residents were able to watch West German television for decades. However, we should not directly copy the German case. Unlike East Germans, North Koreans do not possess even a basic concept of the liberal democratic order, the separation of powers, or human rights. As such, we must develop media content that can gently enter the consciousness of North Koreans without shocking them. It is important to inform them about various aspects of South Korea and the international community, especially the principles of the market economy and democratic politics that operate on the basis of freedom and equality, in a way that is friendly and resonates with their emotions and experiences.

In order to promote the collapse of the North Korean regime, we must help more North Koreans to escape the country. This will help accelerate the process of unification. Tens of thousands of North Korean defectors are hiding in China and waiting for a chance to come to South Korea. We need to start a national movement to enable more North Koreans to come to the South. The very fact that North Korean defectors come to South

Korea is part of the process of unifying the two Koreas. I hope that South Korean society will call them *tongilmin*, or people of unification. They symbolize, in fact, the first step taken toward unification.

I witnessed the tremendous power of South Koreans and their civil society while watching the candlelight revolution at the end of 2016.[3] In order to achieve unification, we need to form a nationwide civic network. The reason the South Korean government's unification policy has not produced great results so far is that previous administrations have failed to implement consistent policies because of the country's left-right political split. This problem can be overcome by strengthening the influence of civil society. It is necessary to form a massive civic network to lead the unification movement. Civil society should become the leading force in the unification movement, and it should guide or place a check on the government's policies toward North Korea. That's the only way South Korea can maintain consistency and continuity in its policies toward North Korea.

I am more concerned about how to achieve reconciliation between different classes within North Korea after unification than unification itself. South Korea should ceaselessly make it known that political retaliation against the core class or leaders will not take place when the Kim Jong-un regime collapses. Unification should be an opportunity for all North Koreans—except the Kim family—to experience joy, stability, and a fresh start. We need to avoid handing them new fears or anxiety.

North Korea could become like today's Yemen, Syria, or Libya if the process of unification consists of cycles of revenge and retaliation for past sins. I believe that we should follow the example of the late South African President Nelson Mandela, who pursued reconciliation, cooperation, forgiveness, and tolerance.

In my mind, the process of unification is that of North Korea's oppressed rising up and holding their own candlelight parade.

The day when the unfree will hold up their candles is not far away. Until that day, I will use all my, albeit small, power to create a practical, energetic, and action-oriented movement for unification.

EPILOGUE

Standing Before the Manin Cemetery of Righteous Fighters

I'm in my late fifties now. According to data released by the Organization for Economic Co-operation and Development (OECD), the average life expectancy in South Korea is 84.6 years for women and 78.0 years for men as of 2015. The average life expectancy in North Korea is 73.3 years for women and 66.3 years for men, respectively, a gap of 11.3 years for women and 11.7 years for men compared to South Korea. I now live in South Korea, and my friends still live in North Korea.

While it may not turn out exactly as the OECD data predict, I could live for another twenty years, and my North Korean friends could die in another ten years. It seems inevitable that the older you get, the more you feel the urgency of time. While in South Korea someone in their fifties isn't necessarily an elderly person, I'm wondering if I'm just missing my own country.

The last time I visited my birthplace of Myeongcheon County was in August 2012. As deputy director of the European Department at the Ministry of Foreign Affairs, I led a diplomatic delegation from Pyongyang on a tour to Mt. Chilbo and stopped by my birthplace on the way. Mt. Chilbo is a famous mountain in the village of Sanggo, Myeongcheon County, and is not far from Punggye-ri, where North Korea has conducted nuclear tests. The diplomatic delegation was taken there to show the international community that nuclear tests had not adversely affected the environment.

I visited my uncle and aunt in Myeongcheon County. I never dreamed it would be my last time. At that time, hundreds of members of the wider Thae clan lived clustered in Myeongcheon County. Even now, things probably haven't changed very much. Digging into one's family tree and studying genealogy is taboo in North Korea because it is seen as a relic of feudal times. Now that I'm in South Korea, I'm going to brag about my family just this once. Please indulge me.

When I was young, my father told me the following story: "The Thaes are descendants of Dae Joyeong, who founded the kingdom of Balhae." After its fall, Crown Prince Dae Gwang-hyeon led tens of thousands of displaced people into exile in the kingdom of Goryeo. King Taejo of Goryeo granted to Crown Prince Dae Gwang-hyeon a government post and the surname Thae. After that, the Thaes were divided into the Hyeopgye and Yeongsungye clans. As part of the Hyeopgye clan, our household had its home in Namwon County, North Jeolla Province, but some of them moved to Myeongcheon County, North Hamgyong Province, to form the Myeongcheon Thae clan.

My ancestors, the Namwon Thaes, were killed en masse during the Japanese invasion of Korea in 1597 to 1598. All the Thaes of Jeolla Province entered Namwon Fortress to defend it, and most of them died heroically. The Manin Cemetery of Righteous Fighters is a joint cemetery in which about ten thousand military and civilian fighters who were killed by the Japanese in the Siege of Namwon were laid to rest. In Chungnyeolsa Temple at the Manin Cemetery, there are fifty-two spirit tablets of generals who fought bravely in that battle at the time, five of whom are my ancestors from the Thae clan.

In 2017, after arriving in South Korea, I stood before Manin Cemetery of Righteous Fighters with my wife and two sons during Chuseok. I cannot help but describe how I felt at the time as just having mixed feelings. Various thoughts whirled around in my head: my roots in the Thae clan, the restoration of Balhae history, the suffering and pain of the Korean nation, the ancestors who sacrificed their lives for the country, my friends and colleagues who remain in North Korea, my children and me, and unification.

As a weak but warm-blooded human being, I have a wish. When the day of unification comes, I want to visit Pyongyang on my own two feet. I want to meet my friends and relatives, and my senior and junior colleagues at the foreign ministry who took care of me like their own blood relative. I want to kneel down and ask them for forgiveness. It is regrettable that they were left behind and only I am here in the Republic of Korea. This alone made me a sinner against them.

The children of my relatives also haunt me. I want to rent a bus from Seoul and pick them all up. If I help them to study at a South Korean university, I think I can alleviate about one-ten-thousandth of the burden I feel in my heart toward my relatives. I also want to invite my parents who lie buried in Pyongyang to the "Thae Clan's sacred mountain" in Myeong-cheon County, where I must return someday.

NOTES

PROLOGUE

1. The author uses the term *jaryeokgaengsaeng*, a commonly used phrase in North Korea that roughly translates to "self-sufficiency."

1. NORTH KOREA'S PATH TO NUCLEAR WEAPONS

1. Stretching from 1994 to 1998, the Arduous March was a period of mass famine in North Korea.
2. The lowest level of organization in North Korea's party hierarchy, party cells vary in size and are tasked with ensuring that decisions made by the party are implemented properly.
3. Part of the Central Committee of the Workers' Party, the Organization and Guidance Department has a broad range of responsibilities, which include directing the activities of all party members, such as ideological education, criticism sessions, and participation in public works projects.
4. Revolutionization, or *hyeokmyeongwha*, is a type of probation for party officials that involves forced labor or ideological training over a set period at "production sites" such as farms, factories, or mines.
5. Nordpolitik was a key policy of the Roh Tae-woo administration to normalize relations with China and the USSR, traditionally close allies of North Korea.
6. A department within the Central Committee of the Workers' Party, the UFD manages espionage, diplomacy, and policy making concerning South Korea, front organizations in domestic and overseas locations, and the country's religious organizations.
7. The Ministry of State Security (MSS) is North Korea's secret police, tasked with investigating political and economic crimes, among other internal security–related duties.

8. The Social Security Department is North Korea's national law enforcement agency. The organization has undergone several name changes over the years and, as of 2023, is called the Ministry of Social Security.

9. The author appears to be referring to Mario Filippo Pini.

10. Bureau 39 is a WPK department that manages foreign currency earnings for the country's leadership; it is also called Room 39 or Office 39.

11. *Gippeumjo* is allegedly a collection of some two thousand women and girls who provide entertainment for the leadership and distinguished guests.

12. In Korea's past, *gisaeng* were women from outcast or slave families trained to be courtesans, providing artistic entertainment and conversation to upper-class men.

13. The ten principles, with sixty-five clauses, act as standards for guiding the behavior of North Koreans.

14. The Pyongyang Foreign Language Institute is a six-year secondary school designed to teach English and other foreign languages.

15. North Korea classifies its people into three classes based on their perceived loyalty to the regime: core, wavering, and hostile.

16. Following four years of primary or elementary school, North Korean students attend higher (or senior) middle school for six years.

2. NORTH KOREAN DIPLOMACY DURING THE ARDUOUS MARCH

1. Reportedly, her family opposed her marriage to a boyfriend and wanted her to return to North Korea.

2. This building was being turned into a mausoleum for Kim Il-sung.

3. Hwang was a high-ranking adviser who had served Kim Il-sung and Kim Jong-il.

4. Also referred to as the Juche Idea or Jucheism.

5. The *Simhwajo* (深化組), literally meaning a "team to intensify the investigation of people's backgrounds and ideological status," was a secret police organization created under the Social Security Department.

6. The *Juche* Farming Method, advocating intensive cultivation, was created by order of Kim Il-sung in 1973.

7. The agency was renamed the Ministry of Social Security in June 2020.

8. In North Korea, preliminary examinations include the entire interrogation process prior to a suspect' being indicted.

9. The North Korean saying is "당원이 돼야 사람값에 든다 (*Dangwoni dwaeya saramgapse deunda*)" which the author compares to the South Korean saying, "사람 구실을 한다 (*Saram gusireul handa*)."

10. Despite North Korean claims that the Gwangmyeongseong 1 was just a satellite, the South Korean government believes that the firing of the Gwangmyeongseong 1 was a test launch of the ballistic missile Baekdusan 1 (otherwise known as the Daepodong 1).

11. The Reconnaissance General Bureau is a North Korean intelligence agency that manages the country's clandestine activities.

12. The Blue House, now a public park, was akin to the White House, serving as the official residence of the country's president. South Korea's Presidential Secretariat is made up of top aides who enjoy special presidential confidence and control access to the chief executive, influencing personnel appointments and even policy decisions.

3. SAVED BY SOUTH KOREA

1. "Unconverted long-term prisoners" is a North Korean term for people who were long imprisoned in South Korea for their political views, namely that they never renounced their loyalty to the North Korean government. These prisoners included North Korean military POWs and North Korean spies caught in South Korea.
2. Panmunjeom is located in the Demilitarized Zone (DMZ), around thirty miles from Seoul.
3. This phrase, in Korean, is *urriminjokkggirri*, which roughly translates—depending on the context—as Koreans solving their own issues among themselves.
4. The Arirang festival is an annual display of mass games and artistic folk performances.
5. Arirang is the name of a Korean folk song. The second act of the Arirang show is "Songun Arirang," which focuses on Korean nationalism and the high position of the North Korean military (*songun* is commonly translated as "military-first").
6. *Choppari* is a common ethnic slur used by Koreans against Japanese people.
7. Ri served as North Korea's foreign minister from April 2014 to May 2016.

4. NORTH KOREA USES THE BRITISH TO CHECK THE AMERICANS

1. Following four years of primary or elementary school, North Korean students attend higher (or senior) middle school for six years.
2. Ri later became foreign minister of North Korea in 2016.
3. Kim Yong-sun served as vice chair of North Korea's Committee for the Peaceful Reunification of the Fatherland.
4. The Blue House, now a public park, was akin to the White House, serving as the official residence of the country's president. South Korea's Presidential Secretariat is made up of top aides who enjoy special presidential confidence and control access to the chief executive, influencing personnel appointments and even policy decisions.

5. FROM KIM JONG-IL TO KIM JONG-UN

1. The branch party is one of North Korea's basic party organizations, which include party cells, branch party organizations, and sub-primary party organizations.
2. The author uses the term *jeongseong jakeop.*

3.   *Songun* is commonly translated as "military-first."
4.   Ho Dam was North Korea's foreign minister from 1970 to 1983.
5.   Ri Han-yeong was born in the DPRK to Seong Hye-rang, the sister of Seong Hye-rim. Ri defected to the ROK in 1982 from Switzerland, where he had been studying. In 1996, he finally disclosed his identity and links to the Kim family by writing the book *Taedong River Royal Family*. He was assassinated in 1997 by unknown assailants. Ri is also known as Yi Han-yong.
6.   *Donju*, literally "money masters," are people in North Korea's class of wealthy entrepreneurs.
7.   The author uses the term *sseogeunssal*, which literally means "rotten rice."
8.   Yeongpyeong Island is a group of islands under South Korean control in the Yellow Sea.
9.   Kim Jong-suk was Kim Jong-il's mother.
10. The Moranbong Band, North Korea's first all-female band, performs interpretive styles of pop, rock, and fusion.
11. These two counties are located in South Hamgyong Province and were considered so remote that the area was used as a place of exile during Korea's modern and premodern history. The phrase *Samsugapsan* refers generally to a "remote or far-off place" or metaphorically to a "difficult situation."
12. This structure is now called the Gumsusan Palace of the Sun.

6. ON THE EVE OF MY DEFECTION

1.   Kang became first vice foreign minister in 1986 and was involved in diplomatic talks with the United States over North Korea's nuclear program. He died in 2016.
2.   Hwang was a North Korean politician and chief crafter of the country's *Juche* ideology. He defected to South Korea in 1997.
3.   This commission was established in 2013 to investigate allegations of crimes against humanity in North Korea.
4.   The *gayageum* is a traditional Korean zither with twelve strings.
5.   A polite greeting used in the Koreas to acknowledge the difficulties or hard work of the listener.
6.   A form of speech Koreans use to others in lower social positions.
7.   News of Thae's defection was first reported in the media in August 2016.

7. STUDYING ABROAD

1.   *Inminban*, or "people's units," are akin to neighborhood watch units. They are the lowest-level administrative units in North Korea and are considered the eyes and ears of the regime at the neighborhood level.
2.   The term used here is *nappeun mul*, literally "bad water," but referring metaphorically to "bad influence."

3. *Jusapa* was a faction of South Korea's student movement that sympathized with North Korea's Juche thought.

4. An organization set up by the Armistice Agreement ending the Korean War, the Military Armistice Commission is tasked with implementing the agreement, settling violations through negotiations, and acting as an intermediary between military leaders on the opposing sides.

5. *Gyeongchip* refers to a period generally falling around March 5 when insects, frogs, and other animals in hibernation for the winter begin waking up and moving around.

6. The official languages of Sri Lanka are Sinhala and Tamil.

7. The author doesn't reveal whether the French student is a female or not, but for readability's sake the student has been deemed a female in the translation.

8. *Donpyo* can be translated as "cash coupons" or "money vouchers."

8. THE THAES OF MYEONGCHEON

1. This phrase, used in South Korea, combines the English word "in" with "Seoul" and "dae." Dae is shorthand in Korean for "university."

2. Shorthand in Korean for *jaeil dongpo*, or Korean compatriot resident in Japan.

3. *Ttakji* is the Korean name for an origami flip toy used in a game in which players try to throw their *ttakji* to flip over the *ttakji* of another player that is lying on the ground. The winner gets to keep the loser's *ttakji*.

4. The reference here is to a passenger flight between Baghdad, Iraq, and Seoul, South Korea, which exploded in midair in November 1987, killing more than a hundred people. Kim Hyeon-hui was one of two North Korean bombers.

5. Otherwise known as Lim Su-kyung, Im was a South Korean university student who visited the Thirteenth World Festival of Youth and Students in North Korea in 1989 without first obtaining permission from the South Korean government. After returning home, she was arrested and sentenced to five years in prison.

9. FOR UNIFICATION AND FREEDOM

1. Yi was a Korean admiral and military general known for his victories against the Japanese navy during the Joseon Dynasty.

2. Kimilsungism and Kimjongilism refer to an ideology based on the theories of the two North Korean leaders.

3. The author is referring to a series of protests in South Korea in 2016 that contributed to the fall of then South Korean President Park Geun-hye.